MUSIC IN AMERICAN LIFE

A list of books in this series appears at the end of this book.

MUSIC AT THE WHITE HOUSE

MUSIC
AT THE
WHITE HOUSE

★ ★ ★

A HISTORY OF
THE AMERICAN SPIRIT

Elise K. Kirk

A Barra Foundation Book

UNIVERSITY OF ILLINOIS PRESS

Urbana and Chicago

© 1986 by the Board of Trustees of the University of Illinois
Manufactured in the United States of America
C 5 4 3 2 1

This book is printed on acid-free paper.

Library of Congress Cataloging in Publication Data

Kirk, Elise K. (Elise Kuhl), 1932–
    Music at the White House.

    (Music in American life)
    Includes index.
    Bibliography: p.
    1. White House (Washington, D.C.) 2. Music—
Washington (D.C.)—History and criticism. 3. Concerts—
Washington (D.C.) 4. Music—United States—History and
criticism. 5. Washington (D.C.)—Dwellings.
6. Washington (D.C.)—Public buildings. I. Title.
II. Series.
ML200.8.W3K57   1986   780'.9753   85-1088
ISBN 0-252-01233-X (alk. paper)

To my mother—my own first lady
whose loving heart and joyous spirit
touched many pages of this book

CONTENTS

*Color illustrations are found
following pages 46 and 270.*

PREFACE

"Pardon me, ma'am, but you'll have to work somewhere else now," said the White House guard politely one morning in 1980. "The president likes to come in here at noon and browse through the books." I left—fast—gathering up my notes, pencils, glasses, and briefcase that had been sniffed both inside and out by two large dogs dutifully searching for bombs. The White House is not equipped to handle researchers. The Office of the Curator is very small and cramped, so that day the staff had situated me in the elegant Federal-style library on the ground floor, where I had been taking notes for several hours with the Gilbert Stuart portrait of George Washington looking over my shoulder and the soft gray and rose tones of the Tabriz carpet under my feet.

I had grown to love this great, white citadel of democracy. Situated among the green parks of Washington, D.C., like a charming "English clubhouse," as Charles Dickens described it when he visited President John Tyler in 1841, the mansion is both imposing and intimate, awesome and warm—the home of every American. I felt that it had been my home, too, for much longer than the eleven years I had worked on this book. For as I left the White House that day I could hear Mrs. John Quincy Adams at her Babcock pianoforte, the young Teresa Carreño playing for Abraham Lincoln, Madame Schumann-Heink serenading Theodore Roosevelt, the legendary Hofmann, Paderewski, Rachmaninoff at the East Room Steinway, and Eubie Blake on the White House lawn. I nodded my thanks to the guard. I would be back—very soon.

How did I come to write a book on the musical history of the White House? The idea occurred to me while I was researching material for my doctoral thesis on the French composer, Charles Koechlin. This erudite master had come to the United States with a mission of French scholars and was entertained at the White House by President Woodrow Wilson in 1918, only two days after the Armistice. Surely there would be ample, accessible information about this event, I thought. But I was wrong. The sources for White House history are widely diffused, and sifting through them to find a specific piece of information is a major undertaking. Official records of the social activities of the White House and its inhabitants were not kept until the turn of the century. But even after this time, published studies of the mansion's social life are rare—and a history of its cultural activities nonexistent. Not until 1961 was the White House curatorial office established by Mrs. John F. Kennedy to amass and preserve the historic furnishings of the mansion. But the *musical* history of our nation's oldest "performing arts center" still needed to be studied and appreciated.

Despite the obstacles, researching a topic that examined American musical practices from a fresh interdisciplinary springboard was tempting. I knew that the White House—both home and governmental institution—could tell us much about our nation if we asked the right questions. But in order to do this, the historian must be willing to roam widely within and beyond his or her own discipline and to chart new landscapes. I would have to become, in the words of Richard Crawford, a mapmaker rather than a prospector, broadening my focus from Music with a capital M to *music-making*—or from the product to the process. Thus, in examining the role of the White House in accepting, reflecting, or promoting certain kinds of music, a new image of America would emerge.

And so the adventure began. I found it essential to explore the resources and insights of several different disciplines to place the details of *Music at the White House* in an appropriate setting. Many of my basic sources were nonmusical: manuscripts and published accounts relating to the White House, presidential papers, newspaper reports, private diaries and letters, oral histories, government documents, and financial accounts. To interpret the facts gleaned from these sources and to relate specific White House events to the musical life of the nation at large, I examined the approaches of various social and cultural historians. Political history was also a vital area to consider; the exigencies of foreign policy, the trauma of war, and the personal lives and tenets of individual presidential families all influenced the musical activities of the White House. Finally, my own experience as a musicologist provided tools for interpreting the various programs, scores, and musical data and determining their significance to the primary theme of my book—that the musical life of the White House is a story of America, of the gradual emergence of the American national character with the growing acceptance of its indigenous creative treasures and lessening dependence upon European culture.

My research, in turn, led to avenues, moments, and memories that have become just as much a part of this book as the documents themselves. Meeting President and Mrs. Reagan. Conversing with Rosalynn Carter, Betty Ford, and Lady Bird Johnson. Chatting with the chief usher, Rex Scouten, in his second-floor office at the White House. Trying out the East Room Steinway as I left the PBS "In Performance at the White House" rehearsal. Interviewing numerous prominent musicians, first family members, and White House staff. But strongest of all is the memory of the great house itself, whose doors opened for me a vital new area of history. As E. V. Smalley, a New York correspondent, wrote in 1884: "There is probably no building in the world where more history has centered than in this shining White Mansion. Heroic men have died here. . . . There have been marriages and merry makings, too, jovial feasts and ceremonial banquets; grave councils of state that shaped the destiny of the nation. . . . The history of the White House is a history of the United States from 1800 to this day."

But no one book can tell the whole story. While I have staked out the territory and unearthed various artifacts, many treasures remain. The scholarly investigation of American music and its role in society is still in its infancy, and the White House offers but one approach to the exploration of this vast panorama. If my book leaves the doors open and invites further research and interpretation, it will have accomplished my aims. It is hoped that readers with both broad and specialized interests will find information in this study that will provide them with new directions and fresh perspectives about America, its people, and the manner in which they perceived their art.

INTRODUCTION

The White House, first inhabited by John and Abigail Adams in 1800, is the nation's oldest important showcase for the performing arts. It is a stage like no other. As both home and office of the president of the United States, it is private, domestic, and intimate but at the same time public, visible, and powerfully linked with the people. While entertainment at the White House is usually presented to only 200 or 300 by invitation, it is open to millions through television. Few edifices in the world can boast the variety and excellence of its music, yet few concert halls or opera houses have been so conditioned by changing political attitudes. No other single arts institution has been as progressive and at the same time as conservative as the great white mansion. No other aspect of White House life can define the presidential image quite like the music performed at the chief of state's residence. Yet this image is a two-way channel. Powerful, elusive, joyous, persuasive, poignant, elegant, and brash, White House musical fêtes are a true mirror of America, a glimpse of court life in a democracy—a barometer of the nation's irrational, romantic, secular spirit.

There is a part of each of us in the music that is performed at the White House: the ceremonial pageantry and tradition that harks back to the age of romantic chivalry; the amateur's joy in making music in the privacy of his or her home; the inspiring thrill of hearing the world's finest performing artists in concert. Where else but at the White House can one find this *Gebrauchsmusik*, this trio of socially "useful" music embodied in a single institution? And if we take a moment to glance back into history, we will note that our American tradition of changing administrations has affected the style of this music in a unique way. The personal and political tastes of the various first families have influenced the choice of music at the mansion, but even more so have the surrounding mood, cultural milieu, and world events of the era. The intensity of the Depression, for example, brought the White House programs at the close of the Hoover era closer to those of FDR, forming a type of cultural bridge between these two politically disparate administrations. The famous Kennedy arts philosophy was forecast by the Eisenhowers, whose White House concerts during their last years reflected the cultural explosion of the late 1950s. Today, however, technology, probably more than any one element, has ensured that the White House is America's stage. New attitudes in journalism and telecommunications have brought the Executive

Mansion as a vital medium of artistic expression closer to the public than ever before.

Music for ceremonies and state entertainment played an important part in the history of the "President's House" from its earliest days. The eight-member U.S. Marine Band was the first musical ensemble to perform at the mansion, functioning as a form of European *Harmonie,* or small social ensemble, for the Adamses' first reception on New Year's Day, 1801. For almost 100 years the Marine Band of from thirty to seventy players performed for thousands in public concerts on the White House lawn. Under Francis Scala, John Philip Sousa, William Santelmann, and other noted leaders, it brought to America the latest Italian operas and newest works of Wagner, Brahms, and other European composers at a time when the city of Washington knew no other regular performing ensemble. The Marine Band, moreover, is our nation's oldest continuous musical organization. Now greatly expanded, it comprises a wide variety of ensemble units to meet the needs of virtually every social, artistic, and ceremonial occasion at the White House.

Despite its location in the culturally primitive capital of Washington, the White House in the early decades of the nineteenth century became an important center for elegant entertainment and informal musical programs. Like the Parisian *salon,* these artistic evenings reflected the fine European tastes of the first six presidents and first ladies. With industrialization and the great railroad expansion, touring artists began to perform at the White House during the 1840s. Among the first were the singing families and balladeers with their social and political messages in song: the Hutchinsons, William Dempster, and the Baker Family. Opera singers, such as the young diva, Meda Blanchard from Washington, Etelka Gerster from Hungary, and the black soprano Marie Selika from Cincinnati, followed under Abraham Lincoln and Rutherford Hayes. Most of these programs were informal musicales, as the Hayeses called them, held in the Red or Green Room with light refreshments following. The White House staged its first formal East Room concert, preceded by supper, during Chester Arthur's administration and saw what appears to be its first printed program under Benjamin Harrison.

In 1903 Steinway & Sons presented the East Room with its first grand piano, and world-renowned pianists came to perform at the mansion—Ferruccio Busoni, Ignacy Paderewski, Josef Hofmann, Olga Samaroff, Fannie Bloomfield Zeisler, Sergei Rachmaninoff, and a host of others. This piano was replaced by another Steinway concert grand in 1938, which remains in the White House today. Guest artists performed for the numerous diplomatic dinners and musicales during the early part of the century but harpist Mildred Dilling, who entertained the king and queen of Siam under Herbert Hoover, was the first to be invited to play for a chief of state. Opera was first staged, albeit modestly, during Franklin Roosevelt's administration, and serious chamber music was performed at the mansion as early as William McKinley's time. But while opera, ballet, chamber music, and jazz all appeared at the mansion before 1940, it was the administration of John F. Kennedy in the early 1960s that gave these styles a clearly defined focus, establishing the White House as a prominent center for America's artistic achievements.

The choice of musical programs at the White House has tended to be more conservative than innovative, more reflective than prophetic. But there have been some notable exceptions. Beginning with Theodore Roosevelt and the assistance of Steinway & Sons in arranging the programs, chamber music, the modern French and Russian schools, and especially American music were featured at a time when these styles were barely recognized in this country. "In this labor of love," wrote the *National Magazine* in 1916, "the Steinways have preserved a patriotic motif. They have maintained the policy that has long distinguished the White House, of encouraging American music and American artists." What other institution can boast this claim over so long and continuous a period in history?

Recognizing brilliant young talent has also been part of White House artistic philosophy from its earliest days. Teresa Carreño, Etelka Gerster, Erica Morini, Vladimir Horowitz, Pablo Casals, Dorothy Maynor, Ruggiero Ricci, and Eugene List are only a few of the noted artists who performed for a president before they were thirty. But obtaining world-renowned talent is not always easy, especially today when artists are in great demand and jet all over the world under tightly controlled contracts. Despite the coveted honor of playing for the president, artists such as Joan Sutherland and Luciano Pavarotti have had to turn down command performances because of their schedules and commitments. Isaac Stern, who has played many times at the White House, recalls the time he barely made it there for a reception. "I had the orchestra in Buffalo change the order of the program so I played in the first half and had a police escort to the airfield where a private jet flew me to Andrews Air Force Base. The White House had a car waiting, and it drove me to the reception." On another occasion, Stern had to apologize to the president, vice-president, and secretary of state: a jet was waiting to take him to his next engagement. If he did not leave, the Washington airport would close down. "Even the White House couldn't get them to hold the airport open for me so that I could stay a few minutes longer and chat with the president," he chuckled.

Television today has opened to the world the first family as arts supporter in a way unparalleled in past decades. We view the president and first lady in the White House enjoying their excellent "Young Performers" series and at various Kennedy Center functions, Ford's Theater, and other cultural affairs. But is presidential interest in the performing arts a mere image-making ploy? Presidents and their families throughout history have genuinely enjoyed music in various degrees as a relaxing diversion, and they have recognized the value of culture to the nation and the human spirit. Thomas Jefferson and Harry Truman were clearly not the only presidents for whom music was a "companion to divert and delight," as our third president professed. Time and again music's persuasive powers have moved the heart and mind of a tormented, weary chief of state. Impulsively. Joyously. Quietly. We need look no further than to George Washington, John Quincy Adams, John Tyler, Abraham Lincoln, Rutherford Hayes, Chester Arthur, Woodrow Wilson, Franklin Roosevelt, Dwight Eisenhower, Richard Nixon, Jimmy Carter, Ronald Reagan, and many others.

Like a vast pendulum swinging back and forth, history ensures that every tone from the past raises an echo today. Thus we can discern certain patterns within the political and cultural climate of the United States and in her leaders. A look backward to five consecutive administrations during the nineteenth century, for example, reveals a striking parallel with five consecutive periods in the twentieth. The Civil War and World War II brought to Lincoln and FDR the musical voices of the troubled masses; the postwar periods of both Grant and Eisenhower enjoyed the military "court" musicians of the mansion; Hayes and Kennedy refreshed the nation with a renewed visibility of the performing arts; Arthur and Lyndon Johnson nurtured those legacies; Cleveland and Nixon added a touch of levity through the popular music they brought to the mansion. And so the pendulum continues to swing—dynamically, creatively. Perhaps one day we will see an important U.S. premiere televised from the White House or a major American composition commissioned by the president. Indeed, there will be many new directions to explore as the performing arts in America continue to gain vitality and significance.

Despite the expanded focus on the presidency by today's media, the perception of this great office has not changed much over the years. Presidential power, performance, and integrity have always been essential to a public that has tended to deify or revere its chief executives from the days of Washington. Harold Laski once said that the president, unique among world leaders, is both "more or less a king and more or less a prime minister." Thus the ceremonial traditions, the pageantry associated with this highest of American offices, still plays as significant a role today as it did during the earliest decades of the presidency—in many ways, even more vital. Through White House musical traditions, our spirits seem to cling to a bygone era, to an age of romantic chivalry in a time of burgeoning technology and commercialism. "In a sense," wrote Anatole Broyard, a critic with the *New York Times*, "America was discovered because European romanticism had nowhere else to go. It had exhausted its poetic impulse in chivalry, kings, castles and cathedrals."

Perhaps then, those words offer an explanation for that unique American phenomenon—White House music. America's early leaders had no indigenous American courtly culture to draw upon, but they had some knowledge of Haydn's work at Esterhazy, aristocratic *Hausmusik* in Vienna, "The King's Private Band" of Charles II, or a Rameau comédie-ballet at the royal palace at Versailles. Curiously, by the early twentieth century, our state musical traditions became more visible and established, as many of those in Europe declined. Certain practices that we borrowed from abroad, such as the "command performance," and the gala after-dinner state entertainment by famous artists, barely exist anymore in the major European countries. Have they been transferred to the New World where they are enjoyed as lingering vestiges of romanticism? Might they be useful tools to gain support for the arts in a nation that lacks the extensive government subsidies found in Europe? Is the music of the White House an image, after all? Perhaps. But it is a lyric image, a joyous vision, and the most graceful language of glory the president will ever know. Music will always be a vital part of the American adventure of discovery, and the White House will remain a prime mover in the voyage.

PART ONE

★ ★ ★

1789–1865

LONG BEFORE the White House was constructed, its colorful history had begun—with the people of America, the explorers, settlers, and pioneers who searched for new frontiers with confidence and an undaunted quest for freedom. Curious, optimistic, and stubbornly independent, the first Americans reflected a spirit underscored by Thomas Jefferson, who wrote in the Declaration of Independence: "We hold these truths to be self-evident, that all men are created equal, that they are endowed by their Creator with certain unalienable rights, that amongst these are Life, Liberty and the pursuit of Happiness." But with these rights came new challenges. The price of freedom was high. Strengthening our national identity was not easy, and America's early decades were fraught with dissension and war. The tradition represented by the Bay Psalm Book—the first book printed in the New England colonies—must surely have lent welcome comfort to those early adventurers.

When the first emigrant ships from northern Europe set sail for America, the continent had already been discovered more than a century earlier. Shortly after the voyage of Christopher Columbus in 1492, the Spaniards founded flourishing colonies in Mexico, and in 1535 Hernando Cortes reached California. English, Dutch, and French settlers in the early seventeenth century soon realized that in this amazing new land grain, fruit, and vines flourished, cattle prospered, and farms yielded a rich return. In 1607 a group of English colonists founded Jamestown, Virginia, and in 1620 Puritans, dissatisfied with the religious situation in England, settled in New Plymouth and later in Boston, where their maxim, "Never waste precious time," became a basic American doctrine. As settlers emigrated northward to the new colonies of Maine and New Hampshire and southward to Rhode Island and Connecticut, a new America arose. For in spite of constant warfare with the Indians and the tensions of world politics, Americans proved that left to their own resources they could fend for themselves. In the words of John Adams: "The Revolution was complete in the minds of the people, and the Union of the Colonies, long before the war commenced."

With George Washington appointed commander-in-chief of the American forces in 1775, the War of Independence cut the ties between the thirteen colonies and the government of King George III of England, whose Coercive Acts had infuriated the independent young nation. On July 4, 1776, the Declaration of Independence was adopted, and after nearly eight years of war, England signed the Treaty of Paris in 1783, thus recognizing the autonomy of a new and important republic— a nation of thirteen colonies that formed a refuge for all who abhorred tyranny or suffered persecution for reasons of religion, race, or creed. In 1787 fifty-five Americans met in Philadelphia to formulate the Federal Constitution, and in 1792 its first ten amendments, the Bill of Rights, went into effect.

After a second war with England that lasted from 1812 to 1814, the westward movement of land-hungry Americans from the East began again with renewed force. Over 5 million people came to the United States between 1820 and 1860, most of them Scandanavians and Germans, and new states reshaped the map of America to the East and West of the Mississippi River. Between 1816 and 1821, Indiana, Mississippi, Illinois, Alabama, Maine, and Missouri were added to the Union. Texas became the twenty-eighth state in 1845 and California the thirty-first in 1850.

During the decades before the Civil War economic expansion occurred as rapidly as territorial growth. In the coal- and steel-producing regions near Pittsburgh, vast mines and steel works came into being. While the nation's industrial center lay in New England and the middle states of the Atlantic coast, the South remained primarily an agricultural area. New demands were made for equality in employment, education, and political life as the first World Conference on Women's Rights took place in 1848 in Seneca Falls, New York. And the young country's national self-confidence found artistic expression through such works as James Fenimore Cooper's *The Leather-Stocking Tales,* William Sidney Mount's *Dancing on the Barn Floor,* and Anton Philip Heinrich's *Dawning of Music in Kentucky.* A new American culture was being formed, and it flourished as the nation prospered.

Yet the faster America developed, the clearer its conflicting interests became. One of the nation's most painful problems was the question of slavery, which threatened to destroy national unity and cast a dark shadow over the country's development. The split in public opinion over Slave State and Free Soil State flared up again and again, with the South defending slavery as an unalterable institution on which the entire economy of its plantations depended and the North demanding its total abolition. In the North the new antislavery Republican Party was founded, and its protagonist, Abraham Lincoln, was inaugurated as president of the United States on March 4, 1861. But while Lincoln refused to recognize the secession of the southern states from the Union and pleaded passionately for the old bonds of friendship to be renewed, war broke out when Confederate troops, led by General Pierre G. T. Beauregard, bombarded Fort Sumter in Charleston Harbor on April 12, 1861. A crucial turning point in the country's history, the Civil War engendered a bitterness between North and South, between blacks and whites, that has not yet been effaced from American history.

Hatred, pride, courage, fear, bloodshed, defeat, and victory all formed the spirit of this nation "divided against itself." And in the culture of the times—in the poetry, novels, plays, paintings, and especially music—the story was retold a thousand times and more. From Harriet Beecher Stowe's *Uncle Tom's Cabin* to the Hutchinson Family Singers' "Get Off the Track," Americans heard their country's messages in voices that rang out all too clearly. They were powerful voices that penetrated even the walls of the White House and formed a unique tale. For the story of the White House is the saga of America. And in the pages to follow, this tale is colored by the rich hues of America's musical voices, instruments, and performers—all reflecting the diversity of a nation and the spirit of its people.

CHAPTER 1

MUSICAL LIFE AT HOME

★ ★ ★

Washington

Nothing is more agreeable, and
ornamental, than good music.

George Washington
June 4, 1777

The windows were thrown open wide at Number 3 Cherry Street
during those warm summer days in 1789. Anyone walking nearby
could hear ten-year-old Nelly Custis practicing on her new pianoforte,
a gift from her stepgrandfather, George Washington, shortly after he
became president. Pleyel sonatas in the incipient stages of virtuosity?
A childish rendering of the "top ten" of the day's ballad-opera tunes?
Scotch, Irish, or English melodies? Perhaps. For Nelly was made to
practice four and five hours a day by her doting grandmother, Martha
Dandridge Custis Washington.[1] Indeed, the White House from its
earliest days resounded with musical tones and airs reflecting early
America's perennial fascination with the keyboard—a family hearth,
a replica of gentility, a burgeoning industry, a titillating idol of the
American inventive spirit. And in the president's mansion, the piano
reigned in yet another fashion—as an elegant image of court life in
a democracy.

Washington occupied three Executive Mansions during his two
terms in office, yet not one of them was in the city that bears his
name. The graceful house on Cherry Street in New York City built
by Walter Franklin, one of the city's wealthiest merchants, afforded
a view of New York Bay, Long Island, and the East River. Washington
took possession of the first "Presidential Palace" only a few days before
his inauguration on April 4, 1789. His wife, the former widow Martha
Custis whom Washington married in 1759, and her two grandchildren,
Eleanor (Nelly) Parke Custis and George Washington (Tub or Little
Wash) Parke Custis, joined him the following month.[2] As winter ap-
proached the family realized that their home was too small, so they
moved to a large mansion on Broadway near Trinity Church. In 1790

7

The first President's Palace at Number 3 Cherry Street, New York, as it appeared in the 1850s, shortly before it was demolished. Ironically, Nelly Custis practiced the piano several hours a day in the building that later housed one of the nation's most flourishing piano manufacturers and music publishers, Firth, Pond and Company (formerly Firth, Hall and Pond). *Leslie's Weekly, 1856.*

Philadelphia became the temporary capital, and there the Washingtons occupied the home of Robert Morris, financier of the Revolutionary War, until the president retired from office in 1797. Washington lived on his beloved plantation at Mt. Vernon, Virginia, for slightly more than two years before his death in 1799 at the age of sixty-seven.

Music at the president's home in those early days was an intimate amusement. If a "concert artist" performed for the Washington family, it would have been one of Nelly's teachers, such as Alexander Reinagle, a long-time acquaintance of Washington. Perhaps this gifted immigrant composer ran through some of the tunes from his latest comic opera for the president or tried out one of the fine new piano sonatas he composed in the 1790s. Reinagle was often at the president's home instructing Nelly. Another early "White House artist" was Nelly herself, who was expected to perform for the ambassadors, foreign dignitaries, and members of Congress who came to visit. Once she played for over an hour in an attempt to "attune the souls" of "two homely Spaniards," one of whom she described as "a crazy count."[3]

At least twice weekly the Washingtons held receptions that became the major social events of both New York and Philadelphia. Criticized by the press hostile to Federalist policies, these gatherings were termed "court-like levees" and "queenly drawing rooms," remarks that offended the president who found the attacks unfair.[4] While he bowed to his visitors rather than shake their hands, he explained that his guests had to remain standing during the levee because there was not enough space for chairs. While we have no records indicating that musicians played during these dinners or receptions, we do know Washington was familiar with the bands attached to the army regiments that often provided music for social functions during the Revolution. When he brought Charles Lee to Valley Forge, for example, both generals were entertained "with an Elegant Dinner and the Music Playing the whole time." "An elegant band of music" also played André Grétry's quartet *Ou peut on être mieux qu'au sein de sa famille?*, most likely a transcription from one of the popular French composer's operas. The piece was played during dinner when Washington met with the Marquis de Lafayette and Comte de Claude Saint-Simon in 1781.[5] The year after Washington left the presidency, the U.S. Marine Band was officially formed on July 11, 1798, but it probably did not function as a social ensemble until it was engaged by John Adams for the White House on New Year's Day, 1801.[6] The musical life of the pre–White House era, however, was linked with the informal joy and ambience of the art in many ways, and its graceful shadow permeated every aspect of the president's spirit and that of his family.

Washington enjoyed music and the theater and was especially fond of dancing. George Washington Parke Custis's *Recollections* noted that the general was conspicuous for his graceful execution of the minuet, a dance associated with European aristocracy and considered old-fashioned by the turn of the century. At a time when some churches called dancing "a pollution of the body," Washington's diaries are filled with accounts of the various balls he attended. During his brilliant inaugural ball on May 7, 1789, he danced with nearly every lady—except Mrs. Washington who could not make the long journey from Mt. Vernon to New York in time to attend. Dancing was also an important recreation at Mt. Vernon where Washington and his family spent two to three months of the year during his presidency. Both Nelly and Tub had dancing lessons, their teacher being the illustrious James Robardet, "lately from Europe" who had "met with the general patronage and applause of the first characters in America."[7]

Whenever he could, Washington attended plays (usually interspersed with music), English ballad operas, or concerts sometimes five or six times a season while he was president and a special box was reserved for him at several of the theaters. In Williamsburg during 1771–72 he often attended the satirical productions of the Virginia Company, whose repertory included John Gay's famous *Beggar's Opera*. With its dialogue and familiar songs, *The Beggar's Opera* (1728) was one of the earliest important examples of the ballad opera, a style of British stage entertainment that flourished in the colonies. On July 10, 1787,

President George Washington dancing the minuet at his inaugural ball, as shown on the cover of *Harper's Bazaar*, May 11, 1889. The issue commemorated the centenary of his inauguration.

in Philadelphia Washington enjoyed James Townley's "sensational" *High Life below the Stairs*, which was billed as a "concert" to circumvent Pennsylvania laws forbidding theatrical performances. Washington was known to have opposed what he felt were narrow-minded restrictions against drama. In 1789 the bans were lifted in Philadelphia and four years later in Boston.

One of the first musical events the president attended after taking office was a bawdy little ballad opera called *The Clandestine Marriage*, presented in New York City by the Old American Company on June 13, 1789. The president also lightened his cumbrous duties periodically with renditions of *Beau Strategem*, *The Lock and Key* (called "a comic opera in 2 acts"), *The Way to Get Married*, and *Animal Magnetism*, all of which he saw in Philadelphia. The last two works were staged on February 27, 1797, by the Reinagle-Wignell Company at the spacious, elegant New Theater on Chestnut Street. But the general's favorite was William Shield's little comic opera *Poor Soldier*, first performed in London in 1783. Seated in an "elegantly fitted up" presidential box, he watched this production at the John Street Theater off Broadway in May 1789, shortly after taking office. Accounts of the event emphasized that a good time was had by all—with the exception of Pennsylvania Senator William Maclay, "an exceedingly straight-laced Republican, who recorded in his diary that he thought the play was 'an indecent representation before ladies of character and virtue,' and wished it had been one 'that inculcated more prudential manners.' "[8]

Sometimes President and Mrs. Washington would enjoy a fashionable early dinner at 3:00 in the afternoon and then attend a long show beginning at 5:00. On December 4, 1796, they saw such a production at the South Street Theater. The Old American Company presented a comedy called *The Young Quaker or The Fair Philadelphian* by O'Keefe, "after which there was a 'pantomimic ballet' of the Two Philosophers, a Musical Piece called The Children in the Wood, a recitation of Dr. Goldsmith's celebrated Epilogue in the character of Harlequin—the whole performance concluding with a Leap through a Barrel of Fire."[9] However unsophisticated these presidential artistic tastes may seem, they reflected what was available to Americans during the colonial and early national period. Long after their decline in popularity in England, ballad operas continued to thrive in the United States as truncated "afterpieces," and their catchy tunes were performed separately in concerts or played on the pianoforte at home.

As more and more skilled European musicians migrated to the United States after the Revolutionary War, concert life began to flourish in New York, Philadelphia, Boston, and other cities as never before. One of the most important immigrant musicians of this period was English-born Alexander Reinagle, a composer, performer, and impresario who dominated the musical life of Philadelphia for over twenty years. Washington, who enjoyed concerts almost as much as theatrical events, attended several of Reinagle's "City Concerts" while in Philadelphia for the 1787 Constitutional Convention. On May 29, for example, he heard works by Haydn and Sarti as well as by the local composers

William Brown, Henry Capron, and Reinagle himself. Two weeks later "a new overture" by Reinagle was featured along with Capron's Violoncello Concerto and overtures by Niccolò Piccinni and Bach, probably C. P. E. Bach, whom Reinagle knew and admired. Presented on June 12, this concert was also attended by Washington. He noted in his journal: "Dined and drank tea at Mr. Morris's. Went afterwards to a concert at the City Tavern."[10]

The associations that Washington made through the City Concerts subscription series resulted in his hiring three of the musicians to teach his adopted granddaughter, Nelly Custis: Reinagle from 1789 to 1792, and John Christopher Moller and Capron for the remainder of Washington's presidency. Moller came to America from London, settling in Philadelphia and later in New York. A codirector of the City Concerts with Reinagle, he was also one of the city's first music publishers and dealers.[11] Shortly after he moved to New York in 1795,

Alexander Reinagle, Nelly Custis's piano teacher, in a drawing by Joseph Muller. Reinagle's piano sonatas, written in ca. 1790, four years after he arrived in America from London, are believed to be the first piano sonatas composed in this country.

he published an edition of Philip Phile's "The President's March" with a march of his own on the same page. Phile's tune, played often for Washington in various editions, was set to verse by Joseph Hopkinson in 1798, thus achieving immortality as the popular national song, "Hail Columbia."[12]

Reinagle, in his turn, also found opportunity to eulogize the president in music. He chose Washington's famous journey from Mount Vernon to New York City to take the oath of office in Federal Hall, April 30, 1789. Reinagle's "Chorus sung before General Washington as he passed under the Triumphal Arch raised on the Bridge at Trenton, April 21, 1789," was "Set to Music and Dedicated by Permission to Mrs. Washington" as the title page indicates. On the other side of this page is a charming description of a group of young girls robed in white, singing as they strewed flowers before the impressed general:

> Welcome mighty chief! once more
> Welcome to this grateful shore
> Now no mercenary Foe
> Aims again the fatal blow.
>
> Virgins fair and Matrons grave,
> Those thy conquering Arms did save,
> Build for thee Triumphal Bowers
> Strew, ye fair, his way with flowers,
> Strew your Hero's way with Flowers.[13]

Reinagle's piece was probably not the version sung by these young women, however. Aside from the fact that it is set in three parts with the lowest part written in the bass clef, a concert presented on September 22, 1789, featured a piece advertised as "a chorus to the words which were sung as General Washington passed the bridge at Trenton—the music now composed by Mr. Reinagle." The key word here is "now." John Tasker Howard believes the words were originally sung to the music of Handel's "See the Conquering Hero Comes" from *Judas Maccabaeus* and that Reinagle's was a later setting, not the music used at Trenton. While this does not agree with Vera Lawrence's conclusions, it does not necessarily refute her assertion that Reinagle's piece is the first music to have been composed for a president of the United States.[14]

More than any other president, Washington has been sentimentalized, emulated, monumentalized, and deified. Even before he began his eight years in office as our first president, Americans thought of him as a demigod. A nation with scant history of its own, America seemed to turn to the epic heroism of classical civilizations to satisfy its political and cultural psyche. Indeed, statesman Francis Hopkinson even composed an allegorical oratorio, *The Temple of Minerva*, that depicted the goddess Minerva joining with the Genius of America and the Genius of France in praise of General Washington and the French-American Alliance. How the good general and his lady must have relished this musical tribute when they heard it first performed at a fashionable private gathering in Philadelphia on December 11, 1781![15]

Washington must have known of his reputation. One of Dodds's important innovations was an improvement in the structure of the pianoforte's hammers and dampers. Having arrived in New York from London in 1785, Dodds advertised in the *Independent Journal* on August 13 that he was an "Organ Builder, Harpsichord, and PianoForte Maker" who also sold and repaired "Violins, German Flutes, Guittars, Hautboys and Clarinets." When Washington bought the pianoforte, Dodds's "Musical Instrument Manufactory" was located at No. 66 Queen Street, an address he retained after he joined in partnership with a German-born luthier, Christian Claus, in 1791.[26]

Nelly's pianoforte, as the early pianos were called, was brought to Philadelphia when the family moved there in 1790. Records show that it was tuned periodically along with the fine new harpsichord Washington bought her in December 1793. The five-octave, two-manual harpsichord was ordered from Longman and Broderip, No. 26 Cheapside and No. 13 Haymarket, London. It stands today at Mt. Vernon and was the first piece of original furniture to be returned to the plantation after the property was acquired by the Mt. Vernon Ladies Association during the mid-nineteenth century.

Five-octave, two-manual harpsichord was purchased by George Washington from Longman and Broderip, London, in 1793. Both this instrument and a Dodds pianoforte were played by Nelly Custis while she lived in the Presidential Home in Philadelphia.

Title page from a collection of keyboard music belonging to Nelly Custis: Six Sonatas for Clavecin or Pianoforte, op. 18, by Johann Christian Bach, published in Berlin by J. J. Hummel ca. 1780. Two of the sonatas are for four hands and with various other compositions are bound into a single volume bearing Nelly's name.

Nelly also owned an English guitar, which bears her initials "E P C" on the ivory rosette that decorates the instrument. Since the guitar, too, came from the firm Longman and Broderip, it may have been ordered about the same time as the harpsichord. It was believed to have been a birthday gift to Nelly from the president. Quite possibly she learned to play it during her lessons with Capron, who instructed "ladies and gentlemen in the art of singing and of playing on the Spanish and English guitars" (or so his newspaper advertisements ran at this time).[27] The instrument, resembling a keyed cither, has a keyboard and hammer mechanism that activates six sets of strings. The action is fitted inside a drawer that can be pulled out of the lower left side of the body.

What did Nelly Custis play on her elegant instruments in the presidential mansions? At the end of the eighteenth century and well throughout the nineteenth, playing the piano was primarily a lady's art, with the gentlemen amateurs aspiring to the somewhat more "intricate" techniques of the violin or German flute. To be educated, a young American woman usually studied history, arithmetic, geography, and languages, as well as music, sewing, and "Dancing with Fancy Work only if required." Nelly's large collection of music is housed at Mt. Vernon, Woodlawn Plantation, the Library of Congress, and Harvard University's Houghton Library. Comprising over ten books, it represents publishers from Paris, London, Dublin, and America, especially Philadelphia. The collection also offers a fine overview of period styles and tastes, as well as Nelly's own musical education. We can envision her at the piano with Reinagle's edition of *A Collection of Favorite Songs, divided into two books containing most of the airs in the Poor Soldier, Rosina etc., and the principal Songs sung at Vaux Hall* (ca. 1789). Published in Philadelphia, the collection includes "I've kiss'd and I've prattled," "The Spring with Smiling Face," "Out of My Sight or I'll box your ears," and "Good morrow to your night cap." The arrangements are very simple, many with fingering written in, suggesting that they might have been used for Nelly's first lessons.

Also part of the collection are several four-hand works undoubtedly selected by Reinagle to instruct his young pupil. Among these are duets in A and F, op. 18 (1781), by Johann Christian Bach, and three sonatas for four hands by Ignace Pleyel (1796). As Nelly progressed, she was challenged by an array of composers popular at the time though largely forgotten today: Johann Vanhal, Johann Sterkel, Leopold Kozeluch, and Theodore Smith. But there can be no doubt that Reinagle—reputed to have introduced to Americans works by Joseph Haydn, as well as a variety of four-hand keyboard music—provided Nelly with "the latest" music. Haydn's Symphony no. 85 in B-flat, "La reine," composed in 1785, was captivating the world with its wit and verve, and Nelly's collection includes a keyboard arrangement of this new masterpiece. On the other hand, Nelly was probably no different from most young players. Chances are she had to plead with her teacher to let her play the real hit of the day—Kotzwara's bombastic warhorse, "Battle of Prague" (1789). With its bugle calls, cannon shots, and other battle appurtenances written into the music, the work's enormous success on both sides of the Atlantic was dubbed "a petty plague that seemed unabatable through the decades."[28] On those warm summer evenings at the "President's Palace" when Nelly tried out this piece, she may have closed the windows. Perhaps it was best.

CHAPTER 2

THE EUROPEAN TOUCH

John Adams to John Quincy Adams

His very foot has music in't
As he comes up the stairs . . .
And shall I see his face again
And shall I hear him speak?

"There's nae Luck
about the House"

"How lonely are my days? How solitary are my nights?" wrote Abigail Adams to her husband John one bleak winter evening in 1778. "How insupportable the idea, that three thousand miles and the vast ocean now divide us!" But an old Scotch song seemed to ring in her ears like a dusty echo of bygone loves. "How oft has my heart danced to the sound of that music?" she wrote: ". . . the native simplicity of it had all the power of a well-wrought tragedy. When I could conquer my sensibility I begged the song, and Master Charles [aged eight] has learned it, and consoles his mamma by singing it to her. I will enclose it to you. It has beauties in it to me, which an indifferent person would not feel perhaps."[1]

Indeed, music became a potion "to divert a melancholy hour" on more than one occasion for Abigail. Long separations often kept her apart from John Adams. Especially during his diplomatic missions abroad as commissioner to France and later minister to the Netherlands and England, Abigail Adams bore the loneliness, responsibilities, and struggles of her husband's ministerial career. Quietly she paid the price for his accomplishments, reflecting the dilemma, still unstudied and unsung, of women in America's early diplomatic life.

Vain, cantankerous, and extremely brilliant, John Adams served for two terms as vice-president under George Washington. On March 4, 1797, he was inaugurated as the second president of the United States. Due to ill health, Abigail remained for long periods at the Quincy farm while Adams served in the capital at Philadelphia. The site for the "Federal City," as George Washington called it, had been determined by Congress in 1790 and formally named the City of Washington the following year. On October 13, 1792, the cornerstone for the "President's Mansion" was laid after a prize of $500 for designing the house was awarded to Irish-born architect, James Hoban. With the capital established at Washington in 1800, President Adams moved into the President's Mansion on November 1 of that year. Abigail arrived two weeks later, only to face what she called a "great castle" in a "wilderness city" of mud, cowpaths, and wooden huts. None of the rooms was finished. Damp plaster chilled the walls, and obtaining firewood regularly was impossible. The main stairway to the second floor would not be erected for months. Still "this house," wrote Abigail to her daughter, "is built for ages to come."[2] How right she was! But could she have realized—as she hung her laundry in "the great unfinished audience-room"—that the future East Room would one day become the stage for the finest performing artists in the world?

The Adamses lived in the White House only about four months when the presidency went to Adams's bitter opponent, Thomas Jefferson, on March 4, 1801. During this short period in the home, the couple hardly had time to unpack, let alone transport a fragile piano or other musical instruments to the drafty, unfinished mansion. There are no records indicating that either John or Abigail owned musical instruments or purchased them for the White House with government funds. Charles Adams sang "with his light and pleasant voice," and John Quincy played the flute, but both boys were grown when their parents lived in the White House.[3]

President and Mrs. Adams, however, were responsible for bringing the first musical ensemble to the new White House, an indication of the importance they placed on music as a vital part of the spirit and social flair of the White House. The young U.S. Marine Band, which later became known as "The President's Own," played for the Adamses'

The President's Mansion (distant left center) when Thomas Jefferson first lived there. At the far right is Blodgett's Hotel, which housed the Capital's first theater of 130 rough wooden seats. Like the President's Mansion, Blodgett's was designed by James Hoban. Watercolor by Nicholas King, ca. 1803.

first reception held on New Year's Day, 1801. This event established the tradition of the Marine Band's performances at the White House that exists to the present day. We cannot be certain of the exact instrumentation of the band at this time. On August 31, 1800, Commandant William Burrows wrote Lieutenant Hall: "Procure and send . . . 2 French Horns, 2 C Clarinets, 1 Bassoon, 1 Bass Drum, 2 feet and 1/2 long and 2 feet in diameter. . . . You will pay $180. . . . I think the price of the Instruments very high." The instruments arrived on November 6, and Burrows urged that "there must be no time lost in instructing them."[4] While the bass drum would not have been used for indoor social events, two oboes and an additional bassoon may have been added later to the ensemble. Thus, like the *Harmonie* of European courts and British military units in America during the Revolution, the Marine Band functioned in a social as well as ceremonial capacity from its earliest days. But for lack of funds and space (the Adams reception was held in the Oval Room upstairs), only five or six players probably composed the first New Year's band, the oboes being omitted.

Dressed in their scarlet coats faced and edged in blue, the musicians must have added a festive image to the scene. An early report specifies their uniforms at that time also consisted of "blue pantaloons with scarlet seams and gaiters to the knees" and "three-cornered hats edged with yellow." What they played, however, must be pieced together from accounts of Marine Band repertory during this early period: "The President's March" ["Hail Columbia"] and some fife and drum tunes from the Revolutionary War, such as "Dog and Gun," "Rural Felicity," and "Yankee Doodle." And there were others: "Friend and Pitcher," "Marseillaise Hymn," "Battle of the Kegs," "Around the Huge Oak," and "He's aye a kissing me."[5] Or could Abigail Adams perhaps have made a special request (as succeeding first families often did)—her favorite Scotch song, "There's nae Luck about the House"?

Unlike John Quincy and Louisa Catherine Adams, the John Adamses had only modest musical talents and interests. Though inherently bright, Abigail lacked the education of her successors. "I was never sent to any school," she said. "In those days it was fashionable to ridicule female learning."[6] Both she and John typified a rather austere Puritanism, reflected in Adams's comment to Mercy Warren in 1795 that he had no pleasure or amusement which possessed any charms for him: "balls, assemblies, concerts, cards, horses, dogs never engaged any part of my [his] attention . . . business alone."[7] Yet his European experiences showed that dogs and concerts were at least put into separate categories within his frame of mind. The varied cultural opportunities abroad must have had a lasting effect on the Adamses' memories and tastes.

When he was in France, John Adams attended a "Concert Spirituel" at the Tuileries on April 19, 1778, where "a vast number of Instruments were performing to an immense Crowd of Company. There were Men Singers and Women Singers. . . . The Musick however did not entirely satisfy me. . . . There was too much sound for me."[8] French grand opera to Adams was "a sprightly amusement, having never seen anything of the kind before." On May 19, 1778, he attended a production in Paris with Benjamin Franklin and noted in his diary that "the Words are unintelligible, and if they were not, they are said to be very insignificant."[9]

Abigail Adams seemed much more receptive to the French operatic sensibility and nuance. On February 20, 1785, shortly after having joined her husband in Europe, she conveyed to her sister, Mary Cranch, her impressions of a production that could have been Gluck's *Armide* (1777) or perhaps his *Iphigénie en Tauride* (1779). Both were being performed in Paris at this time: "And O! the music, vocal and instrumental: It has a soft, persuasive power, and a dying sound. Conceive a highly decorated building, filled with youth, beauty, grace, ease, clad in all the most pleasing and various ornaments of dress which fancy can form; these objects singing like cherubs to the best tuned instruments most skilfully handled, the softest, tenderest strains; every attitude corresponding with the music; full of the God or Goddess whom they celebrate."[10]

But the same letter shows another side of Abigail's nature. Her New England concern for morals led her to describe the ballet almost entirely from the viewpoint of its propriety: "Girls, clothed in the thinnest silk and gauze, with their petticoats short, springing two feet from the floor, poising themselves in the air, with their feet flying, and as perfectly showing their garters and drawers as though no petticoat had been worn, was a sight altogether new to me. Their motions are as light as air, and as quick as lightening; they balance themselves to astonishment." But while she was "ashamed to be seen to look at them," Abigail also admitted that she was growing used to "the habits, customs, and fashions, which at first disgusted me."[11]

The *Messiah* performance Abigail saw later that same year during the Handel Commemoration at Westminster Abbey was "the most powerful effect of music I ever experienced. . . . It is impossible to describe to you the solemnity and dignity of the scene," Abigail wrote to her sister. "When it came to that part, the Hallelujah, the whole assembly rose and all the musicians, every person uncovered. Only conceive six hundred voices and instruments perfectly chording one word and one sound. I could scarcely believe myself an inhabitant of the earth. I was one continued shudder from the beginning to the end of the performance."[12]

After she returned to the United States, Abigail Adams reported hearing a program of a very different nature. One month after John Adams had been inaugurated as president, she attended the first performance of "Hail Columbia" on April 25, 1798, at the New Theatre on Chestnut Street. Internal tension between Federalists and anti-Federalists was mounting daily at this time, and many felt that war with France was inevitable. The singer and actor Gilbert Fox, worried about filling the theater for his benefit performance, had asked Joseph Hopkinson to write a patriotic song adapted to the tune of Philip Phile's popular "President's March." The day after the performance, the first lady described her vivid reactions to Mary Cranch:

My Dear Sister:

I inclose to you a National song composed by this same Mr. [Joseph] Hopkinson. French Tunes have for a long time usurped an uncontrolled sway. Since the Change in the publick opinion respecting France, the people began to lose the relish for them, and what had been harmony, now becomes discord. Accordingly their [*sic*] had been for several Evenings at the Theater something like disorder, one party crying out for the President's March and Yankee Doodle, whilst Cier ["Ça ira"] was vociferated from the other. It was hisst off repeatedly. The Managers were blamed. Their cause was that they had not any words to the Presidents March—Mr. Hopkinson accordingly composed these to the tune. Last Eve'ng they were sung for the first time. I had a Great curiosity to see for myself the Effect . . . they called again for the song, and made him [Fox] repeat it to the fourth time. And the last time, the whole ("Gallery" cancelled) Audience broke forth in the Chorus whilst the thunder from their Hands was incessant, and at the close they rose, gave 3 Huzzas, that you might have heard a mile— My Head aches in consequence of it.[13]

As President Washington was often immortalized in music, the virtues of John Adams became the subject of a song called "Adams and Liberty." "Her pride is her Adams—his Laws are her choice" sounded America's voice in 1798. It was a bold attempt to pit Federalist conservatism against liberal Jeffersonian democracy—bolder still when one considers these words by Thomas Paine, A.M., were set to the tune of an old British drinking song, "To Anacreon in Heaven," which later achieved immortality as "The Star-Spangled Banner."[14]

When Thomas Jefferson moved into the White House shortly after becoming president on March 4, 1801, the mansion was still far from being completed. Benjamin Latrobe, commissioner of public buildings and grounds, reported that the roof and gutters leaked so severely that the furniture had to be protected from damage. By 1804 there were still no cellars, and a few years later visitors were still appalled at the "ancient rude state" of the residence. "In a dark night," described one foreigner in 1807, "instead of finding your way to the house, you may, perchance, fall into a pit, or stumble over a heap of rubbish."[15] The barnlike cavity held little warmth for Jefferson, nineteen years a widower, who lived in the mansion for two terms. He and his personal secretary Meriwether Lewis felt somewhat lugubriously like "two mice in a church."[16]

Jefferson found life in the new capital rather desolate and lonely. For a cultured man, a fine amateur performer, and lover of good music, the city of Washington left much to be desired. He found a population of about 4,000 citizens whose main entertainment consisted of dancing assemblies, magic shows, comic plays, the "Alla-Podrida" (or mish-

Thomas Jefferson, a fine amateur violinist and devotee of the arts, considered music to be his "favorite passion." This well-known painting by Rembrandt Peale (1800) hangs in the Blue Room of the White House.

mash), and a learned pig that could spell, read, and tell the days of the week. Washington's first theater had just opened in the summer of 1800. Called the United States, it was merely a small room seating 130 in Blodgett's Hotel, designed by James Hoban and located near the President's House. Records do not indicate what theatrical events the president attended while in office, although he did buy tickets to a rope-walking show on December 22, 1806, during which Signor Manfredi precariously danced a Spanish fandango over two dozen eggs.[17]

Thomas Jefferson, in fact, regarded music as "the favorite passion of my soul." At the age of seventy-four he considered the art to be "invaluable where a person has an ear. It furnishes a delightful recreation for the hours of respite from the cares of the day."[18] Jefferson's inventive mind, pursuit of excellence, abilities as a performer, and concern for the education of his daughters and granddaughters are well documented in Helen Cripe's *Thomas Jefferson and Music*. His extensive collection of family music is housed in the University of Virginia Library and reflects the tastes of a diligent collector who accumulated every variety and arrangement of music that he, his family, and friends could perform. More than any other president, Jefferson has been recognized by historians as a devotee of the joys of music—his "delightful recreation."

How and when Jefferson learned to play the violin are not known. He was a competent violinist by the age of fourteen, however, and played regularly with the noted gentlemen amateurs of Virginia. He and Patrick Henry often played their fiddles together. During his student and early professional years in Williamsburg in the 1760s, Jefferson performed with harpsichordist Robert Carter, the wealthy planter of Nomini Hall, and violinist/cellist John Tyler, whose bow arm Jefferson had admired. Tyler's son, also named John, became our nation's tenth president in 1841. Musical evenings were also staged by Governor Francis Fauquier, who frequently invited Jefferson to "the palace." Here, with the portraits of the king and queen looking down from the wall, the future drafter of the Declaration of Independence played quartets and trios with the royal governor and his friends.[19]

What compositions did the young lawyer play with his musical confrères? Jefferson's own catalogue, compiled in 1783, provides a clue. Listed under the category "Instrumental Music"—along with a few country dances and Scotch and Irish airs—are over 100 collections of compositions, mostly chamber works, by representative composers of the period. Unfortunately, Jefferson did not always indicate the opus numbers, and even when he did, it is often difficult to determine the pieces he acquired. Many works that exist in the family collection at the University of Virginia, Charlottesville, are not listed, while important items mentioned in the catalogue are lost.[20] The following are merely a few of the compositions Jefferson undoubtedly played or enjoyed, as he listed them:

> Corelli's concertos in parts
> Vivaldi's concertos in parts
> Vivaldi's Cuckoo & Extravaganza
> Handel's 60 overtures from all his Operas and Oratorios, 8 parts
> Corelli's Sonatas op. 7th
> Martini of Milan's Sonatas Op. 1.2.3.4
> Campioni's Sonatas Op. 1.2.3.4.5.6.7
> Boccherini's Sonatas Op. 2. 11
> Figlio's duets

Some authorities believe the catalogue contains entries of items purchased as late as 1814. Certainly several of the works were composed later than 1783, such as the "Haydn 47th. 48th" listed under sonatas. These, in fact, may have been quartets. Along with Arcangelo Corelli, a composer abundantly represented in Jefferson's catalogue, the name

Revolving wooden music stand believed to have been made by John Hemings after Thomas Jefferson's designs. The stand, which folds into a compact box, has music racks for one standing and four seated players.

Carlo Antonio Campioni (1720–88) appears often. Jefferson seemed to be especially fond of Campioni's trio sonatas, opp. 1–6. On a handwritten note in the family music collection he advises: "On this paper is noted the beginning of the several compositions of Campioni which are in possession of T. Jefferson. He would be glad to have everything else he has composed of Solos, Duets, or Trios. Printed copies would be preferred; but if not to be had, he would have them in manuscript."[21]

Jefferson's wife, Martha Wayles Skelton, died at the age of thirty-four after having borne six children. Only two lived to adulthood— Martha (Mrs. Thomas Mann Randolph, Jr., nicknamed "Patsy" like Washington's stepdaughter), and Mary (Mrs. John Wayles Eppes). Both young women lived in the White House for several months during 1802–3 with their husbands who were members of Congress. Like their mother, both girls were talented, and the widower Jefferson gave them every opportunity to develop their musical gifts. "Music, drawing, books, invention and exercise will be so many resources to you against *ennui,*" he once wrote to fifteen-year-old Patsy.[22] He purchased for each of the young women a fine Kirkman harpsichord, and Patsy had lessons in Philadelphia with the noted English teacher, John Bentley.

When Jefferson was minister to France from 1785 to 1789, Paris was the European center of trade, commerce, and the arts. The girls studied harpsichord, guitar, and dancing with the finest Parisian masters. Jefferson took advantage of every concert, opera, private musicale, and dramatic spectacle that he possibly could. The girls, too, became acquainted with a rich new world of artistic expression. Whether an *opéra comique* by Grétry, a new Italian opera by Niccolò Piccinni, a performance by the famed violinist Giovanni Viotti, or a vocal concert at the Tuileries—Jefferson relished all. The Concert Spirituel, which left John Adams dissatisfied, so fascinated Jefferson that he was drawn back time and time again.[23]

But the pomp and elegance of European court life, which attracted both George Washington and Adams, was abhorred by President Jefferson.[24] Adams, who continued the more formal traditions of Washington, sniffed: "Jefferson and Rush were for liberty and straight hair. I thought curled hair was as Republican as straight."[25] When Anthony Merry, His Britannic Majesty's minister to the United States, went in full dress to present his credentials, he was shocked by Jefferson's attire in "an old brown coat, red waistcoat, old corduroy small clothes, much soiled woolen hose and slippers without heels." Jefferson abolished the weekly levees of his predecessors and held more frequent, informal dinners preferring "democratic" circular tables. He was a gracious host—but to the diplomatic circle, his was a "raw and rude court."

Jefferson officially dropped the title "Presidential Palace" when he took office, and informed the citizens that his home was known as the President's House. He held only two official levees at the mansion each year—one on New Year's Day and the other on the Fourth of July. The latter is of special interest to White House musical history. It represents the earliest description of actual performers and musical selections at the mansion. As Jefferson's first reception on July 4, 1801, the event attracted considerable attention—especially the fact that the president shook hands with everyone instead of bowing.

But it was the music, above all, that "awakened patriotic feelings as well as gaiety," recounted Margaret Bayard Smith, wife of the *National Intelligencer*'s publisher.[26] In a letter to her sister, she observed: "Martial music soon announced the approach of the marine corps of Captain Burrows who in due military form saluted the President, accompanied by the President's march [probably 'Hail Columbia'] played by an excellent band attached to the corps. After undergoing various military evolutions, the company returned to the dining room, and the band from an adjacent room played a succession of fine patriotic airs."[27]

And accompanied by the Marine Band, a strong baritone voice rang clear and true—"the ladies said it was divine." The singer was Captain Thomas Tingey, handsome commandant of the newly established Washington Navy Yard. The *Intelligencer* added: "the band of music played with great precision and with inspiring animation. . . . Captain Tingey then sang with happy animation a patriotic song, composed for the occasion by Mr. [Thomas] Law, which was received with loud plaudits."

> Hail Columbia! happy land,
> Hail ye patriots, heaven born land
> Who Independence first proclaimed . . .
> Immortal be that glorious day
> When first we cast our chains away.[28]

This account shows how the term "composed for the occasion" or "newly composed" can be easily misinterpreted unless care is taken by historians to compare texts with preexisting songs. In the early days of our nation especially, parody was very common, particularly in songs that had a great national appeal. Jefferson's Fourth of July gala did not present the first performance of "Hail Columbia" (still

Captain Thomas Tingey, U.S. Navy, first commandant of the Navy Yard, Washington, D.C., and the earliest known musical soloist to perform for a White House program. Print from a painting by Charles Saint Memin.

called "The President's March" for some time to come); rather, it featured a new set of lyrics that celebrated the first Independence Day gala at the White House. Jefferson must have enjoyed vocal soloists, because five years later at the July 4, 1806, White House reception, a "Mr. Cutting" sang a song set to the tune of "Anacreon in Heaven." Eight years later this popular tune was immortalized as "The Star-Spangled Banner," when it received new lyrics by Francis Scott Key.

Smith's description of the Marine Band playing near the dining room during the reception on July 4, 1801, corroborates Benjamin Latrobe's report and design of the White House at this time. According to these documents, the band occupied space in the vestibule as it does today when it performs for state dinners or luncheons. "Leading out of the Hall opposite the 'Porter's Lodge' and 'Pantry,'" states Latrobe in his report of 1807, "was the room for the musicians." The "band" was undoubtedly the same ensemble that played for the Adams reception on New Year's Day, or it might have been slightly enlarged for this important occasion. The East Room, called at this time the "Public Audience Chamber," was still a long way from housing musical groups. Latrobe reports that the whole of the "East Front" was "entirely unfinished"; he adds, "The ceiling has given way."[29]

The Marine Band played at every New Year's and Fourth of July reception during Jefferson's terms. But reports indicate that it may have had to vie for space amid the increasing crowds. Writing to her sister, Catherine Mitchell described the final New Year's Day levee in 1809: "On our arrival at the Castle we found . . . the rooms so crowded that it was with difficulty you could squeeze through from one to the other. . . . An exquisite band of music played at intervals martial, patriotic and enlivening airs, which reverberated through the spacious dome."[30]

There is a legend that Jefferson asked Colonel William Burrows to enlist some musicians in Italy as Marines and bring them back to expand the Marine Band. The tale could indeed be true. Jefferson once had expressed the desire to import from Italy for his Virginia plantation persons who could provide domestic and musical needs simultaneously, in other words, a "court band," American style:

> The bounds of an American fortune will not admit the in-
> dulgence of a domestic band of musicians, yet I have thought
> that a passion for music might be reconciled with that economy
> which we are obliged to observe. I retain, for instance, among
> my domestic servants a gardener . . . , a weaver . . . , a cabinet
> maker . . . , and a stone cutter . . . to which I would add a
> vigneron. In a country where like yours music is cultivated
> and practised by every class I suppose there might be found
> persons of those trades who could perform on the French
> horn, clarinet or hautboy and bassoon, so that one might have
> a band of two French horns, two clarinets and hautboys and
> a bassoon, without enlarging their domestic expenses. . . .
> Without meaning to give you trouble, perhaps it might be
> practicable for you in ordinary intercourse with your people
> to find out such men disposed to come to America.[31]

This plan seems to have been realized after Jefferson became president and about the same time that his conceptions for the dec-oration of the U.S. Capitol Building developed. Jefferson arranged through his friend Filippo Mazzei to bring sculptors from Carrara, Italy, to Washington. The first of these fine artisans arrived in October 1805, and over the ensuing decades the Capitol was emblazoned with the painting, frescos, sculpture, and carving of more than forty Italian specialists.[32]

The story of the Sicilian musicians who arrived in Washington one month before the sculptors from Carrara is less dramatic—but no less colorful. The little "band" not only left its mark on the history of the Marine Band, but ultimately on the cultural life of the city of Washington itself. In 1803 Captain John Hall received orders from Colonel William Burrows, commandant of the Marine Corps, to recruit some musicians from southern Italy where American ships were based during the pirate war with Tripoli. Upon landing in Sicily, Hall scoured the east coast cities of the island for talent and finally enlisted sixteen musicians from Catania, Syracuse, and Messina to serve for a period of three years. They arrived in Washington—several with their wives and children—on September 19, 1805, much to the consternation of Burrows's successor Colonel Wharton who knew nothing of any such orders. "I have been obliged to give the Leader 50 Dolls, and the rest Ten Dollars Bounty, with a ration to eight of their wives," Hall explained, "and this Sir I was obliged to do or could not have got a single man."[33] In addition to this expense Hall had purchased several musical in-struments at Messina, further aggravating Wharton: "The Secretary of the Navy can never consent to allow 2 Military Bands for one Corps."[34]

But arrive they did—tired, dissheveled, frightened, and unable to communicate in a foreign tongue, in a strange new home that their leader described as "a desert . . . a place containing some 2 or 3 taverns and a few scattered cottages and log huts, called the City of Washington, the Metropolis of the United States of America."[35] There was Pasquale, Antonio, Salvadouar, and the Sardo brothers, who, judging from their service records, could not write their names. There were three young boys who were probably placed in the fife and drum corps; two were the Carusis, Samuel aged ten and Ignatio (called Nathaniel) aged nine. Their father Gaetano Carusi was the leader of the band, "a Master of Music who could make his own instruments."[36] Another Carusi, Lewis, was still a babe in arms. All were led off to their quarters in the Marine Barracks, "where men, women, boys and children, 30 or more in all, were obliged to bundle together in a single chamber and sleep upon the bare floor," Carusi himself recalls.[37] Four days later the Sicilians made their debut at the public banquet honoring the victories of Captain Bainbridge over the barbarous Tripolitans. There were seventeen toasts, the *National Intelligencer* noted on September 25, 1805, each accompanied by "the elegant Italian Band" as well as the regular Marine Band.

How elegant the Sicilians felt is open for conjecture. They must have been separated from the main unit because accounts of the time regularly indicate that there was both an "Italian Band" and a "Marine Band." They probably learned "Hail Columbia," "O Dear What Can the Matter Be?" and such typical American fare quite rapidly. But did they long for their vesper hymns, carnival songs, marionette tunes?— the plaintive "Canto del Carcerato" with its modal Arabic inflections?— or the gentle Catanian "Canto de contadini Etnei" (Song of the Peasants from Etna)? Did they miss the numerous *feste* of the Church, the angelus striking at dawn from the cathedral tower, the magnificent Baroque organ at the Benedictine Monastery at Catania? Most of the musicians were from this city situated on the blue Ionian sea. It was here the composer Vincenzo Bellini was born in 1801. What their musical backgrounds were is uncertain. Catania lacked a public theater which would have afforded them orchestral experience.[38] But like Sicilian laughter, music provided an undercurrent of rippling sound on the island day and night.

As for Gaetano Carusi, we can be certain he was a versatile musician. He taught "clarionet, French horn, bassoon, German flute, fife and flageolet as well as every string instrument," as an advertisement said not long after he had left the band.[39] Born in Naples, Carusi grew up in this flourishing operatic center. His professional life in Catania, where he was living when enlisted by the Marines at age forty-two, is unknown, but a notice in the *Baltimore Evening Post* on November 17, 1810, indicates his activities as a civilian in America: "Notice is hereby given to the public that Mr. Gaetano Carusi, Italian Master of Music, is arrived in the city of Baltimore—he and all his family return thanks for the encouragement he received from his friends and the public in general, and offers his services again, to give Serenades, to play at balls, or for any gentlemen that would wish to have Music played in their houses. Him and his family will attend on to arrange any kind of Music for any sort of Instruments. He also copies music, and tunes Forte Pianos. His residence is No. 56, Market Space." Carusi also composed several marches, rondos, and similar pieces that were published around this time in Baltimore and Philadelphia. He was naturalized in Philadelphia in 1820 where he ran a music store. By 1831 he had "resumed his professional business of teaching on the pianoforte" in Washington, according to the *Intelligencer*, commanding high prices for those days—"1.00 per lesson."[40]

It is difficult to know just what interest Jefferson had in the ill-fated Italian Marine Band and its leader. References to their performances at the White House are vague and sporadic. On one notable occasion they played for the reception for Tunisian ambassador, Sidi Mellimelli, with his eight-inch-long black beard, four-foot pipe, and gold-embroidered cloak. They also may have played at the Old Christ Church on G street, then known as the Marine Church. Captain Anthony Gale at Philadelphia wrote Commandant Wharton that he had purchased for the band the best collection of sacred music "that could be found in the City" and strings "for the violincello"[41]—proof that even at this early date, the band had a few orchestral instruments.

But the career of the Italian Marine Band was brief and inglorious. All the members were dismissed from the Corps after only one-half of their three years were served. Several made their way back into the band, however, and one in particular, Venerando Pulizzi, remained with the band for twenty-one years serving as its leader during the presidencies of both James Monroe and John Quincy Adams. A boy of twelve when he enlisted, Pulizzi was undoubtedly one of Gaetano Carusi's star pupils. But Carusi felt differently about his own career in the Marine Corps. He spent most of his lifetime engaged in legal battles with the U.S. government claiming he and his family were abandoned in a foreign land as a result of Hall's mistakes in procuring his services. He felt he had been "lured by false and deceitful promises . . . betrayed, insulted and treated with all the indignity of Barbarians." Even his music, purchased in Sicily with his own money and copied by hand "for the instruction of the band," had been confiscated by the ruthless Wharton. At the age of seventy-two Carusi ultimately petitioned Congress for the sum of $1,000 as compensation for his grievances, but was turned down.[42]

President Jefferson did not appear to get involved in the squabble, nor are the reasons for the band's dismissal known. Wharton felt that the Italians had disgraced the Corps by "mixing with and playing for Characters the most vicious and profligate."[43] The Marines claimed they tried to send the Carusis home, but that the aging maestro refused the offer. Carusi retorted that in order to pick up the ship at Boston, he would have had to have transported his family there in mid-winter with his own meager funds. The ironic grand finale to the Carusi drama is that the maestro's three sons, Lewis, Samuel, and Nathaniel, became very successful as impresarios, composers, and teachers in Washington. In 1822 Lewis restored a building that for several decades was the smartest social center in the city. Called "Carusi's Saloon," it was the scene of many inaugural galas, balls, and concerts attended by the presidents and their families—a kind of primitive John F.

The sons of Gaetano Carusi, the early Marine Band leader from Catania, Sicily (left to right): Lewis, Samuel, and Nathaniel. Lewis built the popular Carusi's Saloon, site of numerous presidential inaugural balls, concerts, and dancing assemblies. Painting by Gardner, 1870.

Kennedy Center for the Performing Arts. When Lewis died in 1872, he was remembered as one who "by intelligence, industry and good management . . . accumulated a handsome fortune and contributed . . . to the advancement of our city and its social and artistic attraction."[44]

Jefferson's enjoyment of music has been studied and documented, and yet his personal musical activities during his eight years in the White House remain a tantalizing enigma. Did he perform music alone or with friends? Did he invite guests to play after his numerous friendly dinner parties?[45] Was there a pianoforte or harpsichord in the White House during his administration? Did the president's musical daughters play when they visited the mansion? True, the presidency weighed heavily upon Jefferson: "He held to a Spartan regimen in his duties, spending from ten to thirteen hours a day at his desk, and allowing himself a bare four hours a day for riding, dining and 'a little un-bending.' "[46] He was fifty-seven years old when he took office and sixty-five when he left. But accounts indicate that he still enjoyed music when he retired to Monticello and played his violin on occasion when not bothered by a bad wrist.[47]

Jefferson managed to escape to Monticello frequently during his presidential years. Even though his daughter Martha kept her Kirkman harpsichord there, and Jefferson probably enjoyed relaxing musical moments at his estate, it is inconceivable he was without a keyboard instrument for the entire time he was president. He was fascinated with the new pianoforte, although he played neither piano nor harp-sichord. In 1771 he wrote to London for a pianoforte for his future wife, Martha Wayles Skelton. While details about the instrument are obscure, Jefferson was among the few Americans to own a piano at a time when the harpsichord was still preferred in more affluent Amer-ican parlors. An inveterate tinkerer and inventor, Jefferson also bought an experimental keyboard instrument from John Isaac Hawkins of Philadelphia for $264 in 1800. The feisty little "portable grand" was promptly returned to Hawkins because it did not stay in tune "a single hour." But when Jefferson was furnishing the White House in 1802 through Thomas Claxton's assistance, he refused Claxton's sug-gestion that a "skilled person" select a pianoforte, an instrument that would be "pleasing to everyone." Jefferson felt that "no doubt a Pian-oforte would be a perfectly proper piece of furniture. But in the present state of our funds, they will be exhausted by articles more indispensable."[48]

It is very possible that the pianoforte made by Astor and Company now at Monticello had been in the White House. It could have been part of Jefferson's personal belongings. Though it does not correspond with any recorded purchase of a piano by the president, its price, Helen Cripe feels, could easily be subsumed in some larger amount paid to one of his agents.[49] The small mahogany and satinwood square has a compass of 5 1/2 octaves and dates from 1799–1815. It was acquired through the Trist decendants, and the curators at Monticello believe it is as reliable as the other Jefferson items of the Trist collection. The piano could also have been given to Jefferson as a gift. The president knew and admired John Jacob Astor and supported his schemes for the establishment of an American fur-trading company in the Atlantic states.[50] Astor's piano-importing business, in fact, was merely secondary to his fur exporting, the foundation of the extraordinary Astor family fortune. German-born, Astor had been a flute maker in London before settling permanently in New York in the 1790s. Many of the pianos he imported during this period were made by his elder brother George of 79 Cornhill Road, London.[51]

Despite the fact that Jefferson was known to have been a good amateur violinist and is believed to have owned at least five violins (one of these may have been a kit, or dance master's fiddle), only scant reference to these instruments exists in Jefferson's correspondence and account books. Perhaps he played a Cremona—or some other fine rare instrument—for diversion during his days in the White House.

While "Jefferson violins" seem to keep emerging over the years, their stories remain only partly credible.[52]

While Jefferson was president, he had several sheaves of music bound into volumes—a sign he valued their preservation. In the family collection at Charlottesville are several volumes with green covers containing some early quartets and trios of Pleyel, Clementi, Mozart, and others. Perhaps the president propped up their parts on the fine stand he designed especially for chamber music and in his casual democratic way invited in a Marine Band player or two. Gaetano Carusi himself may have filled in as flutist or violinist, topping off a relaxing evening with a Sicilian hymn or folk song for the president.[53] Without a doubt the strains of music drifted from the White House on many an evening—when it was dark and the pasture grounds surrounding the mansion were deserted, and Jefferson thought no one was listening. For he was often very tired, and music was his "companion" to divert, delight, and "sweeten many hours."[54]

The White House of Thomas Jefferson had a master but no mistress. The administration of James Madison, from 1809–17, began a new, dynamic period in the history of the mansion. Having assisted Jefferson with his entertaining when her husband was secretary of state, First Lady Dolley Madison continued Jefferson's informal, egalitarian style, but she did so with flair, imagination, and a touch of pomp. With the help of polished Frenchman John Pierre Sioussat, her "master of ceremonies," Dolley managed to maintain an oasis of civilization in a muddy, lonely city that was only beginning to acknowledge its social needs. She transformed Jefferson's cabinet room into a state dining room, expanded the frequency and size of his dinner parties, and established a weekly series of Wednesday night "drawing rooms," in what is now the Red Room, making sure everyone was invited to attend. These were evenings of "blazing splendor," according to Washington Irving who was often a guest during this period. And dressed in her fine French ensembles with their elaborate headdresses, "Queen Dolley," as she was affectionately called, reigned with elegance and ease.[55]

Music under the Madisons became a vital element of their hospitality. The Marine Band played frequently at various events as it did on the New Year's Day in 1811 described by Catherine Mitchell: "When we reach'd the grand entrance the sound of sweet music struck our ears. . . . Upon entering the spacious hall we beheld on one side a number of Musicians seated round a table playing, on different instruments, enlivening airs, for the entertainment of the company as they were ushered into the inner apartments. . . . The Musicians continued playing at intervals, until we had all taken our departure."[56]

There are no indications that either the president or first lady played the piano, but their guests performed often at small receptions and dinners—mostly ladies, in the true American domestic tradition. Margaret Bayard Smith's niece, Mary Kirkpatrick, nearly had her chance in 1816: "Mrs. Madison expressed a wish that she would play and

Oil portrait of Dolley Madison as first lady by Bass Otis, 1816. Mrs. Madison, one of our nation's most gracious hostesses, purchased the first piano and collection of music for the White House.

sing, as she had heard that she played *most elegantly.* But Mary declined."[57] Another guest, Mrs. William Seaton, would hardly have the audacity to refuse the first lady's request, as she relates: "Mrs. Madison insisted on my playing on her elegant grand piano a waltz for Miss S[mith] and Miss M[agruder] to dance, the figure of which she instructed them in."[58] A former Quaker, the first lady had obviously subjugated her strict heritage to the worldly glamour of the waltz, a new dance in America. Europeans at the time were enjoying the shocking intimacies of the waltz, which many called "hugging set to music." Where had Dolley Madison learned her dance steps? Perhaps through the diplomatic circles. But while waltzes were being published in America as early as 1795, they did not become a part of Washington society until the Carusi Dancing Assemblies brought them to life in the 1820s. Still, Dolley Madison's light steps were delightfully immortalized in the earliest piece of music dedicated to a first lady—"Mrs. Madison's Waltz," published by Willig in Philadelphia between 1810 and 1812.

The accounts of Smith and Seaton indicate that there were pianos both in the White House in 1811 and in the Seven Buildings residence occupied by the Madisons after the Executive Mansion was burned during the War of 1812. From the Madison administration, moreover, we have the first evidence that a piano was purchased specifically for the White House. On March 17, 1809, Benjamin Latrobe, who was furnishing the mansion for Dolley, wrote to the first lady that he had found in Philadelphia the answer to her request. After inquiring about two pianos, he settled upon a third "imported especially for a private family." It cost $530, but Latrobe managed to buy it for $450. "It is of such superior tone in strength and sweetness," he said, "that I would by all means recommend its being taken at that price. I have left with my brother Mr. Hazelhurst the necessary instructions."[59] Clementis, Broadwoods, and Astors were being imported at this time, but we may never know the details of the piano's maker. The instrument was destroyed along with the furnishings of four presidents when the British set fire to the mansion on August 24, 1814.[60]

When the Madisons moved to their makeshift quarters at Seven Buildings on Pennsylvania Avenue and 19th Street, NW, Dolley had to furnish the residence on a tight budget. She had only 38 percent of the amount she had spent between 1809 and 1814 in decorating an already furnished White House.[61] Not to be without music for her guests, however, she purchased a pianoforte, possibly a used one, within only a few months. A voucher states: "Received of Mr. George Boyd, agent for the President's furniture fund, the sum of three hundred and ten dollars ($310) for a piano forte. Washington, Nov. 16, 1815." The bill is signed, "F. A. Wagler."[62] Known in Washington as a professor of music, Wagler was also a composer and dealer, who sold "music paper, violins, and pianofortes from New York." It is quite possible that this piano made its way into the White House when the James Monroes took residence there. Reference to a "square gilt-mounted pianoforte" recur in various inventories of White House furnishings during the earlier part of the century, and vouchers indicate that a pianoforte was "repaired" several months before the Erard arrived from France. Tired and outmoded, the little square was probably one of two pianos traded in on July 21, 1841, toward the fancy new Scherr "concert piano" for President John Tyler.

Another purchase that Dolley Madison made for the White House is unique to the mansion's history. Through her agent at the time, Latrobe, she bought a fascinating collection of musical scores—illustrating further the importance she placed on the role of music in her household.[63] The Library of Congress holds a copy of this collection. On the cover, expertly engraved by Godefroy and Tanner, is the designation: "Journal of Musick, Composed of Italian, French and English songs, romances and duetts, and of overtures, rondos, etc. for the Forte Piano, Published by Madame Le Pelletier, Part I, 1810."

Printed by Willig in Philadelphia, the *Journal* was sold by subscription beginning in January 1810. Two "numbers" appeared each month for two years, and each number contained several pieces. Mrs. Madison's copies were purchased through Joseph Milligan of Georgetown, who bound and sold books to Jefferson and gave a "treatise" on gardening to Madison.[64] As for the intriguing Mme. Le Pelletier, she remains a mystery. She is listed in the Baltimore directory for 1810 only and was undoubtedly part of a small French colony in the city. She does not appear in the newspapers of the day, nor is it known that she produced any other musical works. But her elegant *Journal* is an important reflection of the influence of the French in an American culture still largely governed by English practices.

At a time when most American publishers were churning out simple songs on two staves, the *Journal*'s airs are on three, with the vocal line on top supported by a pianistic accompaniment. Most of the composers are French and include such names as Isouard, Berton, Catel, Méhul, and Boieldieu, with representative airs from their operas

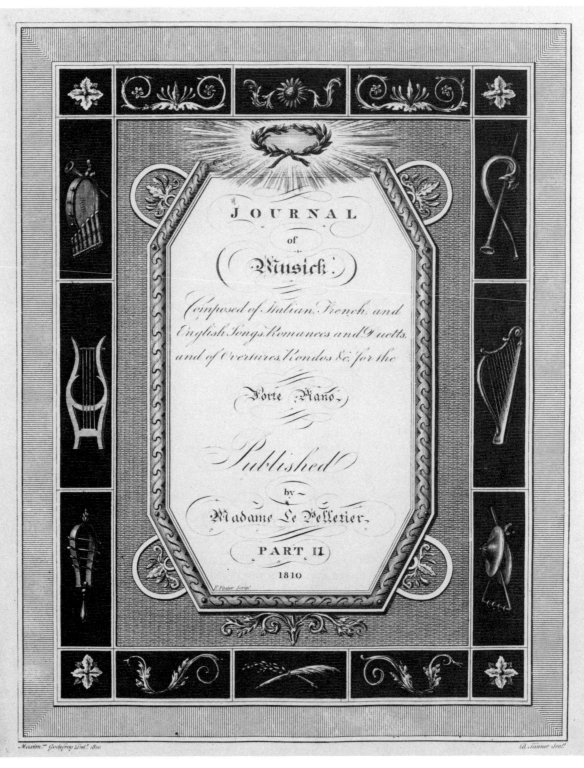

The handsomely engraved cover of Madame Le Pelletier's *Journal of Musick*, Part II, 1810, printed by Willig in Philadelphia. Dolley Madison acquired this fine edition of piano pieces and songs from Joseph Milligan, who sold Thomas Jefferson many books for his library.

unknown in America at this time. Illustrating the rare efforts of a serious woman composer in early America, many of the selections are composed, as well as arranged, by Mme. Le Pelletier herself. One of the most interesting is her set of variations, "Fantaisie sur un Air Russe, composée pour le Forte Piano et dédiée à Madame Daschkoff née Baronne de Preuzar." The work begins with a long introduction in C major that returns in shortened form at the closing. The simple main theme (Andante) in A minor is cast in a classical two-part, sixteen-measure mold allowing the eight variations to show off tremolo passages, rapid runs, octaves, trills, and other virtuosic embroidery in the style of Dussek or Pleyel.

Who would have played this charming piece at the White House for the first lady? Perhaps the assiduous Mr. Wagler, who was giving concerts in the capital at the time—or perhaps Mme. Le Pelletier herself, appearing as Baron Closen described the French ladies of Baltimore: "The freshness and the brilliant vivacity of their eyes are also very captivating. Many have neat and very well proportioned figures, very lovely little hands, white and plump, and sweet feet, wonderfully shod (better than anywhere else). Their hair is dressed with infinite taste, and they value French styles highly."[65]

The Madisons, like Washington and Jefferson before them, enjoyed French furnishings and culture. Elegant imported articles were emblematic of the finest American tastes, and it is somewhat ironic that the pre-fire White House under Dolley Madison boasted hardly any French furniture.[66] Madison was a Republican with pro-French political sympathies, but his taste for French culture was probably stimulated by his good friend, James Monroe. A family of dignity and wealth, the Monroes cherished courtly luxuries. Not long after Monroe took office on March 4, 1817, he purchased a large quantity of furniture from France, and the first family moved into the White House in time to hold a gala reception there on New Year's Day, 1818.

Elizabeth Kortright Monroe had acquired her French sensibilities during a long sojourn in France while her husband was U.S. minister under Washington. During a large part of Monroe's eight years as president, however, she was ill and unable to serve as White House hostess. Her elder daughter Eliza, who had studied harp and other cultural subjects abroad, took her place. If it were not for the festive Marine Band—and the Erard piano—the White House would have been a rather stiff and formal residence; Washingtonians were deprived of the two most popular staples of city parties: dancing and cards.[67] Still the weekly "drawing room" was crowded with "secretaries, Senators, foreign Ministers, consuls, . . . auctioneers and nothingarians . . . some in shoes, most in boots, and many in spurs, some snuffing, others chewing, and many longing for their cigars and whiskey pouch left at home."[68] The Marine Band played in the background, treating guests to some pyrotechnics on the clarinet by leader Venerando Pulizzi. The talented Sicilian, now aged twenty-five, liked to feature his showpiece, Voight's "Tyrolese National Air" with variations.[69] On one occasion a gathering of Pawnee chieftains staged an elaborate ceremonial dance on the White House lawns, attracting a crowd of 3,000, who gazed in awe and astonishment.[70]

Like the Madisons, the Monroes purchased a fine pianoforte for the White House. The graceful furnishing cost 2,200 francs, the most expensive item listed for the Sitting Room (probably today's Red Room), and was shipped on September 15, 1817, with other furniture for the mansion on the *Resolution* bound for Alexandria. It was described as

This grand piano made by Erard frères, Paris, 1818, is very similar to the one purchased for the White House by James and Elizabeth Monroe. It has typically French tapered legs and a multiple pedal mechanism, and it is decorated with especially well-worked ormolu.

"a piano made by Erard Brothers, decorated with bronze, having three legs ('colones') and four pedals and a 'tambourin.' "[71] At this time the prestigious firm of Erard frères (whose first piano was built by Sébastien Erard in 1777) had achieved an international reputation, and its instruments were played by Ludwig van Beethoven and other great artists. The Colt Collection in Kent, England, possesses an Erard dated ca. 1818 similar to the one chosen by the Monroes. It is an exquisite instrument, with well-worked pieces of ormolu and typically French tapered legs. A special feature of the piano was its multiple pedal mechanism, which allowed for theatrical colors and sound effects to serve the era's new descriptive piano pieces. Pedals could render a plucked sound (pizzicato or lute), reedy sound (bassoon), or perhaps more mellow ones (moderator) by means of cloth placed between the strings and the hammers. The "tambourin" of the Monroes' Erard was produced either by a fifth pedal or a sideways-moving "genouillère," which worked a drum (or triangle—or both) built into the bass of the piano. Thus, one can hear the White House halls reverberating with Swiss echo airs, Turkish marches, and battle pieces with their Janissary effects made popular by the European military bands of the time.

Turkish costume, art, and music had attracted the attention of Europeans shortly after the sultan gave a complete band to Augustus II of Poland in 1720. By the close of the century, Janissary effects had become a craze that reached the far shores of America, though its esoteric origins and escapades were received with reservation. The Marine Band, however, was using Janissary instruments by 1812, perhaps brought over by Gaetano Carusi and the Italians. Reports indicate that the band by the time of Madison had—in addition to oboes, clarinets, bassoons, and horns—a bass drum, bugle horn, pair of cymbals, and that raspy predecessor of the bass tuba, the serpent.[72] Parading proudly across the White House lawns on festive occasions, the Marine Band undoubtedly conjured up a curious image, much to the delight of the heterogeneous crowd of onlookers.

Elizabeth and James Monroe appear to be the first presidential couple to have attended the theater in Washington. On March 26, 1819, they saw the *School of Reform* at the Washington Theater (later Carusi's Saloon) during which a "Mr. Russell" danced a "hornpipe in real iron Fetters."[73] What their reaction to this gala spectacle was we may never know. But the first family who succeeded them was a truly musical one, and evidence of the Adamses' interests in the art of music exists in several sources.

Both John Quincy Adams and Louisa Catherine Adams had a broader European heritage than any of their presidential predecessors. John Quincy, son of our second president, spent many vital years of his life in diplomatic service abroad before becoming president in 1825. He lived in Russia, Holland, France, and England, and his revealing diaries detail the numerous operas, concerts, and theatrical events both he and Louisa attended before and after their marriage in 1797. H. Earle Johnson identified many of these performances in his provocative "The Adams Family and Good Listening."[74] From January 10 to April 4, 1815, while in Paris, John Quincy heard twenty-nine operas by Mozart, Gluck, Boieldieu, Catel, Paisiello, Isouard, Cimarosa, and other composers. Music to Adams had a special power and message that remained with him into his most mature years. When he left the presidency in 1829 upon failure of his reelection, he commented bitterly:

> In the French opera of Richard Coeur-de-Lion, the minstrel, Blondel, sings under the walls of his prison a song beginning:
>
> > O, Richard! O, mon roi!
> > L'univers t'abandonne.
> > [O, Richard! O, my king!
> > The universe has abandoned you.]
>
> When I first heard this song forty-five years ago, at one of the first representations of that delightful play, it made an indelible impression upon my memory, without imagining that I should ever feel its force so much closer home. In the year 1829 scarce a day passed that did not bring it to my thoughts.[75]

John Quincy Adams had definite views about the status of American culture. He felt that "American genius was very much addicted to painting ... but that we had neither cultivated nor were attached much to music." Why this was true he was not certain. Perhaps it was due to "some particular construction of our fibres." While the French enjoyed rousing patriotic music, the Americans who fought seven years and more for their liberty did not write a single tune that "electrified every soul." As for his own attitudes, "I am extremely fond of music," he said, "and by dint of great pains have learnt to blow very badly the flute—but could never learn to perform upon the violin, because I never could acquire the art of putting the instrument in tune."[76]

If John Quincy questioned the reasons for Americans lagging behind Europeans in their musical pursuits, his own stern republicanism— reflected vividly and poignantly in his attitudes toward his wife— provided an answer. Born in London of a wealthy Anglo-American family, Louisa Catherine Johnson was our only first lady born outside of the United States. She grew up in a musical family, played the harp and pianoforte as a young girl, and had a naturally lovely singing voice. It was her talent, in fact, that initially attracted twenty-eight-year-old John Quincy Adams while he was in England. His diaries contain many accounts of her entertaining him with her two sisters in their gracious home.[77] During their courtship John Quincy and Louisa sang and played together often; one of their favorite pieces was the aria "Angels Ever Bright and Fair" from Handel's oratorio *Theodora.*

Yet to John and Abigail Adams, Louisa Catherine was never wholly American. She was tainted by the "empty baubles of life connected with courts," the breeding ground of luxury, frivolity and vice. Even music-loving John Quincy once snapped that Louisa's playing the harp was "a trivial accomplishment," providing neither intelligence nor virtue. Music could give little "domestic happiness," he said, and he would willingly give up any of his pleasures in music if she would improve herself.[78] Improve herself, indeed! In the same breath, John Quincy promulgated that intellectualism and politics had no place in the life of a woman. Louisa's biographer, Joan Challinor, summarized her dilemma as follows: "As an ambitious woman, born when ambition was prohibited for women, she could never fully admit to, or act on, her own feelings. Caught in a web spun by the culture and her husband's extreme republicanism, Louisa suffered from ambivalences and a paralyzing guilt. At no time was she able to face herself and her desires squarely and honestly."[79]

Louisa's life as the wife of a diplomat was fraught with struggle, loneliness, and grief. The bouts of deep depression she suffered remained with her all of her life, and there were moments when she feared for her sanity. But she made every effort to be a gracious hostess, and according to Washington society she succeeded. When John Quincy became secretary of state under Monroe, the Adamses opened their commodious house on F Street, offering music and entertainment that consisted of small ensembles. The Adams home was second in importance only to the president's. The famous ball John Quincy and Louisa gave for General Andrew Jackson, hero of the Battle of New Orleans, was the most distinguished social event of the era. When John Quincy became president, moreover, dancing was brought to the White House on December 15, 1828, where it was described as a "novel feature of the evening's entertainment."[80] In every sort of attire, dancers moved to the joyous measures of the cotillion, a popular pattern dance in 2/4 or 6/8 meter executed by four couples. The dance most likely took place in the East Room, recently opened for New Year's Day receptions and large gatherings. A small "social orchestra" from the Marine Band may have accompanied the dancers. Two or three strings with a woodwind or two comprised the usual ensemble for dancing at this time. An earlier major event at the mansion was the visit of the Marquis de Lafayette, whose birthday was celebrated on September 6, 1825, with a festive series of toasts and the "Marseillaise" played by the Marine Band.[81]

The repertory of the band at this time included not only patriotic fife tunes but also many theatrical and sentimental popular songs as well. On July 4, 1828, President John Quincy Adams attended a spectacular ground-breaking ceremony for the excavation of the Chesapeake and Ohio Canal. "Noiseless," reported the *National Intelligencer* of July 7, 1828, "the people moved forward on the bank of the canal, keeping even pace with the long line of boats whilst airs, now animated, now plaintive, from the Marine Band, placed in the forward boat lightened the toil of the walk." Among the selections were "Rural Felicity," "Roslin Castle," "The Star-Spangled Banner," Reinagle's "America, Commerce and Freedom" from his ballet pantomime *The Sailor's Landlady* (1794), Thomas Moore's "The Meeting of the Waters," and a favorite with the first lady, Whitaker's "Oh Say not Woman's Heart Is Bought."

But the most significant piece historically was "Hail to the Chief."

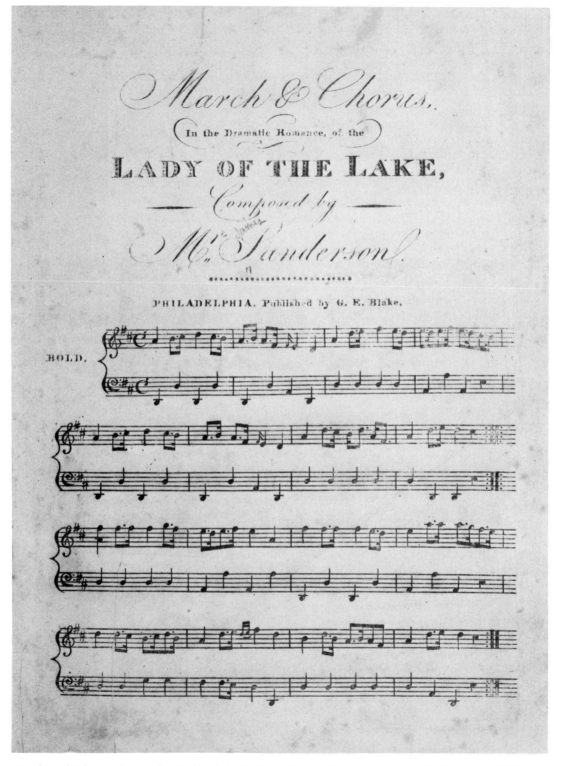

March and Chorus from *The Lady of the Lake* by James Sanderson, published by G. E. Blake ca. 1812. The song was the source for "Hail to the Chief," which was first associated with a president in 1828.

Derived from an old Gaelic air, the tune had been adapted to a scene from Sir Walter Scott's *The Lady of the Lake* by English composer James Sanderson. In Sanderson's version of the play, Highland Chieftain Sir Roderick Dhu (actually an outlaw) is heralded by the lilting boat song "Hail to the Chief." Scott's play had many musical settings, including one by Henry Rowley Bishop. But the Sanderson version, first performed in New York in 1812, caught on instantly and was successful for many years thereafter. The July 4th celebration of 1828 appears to be the song's first association with a president. And this may have been merely by accident. The canal boats—rather than the "Chief"—might have dictated the selection for the day:

> Hail to the chief, who in triumph advances,
> Honor'd and blessed be the evergreen pine!
>
> . . .
>
> Row, vassals, row, for the pride of the Highlands!
> Stretch to your oars for the evergreen pine![82]

A tired, delicate little lady—somewhat resembling Empress Josephine—with her curls bobbing and a faint, elusive smile on her lips, sat at her pianoforte just as she had when she was young. She was afraid to play too often, but the moments she had alone were special. The upstairs drawing room of the president's mansion was very quiet. Louisa Catherine Adams gently fingered one of her favorite pieces, her sweet voice almost a whisper:

> Oh say not Woman's Love is bought
> With vain and empty treasure!
> Oh say not Woman's heart is caught
> By every idle pleasure.[83]

If the evening were not too late, she would try out a French romance or two. Someone named "Mlle Délieu"—a friend from the embassy perhaps?—had given her a collection of handwritten music with the note (in French) that she had sent them as a favor; they were the "six pieces that she had requested" and she hoped Madame Adams would "sing and enjoy them many times." The songs were by Amadea de Beauplan and France's leading opera composer, Adrien Boieldieu. Mlle Délieu's note was signed: "20 Mai, 1824, EBD, Washington," and her gift to the first lady appears in the smaller of two bound albums of music owned by Mrs. Adams. Included also in the albums are more than 100 selections, mainly for voice and piano, and several Mozart arias from operas just becoming known in America, such as *The Magic Flute*, *The Abduction from the Seraglio*, and *The Clemency of Tito*. There are also arias by Andreozzi, Mayer, Paer, Martini, and Guglielmi—composers whose operas Louisa and John Quincy had enjoyed in Europe while they were engaged—and Handel's gentle air "Angels Ever Bright and Fair." At the top of the page was written: "Miss Mary Catherine Hellen from her Cousin George Washington Adams," another betrothed couple. And to Louisa's own doleful words the little-known Italian composer Carusi (Gaetano perhaps?) had penned a song for her called simply "Hymn":

President's House in 1825. Aquatint by H. Stone, 1826.

Oil portrait of Louisa Catherine Adams, wife of John Quincy Adams, by Charles Bird King, ca. 1824.

Fanny Elssler in her celebrated Spanish dance, the cachucha. Lithograph designed by N. Sarony.

"Swedish Nightingale" Jenny Lind presented concerts in Washington on December 16 and 18, 1850. Both were attended by President and Mrs. Millard Fillmore, who later received the celebrated soprano at the White House. Hand-tinted lithograph.

(Top) American soprano Clara Louise Kellogg was only twenty when Abraham
Lincoln heard her in Donizetti's *La figlia del reggimento* in Washington.
(Bottom) New York's Academy of Music where, as president-elect, Lincoln
attended his first opera.

Title page of the 108-page, hand-tinted register: "Record of the Social Events at the Executive Mansion during the Administration of President Hayes. Executed with pen and pencil by Mr. O. L. Pruden, Assistant Secretary to the President."

Emma Abbott, an American soprano who sang for Presidents Hayes, Arthur, and Cleveland. Hand-tinted photograph, ca. 1880.

Caroline Scott Harrison was the earliest first lady to have been a professional musician. This posthumous portrait by Daniel Huntington, 1894, hangs in the White House.

This portrait of John Philip Sousa, painted by J. J. Capolino in the 1950s, hangs in the Sousa Band Hall at the Marine Barracks in Washington, D.C. The painting was inspired by a photograph of Sousa taken while he was leader of the U.S. Marine Band from 1880 to 1892.

Lord, listen to my great distress,
Oh hear my feckle plaint.
Could language all my griefs express
Those words that griefs could paint.

She would sing these words mournfully. The manuscript is dated April 21, 1828—shortly before her sensitive, tormented son George Washington Adams committed suicide.

"Melancholy is the soul of music," Thomas Moore once said. Louisa had a fine edition of the popular Irish poet's plaintive songs entitled: *A Selection of Irish Melodies with Symphonies and Accompaniments by Sir John Stevenson, Mus-Doc. and Characteristic words by Thomas Moore, Esq* (published by Blake, Philadelphia, ca. 1808). But the feisty little poet, who, on more than one occasion raised the ire of Jefferson,[84] detected perhaps the tragic inhibitions that confined Louisa's creative spirit. The first lady recalled in her memoirs Moore's visit to Washington in 1806: "Sometime before the birth of my Child Mr. [Anthony] Merry introduced at our house the celebrated Thomas Moore. . . . I heard him sing many of his Songs and two or three Evenings sang with him. He said that I sang delightfully but I wanted Soul. . . . [H]is style was so full of sentiment it would not have been very becoming or suitable for Ladies generally to echo his tones or

Five- and one-half octave mahogany and rosewood pianoforte made by Alpheus Babcock, Boston, 1825–29. Mrs. Adams's pianoforte, harp, and two volumes of music are on exhibit in the First Ladies Hall, National Museum of American History.

the expression of his words or his manner!"[85] Yet Louisa understood Moore more than he realized. Underneath the façade, their spirits shared "the language of sorrow" that the poet's fluid songs expressed— that "characteristic wildness and melting pathos of Irish music,"[86]

> The harp that once, thro' Tara's halls,
> The soul of Music shed
> Now hangs as mute on Tara's walls
> As if that soul were fled:—

Both volumes of Louisa Catherine Adams's music bear the name "L. C. Adams" tooled in gold on the covers. They are on exhibit at the Smithsonian Institution's Museum of American History along with Mrs. Adams's harp, music stand, and pianoforte. The collection comprises the first musical objects owned by a presidential family member during their years at the White House that are still preserved. Louisa's pianoforte, made by Alpheus Babcock of Boston, dates about 1825–29 and is believed to have been in the White House during the administration of John Quincy Adams. It is uncertain whether the piano was Mrs. Adams's own or purchased for the White House. Louisa enjoyed her American-made piano at a time when the Monroes' French tastes were criticized, and Congress had directed that the president's house should contain American-made furniture "as far as practicable."[87] The 5 1/2 octave mahogany and rosewood instrument lacks the one-piece cast iron frame for which Babcock and his partner John Mackay achieved national recognition on December 17, 1825. But Babcock's pianos of this time won several prizes for their "excellent finish, tone and touch."[88]

When John Quincy Adams left the White House, defeated and bitter, an era had ended. The old customs soon would be modified and incorporated into a new stream of entertainment styles; the intimate family drawing rooms would open their doors to famous guest performers as technology, industry, and transportation carried their musical messages—sometimes graceful, sometimes brash—to the Executive Mansion. Presidents would be sung into office. Gentle serenades would become screaming protest. A civil war would bring to the White House music with a depth and intensity the nation had never known. For the history of the White House is the history of America. And underpinning this heritage are the ubiquitous sounds of music—tones which captured the event and the human spirit simultaneously.

CHAPTER 3

POLITICS, PROTEST, AND THE CHANGING AMERICAN CULTURE

★ ★ ★

Jackson to Taylor

Liberty is our motto,
And we'll sing as freemen ought to
Till it rings through glen and grotto
From the Old Granite State
That the tribe of Jesse,
That the tribe of Jesse,
That the tribe of Jesse,
  Are the friends of equal rights.

Hutchinson Family
"The Old Granite State"

In his sociable, democratic dealings with the American people, Andrew Jackson was closer to the spirit of Thomas Jefferson than to that of his stately predecessor, John Quincy Adams. Jackson was the product of pioneer philosophy, a self-educated man who had risen to affluence as a prosperous Tennessee planter. His father was a farmer in a backwoods area of the Carolinas, and Andrew Jackson's popularity with the voters was founded on his rough, fearless career as soldier and statesman. Like the presidents before him, Jackson was welcomed into office with the usual run of dedicatory marches, gala parades, and balls. For "Old Hickory," however, there was something extra. His inauguration on March 4, 1829, featured a performance of *Belle's Strategem*, an "elegant comedy" (and one of George Washington's favorites). The evening opened with "a new Jackson Overture composed by Henry Dielman, leader of the Orchestra," and concluded with a song sung by "Mr. Heyt of the Hunters of Kentucky with an additional stanza in honor of General Jackson now President of the United States."[1]

    The White House of Andrew Jackson was simpler in its customs,

President's House from an English engraving of 1831, showing oval portico and French-style gardens.

ambience, and attitudes than it had been under Adams or Monroe. It was the people's house and its public receptions with doors open to one and all were clearly the people's pleasure. The designation "White House" was used now with more regularity, gradually replacing the term President's Palace or President's House until eventually it became the legal name under Theodore Roosevelt. The East Room was tastefully furnished; however, "it was mortifying to see men with boots heavy with mud, standing on the damask-satin-covered chairs and sofas," wrote one eyewitness about the inaugural reception. "Negroes, boys, women, and children took possession of the house and scrambled, romped and fought in the rooms," commented another.[2] During the Jackson terms food, music, and congeniality were abundant. At his first Fourth of July reception the general treated his guests to a 1,400-pound "Mammoth Cheese" while the Marine Band played the president's favorite tune, "Auld Lang Syne."[3]

Jackson's wife, Rachel Donelson, died on the Christmas Eve before the general's first inauguration, and his niece, Emily Donelson, and later his daughter-in-law, Sarah Yorke Jackson, served as hostesses. Music was enjoyed informally during these years. Sarah Jackson played the guitar, and her fine imported six-stringed instrument, made by Cabasse Visinaire l'aîné, is the property of The Hermitage, Jackson's home in Tennessee. On November 21, 1831, a "rosewood pianoforte of six octaves" was purchased for the White House from Thompson and Homans "for $300 less $100 for second hand piano exchanged."[4] As prosperous merchants in Washington, Thompson and Homans sold books on ornithology, law, medicine, and fine arts as well as pianos, sheet music, music stands, and "genuine Naples violin strings." The firm also had the added distinction of having sold Jackson three volumes of the first edition of the *Encyclopedia Americana* the same year as the piano.[5] As to the maker of the "rosewood pianoforte," the Smithsonian's Worch Collection possesses an instrument similar to the styles Thompson and Homans were advertising for sale in the *National Intelligencer* at this time. It is made by D. B. Grove of Philadelphia, dates ca. 1830–34, and has a range of six octaves (FF-f[4]) with two pedals and an elaborate scrolling on the nameboard. Especially intriguing is the American eagle gracefully carved into one corner of the case. The new piano was probably exchanged for the "French grand piano," the old Erard that was still in the mansion on March 12, 1830.[6]

Music and pretty ladies seemed to have gone hand in hand with President Jackson. Some of them played the piano—others danced. John Campbell of the Treasury Department wrote to his brother David in Virginia about his visit to the White House: "There were some 20 or 30 ladies & gentlemen seated and standing. He [Jackson] was in the midst of the ladies in as fine a humour as I ever saw him. He took me by the arm in his usual gallant style and introduced me to all the Ladies with whom I was not acquainted. He then handed a young lady to the piano and stood by her while she play'd several airs. . . . He paid her some pretty compliments and then handed her back to seat again."[7]

Whether or not it was Jackson's fondness for feminine glamour that attracted him to the graceful ballerina "Mlle. Celeste," we may never know. But during the 1836 campaign, well-known political caricaturist Henry R. Robinson used an imaginary scene at the White House for some whimsical anti-Jacksonian propaganda. He showed the charming French dancer performing for the president and members of the cabinet. Barely sixteen when she arrived in New York from Paris in 1827, Celeste Keppler was one of the first to dance *en pointe* in the United States. With her spectacular pirouettes and other tours de force, she exhibited her well-rounded legs to the delight of her audience.[8] The lithograph, called *The Celeste-al-Cabinet*, was an obvious spoof on the notorious scandal between Secretary John Eaton and Peggy Timberlake—a political war of nerves that split Jackson's cabinet in 1831.

Ironically the year after the *Celeste* caricature appeared, another famous ballerina actually did visit the White House. Fanny Elssler and her voluptuous, hip-swaying cachucha complete with Spanish castanets took Washington by storm. So popular was the provocative Fanny that during one of her tours it was decided that Congress would meet only on the days she was *not* dancing. Martin Van Buren, a widower who was inaugurated as president in March 1837, attended one of her performances and promptly invited the pretty dancer to the Executive Mansion the next morning. "I think his demeanor is very easy, very frank and very royal," she noted respectfully.[9]

Not all agreed. And the president's "royal" attitude became the subject of satire and song as the campaign of 1840 took firm hold on the nation. Whig voices denounced Van Buren as the corrupt, champagne-guzzling "King Matty," decadent despot of the Presidential

Popular ballerina Celeste Keppler dances for President Andrew Jackson and his cabinet in a caricature by H. R. Robinson, 1836. "I've not lost all my penchant for pretty women," says Jackson in the drawing. Seated at far right is Vice-President Martin Van Buren.

Palace. The White House was no longer the people's shrine; it would be restored to its rightful position by William Henry Harrison ("Old Tip"), knight of the log cabin. To the tune of "The Mistletoe Bough" rang the words: "Van Buren sits in his marble hall, / And liveried slaves come forth at his call, / The banquet is spread—the silver gleams, / The dark wine flows in purple streams."[10] Indeed, these were the days of "The *Supreme* Court," or so it seemed.

To these vitriolic verses Congressman Charles Ogle of Pennsylvania added his own discordant counterpoint. He lashed out at Van Buren's New Year's receptions, complaining that one, stiff ceremonious assembly each year was a poor replacement for weekly public receptions with an abundance of food and wine for all. He branded Van Buren as an effete voluptuary whose "Asiatic Mansion" contained imported carpets, exotic artificial flowers, and even a "bathtub!" In the "yellow drawing room" (Red Room) stood an "elegant gilt-mounted pianoforte" with "damask satin-covered music stools." At the eastern end of the hall during receptions, noted Ogle, the Marine Band was stationed and "with all their fine instruments in full tune 'at the same identical moment' [they] strike up one of our most admired national airs."[11] Benjamin Perley Poore, however, thought differently about these "admired airs": "The Marine Band . . . is always ordered from the Navy Yard and stationed in the spacious front hall, from whence they swell the rich saloons of the palace with 'Hail to the Chief!' 'Wha'll be King but Charley?' and other humdrum airs, which ravish with delight the ears of warriors who have never smelt powder. As the people's cash, and not his own, pays for all the services of the Marine Band, its employment at the palace does not conflict with the peculiar views of the President in regard to the obvious difference between public and private economy."[12]

Poore's reference to "Hail to the Chief" indicates that the presidential march was played in the White House during Van Buren's administration. The piece had been in the Marine Band repertory, as noted earlier, as far back as John Quincy Adams, but there is no way of knowing how closely it was identified with the chief of state. During these years it may have been just another underpinning of the festive social scene—just another "humdrum" air.[13]

The Whigs' effort to elect William Henry Harrison and John Tyler in the "log cabin and hard cider" campaign of 1840 evoked a frenzied and persuasive outburst of song and singing. Henry Russell's famous interpretation of Alexander Ross's "Tippecanoe and Tyler, too" resounded in all the glee clubs and rallies, and "spirit-stirring" brass bands were so essential to a political meeting that gatherings were sometimes cancelled when a band was not available. "Van, Van, Van's a used up man!" chanted the Whigs. On March 4, 1841, Harrison was inaugurated. Exactly one month later he was dead. Overnight the joyous bursts of song changed to mournful dirges. Starting at the White House six white horses, each led by a black groom dressed in white, with white turban and sash, drew the hearse bearing the stricken president's remains. The funeral procession was two miles long "eclipsing the inaugural pageant which had so recently preceded it."[14]

It was not until late in the century that music was used during the simple funeral services held inside the White House. During the lengthy Harrison procession, the traditional dead marches were played by bands from the many military units that assembled outside the mansion. Music was composed and published hurriedly to commemorate the occasion, such as Henry Dielman's "President Harrison's Funeral Dirge, as performed on the occasion of his burial at Washington City, April, 1841" (Philadelphia, Osbourn's Music Saloon). The piano arrangement of Dielman's march traveled into thousands of American homes, complete with fanfares ("The last trumpet peal"), diminished seventh chords ("The Widow's Shriek"), and other programmatic devices. The public heard the somber tale again and again through music in a way that surpassed any newspaper. But the historical value of the piece lies in the lithograph on the cover depicting bands marching in procession from the White House—the earliest known iconographical source linking music with the president's home.

What else the bands played on this day is hard to determine. Sources barely mention the music: "The music was excellent," noted one account, "several fine bands playing mournful airs, giving place from time to time to the muffled drums of the military beating slow marches."[15] One of these marches may have been "Roslin Castle." The ancient Scottish bagpipe tune was often associated with funerals in New York during the Revolution,[16] and it was part of the repertory of the Marine Band in the 1830s. More than a century later elegaic

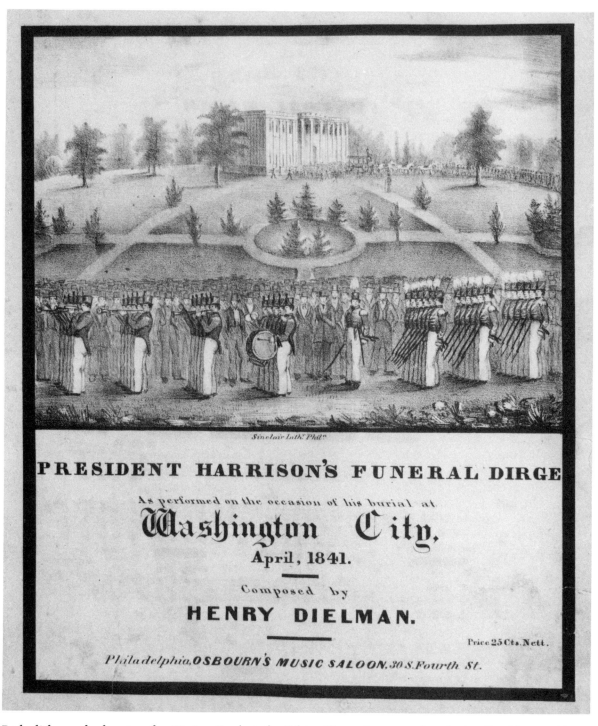

Early lithograph showing the Marine Band at the White House in procession during President William Henry Harrison's funeral ceremonies. Cover of sheet music published in Philadelphia in 1841.

Scottish bagpipe tunes would dolefully begin the funeral procession assembled at the White House for President John F. Kennedy.

The decade of the 1840s—the terms of John Tyler, James Knox Polk, and Zachary Taylor—was forecast eloquently in John Greenleaf Whittier's *Ballads and Anti-Slavery Poems* written in 1838. His popular "Stanzas" and "The Moral Warfare" were grim, moving messages of a self-conscious era. The opera house, gala new site of both culture and social persiflage during Jackson's terms, became the stage for one of the century's most spectacular riots on May 10, 1849. At least twenty were killed in the Astor Opera House in New York during the infamous Macready-Forrest feud caused by anti-English sentiments. Through their heated promulgations, the actors managed to ignite the emotions of the audience in a way like no other. Even singers such as Henry Russell and the Hutchinson Family were making strong social statements in song during this period, as were the newly founded Christy Minstrels of 1842 and the Virginia Minstrels of the following year, who toured in various parts of the country. It is little surprise, then, that among the earliest guest artists to perform at the White House were those whose musical pleasures had political overtones.

John Tyler, the Democrat-turned-Whig who followed Harrison in the White House, came from a distinguished line of Virginia planters as had his predecessor. He had fifteen children, eight by his first wife, Letitia Christian, who died in 1842, and seven by his second wife, Julia Gardiner, whom he married in 1844 a few months before he left office. Tyler inherited his father's love of music. As a boy on the family 1,200-acre Virginia estate, he found great joy in playing reels, hornpipes, and breakdowns on his violin. Julia Gardiner Tyler was also talented and set to music a poem, "Sweet Lady Awake," that her husband had written for her during their courtship. She also attempted to get the work published to no avail. While the music has not survived, a copy of the verses in Tyler's handwriting may be found in the John Tyler Papers at the Library of Congress. The opening lines are as follows:

> Sweet lady awake, from your slumbers awake,
> Weird beings we come o'er hill and through brake
> To sing you a song in the stillness of night,
> Oh, read you our riddle fair lady aright?[17]

Tyler turned to music "to escape from all the environments of political and social cares and duties," his daughter Letitia ("Letty") recalled: "In spite of the comparatively quiet life at the White House, my father's time was rarely ever his own. 'Now sing, Letty,' he would say when we found ourselves far from the maddening crowd enjoying the quiet of some country road. And then I would sing his favorite songs, the old Scotch ballads we loved so well. ... Nobody sings 'Barbara Allen' and 'Ye Banks and Braes' these days."[18] The Tylers continued to enjoy music during their years at Sherwood Forest plantation following the presidency. The former chief of state practiced his new violin, acquired in 1848, daily, and reports indicate that in 1855 he was still "fiddling away every evening for the little children black and white to dance."[19] The family also found special pleasure in forming their own quartet modeled after the Virginia Minstrels and other blackface minstrel troupes who were capturing the American stage at this time. With John Tyler playing violin, Julia on guitar, son-in-law William Waller on banjo, and young Tazewell Tyler playing the bone castanettes, the distinguished family had a true "Ethiopian band," as Julia called it, reflecting America's joy in this spirited art form.

The Tyler White House was socially active. While Congress was in session two dinner parties were given each week, and informal "drawing rooms" were held every evening. In addition there were public levees each month and the usual public receptions on New Year's Day and the Fourth of July. And then there were the balls. Jessie Benton Frémont described the party for the Prince de Joinville of France during which the guests formed a "Quadrille d'honneur in the East Room."[20] An elaborate children's masquerade ball took place for the Tyler grandchildren, and a gala "Farewell Ball" was held on February 18, 1845, shortly before the Tylers left the White House. For this occasion the scarlet-coated Marine Band played waltzes, cotillions, and the polka, a dance recently introduced in America.

Julia Gardiner, a queenly woman whose regal attitudes earned her the title "Mrs. Presidentess," reputedly gave instructions to the Marine Band to play "Hail to the Chief" whenever the president made an official appearance. By the time of Polk's inauguration, the piece was associated with the president in a ceremonious tribute maintained to the present. President and Mrs. Tyler enjoyed the weekly outdoor Marine Band concerts initiated earlier during their administration by Francis Scala, who later became leader of the Marine Band. The concerts, open to the public, were held from spring to fall on the South Lawn of the White House on Saturday evenings—a custom that continued until the administration of Herbert Hoover.[21]

Records of the instrumentation and repertory of the Marine Band during the Tyler period are detailed and accessible. The Francis Maria Scala Collection at the Library of Congress contains 342 compositions or arrangements for the Marine Band, dating primarily 1842 to 1871, among other catalogued items. Scala came to America on the cruiser *Brandywine* from his native city of Naples, a stocky young man of nineteen with gray eyes and dark hair who spoke no English. His story reads like a sequel to the Carusi saga, with a happier ending now that Washington and the Marines seemed more ready to accept the Italian immigrant musician as a cultural asset. On August 11, 1842, Scala enlisted in the Marine Corps and joined the band, vowing never to set foot again on another ship after suffering from violent seasickness. Eventually he became the first to be honored with the formal designation "Leader of the Band," having held the position of fife major for several years.[22] When Scala left the band in 1871, he had served under nine presidents and had decidedly improved the balance, technique, and repertory of the ensemble during these formative years. In 1842 the band had been just a "small reed affair," he recalled. "We had one flute, one clarionette, one French horn, two trombones, one bugle, one bass drum, and one cymbal player. The nation's [sic] represented were America, England, Germany, Spain, Italy and Austria. Why, the bass drummer couldn't read music and while I led the band with my clarionette, I directed the drummer by stamping my feet. . . . Tyler was a friend of mine, and he did much to improve the band."[23]

The size and instrumental balance of the band appears to have varied considerably at this time, because the Scala collection contains some pieces with eight to ten parts and others with parts for more than twenty players. Most likely the occasions dictated the music as it does today, and these events ranged from intimate dinners to large ceremonial receptions and outdoor concerts. There are parts for strings in the collection and indication that the band ordered eighteen instruments, mainly brass and winds. Among these were the somewhat old-fashioned "Turkisch [sic] Bells," the new valve trumpet, and the fashionable "Oficlayde" (ophicleide), a bass-baritone keyed brass instrument that was priced at $30.[24] A few years later a request was made for funds for "copying 64 opera pieces for full band at $1.00 per piece." But the order was returned with a note on the back saying, "Cannot ask payment for copying opera pieces. The musicians must do that for themselves."[25]

A survey of the Marine Band repertory of this period indicates a balance of musical styles represented by polkas, waltzes, quickstep arrangements of popular songs, and especially operatic selections. David Ingalls in his study of the Scala materials found that nearly one in every three pieces had some connection with grand opera.[26] For Italian opera—new to American shores in the 1820s and 1830s—became immediately popular and was transformed into piano parlor pieces, dances, and other arrangements. Indeed, Scala, born into the traditions of Italian opera, often arranged for band an operatic aria or chorus shortly after its European or American premiere. The parts of "Scena e aria" from Donizetti's *Lucia di Lammermoor*, for example, are dated 1842, and the opera was given its American premiere in New Orleans only the year before—with its New York premiere the year *after*. Band parts for operas by Auber, Bellini, Boieldieu, Donizetti, Flotow, Gounod, Meyerbeer, Offenbach, Rossini, Verdi, and von Weber are represented in the Scala archives. Thus under the baton of Francis Scala, White House guests were treated to all the titillating operatic airs that were invading America at this time.

Shortly after he became president, Tyler purchased two pianos for the White House from Emilius N. Scherr, a Philadelphia piano and guitar maker who had migrated from Denmark. The instruments cost $600 and $450 and were bought "by two second hand pianos taken in exchange" on July 21, 1841. The new pianos probably remained in the White House, at least through James Polk's term, because there are no further records of piano transactions until Millard Fillmore's administration. An "Inventory of Furniture in the President's House," dated January 1, 1849, states that "1 Piano Forte and music stool" stood in the "Receiving or Red Room" and "1 Piano Forte" was in the "Red Circular Chamber" (second floor oval room). The interesting voucher for this transaction provides details.[27]

Bot of E. N. Scherr

1841 July 21st. For the President's House at Washington D.C.
One large new concert piano with double grand action, metallic plate, tablet front, large new fashioned legs, iron frame, Rosewood case, nearly 7 octaves—down from Contra C, up to G at $600
One piano do[down] 6 octaves $450
$1040

July 21st, 1841. By two second hand pianos taken in exchange
$400
$650

Who performed on this new "concert piano" purchased from one of America's most prestigious makers? Undoubtedly "America's Bee-thoven," as he was called, the eccentric Bohemian-born artist, Anton Philip Heinrich. A composer in the expressive Romantic tradition, Heinrich wrote a large quantity of descriptive symphonic music at a time when there were few orchestras or singers capable of executing these complex works. In 1841 he completed his *Jubilee*, a vast fresco for orchestra, chorus, and soloists, commemorating "events from the landing of the Pilgrim fathers to the consummation of American liberty."[28] It was probably this work that Heinrich played for Tyler. He had spent several years lining up patrons for the piece and even journeyed to Washington to get support from high government officials, including the president. In his *Shadows on the Wall*, John Hill Hewitt describes accompanying Heinrich to Washington: "Poor Heinrich! I shall never forget him. He imagined he was going to set the world on fire . . . two or three hours of patient hearing did I give to the most complicated harmony I had ever heard . . . wild and unearthly passages." Hewitt goes on:

At a proper hour we visited the President's mansion, and . . . were shown into the presence of Mr. Tyler, who received us with his usual urbanity. I introduced Mr. Heinrich as a professor of exalted talent and extraordinary genius. The President after learning the object of our visit, which he was glad to learn was not to solicit an office, readily consented to the dedication, and commended the undertaking. Heinrich was elated to the skies, and immediately proposed to play the grand conception. . . .
We were shown into the parlor. . . . The composer labored hard to give full effect to his weird production; his bald pate bobbed from side to side, and shone like a bubble on the surface of a calm lake. At times his shoulders would be raised

Anthony Philip Heinrich, a Bohemian composer who emigrated to America in 1810, performed for President John Tyler in the 1840s. Anonymous drawing made from a contemporary silhouette.

to the line of his ears, and his knees went up to the keyboard, while the perspiration rolled in large drops down his wrinkled cheeks. . . .

The composer labored on, occasionally explaining some incomprehensible passage, representing, as he said, the breaking up of the frozen river Niagara, the thaw of the ice, and the dash of the mass over the mighty falls. Peace and plenty were represented by soft strains of pastoral music, while the thunder of our naval war-dogs and the rattle of our army musketry told of our prowess on sea and land.

The inspired composer had got about half-way through his wonderful production, when Mr. Tyler arose from his chair, and placing his hand gently on Heinrich's shoulder, said:

"That may all be very fine, sir, but can't you play us a good old Virginia reel?"

Had a thunderbolt fallen at the feet of the musician, he could not have been more astounded. He arose from the piano, rolled up his manuscript, and taking his hat and cane, bolted toward the door, exclaiming:

"No, sir; I never plays dance music!"

I joined him in the vestibule. . . . As we proceeded along Pennsylvania Avenue, Heinrich grasped my arm convulsively, and exclaimed:

"Mein Gott in himmel! de peebles vot made Yohn Tyler Bresident ought to be hung! He knows no more about music than an oyshter!"[29]

The elegant Scherr piano was treated more subtly, though no less expressively, when two noted singing families and a balladeer came

Public Exhibitions.

THE HUTCHINSON FAMILY.

A SKETCH, BY MARGARET GILLIES.

No. 17.   April. 25, 1846.

Hutchinson Family Singers, known as "The Tribe of Jesse," in a sketch by Margaret Gillies, 1846. In various combinations, the group sang for seven presidents.

to the White House with messages ringing loud, clear, poignantly—
with voices of reform, humanitarianism, rugged nationalism, and
idealistic sentiment. "We have come from the mountains ... of the
" 'Old Granite State,' " sang the Hutchinsons. "We're a band of brothers
... And we live among the hills. With a band of music ... We are
passing round the world."

For over a period of twenty years, the "Tribe of Jesse," as the four
(sometimes five) singers were called at first, became a stirring symbol
of the Yankee spirit in music. The ensemble came from rural New
Hampshire and were the most popular of the singing families of the
1830s, 1840s, and 1850s, such as the Rainers (the "Tyrolese Minstrels"),
the Bakers, the Cheneys, the Peakes, and the Gibsons. Through their
rich harmonizations and clear diction, the Hutchinsons expressed their
genuine concern for human misery and social reform in subjects involving woman's suffrage, alcohol, war, prisons, and especially slavery.
One of their songs, the controversial "Get Off the Track," was so
militant that publishers refused at first to print it. "Ho! the car Emancipation," as the song began, had abolitionists shouting their approval
and the opposition hissing and screaming in derisive anger. Some
historians have even gone so far as to say that the Hutchinsons' music
hastened the confrontations and conflicts that led to the Civil War.[30]

Tyler was the first of seven presidents who would hear the Hutchinsons sing in the decades ensuing. But the ensemble's first concert
in the White House, on January 30, 1844, was rather subdued in tone,
more patriotic than polemic. The reception packed numerous guests
into the East Room, and Asa noted that there were "many pretty good
looking maidens there but I pitied them laced up as they were so that
they could scarcely breathe and with their dresses and shoes hardly
fit for summer wear. I can't describe—music by a poor band, some
dancing. ... I hate false fashions. 'A life in the wildwood free.' "[31]
The singers' program included "The Land of Washington," "Happy
and Free," "A Little Farm Well Tilled," and "The Origin of Yankee
Doodle." At the close of the program was the perennial "The Old
Granite State," which the group often sang in antiphonal style—solo
with chorus in echo fashion—characteristic of gospel hymnody. There
was scarcely a program given by the Hutchinsons that did not open
or close with this piece; it became their theme song. Frequently they
added or changed its verses to suit their moods. Whether or not they
sang their most controversial text when they appeared before Tyler,
we may never know. It was:

> Liberty is our motto,
> And we'll sing as freemen ought to
> Till it rings through glen and grotto
> From the Old Granite State
> That the tribe of Jesse,
> That the tribe of Jesse,
> That the tribe of Jesse
>   Are the friends of equal rights.[32]

William Dempster was a ballad singer of the same era as the Hutchinsons, but with a message far less urgent. About a year after James Knox Polk became president, Dempster sang in the White House. The president jotted down a few notes about the event in his diary for March 7, 1846: "At this stage of the conversation I was sent for by Mrs. Polk to go to the parlour to meet company who were there. . . . I found 50 or more persons, ladies and gentlemen, in the parlour; Mr. Dempster, a celebrated musician, entertained the company by singing and playing on the Piano."[33]

The musical style of Dempster—like that of Henry Russell and John Braham, other popular balladeers of the day—harked back to the sentimental Scotch and Irish traditions still popular in America at this time. Born in Scotland in 1809, Dempster lived in America for a number of years but was constantly traveling back and forth to England, where he died in 1871.[34] George Odell's *Annals* show that he sang often in New York from 1834 to 1864 where "he brought music to the hearts of the people."[35] On March 6, 1846, he sang at Carusi's and his program was undoubtedly the one he gave at the White House the following night. According to the *National Intelligencer* of March 7, 1846:

> Dempster who is about to return to Europe sang his most popular compositions.
> When the Night Wind Bewaileth
> Lonely Auld Wife
> Blind Boy
> Lament of the Irish Immigrant
> I'm alone—all alone
> and his favorite cantata "The May Queen," a song in three parts which represents the gradual decay of a lovely girl from the bloom of health to a premature grave.

"The May Queen" is an interesting sentimental musical cameo in the style of the European art song. It is constructed in three subdivisions with each part related by common musical motives. Closely allied to the text by the great English poet Alfred Tennyson, the music seems genuinely Schubertean in its overall lyrical expression and piano accompaniment. The piece was published by Oliver Ditson in 1846 and has on its cover an especially beautiful lithograph in finely drawn colors. "The Lament of the Irish Immigrant" (Boston: William Oaks, 1840), on the other hand, was written at a time when the Irish began to arrive in America in large numbers. It tells of loved ones lost and a cherished homeland in a melancholy little mood piece.

President and Mrs. James Knox Polk allowed no dancing, cards, or "frivolities of any kind" during their term in the White House from 1845 to 1849. Sarah Childress Polk was a talented woman whose father had given her a fine Astor pianoforte when she was a young girl.[36] As a student at the Moravian Female Academy in Salem, North Carolina, she composed music and was especially well educated in the arts. Music to Mrs. Polk had a significant place in American life, but its graceful tones were meant only to be listened to, and it was not until

"The May Queen," a new "cantata" by William Dempster, was a three-part sentimental ballad with poetry by Alfred Tennyson. It was most likely included on Dempster's program for President James Knox Polk at the White House. Boston: Oliver Ditson, 1846.

the administration of Benjamin Harrison that dancing became an active part of White House social life again.

Scala recalled that "Polk did not care much for music and he gave the Marine Band little attention. He was of a kindly disposition, however," as the bandmaster testified. Scala related that one of the young Italian bandsmen, after a reception at the White House, "opened a piano and began to play an accompaniment to a young Neapolitan who started to sing a passionate love song. About the middle of the ballad President Polk appeared. The bandsman made a break for the door. The President laughed and asked them to continue. When they concluded, he returned to his room upstairs, from which he had emerged to learn the cause of the music."[37]

Music to the president, however, was a mystical language that fortified the spirits of those who knew no other means of communication. On April 30, 1846, he wrote in his diary that between twenty and thirty blind and deaf-mute children called on him and demonstrated their skills in literature, mathematics, and music. America at this time was only beginning to form an awareness of her less fortunate brothers and sisters; the Perkins Institute for the Blind, for example, was a searchlight for those deprived of sight. The president does not say from what institution the pupils came, only that "altogether it was an interesting exhibition, and impressed me sensibly with the benevolence and great value of the discovery by which these unfortunate persons could be taught to communicate their thoughts. . . . One of the females performed on the piano; one of the males (a boy) on the violin, and several of them sung very well."[38]

On March 4, 1849, Zachary Taylor was inaugurated as the nation's twelfth president. He served until his sudden death on July 9, 1850. Like Harrison, Taylor was a soldier and had won the respect of a grateful nation for his bravery during the war with Mexico. "Old Rough and Ready" became America's idol, and his feats were eulogized in a panoply of songs and parlor piano pieces churned out by American publishing houses in vast quantities. "General Taylor was an old-fashioned soldier who put on no airs whatever," said bandmaster Scala. "In fact, he was rather gruff than otherwise. . . . He was fond of older martial music."[39]

The White House Office of the Curator possesses three bound albums of music from the estate of Betty Bliss Dandridge, Zachary Taylor's youngest daughter. Recent bride of Lt. Colonel William Bliss, Betty Taylor served as White House hostess for her mother, Margaret Smith Taylor, during the family's brief period in the mansion. It is uncertain whether the music was used in the White House or whether it was merely part of the family collection over the years; the pieces date mainly from the 1840s, but there are some from the 1820s, notably "Washington's Favorite, the Brave La Fayette [*sic*] written by a Gentleman of this city [Washington] to a Favourite Air arranged with a Chorus in three parts and an accompaniment for the piano." The author's identity is not given, but the piece was published by John Cole of Baltimore in 1824. Other works in the collection are

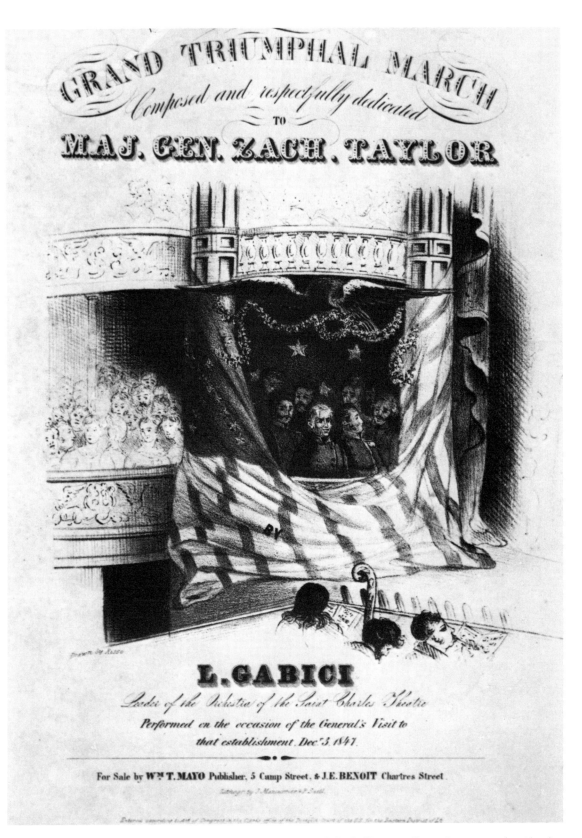

Major General Zachary Taylor attending a performance of the ballet *Giselle* at the new Saint Charles Theatre, New Orleans, on December 3, 1847. Taylor is shown on the cover of "Grand Triumphal March" by L. Gabici, leader of the orchestra, published by William T. Mayo.

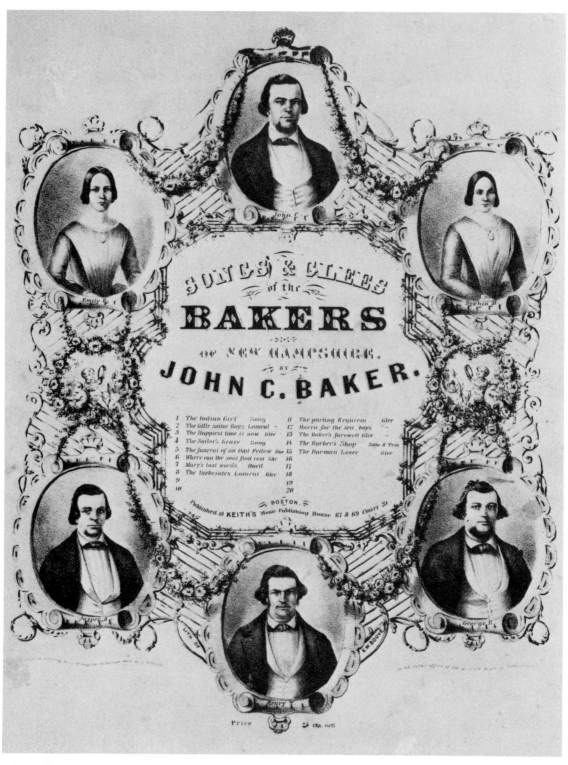

The Baker Family from New Hampshire, four brothers and two sisters, sang several songs and arrangements by John C. Baker for President Zachary Taylor. Boston: Keith's, 1847.

also linked to the city of Washington. A rare copy of "French Air" by Nathaniel Carusi indicates that the piece was "Published and sold by Sam Carusi and Brothers, Washington." There is also a copy of Charles Grobe's programmatic memorial to the heroism of the Mexican War, "The Battle of Buena Vista" (Willig, 1847).

Not long before the century reached its halfway mark, President Taylor and his family heard a singing group at the White House that resembled the Hutchinsons in style and origins. On April 24, 1849, the Baker Family presented a program that included some of their most popular songs.[40] Like the Hutchinsons, the Bakers came from New Hampshire, but their four-part harmonizations and moralizing verses, composed or arranged by John C. Baker, bore more sentiment than social commentary. Likenesses of the family appear on the decorative covers of the sheet music: two sisters—Emily and Sophia—and four brothers—John, George, Henry, and Jasper.[41] The young musicians sang at Carusi's Saloon, and like Dempster when he sang in Washington, they presented a program the following night at the White House. We have no review of their performance for President Taylor, but the *National Intelligencer* of April 30, 1849, mentions that their Washington concert included "Death of Washington," "Happiest Time Is Now," "Is There No Comfort for the Sorrowing Heart," and "The Mountaineer's Farewell, or The Granite Mountain State," a subject set by the Hutchinsons as well.

"Rarely has it been my happiness to be more agreeably entertained than at the concert given by these charming vocalists on Wednesday night last," said the *Intelligencer.*

> The "family" consists of two sisters and four brothers, of youthful appearance, each possessing a natural, strong, and finely-cultivated voice, blended with unassuming manners; and, when united in sound, produce the roundest, fullest, and sweetest music I think I ever listened to. The bass voice, and I may add those of the air, I venture to affirm, are rarely surpassed in our country. . . . and it is the "moral influence" inculcated in these concerts, that, to me, gives them their chief charm and renders them so inviting; for what are sweet sounds and a brilliant audience, and the joy and happiness of the occasion, if no good and lasting impressions are produced on the mind? . . . no one can hear them, as well as many of those sung by the "Hutchinson family," without having his feelings awakened, and who will not leave the concert in heart a better person.

A "better person"? The value of the "moral influence"? America's feelings were being awakened, to be sure. But something else was emerging—something like "a war between intellect and affection; a crack in Nature which split every church in Christendom," as Ralph Waldo Emerson wrote—"The key to the period appeared to be that the mind had become aware of itself. . . . The young men were born with knives in their brain."[42]

CHAPTER 4

A HOUSE DIVIDED: PROSPERITY AND WAR

Fillmore to Lincoln

When the battlefield is silent,
  You can go with careful tread,
You can bear away the wounded,
  You can cover up the dead.

S. M. Grannis
"Your Mission"

"The early 1850s shed a warm glow of hope and satisfaction over the American scene," wrote the historian Samuel Eliot Morison.[1] Industry prospered, railroads extended to the West, and immigrants continued to reach out to America's golden door of freedom and opportunity. During the second half of the century, concert and operatic life quickened, and noted European artists began to travel to the eastern seaboard and eventually venture out into the trans-Appalachian urban frontier. Sensational and eccentric entertainment appealed to Americans who demanded a real "show" for their money. The fine musicianship of conductor Louis Antoine Jullien was too often subjugated to his quest for the extravaganza, his love of the "monster" concert that exploded in volumes of instrumental forces and sound. Pleasurable humbug was offered the gullible public by master conjuror, P. T. Barnum, and opera and concert stars were advertised as musical wonders of the world. Did it really matter whether or not the great De Begnis could sing 600 words and 300 bars of music in a minute, as claimed? The thrill lay in the anticipating, the daring—that emboldening promise that Americans took for granted as their undisputed right.

As the nation expanded westward, discussions about moving the capital to the geographical center of the new republic persisted. From 1840 to 1850, however, Congress showed a tendency to improve District conditions, and fear of relocation subsided. Large sums of money were appropriated for new public buildings and general civic development.

By the mid-nineteenth century, moreover, the local population had increased to 40,000 (10,000 of whom were black), and while a full orchestral concert was still a rarity, touring grand opera companies began to allot the city seven or eight performances a year.

From New York the Seguin troupe, which had been presenting foreign operas in English, arrived in Washington in 1851. About the same time, impresario Max Maretzek of the Astor Place Opera House brought to the capital the Italian soprano Teresa Parodi, who sang with a troupe of singers and instrumentalists in a concert devoted mainly to operatic selections. Washington in 1852 also heard two of the nineteenth century's greatest prima donnas sing within five days of each other when Maria Alboni and Henrietta Sontag attracted even President Millard Fillmore and his family to the theater. By 1858 the *Washington Weekly Star* was describing the city's characteristic enthusiasm for opera as it had predicted the reaction to Maretzek the Magnificent's arrival with his troupe on October 17: "The Washington theater will, of course, be crowded to its utmost capacity, for in no other American city is a larger portion of the community competent to appreciate such music as they render."

The excitement of the decade, however, had come with the arrival of Jenny Lind, who disembarked in New York on September 1, 1850, to begin a concert tour under the auspices of Barnum. Barely thirty at the time, she had reputedly sung in opera over 700 times and had just announced her retirement from its "immoral and evil roles." A contemporaneous young lawyer, George Templeton Strong, recounts her wild welcome by no less than 20,000 screaming spectators in New York harbor.[2] Lind's two concerts in Washington on December 16 and 18, 1850, were an enormous success. She was accompanied by an orchestra of sixty "professional men of New York and this city," directed by Julius Benedict. Arias and the ballad "Home Sweet Home" comprised the program, and on the December 18 playbill the final selection was the ever-popular "Hail Columbia."[3]

President Fillmore and his family occupied choice seats at both concerts held in the National Theater, its reconstruction barely finished after the fire of 1845. The audience, deemed "ill-mannered" by a local critic, disturbed the music with raucous applause at the late arrival of Daniel Webster and Henry Clay, since Washington society—southern and slave-holding in outlook but almost by definition committed to union—considered them heroes. After all, had they not been instrumental in halting a strong southern secessionist movement through their involvement in the Compromise of 1850 just two months prior to the concert? The president invited the diva to visit him and Abigail Fillmore, a great lover of music and literature, in the Executive Mansion. Jenny Lind's biographer C. G. Rosenberg describes her reaction: "She had sat and chatted with him, and with his wife and daughter—she had utterly forgotten his position for the time, and only when she retired did she recollect that she had been in the presence of the man who controlled the most powerful and vigorous government that had ever arisen in the short lapse of a single century."[4]

Fillmore, who served as vice-president under Zachary Taylor, succeeded to the presidency upon Taylor's death in July 1850 and served until March 1853. The Fillmores found the White House in need of immediate care: "The great room over the Blue Room was covered with a straw carpet made filthy by tobacco-chewers. Underneath this was found a good Brussels carpet of the old pattern, a basket of roses upset. Mrs. Fillmore had this cleaned; she sent to Buffalo for her piano and Abigail's harp, shut off much of the space with screens, and with a wood fire and comfortable surroundings, made the place very pleasant."[5]

Mrs. Fillmore, the former Abigail Powers, was responsible for selecting books for the first White House library, and the "great room over the Blue Room" became a comfortable music room and library. The Fillmores' daughter, Mary Abigail ("Abbie"), was an accomplished linguist and pianist who also played the harp and guitar. She was eighteen when she first came to the White House, and the year after she left at age twenty-two, she died—one year after her mother. The upstairs oval room resembled the family music room of the Rutherford Hayeses several years later. Here, wrote a friend, Mrs. Fillmore "could enjoy the music she so loved, and the conversation of . . . cultivated society."[6] The first lady often invited talented friends to perform for her, such as the daughter of Congressman James Brooks of New York. A guest at the White House during this era recalls one of these evenings: "Mrs. Brooks' daughter, then quite too young to appear in general society, was there by special request of Mrs. Fillmore, who so enjoyed her wonderfully sweet singing, that she relied upon her as one of the attractions for this evening. Miss Fillmore played the piano with much skill and exquisite taste. Indeed, few ladies excelled her in this accomplishment; and this evening she was particularly successful in her efforts to please. Mrs. Brooks accompanied her upon the harp, which instrument she played with much grace."[7] Occasionally the president would join in the singing; a particular favorite of his was a new tune called "Old Folks at Home."[8] Composed in 1851, Stephen Foster's immortal song was popularized by the Christy Minstrels, but its nostalgic themes of longing for bygone days gave it universal appeal.

The music that the Fillmores owned is bound into five large volumes with "Mrs. M. Fillmore" or "M. A. Fillmore" (Mary Abigail) tooled in gold on the covers.[9] The pieces date mainly from the 1830s and 1840s and are generally for piano alone or piano and voice. A large percentage of the selections are stamped: "Sold at J. D. Sheppard's Music and Fancy Store, Buffalo"—the city in which the Fillmores lived for many years. One of the volumes contains an index in a child's handwriting with the signature "Abbie Fillmore." Abbie was born in 1832 in Buffalo and studied and played a large quantity of the music—an indication of her talent and motivation. No music appears to have been added to the collection after the deaths of mother and daughter in the early 1850s.

The five volumes of music in the Fillmore collection are a fine representation of the tastes of an artistic and educated American family

Portrait of Mary Abigail Fillmore, daughter of Millard and Abigail Fillmore, is believed to be a daguerreotype from her White House years. Mary was a talented amateur performer who played the harp, piano, and guitar.

during this period. There are the ubiquitous Scotch and Irish airs, operatic transcriptions, patriotic songs, variations, battle pieces, and the popular Henry Russell tunes. But in addition are a number of piano duets, no doubt enjoyed by mother and daughter, and a well-penciled copy of J. B. Cramer's "Instructions for the Piano Forte." And to captivate a young girl's imagination is a jaunty little piece called "Fanny Grey—a ballad of real life." Its verses begin: "I saw you making love to her/You see I know it all/I saw you making love to her/At Lady Glossop's ball!"

Government records show that there were three pianos tuned in the White House during Fillmore's term of office. One may have been the Tyler Scherr, the other Mrs. Fillmore's own piano brought from Buffalo, and the third a new piano purchased for the White House on March 22, 1852, from William Hall and Son. The voucher indicates that "one Rosewood, seven octave piano forte" was purchased for $475 and a "white printed india rubber piano cover" for $8.[10] The Aurora Historical Society owns a seven-octave rosewood Boardman and Gray square whose provenance dates to the Fillmore White House years. The piano's number 2,731 indicates that it was made about 1850 or 1851. William Hall of the piano dealers and music publishers, Firth and Hall, was the tutor of James A. Gray of Boardman and Gray, Albany.[11] Hall undoubtedly procured the piano from Albany for the Fillmores or sold them a Boardman and Gray instrument from his New York store.

Between October 31, 1851, and December 7, 1852, piano tuner Jacob Hilbus was at the White House on nine occasions. The name Hilbus, in fact, reappears on vouchers for piano maintenance from the administrations of James Monroe through Franklin Pierce—a span of over thirty years. Hilbus is listed in the Washington directory of 1822 as an "organ builder," and he built the chamber organ for Christ Church, Alexandria, now at the Smithsonian. But the musical Fillmores kept the versatile tuner busier than any other presidential family: there were three pianos to tune, strings to repair, and "superintending the moving of pianos and tuning same"—all "to Miss Fillmore's order."[12]

The Franklin Pierce administration, from 1853 to 1857, while politically important, was socially quiet. There were the usual public receptions, levees, and dinners, but no brilliant entertainment of foreign dignitaries. The outdoor Marine Band concerts continued to draw crowds, with leader Francis Scala providing many of his own new arrangements. "The most fashionable gatherings in Pierce's and Buchanan's administrations occurred during these concerts," noted a former *attaché* of the White House.[13] Indoors, guests continued to enjoy the band at the weekly receptions. On April 26, 1856, recalled the *Star*, "a delegation of Seminole Indians was present, but they seemed to care little for the display of fashion; and stationing themselves as near as possible to the Marine Band, were oblivious to nought else but the music, for the entire evening."[14] The often somber overcast of the White House under Pierce was due in part to the family's loss of their only son "Benny" in a railway accident only a few weeks before the inauguration. "But if, for that, my first winter in Washington, the White House was sober," wrote Virginia Clopton, "the houses of the rich Senators and citizens of Washington, of the brilliant diplomatic corps, and of some of the Cabinet Ministers, made ample amends for it."[15]

James Buchanan, whose term of office was overshadowed by that of his successor, Abraham Lincoln, was sixty-six years old when he reached the White House. A tired, once-brilliant lawyer, Buchanan spent four years trying to satisfy both North and South but failed to grasp the political realities of the stressful times. Buchanan was the only president who never married, and his niece and ward, Harriet Lane, served as White House hostess. Under her direction the Buchanan period saw some of the most brilliant receptions in the annals of the White House during the nineteenth century. The Marine Band and

Title page of music belonging to Mary Abigail Fillmore: *Firth and Hall's Occasional Selections of Celebrated Duets for Two Performers on One Pianoforte.* New York: Firth and Hall, (n.d.).

Scala were at the president's several times a week, and the outdoor concerts continued to draw hundreds. An account in the *Star* on May 7, 1859, paints a provocative image of the season's first concert on the grounds south of the mansion: "When they [the Marine Band] played waltzes or other dances, hundreds of happy children instantly went to capering . . . while the multitude of colored nurses, of all ages, catching the inspiration, danced as enthusiastically as their several charges. These scenes formed very interesting features in the constantly varying picture. The part in them taken by the servants struck us as embracing an effective practical argument against the soundness of the anti-slavery theory concerning the unhappy condition of the African race in the South."

Another band concert held outdoors was the gala event honoring the visit of the prince of Wales ("Baron Renfrew"), later King Edward VII. The young statesman arrived in Washington in early October 1860 and stayed about one week. Scala and the Marine Band played a special program featuring Scala's arrangement of "Listen to the Mocking Bird" by Richard Milburn, a Negro barber noted for his whistling and guitar playing. Scala dedicated his arrangement to Harriet Lane:

> On the afternoon it was to be first played in public, Scala came to the grounds with a handsome program of the selections. On it was painted a mocking bird. Miss Lane did not know of the honor, and was not there; but a messenger was sent after her, out to the Soldier's Home, and she was on hand when the "Mocking Bird" was played. There was a good crowd present, and much applause followed. Miss Lane bowed and bowed, and Scala bowed and bowed; but it had to be repeated. In less than a week every man was whistling, and every lady who could play it was playing and singing it. But I don't think I ever heard it played as well as it was played that afternoon, though the same band played it often during the summers.[16]

Time and again reports of this event have been convoluted, crediting the occasion with the first performance of Milburn's famous song. The piece, in fact, had been published five years earlier by Septimus Winner (who also wrote the words under the pseudonym Alice Hawthorne). Undoubtedly the "premiere" writers refer to was the new band arrangement that, coupled with its White House appearance, set the piece firmly on its path to popularity.

The indoor receptions continued to be mobbed, despite President Buchanan's efforts to change the order of the New Year's Day reception. He staggered diplomats, justices of the Supreme Court, high-ranking military officers, and the general public and put police in charge to guard against theft. The plan did not always work. One visitor recorded that he called on the president on New Year's Day, "and had the privilege of shaking hands with Miss Lane and having his pocket picked simultaneously in the presence of a strong force of Irish police. All this was accompanied to the tune of the *Star-Spangled Banner* played by a feeble band in an invisible chamber."[17]

Opera stars and concert artists occasionally came to the White House during this period as they did under Fillmore. We have no verification that they performed for the president, but their invitations to small gatherings and appearances at large public receptions show that their link with the president and his family was growing stronger as America's cultural life flourished. Harriet Lane had a box at the theater and heard seventeen-year-old Adelina Patti in her Washington debut in Donizetti's *Lucia di Lammermoor*. People were clamoring for seats at $90 apiece at the time. But to an artist there was something very special about visiting the presidential family in that most distinguished of all homes—the White House.

In mid-February 1859 the Washington papers were full of the glitter of Ullman's Opera Troupe and its star, Mlle. Marietta Piccolomini. The twenty-year-old Italian diva, who had just sung in *Don Pasquale* in Washington, attended a reception at the White House on February 19, during which she shared the honors with a delegation of Potawatomie Indians. Several modern accounts have erroneously magnified her White House visit into a full-scale operatic production of *La traviata*. She may have sung a tune or two, but all we know of the incident is the following vignette:

> But who is this rising out of a cloud of pale yellow lace, a red rose in her bosom, a short budding vine drooping beneath her waist, her hair simply braided over her head, wearing no ornaments? Piccolomini for all the world, escorted by the Sardinian Minister. . . . Mr. Buchanan . . . made a gallant remark to the *prima donna* to the effect that he did not understand and could not speak French. Piccolomini smiled, and used her eyes. Mr. Buchanan went on to say that he did spend three months in France five years ago, but that he had no ear nor tongue now. (His worst enemies who speak of him as in his dotage, never said anything so severe.) Piccolomini smiled, and used her eyes again. Then the President informed the Sardinian Minister that his country was going to war—adding that he hoped Piccolomini would not be impressed into the service. How the little coquette used her eyes and her smiles when this remark was translated to her only those who have seen her in *Traviata* can imagine. Mr. Buchanan would probably have stayed till daylight did appear, had not Mrs. Gwin intimated that it was time to go. Thereupon he shook hands with the several members of the family and disappeared.[18]

How she used her eyes! So did another—but his had no vision. He was blind. His distended "sightless eyeballs seemed to be searching in the stars and the great opera ear seemed to be catching harmony from the celestial spheres." He was labeled an idiot. "He claws the air with his hands, whistles through his teeth, capers about and see-saws up and down."[19] Yet at the age of ten he was playing the piano like Gottschalk, Mozart, or Beethoven. He was called "Blind Tom" and was presented at the White House to President Buchanan for whom he played a twenty-page piece of music shortly after hearing it for the first time.[20]

Thomas Greene Bethune ("Blind Tom"), an amazing idiot savant who toured Europe and America as a concert pianist and performed at the White House for President James Buchanan.

An excellent article by Geneva Southall discusses some of the inaccuracies written about Tom, a black musical genius whose strange antics may have been deliberately cultivated by his concert managers, who sent him on tours throughout America and Europe claiming his musical abilities derived from occult powers.[21] Certainly the way Tom's publicity was handled suggested charlatanism. Judging from the many accounts written about him, Thomas Greene Bethune, born a slave in 1849, was perhaps the most exploited figure of this era of the American extravaganza. He was a sensitive, naturally gifted musician and composer, who was far more than a mere musical curiosity. Edgar Stillman Kelly, noted American composer, claimed his career diverted from painting to music after he heard Blind Tom perform Liszt's transcription of Mendelssohn's "Midsummer Night's Dream" Overture. And not long after Tom played for Buchanan, William Knabe, a well-known American piano manufacturer, gave the ten-year-old slave a grand piano, which bore the inscription "a tribute to genius."[22]

The piano Tom undoubtedly played at the White House, however, was a superb "full grand" made by Jonas Chickering, one of the first firms in America to make grand pianos. This style of piano was still quite rare in America, and it was considered a sign of great affluence and prestige for a home or concert hall to possess one. On June 22, 1857, John Blake, commissioner of Public Buildings and Grounds, wrote to Chickering: "Gentlemen—I wish to purchase for the President's House a *first rate* grand piano of elegant appearance, but not elaborately carved or inlaid with pearl or papier maché nor in any other manner decorated so as to give a tinsel appearance." The firm replied, giving three choices, and Blake selected the medium-priced model for $800.[23] Harriet Lane enjoyed playing the piano, and a large album of her music, with her name tooled in gold, is property of the Wheatland home of

William Batchelder Bradbury, music educator and composer, brought his well-trained choir to the Executive Mansion in 1859. Engraving by F. Halpin.

Buchanan in Lancaster, Pennsylvania. The collection comprises mainly piano arrangements of Italian opera arias and overtures dating from the presidential period.

Under Buchanan, William Batchelder Bradbury began an association with U.S. presidents that was to last for over forty years. He founded the Bradbury Piano Company, which supplied the White House with pianos from Ulysses S. Grant through William McKinley. But his appearance before President Buchanan in the East Room on Friday, April 22, 1859, was important for a different reason. He conducted a choir of musicians attending a week-long music convention in Washington in a rare performance of Handel, probably a chorus from one of the master's oratorios that the choir was then performing in the city.[24] Bradbury, a pupil of American music educator Lowell Mason, went even further than his noted teacher in introducing music to the New York public schools. He directed annual festivals in New York with 1,000 children singing, and his tunebook, *The Jubilee* (1858), sold over 200,000 copies. The president must have been pleased with Bradbury and his choir because he personally conducted the group on a tour through the mansion, inviting them to sing an encore before they left. What might they have chosen? Perhaps Bradbury's own "Woodworth" of 1849. It was a far cry from Handel, this newly emerging style. It resembled a soul-stirring, evangelistic gospel song—with a modicum of urban commerciality about it.[25]

But the 1850s saw hardship as well as prosperity. The North and South were moving in perilous directions that would one day collide. There set in "one of those terrifying, and rationally unaccountable, decades in American life when all the ingenuity, vigor, and hot blood of the country seem to concentrate into opposing channels of fear and self-righteousness," writes Alistair Cooke.[26] In 1858 Abraham Lincoln, candidate for U.S. senator from Illinois, preached his vital testament of antislavery: "A house divided against itself cannot stand. I believe this government cannot endure, permanently half *slave* and half *free.*"[27] Two years later at Cooper Union, New York City, Lincoln reiterated his views that no compromise with slavery was possible. When he was inaugurated on March 4, 1861, Lincoln became president of what was no longer the *United* States. The first gun of the fratricidal Civil War was fired against Fort Sumter the next month. As James P. Shenton noted, two brothers became separated by boundaries drawn in blood.[28]

The music that made its way to the White House during Lincoln's tenure from March 4, 1861, to April 14, 1865, reflected the spirit of the times more than it did during any other period in American history. For soldier or civilian, music's message was persuasive and powerful. Tones rang clear, thousands of songs captured the moment—tearful, tense, jubilant, courageous. Americans communicated through bands, songs, and choruses, at home by the fire, on the battlefield, and in churches, schools, and taverns. They told all through music; and music, in turn, sustained and diverted their spirits throughout the grim struggle. In his *Lincoln and the Music of the Civil War*, Kenneth Bernard writes: "Abraham Lincoln, like other Americans of that chaotic time, became absorbed in the music of the war that so well fitted every occasion, every mood. He heard it in the White House, throughout the city, and in many of the 'hundred circling camps.' He felt its strength and realized its power and influence. More than once he had been thrilled and moved to tears by it. Coming from the hearts of men and women whose lives were torn asunder by war, this music touched the heart of the wartime President time and again."[29]

Lincoln had been responsive to music from his early boyhood days in the wilderness frontier cabin. Friends recalled that certain sentimental ballads would "mist his eyes with tears and throw him into a fit of deep melancholy."[30] Noah Brooks, Washington correspondent for the *Sacramento* [California] *Union*, wrote that in later life Lincoln's "love of music was something passionate . . . [and that] his tastes were simple and uncultivated, his choice being old airs, songs, and ballads. . . . All songs which had for their theme the rapid flight of time, decay, the recollection of early days, were sure to make a deep impression."[31] Among Lincoln's favorites were "Barbara Allen" (or "Barbary Ellen"), believed to have been sung by his mother Nancy Hanks in the Kentucky hill country of his youth, "Mary of Argyle," "Kathleen Mavourneen," "Old Rosin the Beau," "Annie Laurie," and "Twenty Years Ago."[32] Concerning the last song, Ward Lamon, Lincoln's musical friend from the Shenandoah Valley, recalled: "Many a time, in the old days on the Illinois circuit, and often at the White House when he and I were alone, have I seen him in tears while I was rendering in my poor way that homely melody." Lamon noted one of the verses that affected Lincoln most deeply:

This official portrait of Abraham Lincoln, painted by George P. A. Healy in 1869, was bequeathed to the White House in 1939 and hangs today in the State Dining Room. While not musically talented, Lincoln was deeply moved by patriotic songs, sentimental ballads, and grand opera.

> My lids have long been dry, Tom, but tears came to my eyes;
> I thought of her I loved so well, those early broken ties:
> I visited the old churchyeard, and took some flowers to strew
> Upon the graves of those we loved, some twenty years ago.[33]

But Lamon also had a way of cheering Lincoln with his spirited banjo tunes from the new blackface minstrel shows then in vogue. Special favorites with the president were "The Blue-Tail Fly" (or "Jim Crack Corn") and "Picayune Butler," whose comic lyrics and syncopated beat provided contrast with the sentimental Scotch and Irish ballads of the day:

> I'se gwine some day to buy a farm,
> An a band of niggers I'll take along, Yah-ha.
> An ebry day we'll sing dis song,
> Ob Picayune Butler come to town, Yah-ha.[34]

Little did Lincoln realize that Lamon's rendition of "Picayune Butler" would become a controversial national incident. The sensitive president asked Lamon to sing a song to cheer him during their exhausting ambulance ride through the blood-strewn battlefield of Antietam. Twisted and misinterpreted, the incident was magnified into a malicious vehicle for criticism by Lincoln haters.

Lincoln also loved opera. As president he attended grand opera nineteen times, sometimes without Mrs. Lincoln, and he is the only president in history to have attended an inaugural opera when Flotow's *Martha* was staged for his second inauguration in 1865. Lincoln also enjoyed in Washington such productions as *The Magic Flute, La dame blanche, Norma, Der Freischütz,* and *Faust,* whose famous "Soldiers' Chorus" was a special favorite.[35] On February 20, 1861, shortly before his inauguration, Lincoln witnessed at the Academy of Music in New York a chilling prophecy of his assassination. *A Masked Ball,* Lincoln's first opera and the American premiere run of Verdi's dramatic masterpiece, is the story of a Swedish monarch's brutal murder.[36] Four years later, Lincoln's own assassination was enacted in a theater— dramatically and with tragic realism. The president was fatally shot by John Wilkes Booth while attending a performance of *Our American Cousin,* a play with music starring Laura Keene, at Ford's Theater on April 14, 1865.

There were times when the president was criticized for attending the opera when the real life dramas of Bull Run and Harpers Ferry were raging, but he retorted, "The truth is I must have a change of some sort or die."[37] But even grand opera was subject to the current wave of public sentiment, especially in the nation's capital, where the war fever was at its peak. The performance of Donizetti's *La figlia del reggimento,* which the president heard in May 1862 featured South Carolina–born Clara Louise Kellogg. The young diva related in her memoirs how the cast introduced American national airs and additional drum rolls and bugle calls to turn the patriotic French opera into an American pageant: "The audience cheered and cried and let themselves go in the hysterical manner of people wrought up by great national excitements. Even on the stage we caught the feeling. I sang the Figlia better than I had ever sung anything yet, and found myself wondering as I sang, how many of my cadet friends of a few months earlier were already on the front."[38]

Whenever Lincoln could attend a concert by the popular pianist and composer Louis Moreau Gottschalk, he would do so. Born in New Orleans in 1829, the legendary matinee idol was touring at his typical pace of eighty-five recitals within a four- to five-month period when Lincoln heard him in Washington on March 24, 1864.[39] Gottschalk, an abolitionist whose sympathies were with the North, was America's first important pianist. His original compositions prophesied the coming of ragtime and jazz and the practice of musical quotation characteristic of Charles Ives.[40] Gottschalk's *Notes of a Pianist* is a remarkable commentary on American life and manners, especially during the Civil War. About Lincoln he says candidly: "President Lincoln is the type of American of the West. His character answers but little to the idea which they have of a nation's ruler. Tall, thin, his back bent, his chest hollow, his arms excessively long, his crane-like legs, his enormous feet, that long frame whose disproportionate joints give him the appearance of a grapevine covered with clothes, make of him something grotesque and strange, which would strike us in a disagreeable manner if the height of his forehead, the expression of goodness and something of honesty in the countenance, did not attract and cause his exterior to be forgotten."[41]

Neither Abraham nor Mary Todd Lincoln could read music, sing, or play an instrument. Shortly after moving into the White House, however, Mrs. Lincoln traded an older piano, "free of all expense for exchange, labor or transportation," for a fine new one made about 1860 by the Schomacker Company of Philadelphia.[42] The piano had a compass of seven octaves plus a minor third, a one-piece cast-iron frame, and was supported by three cyma-curved, scroll-carved legs. Its attractive top was edged in graceful leaf carving. Seated often at the "grand Schoomaker," as government records were prone to call it, were the two unruly Lincoln boys, Willie and Tad, with scholarly Professor Alexander Wolowski patiently guiding them. Perhaps they fingered some of their father's favorite tunes, but if they followed the professor's "special simplified method," as advertised in the *National Intelligencer* at the time, they would have been able to "execute operatic as well as classical music with rare perfection." The Polish pianist had recently set up a studio in Washington and considered himself a court musician to the Lincolns. Apparently he had the "run of the Executive Mansion, a priviledge he did not abuse."[43] The Schomacker piano occupied a prime spot in the lush Victorian-style Red Room, Mrs. Lincoln's favorite sitting room. A description of the White House furnishings two years after the Lincolns moved in indicates that there was "a grand piano in this room and a full-length portrait of Washington" [the Gilbert Stuart painting].[44]

If the president readily attended musical entertainment outside the White House, how he must have enjoyed the programs within the

Rosewood grand piano (#1,900) made by Schomacker and Company, Phila-delphia, as it stands in the Chicago Historical Society today. The piano was placed in the White House by the firm of William H. Carryl in 1861 and remained in the Red Room until the beginning of Rutherford B. Hayes's administration (1877–81).

mansion! These events, while not numerous, were as varied as the president's own artistic preferences and as kaleidoscopic as American taste itself. The first guest artist to perform at the White House for the Lincolns was a young American opera singer, Meda Blanchard. Forgotten today, the aspiring diva also appears to be the first opera singer to have performed in the Executive Mansion. That the young soprano was a native of Washington attracted the attention of the press, which noted that she had sung in local churches, then went abroad to study with "the most eminent Italian masters." When she returned to the city in 1861, the *Sunday Morning Chronicle* proudly heralded her first concert: "the results of her industry, we are assured, are very manifest in a great accession of melody and power. She returns to America laden with the highest encomiums."[45] The *Chronicle* also printed a public letter signed by twenty-two leading citizens, including William Seward and Salmon Chase, inviting her to present the concert. With this support, as well as the interest of the Lincolns, how could she lose? Her program took place on July 6 at Willard's Hall, but more important, she presented a preview a few days earlier at the White House.

> Urged to sing for Mrs. Lincoln's guests, she did so. Playing her own accompaniment, she sang in a manner that charmed everyone present. Just as she had finished and was about to leave, the President appeared. The music had reached his office upstairs, and he had now come down to listen. Mrs. Blanchard was recalled with the request that she sing for the President. She agreed, again went to the piano and, as one observer put it, ". . . having laid off the shawl from shoulders that no 'South' would ever have seceded from, (with its eyes open)," sang the "Casta diva" [from Bellini's *Norma*] and one or two ballads, and then, at the President's request, the "Marseillaise." The President was delighted and thanked her enthusiastically.[46]

Four days later the Lincolns attended Mme. Blanchard's concert at Willard's. The *Star* noted that "our Republican President seemed to have been oblivious to the cares of office and wholly absorbed by the syren [*sic*] voice of the fair cantatrice." Did it matter that the young singer would never soar to stellar heights? She had sung for the president—and he had sent her a bouquet of flowers![47]

If the president craved diversion from the increasing gloom of the war, he found it in three disparate entertainers whom he welcomed on different occasions at the Executive Mansion: an Indian songstress, a midget song-and-dance man, and a nine-year-old prodigy destined to become one of the century's finest pianists. Several months before Blanchard sang, another young woman presented a few numbers for the president and his guests at a White House reception in late March. Her name was Larooqua; she was an American Indian. There would not be another like her to fill the mansion with such "wood notes wild" nor "mellifluous voice," as the papers described her Washington program, until Princess Te Ata would sing for President Franklin Roosevelt in 1939. Larooqua was called the "aboriginal Jenny Lind," and her voice was described as "somewhat thin, but pleasant and of considerable cultivation."[48] Probably politics more than artistry brought her to the White House. She was in Washington assisting John Beeson, who was giving a series of lectures on the plight of the Indians in Oregon.

Commodore Nutt, a talented midget brought to the White House by Phineas T. Barnum in 1862, sang for President Abraham Lincoln and members of his cabinet.

When Commodore Nutt entertained President and Mrs. Lincoln, the distressed chief of state had just witnessed his "darkest hour" through the disastrous carnage at Fredericksburg. On October 17, 1862, the great showman Phineas T. Barnum brought one of his $30,000 stars to the White House—a twenty-nine-inch-high midget that probably barely reached the president's knee. Advertised in the *National Republican* as the "smallest man in the world," George Washington Morrison Nutt was considered intelligent, enchanting, and a fine entertainer—"a most polite and refined gentleman."[49] The little performer delighted Lincoln and members of the cabinet by singing Thomas à Becket's popular "Columbia the Gem of the Ocean."

Another small artist was the amazing Venezuelan prodigy, Teresa Carreño, who was only nine when she was brought to the White House by her father in the fall of 1863. But she exhibited the temperament that was to become her hallmark. Recalling the event in her later years, she wrote:

> The President and his family received us so informally, they were all so very nice to me that I almost forgot to be cranky under the spell of their friendly welcome. My self-consciousness all returned, however, when Mrs. Lincoln asked me if I would like to try the White House grand piano. At once I assumed the most critical attitude toward everything—the stool was unsuitable, the pedals were beyond reach, and when I had run my fingers over the keyboard, the action was too hard. My poor father suggested a Bach Invention would make me more familiar with the action.
>
> That was quite enough to inspire me to instant rebellion. Without another word, I struck out into Gottschalk's funeral

Marche de Nuit, and after I had finished modulated into *The Last Hope*, and ended with *The Dying Poet*. I knew my father was in despair and it stimulated me to extra effort. I think I never played with more sentiment. Then what do you think I did? I jumped off the piano stool and declared that I would play no more—that the piano was too badly out of tune to be used.

My unhappy father looked as if he would swoon. But Mr. Lincoln patted me on the cheek and asked me if I could play *The Mocking Bird* with variations. The whim to do it seized me and I returned to the piano, gave out the theme, and then went off in a series of impromptu variations that threatened to go on forever. When I stopped it was from sheer exhaustion.

Mr. Lincoln declared that it was excellent, but my father thought I had disgraced myself, and he never ceased to apologize in his broken English until we were out of hearing.[50]

Carreño was not the only artist to complain about the White House piano being out of tune. John Hutchinson did also. But his reference to the "rickety box of wires" could hardly have been the fine new Schomacker—even if it were not kept in tune. (No tuning vouchers can be found during the Lincoln term.) Perhaps another, older piano was kept on the main floor, in the oval room (Blue Room), shown in the drawing in John Hutchinson's *Story of the Hutchinsons*, where one of the family members appears seated at the Hutchinsons' melodeon. For the reception of January 7, 1862, the Hutchinsons—who literally had sung Lincoln into office with their popular campaign music—chose "The War Drums Are Beating," "Up, Soldiers, and Fight," and Henry Russell's "Ship on Fire," by request of the president. "We suffered a slight inconvenience in singing," wrote John, ". . . the piano was in shocking bad tune." In addition,

No music stool could be found, and altogether it was evident that Mr. Lincoln and his family were thinking of something else than music in those days. . . . "There's nae luck aboot the house," might perhaps have been played upon the rattling old keys, but it would have been little less than treason to have attempted "Yankee Doodle" on such a rickety box of wires. At President Lincoln's request, I sent for my melodeon, and sang the "Ship on Fire," he having heard me sing it before at Springfield, Ill. I can seem to see our martyred President now as he stood only a few feet from me, holding his sweet boy, "Tad," by the hand. We were warmly applauded as our songs concluded. The room was as full as it could be.[51]

Henry Russell's melodramatic "Ship on Fire" was labeled "a descriptive scene" on its cover, probably after its contemporaneous Italian operatic models, but the piece actually had all the earmarks of a D. W. Griffith silent film score: "agony" (triplets in C minor); "she flew to her husband" (staccato repeated chords, FFF); "smoke mounting higher and higher" (sixteenth-note runs); "thank God we're saved!" (p to pp in E-flat major). It was pictorial music, and it moved the president greatly.

But the music closest to Lincoln were those tones bound most intimately with the people during their turbulent war years. Practically every familiar and lesser-known national tune encircled the White House in those days—melodies that revealed the soul of a people who knew the powers of both tragedy and joy, defeat and victory. One hundred years before Woodstock and the Rolling Stones, America's propensity for self-expression through song escalated to dramatic new heights: "We are coming, Father Abraham, Three hundred thousand more!" sang mobs of soldiers before the White House as they responded to the president's call; strong men cheered, cried, and bellowed out George F. Root's immortal "Battle Cry of Freedom"—"Yes, we'll rally 'round the flag boys, we'll rally once again!" Thousands of black people gathered to sing spirituals on the White House lawn on July 4, 1864, in joint commemoration of Independence Day and the Emancipation Proclamation; 500 members of the Christian Commission called on the president on January 27, 1865, singing "Your Mission," the "Soldiers' Chorus" from *Faust,* and various hymns; far into the night crowds gathered at the White House after the fall of Richmond, waving flags and serenading victory with Julia Ward Howe's "Battle Hymn of the Republic" and Dan Emmett's "Dixie." "Let's have it again!" cried the president, who had first heard "Dixie" at a minstrel show in Chicago. "It's our tune now!" he said, implying that both North and South would find unity and fellowship in a common musical expression.[52]

How deeply the president was moved by these ubiquitous musical demonstrations has been recorded by those close to him. He was known to have called for certain pieces again and again. There were those special songs and singular incidents that drew mist to his eyes, such as Chaplain Charles C. McCabe's interpretation of the "Battle Hymn of the Republic," sung in the hall of the House of Representatives in February 1864, for the anniversary meeting of the Christian Commission. At the same meeting the following year, the president heard the talented Philip Phillips sing words that sent tears streaming down his face:

> If you can not in the conflict
>   Prove yourself a soldier true,
> If, where fire and smoke are thickest,
>   There's no work for you to do;
> When the battlefield is silent,
>   You can go with careful tread,
> You can bear away the wounded,
>   You can cover up the dead.

During the meeting Lincoln jotted off a quick note to Secretary of State William Seward: "Near the close let us have 'Your Mission' repeated by Mr. Philips [*sic*]. Don't say I called for it. Lincoln."[53]

War songs and patriotic music were performed often in the White House during the Lincoln receptions. The Marine Band, under Scala's direction, was on hand to play at all levees, described as "a curious mixture of fashion, elegance and the crudity of everyday frontier life."[54]

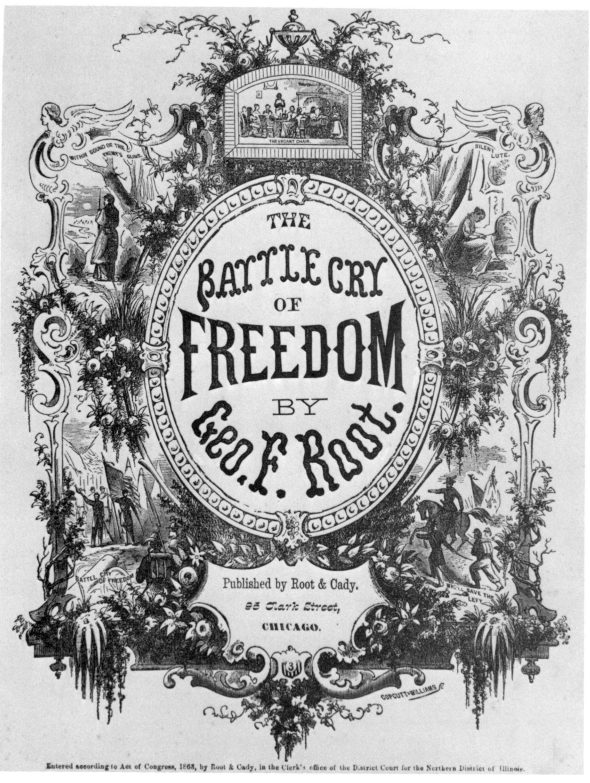

George F. Root's "Battle Cry of Freedom" was a favorite song of Abraham Lincoln. The cover of one of its earliest editions was decorated with scenes depicting the meaning of war to the soldier and his family at home. Chicago: Root and Cady, 1863.

The Marine Band performing in its bandstand on the White House grounds during the visit of Prince Napoleon of France. In the distance is the unfinished Washington Monument. *Frank Leslie's Illustrated Newspaper*, August 17, 1861.

Except for the period of almost two years when Mrs. Lincoln allowed no Marine Band programs in the White House or on the grounds following the death of her son Willie, social events went on fairly regularly during the war years and music played an active part. Mary Lincoln, an elegant, educated, though emotionally unstable, woman, was criticized regardless of whether she entertained too much or too little. The public objected to the long periods without their popular band concerts on the mansion grounds.

Lincoln was fond of the Marine Band and appreciated Scala's contribution to its excellence. On July 25, 1861, he established the first act to recognize the Marine Band by law. He also supported Scala's choice of repertory at a time when the band was being criticized for playing too many operatic selections rather than "national and martial music." The rift was vaguely reminiscent of the eighteenth-century War of the Bouffons, with John G. Nicolay, the president's secretary, favoring the "cultivated" sound of Italian and German music," and Secretary of the Navy Gideon Welles retorting that this "sentimental music . . . was unsuited to most of our fighting men, [and] inspired no hearty zeal or rugged purpose."[55] Nevertheless, the president attended the concerts whenever he could, and the following account only under-lines what little peace the head of state had to pursue his own pleasures: "One Saturday afternoon when the lawn in front of the White House was crowded with people listening to the weekly concert of the Marine Band, the President appeared upon the portico. Instantly there was a clapping of hands and clamor for a speech. Bowing his thanks, and excusing himself he stepped back into the retirement of the circular parlor, remarking to me, with a disappointed air, as he reclined upon the sofa, 'I wish they would let me sit out there quietly, and enjoy the music.' "[56]

Did the president ever tire of hearing "Hail to the Chief"? It seemed to follow him around like a shadow during his entire presidency. It was the first piece of music he heard as he stepped into his carriage and started for the Capitol on the day of his first inauguration—and it was the last piece he heard before he died. The orchestra struck up the presidential march as Lincoln entered Ford's Theater on that fateful night of April 14, 1865. But the special feature of the evening, the "Patriotic Song and Chorus, Honor to Our Soldiers," was never played. Lincoln was assassinated by John Wilkes Booth; a stunned nation poured forth its grief through music—solemn hymns and dirges that numbered in the hundreds.

The funeral ceremony at the White House had no music, but the thirty-five-piece Marine Band played as the impressive cortege left the mansion for the Capitol, led by a drum corps shrouded in quiet dignity. One thousand singers chanted as the martyred president lay in state in the Springfield City Hall, and when the funeral train arrived in Chicago, selections from Mendelssohn's *St. Paul* and *Elijah* were sung by a large choir. But the most impressive service of all was the quiet ceremony at Springfield's Oak Ridge Cemetery. George F. Root, com-poser of Lincoln's beloved "Battle Cry of Freedom," had composed an elegiac tribute, a simple song like those Lincoln loved:

> Farewell Father, Friend and guardian,
>   Thou has joined the martyr's band;
> But thy glorious work remaineth,
>   Our redeemed, beloved land.[57]

PART TWO

★ ★ ★

1865–1901

RECONSTRUCTION BEGAN with the surrender of the Confederate forces in 1865 and ended with the removal of the last Union occupation troops in 1877. It was a grim period. The Confederacy had collapsed, and the South was totally devastated. From Virginia to Texas, farms, railroads, and entire towns had been destroyed. Carpetbaggers plundered what remained of once-graceful plantations, and the Ku Klux Klan terrorized former slaves in the dark of night. Despite bitter altercation among political leaders over plans for rebuilding, new patterns of government and economic directives eventually managed to rebuild the South, but the haunting memories of a defeated people remained for generations.

With at least some of the problems concerning Reconstruction settled, America turned its attention elsewhere. From the end of the Civil War to the turn of the century, the United States rose as a new industrial society and an important world power. In 1860 one American in every six lived in a community of more than 8,000 persons; by 1890 this ratio had become one in three. In 1860 there was not a single city in the United States with more than a million inhabitants; by 1890 New York, Chicago, Philadelphia, and Baltimore had all exceeded that figure. The population of the United States, recorded as 65.5 million in 1890, was greater than that of Germany, France, or England. Between 1860 and 1900, moreover, more than half a million inventions had been patented, among them the light bulb, the phonograph, the telephone, the typewriter, the cash register, and the Wright brothers' flying machine.

Increasing urbanization, industrialization, and economic prosperity brought difficulties, too: bitter conflict between labor and capital and a ruthless struggle for the country's riches. Organized corruption, operating through influential rings with their "bosses," exercised its powers through broad networks that involved even President Ulysses S.

Grant. Once primarily an agricultural nation, America became within a few short decades a nation of businessmen. "The Great God Dollar" was born. Under the banner of economic expansionism, President Andrew Johnson purchased Alaska from the Russians for $7.2 million, paving the way for the thousands of adventurers who would explore the mineral-rich wilderness in the gold rush of 1896. Interests in Cuban sugar plantations by American entrepreneurs became a factor in the Spanish-American War of 1898, which resulted in the American acquisition of Cuba, Guam, Puerto Rico, and the Philippines from Spain.

And the American people? Where did they come from? What did they accomplish? What were their dreams? Lured by the railroad systems that were expanding across the continent, immigrants, homesteaders, cattlemen, and farmers pioneered the unsettled territories between the Mississippi River and California. Mining towns sprang up in the Rocky Mountains, and the Homestead Act of 1862 promised every citizen 160 acres of free land, providing that he was willing to occupy and improve the land for five years. Most of the immigrants during this period—the Germans, Irish, English, Canadians, and Italians— came to America because of hard times in their homelands. Between 1860 and 1890 there were more immigrants from Germany than from any other country, and they provided the nation with a wide variety of professionals, scholars, and musicians. From the "rousing songs" of the German singing societies to the Wagnerian glories of Mme. Ernestine Schumann-Heink, Germanic traditions played a significant role in shaping and defining American cultural life.

Many immigrants became homesteaders, whose life was rough and raw. Women served as mothers, teachers, nurses, cooks, and comforters. But in time their simple homes boasted wallpaper, carpets, and an upright piano. For as Alistaire Cooke points out, "It was the mother who accompanied the family hymn singing . . . maintaining the frontier tradition, which lasted long—too long, perhaps—in American life: that culture belonged to the women." One such person was Dwight D. Eisenhower's mother, who went to Abilene, Kansas, in 1892. Her modest home on the corner is preserved today as a national monument—the president's boyhood home.

Blacks and European immigrants filled American life with a rich and variegated culture that was unlike any in the world. It permeated all genres of music from operatic and concert styles to popular, ragtime, folk, and other vernacular forms. The American Indian, by contrast, played a much less significant role in the development of the nation's music. Living in relative isolation, their population having fallen drastically by the end of the century, Indians practiced a form of ancient tribal music that was not understood by other Americans. While the culture of the native American came to be valued and preserved, mainly through the efforts of Theodore Roosevelt, Indian traditional music was either ignored or Westernized through its incorporation into art music.

By the close of the century America was linked by a chain of states from the Atlantic to the Pacific, and 6 million people were living where only decades earlier bison had grazed. The days of the Wild West were over.

CHAPTER 5

MUSIC ON THE LIGHTER SIDE

Johnson and Grant

Oh, it's really shameful! 'tis most scandalous,
  The sorrows and hardships poor females must endure.
  Those dreadful cabmen! swear, swear, grumbling!
. . . Or if you hail an omnibus, conductors will deride,
With "Very sorry, ma'am we're full,—but won't you go outside?"

Mr. and Mrs. Howard Paul

Mary Todd Lincoln sat upstairs in the White House wringing her hands, half-demented, unable to pack her belongings and leave. There was no hurry, the new president assured her. Not long after the tormented Mrs. Lincoln had left for her lonely life ahead, Andrew Johnson moved into the mansion. It was June 9, 1865. The war was over, but the fires had left burning embers. Johnson faced some onerous tasks of his own—reconstruction of the devastated South and establishment of viable relationships between whites and newly freed slaves. There were at least four million of the latter, who had nowhere to go. Johnson adopted what he thought would have been Lincoln's program—faith in the South—but his policies clashed with those of Radical Republicans in Congress, and he was impeached, barely escaping removal from office.

The patriotic fervor, heartbreaks, and pride of Civil War music had little place in an America that wanted to forget. Even the songs of the Hutchinson Family carried a social message less urgent, less acidulous now. When they sang for Rutherford B. Hayes in the White House on April 18, 1878, the Hutchinsons featured such pieces as their "Lullabye Glee" and Henry Work's "Grandfather's Clock." Work's enduring song about the clock that "stopped short, never to run again" at the moment the old man died reflected the new postwar spirit: affectionate and nostalgic, rather than stirring or passionate—looking backward for solace, rather than forward for dramatic action. Charles Hamm summarizes this philosophy in his *Yesterdays: Popular Song in America:* "In deliberately turning away from contemporary issues, our songwriters made of popular song something it had never been before—escapism."[1]

Music at Johnson's White House often took the form of entertainment with a special appeal to children and youth. The mansion was described by staff members during Johnson's administration as "an old-fashioned, hospitable, home-like farm house," which rang with children's voices, games, good spirits—and most certainly, music. "We are plain people from the mountains of Tennessee," the Johnsons' daughter Martha once said. "I trust too much will not be expected of us."[2] The family was large. It comprised the President and Mrs. Johnson, their two sons, two daughters (the widowed Mary Stover and Martha Patterson with her husband), and five grandchildren, the oldest being about ten when Johnson became president.

All the Johnson grandchildren studied music and attended Marini's Dancing Academy during their more than three years in the White House. Mary Johnson Stover's children learned to play the violin and guitar, and many entries for strings are to be found in their mother's old account books.[3] One of Mary's boys, Andrew J. Stover, found pleasure in his violin well into his later secluded years spent in the Tennessee mountains; people in the valley recounted hearing his playing on many warm summer evenings. Belle (or Mary Belle) Patterson, Martha's daughter, undoubtedly continued playing the piano as a young girl when her family left the White House for the Johnson home near Greeneville. Her album of bound sheet music consists of twenty-eight pieces dating from the 1840s to about 1880 and reflects the sentimental parlor music typical of American home life at this time. Selections in the book include "Silver Threads among the Gold," "Robin Adair," Franz Abt's "Embarrassment Song," and—new to presidential collections—some short piano pieces by Robert Schumann, among them "Träumerei" from *Kinderszenen,* op. 15.[4]

When Andrew Johnson took office on April 15, 1865, the Schomacker grand piano from the Lincoln administration was still in the Red Room. According to an inventory of February 28, 1867, it had been decked with a "new cloth cover with a rich silk fringe."[5] If the Hutchinsons could find no stool for their program for Lincoln, Johnson's household had the problem rectified. The inventory also stated that there were "two stools and one music rack," no doubt for the aspiring piano-duet players and violinists in the large family. The piano was also given a fair amount of care, judging from correspondence a few weeks after Johnson moved into the White House and shortly before his family arrived. The commissioner of public buildings found himself writing to the Schomacker representatives:

> I have consulted with the Ladies at the President's as to your proposition to take the Piano belonging to the U.S. in the House, to Philadelphia and putting it in perfect order.
>
> They instruct me to say that you can take it at your convenience.
>
> It is understood that it is to be taken away and returned in a reasonable time, and entirely without expense to the United States.
>
> On these conditions you will please send for it as soon as you can.[6]

The Schomacker grand piano is seen in drawings and photographs of the Red Room during Andrew Johnson's and Ulysses Grant's administrations until it was removed to make space for the Hallet and Davis upright during the Hayes term.[7]

But Johnson cared enough about his "Ladies" of the White House, and about the joys and diversions that music brought them, to purchase for each of his daughters a fine Steinway square pianoforte. Neither instrument, however, became part of the White House furnishings. The first (#16,214) was sold to Johnson in 1868 for Mary Stover to use in the Johnson home at Greeneville. The second (#16,651) was also purchased by Johnson, on April 6, 1869, and shipped to his second daughter's home, that of Martha Patterson in Henderson Station (now Afton, near Greeneville) for the sum of $575. Martha states in her will that this piano was purchased for her daughter Belle. The pianos are practically identical, and both were sold by Wm. G. Metzerott and Co. of Washington, D.C. They are also fine, early examples of the overstringing technique for which Steinway & Sons won a gold medal at the 1855 American Institute Fair.[8]

As the war clouds gradually dispersed, the gala White House receptions of prewar years returned. The Marine Band was kept busy, and leader Francis Scala noted in his memoirs that both President and Mrs. Johnson supported and helped the organization immeasurably. "Every time the band played, Mrs. Johnson sent me a bouquet and in return I dedicated a march to her," Scala said.[9] The Marine Band programs were some of the few events Eliza Johnson enjoyed. Due to a chronic illness, this small, quiet woman kept to her room upstairs in the southwest corner of the mansion for most of her days there. But it was a pleasant time, indeed, when the frail lady could see and hear the band as it played under her window on the lawn.

Martha Johnson, wife of Senator David T. Patterson, took over most of the mansion's social activities for her ailing mother and proved to be an efficient, yet unpretentious hostess. For over twenty years there had been no dancing at the White House. Now it was the younger crowd who set the pace with the rollicking "Juvenile Soiree" held on December 28, 1868. Four hundred members of Marini's Dancing Academy tripped to the measures of the Marine Band amid flowers, shimmering candles, and sumptuous repast. What did they dance? The small engraved program preserved in the White House Curator's Office tells us. Bound with a white satin ribbon, the little card is the earliest memento of White House entertaining to print a complete program. It lists the basket quadrille, the esmeralda, varsovienne, lancers, polka redowa, galop, and, of course, the waltz. But Dolley Madison's bequest to American society was given some precise guildelines by Thomas Hillgrove. Writing in 1863, Hillgrove observed that "it is improper for two gentlemen to dance together when ladies are present." He also noted that "in waltzing, a gentleman should exercise the utmost delicacy in touching the waist of his partner. Dance quietly," he added. "Do not jump, caper or sway your body."[10]

As for the remaining dances, they had been popular, like the waltz, earlier in America and all originated in Europe. The lancers came from Dublin and was a type of square-dance variant of the quadrille. One of the most popular dances of the nineteenth century, the quadrille comprised five distinct parts and was danced by sets of four, six, or eight couples. The varsovienne (from the French for "Warsaw") resembled a slow waltz, and the polka, having come to the United States in the early 1840s, gave rise to numerous jokes about presidential candidate James Knox Polk. Along with the waltz, it was the staple of military bands and mid-nineteenth-century popular sheet music. And the galop? To music suggesting the galloping of horses' hoofs, couples bounded with springing steps in an exhausting dance that lasted only two or three minutes—a rousing finish to the ball.

One of the most unusual programs that the Marine Band ever accompanied took place on July 28, 1866—a gymnastic exhibition. The event itself was not especially unique when one considers that the *Turnverein*, brought to America by German immigrants, was attracting national attention. But at the White House? And why not? Abner Brady, noted turning professor, had just presented his bevy of talented pupils at Grover's Theater. The papers advertised the big event as a "Grand Gymnastic Exhibition and Instrumental Concert," and from Grover's the next stint was the president's. On the south lawn of the White House a clever system of identification was devised to let the audience (and gymnasts) know what pieces were being played. *The Evening Star* of July 28, 1866, reported that the names of the pieces would be displayed "from the east side of the music stand." In the National Archives is a voucher of this date for the printing of "12 cards: designations of music pieces to be played at the President's,"[11] but we have no record of what these selections were, nor whether they were played during or between the acts. And the gymnasts? One can only speculate. Women athletes, however, were not uncommon during this time: "They do their contortions in slippers, striped stockings, loose pants, and other things, in which costume they are said to 'look sweetly pretty.' They run, jump, swing, pull weights, and do lots of difficult things. The school mams are given to practice on the horizontal bar, while it is noticed that the married women mostly devote their efforts to practice in swinging the heavy clubs."[12]

But along with this rather indecorous cavorting, there were some "chaste and elegant divertisements" at the White House in those days, as the papers noted, such as the program of Mr. and Mrs. Howard Paul on January 12, 1867. Forgotten today, this team came from England and apparently created quite a stir in America—albeit short-lived—during the 1860s and early 1870s.[13] Their six-night run at Metzerott's Hall in Washington beginning Monday, January 7, 1867, was described by the *Evening Star* as a series of "concerts in costume, an entertainment which is by turns gay, serious, fanciful, grotesque and always amusing. Mrs. Paul is not only a great actress, but a singer of wonderful power, and Mr. Paul is an accomplished actor and vocalist. They have given great satisfaction wherever they have appeared."

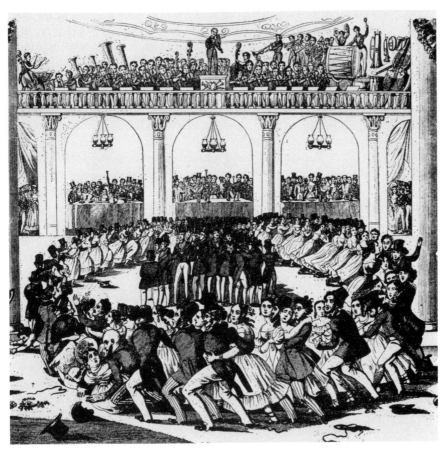

"The Grand Galop" by Johann Strauss (the Elder) in an engraving by A. Geiger, 1839. The rapid motion and lively spirit of the dance kept it popular at the White House until the end of the century.

If we wonder what the Pauls sang for the president and his family, we need only to consult their current program at Metzerott's Hall. Undoubtedly some of these works would have made their way to the White House. "The Life of Julius Caesar" was a satirical impersonation of Napoleon III with Howard Paul dressed in "imperial costume." It opened with the lines:

Friends, countrymen, and lovers, will you kindly lend an ear,
To a little ancient history, describing the career
Of the late lamented Caesar, who, I think you'll all agree,
Was exactly like my *uncle*, who was very much like me.

Each verse was then sung to a different tune, such as "Home, Sweet Home," "Paddle Your Own Canoe," "Tight Little Island," "The Ratcatcher's Daughter," and so on. Another number that captured the fancy of Washingtonians was a song called "Mr. and Mrs. Doubledot (a quarrelsome couple who are known among their friends as the Dog and Cat)." And the *National Republican* of January 10 noted that "the humorous side of the Irish character is given with much effect ... illustrated by a Hibernian rendering of 'The Bold Soldier Boy' with drum accompaniment." With a touch of satire Mrs. Paul exposed "The Sorrows and the Hardships Poor Females Must Endure" ("For she's pushed about, insulted, and imposed upon by all. . . . Or, if you hail an omnibus, conductors will deride: With 'Very sorry, ma'am we're full,—but won't you go outside?' ").

Several of the Pauls' songs had a more serious message. Particularly popular numbers were Henry Russell's epic "The Dream of the Reveller," which the *National Republican* called "a triumph of impassioned lyrical expression," and also his "Ship on Fire," a favorite with Abraham Lincoln. Apparently Mrs. Paul (we never learn her first name) possessed a contralto voice of particular beauty and excelled in her impersonations of Sims Reeves, a noted English actor and singer, "entirely free from any caricature."

But one piece was certainly sung for the president, as the *Evening Star* reported on January 12, 1867: "His excellency was very much struck with Mrs. Paul's singing of the 'Star Spangled Banner' which she rendered superbly." In Howard Paul's anthology *Comic and Musical Entertainment* is the additional commentary: "During the late Rebellion Mrs. Howard Paul sang this splendid National Lyric in almost every town and city of Great Britain, not for any political or partisan reason, though occasionally audiences would insist on taking this view of it. . . . [She] must have made the melody of the 'Banner' familiar to tens of thousands of English people."[14]

While Mr. and Mrs. Howard Paul might be considered a British version of the American singing families who were at the height of their popularity during the 1840s and 1850s, they could also be considered the forerunners of modern popular duos such as Captain and Tennille, who would belt out their ballads and musical messages for Gerald Ford in the White House more than 100 years later. By the 1860s and 1870s, however, families such as the Peakes, Alleghanians, Bakers, Bergers, and Barkers had joined forces with other entertainers to provide more variety and better "show." This was the type of program Johnson and his family heard on January 21, 1867, when the Peakes performed with the Swiss Bell Ringers. Undoubtedly the president brought along the grandchildren. There were special matinees for children and even children in the show itself.[15]

The performance that the president heard at Metzerott's ran for a season of two weeks commencing on January 17. It combined three distinct companies: the two Peake Families, the Swiss Bell Ringers, and the Berger Family in a "Grand Consolidation of vocalists, harpists, violinists and silver cornet band." The *Intelligencer* defined the total number of performers as twenty-five with "280 silver table bells" gleaming on the long counter at the front of the stage. There were also two featured bell-players, "the only solo staff bell-players in the world."

Bell-ringing shows remained popular in America well up to the close of the century. In 1881 the *Washington Post* reported that the Hand Bell Ringers of London, who had appeared to crowded houses during their American tour, would perform in Lincoln Hall on December 28 and 29. A few years later, the Benjamin Harrison family held a "grand musicale" in the East Room of the White House, which featured a group of bell ringers that apparently fascinated Baby McKee. The president's famous grandson made up his mind that he was too far from the music, broke away from the president, and tried to get closer to the performers—despite his grandfather's unsuccessful attempts to keep him from upsetting the program.[16]

By the time Ulysses S. Grant became president, the nation was ready for a grand celebration. The military hero of the North during the Civil War, General Grant was inaugurated on March 4, 1869, amid gala parades and the most brilliant inaugural ball to date, held in the just-completed Treasury Department building. The new wing was mobbed. There was plenty of music but little dancing due to the "crush." The affair was prophetic nonetheless. During their two politically tormented terms in office, the Grants held dinners and receptions that were equally lavish. While Thomas Jefferson had entertained sixteen for dinner, Grant had thirty-six (and McKinley was to have eighty!). He spared no expense; the dinner for Queen Victoria's son Prince Arthur was estimated to have cost $1,500. The Grants also employed a fine steward to work at the White House—an Italian who planned sumptuous meals of up to twenty-nine courses to satisfy a society quite ready for new diversions after the devastations of war and reconstruction.

All this suited Julia Grant, who enjoyed Washington society. But the general? According to that ineffable capital gossip, Ben Perley Poore, President Grant found the social season less than bearable. He would take his stand in the Blue Room and for two hours wear his "fight it out on this line" expression.[17] But even visitors to Washington at this time noted that social life seemed to revolve in a constant, meaningless whirl where "vulgar ostentation mingled with Doric simplicity." Could it be that public taste was passing through the confusion of youth, as William Hesseltine noted? Perhaps out of the clashing elements "a new society, and a new America would be born."[18]

Visiting artists and guest entertainers at the White House during Grant's two terms were rare indeed. Like another military president, General Dwight D. Eisenhower, Grant preferred military music and musicians, and his "in-house" court ensemble, the Marine Band, received a place of high accord. But the general had little eye for art and less ear for music. He openly avoided grand opera and theater and Gottschalk's quip that he knew only two tunes—"One is 'Yankee Doodle' and the other isn't"—may not have been too far off mark. Still the president must have enjoyed hearing the Hutchinson Family. According to the records of this famous singing family, the president attended

Julia Dent Grant, General Ulysses S. Grant, and their four children (left to right): Fred, Jesse, Buck, and Nellie. Lithograph by P. S. Dural shortly before Grant became president.

several of their concerts: "we gave many concerts in the capital, a large number in Dr. Tiffany's Metropolitan M.E. Church. F. Widdows, whom I have spoken of as agent for Ole Bull, usually had some connection with these concerts. He at this time played the chime of bells in the Metropolitan Church, and as he was very friendly to us would often play on the bells some of our melodies, 'The Old Granite State' and others. We were somewhat restricted in our selections when singing in this church, as the trustees objected to anything of a secular nature. Our entertainments were therefore sacred concerts. President Grant often came to these concerts."[19]

President Grant may also have enjoyed the rousing "songs of the fatherland" on July 16, 1870, described by Esther Singleton: "There were numerous visitors today, however, to see the premises, among them a German society just returned from the Saengerfest who gave in the East Room, to the few listeners, a brief concert in chorus, including some of the loudest and most enthusiastic songs of [the] Fatherland."[20]

The German society to which Singleton refers was most likely the Washington Sängerbund, who were participating in a local festival at the time and had sung at President Grant's inauguration. Founded on April 20, 1851, the all-male organization enjoyed an active eighty-year performing history and in 1911 celebrated its silver anniversary by singing once again in the White House, this time for President William Howard Taft. The group was probably the oldest singing society in the District, which also hosted the Masonic Choir, Amphion Glee Club, Germania Männerchor, Washington Operatic Society, Arion Singing Society, and several other groups founded during the nineteenth century. But the joyous German institution known as the Sängerbund was not confined to Washington. Before mid-century had passed, German art, spirit, and camaraderie had been powerfully transplanted to American soil through these influential choral groups. They took root in numerous American cities from St. Louis to Philadelphia, Louisville to Baltimore; New York could boast one of the finest—the famed German Liederkranz that years later would present a recital with the great Wagnerian contralto Ernestine Schumann-Heink for President Theodore Roosevelt at the White House.

As to what selections were included in the rousing "songs of the Fatherland" sung at the president's mansion in 1870, we can only speculate. Undoubtedly the program included one or two songs by Franz Abt, the German composer whose great popularity in America began with the male singing societies' renditions of his part-songs. A composer of over 3,000 pieces, most of them for voice, Abt came to America in 1872 as a participant in the World Peace Jubilee, organized

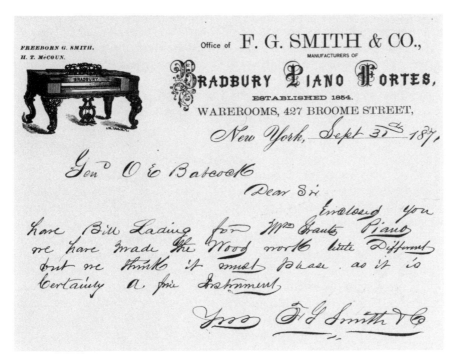

A bill for the Bradbury piano made for Julia Grant and delivered to the White House in September 1871. This was the first of nine Bradbury pianos to be placed in the White House before the turn of the century.

by Patrick Gilmore. On one of his conducting tours, he visited Washington where he was received at the White House by President Grant as a respected guest.[21]

With the increase in both the frequency and importance of White House social events, the Marine Band's reputation as "The President's Own" became more visible than ever before. It played for all the galas, receptions, banquets, serenades, and holidays and added special luster to the wedding of the Grants' eighteen-year-old daughter Nellie to Algernon Sartoris on May 21, 1874. And while distinguished foreign guests had been entertained at the White House as early as Lafayette's visit in 1825, during Grant's terms, the first heads of state came to visit our nation. King Kalakaua of Hawaii began his two-week stay on December 12, 1874. Dom Pedro, emperor of Brazil, arrived on May 8, 1876. And there were other important guests during Grant's administrations: Prince Arthur of Connaught, Grand Duke Alexis of Russia, and the staff of the Japanese embassy. All were entertained with elegance and aplomb by the president and the festive airs of the Marine Band, now forty strong. King Kalakaua's historic entrance into Washington was heralded in due royal fashion with "Hail to the Chief." While today's ears may find this tribute surprising, it was perfectly natural to Americans who were honoring their first foreign chief.

During the official dinners of this period, the Marine Band was stationed in the large corridor outside the state dining room as it is today. But while some White House guests dined elegantly to the pleasant tunes of the band, others promenaded, jostled, elbowed, shoved, and nearly suffocated to the melodious "soul-stirring airs" played during the public receptions. It is difficult for us to envision the doors of the White House being thrown wide open to everyone as it was, for example, every New Year's Day. But it must be remembered that this was virtually the only way for a nation—before modern methods of mass communication, such as commercial photography, radio, motion picture, and television—to see and hear its president. Public receptions continued well into the twentieth century and were not abolished until President Herbert Hoover's administration.

And who were the people who filed past the president? To one observer they resembled the "march of the centuries where Civilization and Barbarism once more embrace. . . . High and low, rich and poor, all shades, all colors, from the blanched cheek of the haughty Circassian belle to the Ethiopian's polished ebony, may be found waiting in the ante rooms of the White House."[22] By January 1, 1889, the crowds had reached 9,000, and Mrs. Grover Cleveland would have to have her aching arms massaged after shaking so many hands. Long lines formed outside, reaching all the way to the War Department—callers with "a look of New Year's gaiety on most of their faces. . . . The event was one of the greatest experiences of their lives. In the tiled vestibule the Marine Band, clad in gorgeous costumes of red and silver, sat along the Tiffany mosaic wall which shuts off the corridor. Professor Sousa was at the head, beating time for the musicians as the visitors passed."[23]

One wonders how the band avoided the crush and managed to play at all. Apparently there were times when it did not: "Mrs. McElroy's last reception was one of the greatest social triumphs any woman ever enjoyed in the White House," said one reporter ecstatically during Chester Arthur's presidency. "The crush was so great that the Marine Band was swept from its moorings and could not continue playing because of the pressure of people. So famous a hero as General Phil Sheridan got in only by being helped through a portico window by two policemen."[24] Like President Buchanan ten years before him, Grant had temporarily alleviated the problem by removing the band from the large anteroom or vestibule to the East Room, where a stand had been erected for it, "handsomely festooned with white lace and elaborately decorated with flowers."[25] This freed the large entry hall for the visitors, but the problem of handling the multitudes persisted.

Almost as popular as the receptions were the public concerts presented by the Marine Band on the White House grounds every Saturday during summer and early fall. They usually alternated with the programs held at the Capitol each Wednesday. On May 1, 1872, the *Evening Star* announced that General Babcock, commissioner of Public Buildings and Grounds, was preparing the South Lawn for the concerts. Now greatly enlarged, the lawn extended "throughout the entire space north of Executive Avenue." That the newspapers often listed the programs for these hour-long concerts indicates how attractive and important they now were to the public. For the open-air program on October 25, 1873, the *Star* gave the following: "1. March   2. Aria from the opera *I Masnadieri*, by Verdi   3. Overture *William Tell*, by Brossini [*sic* Rossini]   4. Waltz, Le Tourn [*sic*] du Monde, by Metra   5. Selection from *La Favorita* by Donizetti   6. Grand Galop, Battle of Inkermann, by Ed. van Buggenhout."

As an encore the band might have played a tune familiar to every U.S. Marine Corps member and all Americans as well—"The Marines' Hymn." At that time, however, it was known by a different name, "Couplets des Hommes d'Armes" (Duet of the Queen's Guards), sung by Pitou and Grabuge, two gendarmes in Jacques Offenbach's comic opera, *Geneviève de Brabant* of 1859. Like other songs that made their way into the American patriotic repertory via a folk tune transferred to opera (for example, "Hail to the Chief"), "The Marines' Hymn" is believed to have derived from a century-old Spanish folk song. A "Potpourri-Fantaisie" from the opera containing this tune dated 1868 is in the Scala Collection at the Library of Congress, and John Philip Sousa's autograph appears on an early copy of the duet in the Marine Band Library. But while both duet and hymn share the same musical spirit and vigor, they differ dramatically in their texts. "The Marines' Hymn" closes with the confident lines: "We are proud to claim the title/Of United States Marine"; the jolly little *buffa* duet: "Ah, it's fine to be a gendarme, but it's such a grueling curse!"[26]

Francis Scala, leader of the Marine Band from the time of President Pierce, was honorably discharged on December 13, 1871, at age fifty-one. He was succeeded by Henry Fries and on September 2, 1873, by

Popular Marine Band concerts on the White House lawn included works such as operatic excerpts by Verdi and Rossini and Van Buggenhout's "Grand Galop, Battle of Inkermann." *Harper's Weekly*, July 4, 1868.

Louis Schneider. Scala's arrangements dating from his last years as leader under President Grant show the number of his players to range from twenty-five to forty-five, depending most likely upon the occasion. A Neapolitan by birth, Scala retained his country's custom of holding the clarinet to be the principal band instrument. He was a fine virtuoso on the E-flat clarinet and played several other instruments as well, including the guitar and piano. His earlier band arrangements called for an instrument that he dubbed the "hippocorno," sometimes seen as "ipocorno," which seems to have been a brass instrument in E-flat playing an alto part.[27] Scala also employed the side-ranging saxhorn family with the bells pointing forward, upright, or back over the shoulder (common with marching bands). Saxophones and cornets (cornetta) are also indicated in some compositions.[28]

Cover from the piano/vocal edition of Offenbach's comic opera, *Geneviève de Brabant*, Paris: Heugel, 1861. The melody of the "Duet of the Queen's Guards" was most likely the origin of "The Marines' Hymn."

Francis Maria Scala, born in Naples, Italy, was leader of the Marine Band from 1855 to 1871.

On June 9, 1870, President Grant held a gala reception for Red Cloud and his Indian delegation of Ogallallas. They were shown through the White House and treated to a fine feast at which all the foreign ministers and many cabinet members with their wives were present. The Indians, delighted with what they saw, "expressed themselves as having a good heart toward the man who could have 'so much good eat and so much good squaw.' "[29] Many tried to get as close as possible to the Marine Band rendering the novel sounds of Verdi's *Attila*.

President and Mrs. Grant recognized the vital contribution of the Marine Band to the success of their entertaining and to the spirit of the people—but did Congress? These were rough years for the band. Problems mounted. Many players became disenchanted with the pay, which was considerably lower than civilian jobs in cities like New York and Philadelphia. A first-class musician in the Marine Band earned $34 per month with an additional $4 for his performances at the Capitol and on the White House grounds.[30] Along with his musical duties, the Marine Band player was required to "work on fortifications, surveys, roads, barracks, quarters, storehouses or hospitals, or as clerks at division or department headquarters and on constant labor."[31] When Congress refused to increase the pay of the band members, many submitted applications for discharge and left.

The losses were significant both in the numbers and the quality of the band. Andrew Coda, "1st Clarionetist," left to take an offer of $64 per month in a theater position; Lorenzo Schneider, brother of the leader, went back to his $200 per month orchestral job in New York; Charles Thierback found his present pay to be totally inadequate to support his wife and children, and he opted for "a large outside practice as teacher of music to which I wish to give my entire attention, as it will pay me better than 1st Class Musician in the Marine Band."[32] Even William Jaeger, who had acquired a considerable reputation as solo cornetist with the band, resigned for a position in New York that paid almost ten times his military salary. But it was many years before the band's prestigious position was filled by another brilliant cornetist, Walter Smith from Kalamazoo, Michigan, who eventually became second leader.[33]

The Treasury Department also frowned upon the expensive instruments purchased by the band for President Grant's grand parties. These included "two cases of German Silver Instruments and a second lot of wooden instruments" that were shipped via Southampton, England, in August 1879, and another large purchase on October 9, 1876, from P. Goumas & Cie of Paris, the firm that supplied instruments to the Conservatoire del'Académie Nationale de Musique.[34] Even the horse-drawn streetcar transportation that the band used weekly to travel from the Marine Corps Barracks to the White House came under attack by the fourth auditor. The secretary of the Navy, however, supported the request to continue each man's $4 allowance for this cause, and the streetcar stayed.

But there were other problems. These concerned the leader of the Band, Louis Schneider. The Italian-born maestro spoke only French and his native language, but his inability to communicate with the band was more than a problem of language. Schneider was called a fraud, a "wolf in sheep's clothing," and an imposter whose band experience derived from a small group he formed while serving a stint in the French State Prison in Paris.[35] On October 1, 1880, under President Rutherford B. Hayes, Schneider was discharged by the secretary of the Navy as "unfit for service."

The biggest blow of all to the band, however, came with the bill during the last months of Grant's presidency to "reorganize" the time-honored institution. Section 12 of the bill expressed this desire bluntly: "The band known as the 'Marine Band' must be abolished at once, mustered out of service, the instruments sold, and the money turned into the Treasury of the United States." This time Congress rallied to the cause. On June 3, 1876, Charles Harrison of Illinois rose to defend what he call "the Athenian concept of music . . . which ennobled the heart and purified the soul":

> Mr. Chairman, for fifteen long dreary years at the other end of Pennsylvania avenue the White House has been occupied by a Republican, and during the winter months, of evenings, the Marine Band has been up there at receptions to discourse sweet music for the delectation of a Republican President, and for the delectation of his friends. . . . For long years, of summer Saturday afternoons, twenty-four gentlemen in scarlet coats have caused twenty-four silvered instruments, on the green in front of the White House, to belch forth martial music for the delectation of a Republican President.
>
> On the 4th of March next, sir, there will be a Democratic President in the White House. Sir, is the Democratic President to have no music? (Laughter). . . . And from deep down in my heart came a reply, "No! No!" I will see a Democratic President in the White House. He shall receive his friends to the music of twenty-four silvered instruments filled with the breath of twenty-four gentlemen in scarlet coats. The Marine Band shall play Democratic music for a Democratic President (Laughter); and out there on that south portico I want to see a Democratic President sitting with his feet on the balustrade listening to the music poured forth by the Marine Band, and I hope to be one of his friends; and will sit there with my feet on the balustrade enjoying one of his Partagas [cigars]. But they wish to abolish the Marine Band. Think of this being done, Democrats, before the Democratic President goes into his position.[36]

Roars of laughter and applause from both sides of the house instantly brought defeat to the bill. Congressman Harrison won—and the Marine Band was saved. But there would be no Democratic chief executive with his feet on the balustrade enjoying the music. On March 4, 1877, Rutherford B. Hayes was inaugurated as the nineteenth president of the United States—a Republican!

CHAPTER 6

PRIMA DONNAS
FOR THE PRESIDENT

Hayes, Garfield, Arthur

Music, you know, is the pet of both
your mother and father.

Rutherford B. Hayes to Fanny Hayes
January 24, 1886

During the second half of the nineteenth century grand opera and that timeless cynosural delight, the diva, were becoming increasingly a part of the national artistic scene. And Washington, according to critics of the time, was turning into a "real center of culture." In the 1860s true opera seasons were evident in the nation's capital; John G. Nicolay, secretary to President Lincoln, found in opera "one of the most pleasant and useful auxiliaries to social pastime and enjoyment." By the final two decades of the century, Washington amusement pages were filled with notices of local and visiting opera companies, and reviews were emphasizing theaters packed with the wealth and beauty of the city. The National Theater, having given Washington premieres of both Gluck's *Orfeo ed Euridice* and Delibes's *Lakmé* in 1886, presented Mascagni's *Cavalleria rusticana* in 1891. The same year marked the opening of the Academy of Music on the corner of Ninth and D streets, which housed troupes of modest dimension until 1894, when the Hinrichs Company of Philadelphia gave two month-long seasons there. Divas and semi-divas frequently passed through the capital on the New York-Boston-Philadelphia-Chicago circuit, appearing in operatic productions as well as solo recitals. If one could manage a program at the White House, it was considered a coup. And many did.

Rutherford and Lucy Webb Hayes appeared to enjoy music and America's new cultural image more than any other first family of the century. If the Republicans wanted an upright president who would erase the taint of scandal lingering after Grant's administration, they found him in the conscientious, devout Hayes. One hundred years later President and Mrs. John F. Kennedy would reestablish the White House as a focal point for the performing arts in America. But the Hayeses were the pioneers. Nearly fifty musical programs were reported at the mansion during their one term in office, 1877–81. At least half of these were presented by guest artists: opera singers, instrumentalists, and choral groups that represented the finest in American taste in the latter part of the century.

The Hayeses entertained with elegance, grace, and conservatism (no liquor was served at the White House during their term). A fascinating replica of their taste is the beautiful hand-painted social register kept by O. L. Pruden, secretary to the president, now at the Hayes Presidential Center in Fremont, Ohio. The 108-page book—a far more decorative record than the later typewritten versions of William McKinley's and Theodore Roosevelt's terms—provides an accurate source for White House entertaining at this time, the earliest of its kind. While the guest artists and their selections are not indicated in the register, these programs were generally informal and homelike in the true sense of the word "musicale"—a term that had been used in Europe from the late eighteenth century to denote a private concert with social entertainment. The concept of the musicale, so vital to White House history to the present day, appears to have been inaugurated by the Hayeses, who were the first to use the term at the mansion.

One way in which the Hayeses incorporated music into their social scheme is recounted by opera singer Lillian Hegermann-Lindencrone, a former pupil of Gioachino Rossini.

Washington, March 1877

The question of the annual diner diplomatique was cleverly managed by Mr. Evarts. Mr. Hayes wanted to suppress wine and give tea and mineral water, but Mr. Evarts put his foot down. He said that the diplomats would not understand an official dinner without wine, and proposed, instead, a *soirée musicale*—in other words, a rout. The diplomats had a separate entrance (a novelty) from the garden side. There was an orchestra at the end of the blue Room which drowned conversation when you were near it. I noticed that most of the young ladies found it too near, and sought other corners. The supper *ne laissait rien à désirer,* and there was a sumptous buffet open the whole evening; punch-bowls filled with lemonade were placed in the different salons. On the whole, it was a great success.

I think that the teetotality of the White House displeases as much our country-people as it does the foreigners. At one of our musical parties Mr. Blaine came rather late, and, clapping his hands on John's shoulder, said, "My kingdom for a glass of whisky; I have just dined at the White House." Others call the White House dinners "the life-saving station."

Mrs. Hayes was very nice to me. She sent me a magnificent basket of what she called "specimen flowers," which were superb orchids and begonias. On her card was written, "Thanking you again for the pleasure you gave my by your singing."[1]

President and Mrs. Hayes also enjoyed family gatherings. Lucy Hayes sang and played the piano frequently to pass an evening, and the president once wrote to her before they were married: "With no musical taste or cultivation myself, I am yet so fond of simple airs that I have often thought I could never love a woman who did not sing them." He also remarked to his daughter Fanny: "Music, you know, is the pet of both your mother and father."[2] For the Hayes administration, Sunday evenings at the White House had a character of their own. Often intimate friends were invited to participate in the dinner and family hymn-singing sessions that followed: "Hymn books were distributed and with someone at the piano, one favorite hymn after another would be sung in one of the parlors."[3] Hymns could accomplish miracles, satisfying social, recreational, and religious leanings. Little did it matter that President Hayes could not sing very well. The spirit was there. "Hayes can't sing any more than a canal-boat," expounded the *Ohio State Journal* when Hayes was major general with the Ohio Volunteers during the Civil War. "He stampeded Averill's whole cavalry division once by trying to sing 'John Brown's Body.' They thought it was the long roll."[4]

With the family's love of hymns it is not surprising that an opera company visiting the White House should sing some of them for the president. Giuseppe Operti, "Celebrated Chef d'Orchestre," and other members of the C. D. Hess English Opera Company (more accurately,

Secretary of the Interior Carl Schurz plays the piano for President Rutherford B. Hayes, Lucy Webb Hayes, and their guests during one of the weekly hymn-singing sessions in the family library upstairs (today's Yellow Oval Room). *Frank Leslie's Illustrated Newspaper*, April 3, 1880.

English-Language Opera Company) called on President and Mrs. Hayes on April 19, 1879. According to the *New York Times* the following day, they "sang a few hymn tunes to the delight of the Executive household in the library upstairs." Operti's fame had come several years earlier as composer of some of the songs for the 1870 revival of *The Black Crook*, America's naughty, controversial extravaganza.[5] With this visit the Hess troupe became the first opera company to perform in the White House. That Verdi's complete *La traviata* was performed during Buchanan's term, as some modern sources claim, is clearly a misconception.

Who were the singers in Hess's troupe who would have entertained the president? The featured artist during the 1878–79 Hess season was "the emotional and popular prima donna, Miss Emma Abbott." Another "distinguished lyric artist" of the troupe was Annie Montague, who had sung "Kathleen Mavourneen" at the White House for the Hayeses on May 1, 1877, while accompanying herself on the piano.[6] Montague, a Baltimorean, had been a member of the Clara Louise Kellogg English Opera Company. She sang Serpolette in the Hess production of Robert Planquette's *Chimes of Normandy* during the 1878–79 season and Oscar in Verdi's *Un ballo in maschera* on May 7, 1878, to a packed National Theater in Washington. Her voice was considered "strong, melodious and honest."

Other members of the Hess Company were Zelda and Edward Seguin, William Castle, Harry Bragaw, and "a grand chorus and orchestra." Some of these artists probably comprised the group that sang for the Hayeses in April 1878. The organization had been touring from New York to St. Paul and was greeted everywhere with enthusiastic and capacity audiences, according to the press. During the 1879–80 season, Hess's star and "most successful Prima Donna Assoluta," Emma Abbott, formed her own opera company. She doubled the Hess repertory from eight to sixteen operas, translating most of them herself. Her enterprising company opened no fewer than thirty-five opera houses throughout the United States and toured as far west as San Antonio, Texas.[7]

Though Miss Emma was apparently fond of interposing hymns, such as "Nearer My God to Thee," within her opera performances (to the disdain of some New York critics), she introduced Rossini's *Semiramide* with "The Star-Spangled Banner" for the opening of Albaugh's Grand Opera House in Washington on November 10, 1884, as a huge American flag was lowered over the entire stage. Miss Abbott bowed her acknowledgments to repeated rounds of applause, and shortly thereafter President Chester Arthur, the assistant secretary of state, and the assistant postmaster general entered and took their seats.

The programs were printed on cerise silk, the walls of the new opera house were cream-colored, the proscenium was gilded, and a blue-velvet, gold-fringed curtain divided at the center for the first time in the city's history. Costumes and scenery for the production were equally elegant. According to the *National Republican*, "Miss Abbott, wearing a crown that literally blazed with diamonds . . . sang the 'Bel raggio' with excellent effect, introducing variations by Arditi that showed the flexibility of her voice and purity of her method."[8] But the elegant new opera house must have heard some less graceful countermelodies at times. On its lower level was the armory or drill room of the Washington Light Infantry Corps, which had constructed the building.

While the English translations of the Hess, Kellogg, and Abbott companies were significant in spreading the enjoyment of opera throughout the United States, the great Hungarian dramatic soprano, Etelka Gerster, specialized in singing Italian opera in the original language. At the age of twenty-three she made her highly successful American debut as Amina in *La sonnambula* at New York's Academy of Music on November 18, 1878. Three months later she sang selections from Bellini's opera at the White House. The diva was invited to sing there two years before she made her public Washington debut on January 24, 1881, once again as Amina. The *Cincinnati Gazette* described this memorable appearance in the Executive Mansion when she sang for President and Mrs. Hayes.

> Madame Gerster, the Hungarian prima donna, accompanied by Signor Gardina, her husband, came from Baltimore today to visit Mr. and Mrs. Edwin Sherman of Boston, who had met her in Paris, and to be presented at the Executive Mansion by invitation of the President and Mrs. Hayes. The party visited the White House at 5 o'clock, spending an hour. Madame Gerster wore a black velvet visiting dress with white bonnet; Mrs. Hayes a black silk. The President and Mrs. Hayes received the party in the Red Parlor, thence adjourning to the Green Parlor. Madame Gerster, who was in fine voice, sang several airs from *Sonnambula* and the jewel song from *Faust*. The party then went through the mansion. Mrs. Hayes and the prima donna were mutually charmed. At dinner, an hour later, Madame Gerster received from Mrs. Hayes a basket of flowers with a cordial note. The party then attended the brilliant closing reception of the series given by Senator and Mrs. Matthews.[9]

America was slow to accept Negro performers outside the confines of the minstrel shows in the years after the Civil War and throughout Reconstruction. There were exceptions: for example, the black prima donna Marie Selika pursued her remarkable career during the 1870s and 1880s. And the power and pathos of the black voice were recognized in the wide reputation of the Fisk Jubilee Singers, who sang for President Arthur at the White House in 1882. In Washington blacks were usually not admitted to musical events held for whites, but many Negro churches boasted excellent choirs, which drew an occasional white person to the audience. The reputedly fine Colored Opera Company, with John Esputa (John Philip Sousa's violin teacher) as director, received warm eulogies from the *Philadelphia Inquirer:* "Their singing is really unsurpassed by the finest choruses in the best companies." The troupe was founded in 1872, ten years before the Metropolitan Opera of New York.

Coloratura Marie ("Selika") Williams appears to be the earliest black artist to have presented a program at the White House. Photo from cover of "Selika, Grand Vocal Waltz of Magic" by Frederick G. Carnes, San Francisco: Sherman and Hyde, 1877.

Etelka Gerster, a Hungarian soprano, sang in the White House
three months after her American
debut at age twenty-three.

It would be fascinating to know just what circumstances brought
Marie Selika to the White House. The papers said she sang "by appointment of the President." Like both Rutherford and Lucy Hayes,
she was from Ohio where Hayes also served two terms as governor.
The talented Cincinnatian sang for the Hayeses on November 13,
1878. Since the Colored Industrial School Children had sung in the
East Room a few months earlier, Selika's program in the Executive
Mansion appears to reinforce Hayes's endorsement and encouragement
of black talent. Biographical sources for the young artist, who apparently
took her name from the heroine of Giacomo Meyerbeer's *L'africaine*,
are scant and often in disagreement. She must have been at the beginning
of her career when she sang for the president because most of her
press clippings come from the 1880s, when she toured throughout
Europe with great acclaim and even sang for Queen Victoria. Before
her program in the Green Room, Selika was introduced to President
and Mrs. Hayes by Marshall Fred Douglass. She then sang Verdi's
extraordinary showpiece for technical prowess, "Ernani, involami,"
with its two-octave range from high C to the B-flat below middle C.
Following the aria she sang Thomas Moore's popular "The Last Rose
of Summer" from his *Irish Melodies*, Harrison Millard's "Ave Maria,"
and Richard Mulder's "Staccato Polka," all accompanied by "Professor
Richter." Selika's husband, baritone Sampson Williams, "sang by request
the popular ballad 'Far Away' by Bliss"; the papers added, "The singers
were warmly congratulated by President Hayes, Mrs. Hayes and their
guests."[10]

Called the "Queen of Staccato," Selika apparently became famous
for a coloratura style characteristic of Mulder's "Staccato Polka"—a

tricky little ditty whose frothy exterior belies the agility essential for putting across the song effectively. Perhaps the most interesting account of Selika is found in the memoirs of James Henry Mapleson. Writing at a time when blacks were hidden, segregated, or excluded from the concert hall, the English impresario tells about Selika's singing "in the extreme quarters" of Philadelphia.

> On entering, I was quite surprised to find an audience of some 1,500 or 2,000, who were all black, I being the only white man present. I must say I was amply repaid for the trouble I had taken, as the music was all of the first order.
>
> In the course of the concert, the prima donna appeared, gorgeously attired in a white satin dress, with feathers in her hair, and a magnificent diamond necklace and earrings. She moreover wore white kid gloves, which nearly went to the full extent of her arm, leaving but a small space of some four inches between her sleeve and the top of her glove. Her skin being black, formed, of course, an extraordinary contrast with the white kid. She sang the Shadow Song from *Dinorah* delightfully, and in reply to a general encore, gave the valse from the *Romeo and Juliet* of Gounod. In fact, no better singing have I heard.[11]

This fascinating account raises some doubts about opera being purely an elitist art for white society. But, however impressed he was with Selika's singing, Mapleson did not offer the diva an engagement. Reviews mention only her concert performances, never an appearance in a fully staged opera.

There were other great singers who performed at the White House in those days: the American oratorio artist, Emma Thursby, accompanied by Silas Gamaliel Pratt (founder of Pittsburgh's Pratt Institute of Music and Art) on November 28, 1877; German soprano Teresina Singer on January 9, 1880; and the great Italian tenor, Italo Campanini of Her Majesty's Opera Company, on February 26 of that same year. Campanini had fought in Garibaldi's army in the Italian struggle for unification before his successful debut in 1871 in London. But in America his fame came when he sang the role of Faust in the inaugural production of the Metropolitan Opera Company in 1883. At his program for the Hayeses, the president gave the noted singer an "autograph letter expressing his thanks with the wish that the Washington public should hear Signor Campanini and the other members of the company in opera in Washington."[12] "And," a reporter added, "if musical receptions were common at the White House it would not be long before they would become fashionable in the Society of the Capital."

But as musicales at the White House became more frequent, they required more planning, finesse, and "connections" with the local artistic community. Someone was needed to assist the president and first lady, someone who knew the artists, was aware of who was in town, and could act as a sort of "White House impresario." A natural was black-bearded Professor Frederick Widdows, a virtuoso on the chimes of the Metropolitan Methodist Episcopal Church. The stately gentleman can well be considered the first in a long line of presidential impresarios, which included Henry Junge, Alexander Greiner, John Steinway (and even Frank Sinatra), who brought entertainers to the attention of the first family and arranged their appearances at the White House.

Born in England, Widdows was not only a clerk in the Office of the Comptroller of the Currency earning a salary of $1,400 a year, but also a composer, performer, and teacher of music. He wrote music for Jullien's American Monster Concerts and composed a hymn called "Rock of Ages," which Mrs. Hayes often enjoyed hearing at the Foundry Church.[13] It was Widdows who introduced singer Annie Montague, the noted Remenyi Concert Company, Emma Thursby, the harpist Aptommas, and many others to the first family. That he must have been quite an entrepreneur is illustrated in the following excerpt from the Hutchinson family memoirs regarding their tour in January 1868: "Ole Bull had a sagacious advance agent named Widdows. He had possessed himself of one of my lists of advance dates, and was politely putting the great virtuoso in about two days ahead of us as fast as we went along. His prices were a dollar a ticket, and ours only 50 cents, to be sure, but it was too much to ask the average concert goer to pay one dollar and a half so nearly at one time. So we concluded to change our plans, and give a few concerts near Chicago, until Ole Bull's tour had carried him a little farther away."[14]

Widdows scored a triumph, however, when he brought the famous Welsh harpist Thomas Aptommas to the White House. On February 18, 1879, Aptommas played for the "Social Reception of Mrs. Hayes, in company with Mr. F. Widdows . . . and having sent his instrument in advance, delighted Mrs. Hayes and her visitors with some of the most exquisite music ever heard at the White House," said the *National Republican*.[15]

Information about Aptommas is scant. The Music Division of the Library of Congress possesses his beautifully illustrated *History of the Harp*, which informs us that he was a composer and an importer of European harps and that he ran a "Conservatoire de la Harpe" in New York City.[16] As for his "exquisite music" we turn to Washington Steinway dealer Edward F. Droop, who had penciled in his friend Leo Wheat's "Album" the following eulogy: "The distinguished Welsh harpist—a wonder!! No greater ever has been. One evening he played for me Beethoven's 'Moonlight' and the Rondo Capriccioso of Mendelssohn, besides many beautiful Chopin numbers."[17] How Aptommas came to perform in the Executive Mansion is detailed in part of Widdows's letter to Mrs. Hayes, dated February 12, 1879: "Mr. Aptommas the celebrated Harpist contemplates giving a harp recital in this city during Lent previous to his return to Europe. When here last year he expressed a great desire to have the honor of playing before the President and yourself and Friends, before returning to Europe, he having had the honor of playing before nearly all the Crowned Heads of Europe. I received a letter from him this morning stating that being in Baltimore he would visit this city on Saturday and if it was the pleasure of the

Thomas Aptommas, a Welsh harpist, from a drawing in *Aptommas' History of the Harp*, which was published by the author in New York, 1859.

President and yourself, would be pleased to arrange for some evening next week."[18]

A few months later Aptommas played again at the White House, and Donaldson's *Memoirs* provides the details:

—I was at the White House this evening after 7:30. Mayor (Ray Vaughn) Pierce, of Buffalo, N.Y., Member of Congress elect to the 46th Congress, and Dr. (J. M.) Bedford, Post Master at Buffalo, were in the Cabinet room when I went in. The President came out of the library and introduced us. He then said that there was to be some music below and insisted that we would go down. We went with him.

In the Red Room we found Mrs. Hayes, Prof. (F.) Widdows, and Prof. (Thomas) Aptommas, the Welsh harpist. We then followed Mrs. Hayes, who was dressed in a gray suit trimmed with black, to the Blue room. Here the harp was gotten out and the music began. Guests began to arrive, and on entering paid their respects to Mrs. Hayes who sat to the right near the Red room door, and then to the President who sat near the rear door. The guests who thus came in were not presented to any other persons, but were seated. Murat Halstead, Col. Jack Wharton (died in 1882), Gen. G. A. Sheridan, Judge (Joseph P.) Bradley and ladies, and others came in. Mrs. Hayes was as usual genial and courteous. When any guest departed, he simply shook hands with Mrs. Hayes and retired. The President retired after the first air was played. Aptommas was a wonderful musician. During the first air he unfortunately broke a string. He became flushed, stopped, and explained.[19]

Three days after the inauguration the famous Norwegian violinist Ole Bull called upon the president at the White House, but he did not perform. The first family heard him later that evening, however, at his concert in Washington. The legendary Eduard (Ede) Remenyi appears to have been the first concert violinist to perform at the White House. A Hungarian with a particularly restless, romantic spirit, the great Remenyi had more adventure packed into his long life than all the historic violinists together. Born in 1828, he fought in the insurrection of 1848 and as a result was exiled and fled to the United States. He managed after bouts of poverty and depression to resume a reputable career as a virtuoso in America. But his mercurial disposition did not seem to allow his remaining very long in one place. He went to Weimar in 1853 where he became friends with Franz Liszt, then to London as a solo violinist in the queen's band. By the time he played for President Hayes, he had lived in eleven cities of the world and during one journey suffered shipwreck and near drowning. The year before Remenyi played for Hayes he had performed a fantasia on themes from Meyerbeer's *Les Huguenots* at the Crystal Palace in London to a wildly cheering, packed house. He died in 1898 while playing a concert in San Francisco during his world tour.[20]

On December 6, 1878, Remenyi and his little company of performers entertained in the White House at the request of Mrs. Hayes. Accounts do not identify the solo singer who performed Sullivan's "The Lost Chord" and Barry's "Saved from the Storm," or the pianist who rendered

The fiery Hungarian violinist Eduard Remenyi entertained at the White House on December 6, 1878, for President Rutherford B. Hayes and his guests.

works by Chopin. Remenyi's selections also were not recorded. But his repertory during this year included an "Otello Fantasie," "Swanee River," and "Grandfather's Clock," the papers reported. From additional publicity we learn of his "mocking disposition which rebels against monotony," his fluency in six languages, and especially the effect that his playing had upon the audiences: "In the wild rhythms of the gypsy dance, in the fierce splendor of the patriotic hymn, the player and audience alike are fired with excitement. The passion rises, the tumult waxes furious; a tremendous sweep of the bow brings the music to an end; and then we can say that we have heard Remenyi."[21]

White House guest artists often included prodigies and youthful entertainers. Lulu Veling, a "remarkably skilled child pianist," played on January 16 and 17, 1880, for twelve-year-old Fanny Hayes, and the McGibeny Family performed their choicest selections before President and Mrs. Hayes on February 10 of this same year. The McGibenys comprised a father, mother, and eleven children; the oldest was sixteen and skilled in playing the violin, tuba, and cornet. They toured the East Coast with rave reviews, offering a program arranged for various vocal and instrumental combinations that would have challenged the famous Trapp Family Singers: Mozart's Minuet from the Symphony in E-flat Major, Beethoven's Scotch song, "Faithful Johnny," J. S. Bach's Prelude No. 1 in C Major, a comic opera scene called "The Professor at Home," and the entire family in the Anvil Chorus from *Il trovatore*.[22]

Solo pianists were infrequent at the White House, but twenty-six-year-old Julie Rivé-King, one of America's finest women virtuosos, performed on March 17, 1880, for the women in Carl Schurz's family.[23] A few years earlier, Cincinnati-born Rivé-King had made her American debut with the New York Philharmonic. Her mother, Caroline Rivé, had been Lucy Webb Hayes's piano teacher, and it is possible the young artist was a family friend.

As to what piano Rivé-King might have played at the White House, her choices were excellent. Keeping up with the pianos coming in and out of the White House under the Hayeses, in fact, is like following a fast-moving shell game. There were at least four in the mansion at that time: a Bradbury upright in the oval library upstairs; a "cabinet piano" (possibly another Bradbury) in twelve-year-old Fanny Hayes's room "so that she could practice undisturbed";[24] a Hallet and Davis "grand cabinet upright downstairs in the Red Room"; and in the Green Room a Knabe grand, the fine instrument that would have accompanied Etelka Gerster, Marie Selika, Eduard Remenyi, and others.

Pianos had always been an important part of White House furnishings as we have seen, but up until now they either had been brought to the mansion with the first families' personal possessions or were purchased for the White House with government funds. With the musical Hayeses—and possibly even with President Grant—a new trend began, coincident with the great boom in American piano production, structural development, and mass marketing techniques after mid-century. Some manufacturing firms realized that donating

The cover of the promotional flyer of the McGibeny Family—father, mother, and eleven children—who performed for President and Mrs. Rutherford B. Hayes on February 10, 1880.

a piano to the president was a great honor (the carriage manufacturers, for example, had been doing it for years). One year after President Hayes took office, the Knabe Company, founded in 1837 and the leading piano maker for the southern states until the Civil War, made such an offer.

Gentlemen,

In reply to your communication of the 1st inst. I have to state that your firm will be allowed to place at your own risk, one of your Grand Pianos in the parlors of the Executive Mansion, subject to your future orders. It being distinctly understood that the said use and disposition of the piano shall in no way create or give rise to any claim of any description whatever against the United States.

Lt. Col. Thos. L. Casey

Dear Sir:

We beg to acknowledge receipt of your esteemed favor of 25th and to thank you for the privilege kindly accorded to us. We shall proceed at once to place the Grand Piano in the Parlors of the Executive Mansion on the Conditions stated by you in your letter.

Wm. Knabe and Co.[25]

Almost a year later this same piano was purchased for $800 with "appropriations available for furnishing the Executive Mansion" by Thomas Casey, on March 15, 1879.[26] Chester Arthur, however, felt that a new Knabe was in order when he decorated the White House to his elegant, sometimes extravagant tastes. On December 13, 1882, the three-year-old Hayes Knabe was removed, and a new seven-and-one-third octave, rosewood grand piano was delivered to the White House. This Knabe remained at the mansion for about twenty years—at least well into the early part of McKinley's administration.[27]

But one of the most fascinating White House piano tales concerns the great entrepreneur, Freeborn Garrettson Smith, who took over William Bradbury's flourishing piano firm in 1867.[28] Clever and resolute, Smith managed to place at least nine pianos in the White House before the century turned. On March 4, 1897, the day of McKinley's inauguration, an advertisement appeared in the *Washington Star* showing the likenesses of Presidents Grant, Hayes, Garfield, Arthur, Harrison, and Cleveland encircling an image of the White House. At the bottom of this laurel of luminaries was none other than Freeborn G. Smith himself. But for all his promotional drive, Smith did not lie. The Bradbury really *was* "The Administration Piano" as the ad claimed.

What the Steinway piano was to the White House in the twentieth century, in fact, the Bradbury was during the nineteenth. Smith wasted no time when he took over the firm in 1867. He delivered his first piano to Mrs. Grant at the White House in September 1871, although it is unclear whether it was a gift or purchased for the mansion. "We have made the wood a little different but we think it must please, as it certainly is a fine instrument," he boasted to Orville Babcock, commissioner of Public Buildings and Grounds.[29] Mrs. Grant's piano may have been a square similar to the ones pictured on the Bradbury company stationery at this time. But on March 22, 1877, it was replaced with a new upright that had been donated to the White House. It was the first piano to be made specifically for the mansion. "I have been at work on a piano," Smith wrote to Thomas Casey, "the case of which has been designed fitted up with special reference to that apartment [Red Room] in dark finish ornament with wines [*sic*] of gold leaf. The center panel has a beautiful eagle made of a great variety of woods in some 5000 different pieces. This piano I have just completed and sent forward."[30]

But the fancy new Bradbury upright, a style so newly fashionable, never made its way to the Red Room. Freeborn Smith did not know that about this same time the prestigious old Boston firm of Hallet and Davis asked to place *its* upright in the presidential lower parlor. Result—a veritable piano war broke out at the White House. The winner, replacing the old Schomacker from Abraham Lincoln's period, was Hallet and Davis, and Smith's eagle-decorated Bradbury was relegated to the upstairs oval library. According to the gossipy Miss Grundy: "A Bradbury upright piano is in this room (library, oval room) which is used more especially as a family sitting room. As it adjoins the President's office (cabinet room), he sometimes comes in here with those he wishes to see privately."[31]

Smith fared much better with the Hayeses than he did with the Garfields. Shortly after he took office on March 4, 1881, President James Garfield requested that the fine eagle piano be removed, much to the annoyance of Smith who did everything he could to keep it there—including ignoring the request. His stubborn defiance resulted in Colonel Casey's shipping the piano back to the Washington, D.C., warehouse where it went the way of many other White House pianos: it was sold at auction.[32] "Between you and me," complained Casey, "we had some trouble at the Executive Mansion with Smith's Bradbury and he proved very disagreeable to work with. He was not polite to Mr. Garfield."[33]

Perhaps Hallet and Davis's agent was more gracious, certainly she was equally as enterprising as Smith. A highly determined lady in her own right, Helen Sumner wrote to Colonel Casey as President Garfield took office and offered to give the White House *another* piano, this time "a grand horizontal" as she called it. She recommended the instrument be placed in the Blue Room near the window to take away the lonely, stiff "company look." When this did not work, she tried the East Room, where no piano regularly stood: "I will have a special lock and key so it shall not be opened except by Mrs. Garfield's order. I will have an elegant chord attached to the desk with the words 'Visitors are requested not to play on the piano.' " Casey tactfully replied that the services of the mansion would not permit the introduction of another "concert grand piano." The Knabe grand was in the Green Room at this time.[34] After Garfield died in fall of 1881, Helen Sumner removed the Hallet and Davis upright from the Red Room. But the important parlor, used so often for musical events, did not remain without a piano for long. On May 13, 1882, the period of Chester Arthur, it housed an ebony grand—once again, a Bradbury.[35]

Under the musical Hayeses, even the polish of the Marine Band took on a new glow. In October 1880 Louis Schneider was replaced by one of the most distinguished band masters of all time—John Philip Sousa. Clearly the credit for building the modern repertory and reputation of the Marine Band goes to this famous showman who molded the somewhat mediocre unit into a superb marching and concert band. From the time he became leader during the last few months of the Hayes administration to the day he left to form his own world-famous touring band in 1892, he had raised the band's level of musicianship, modernized its instrumentation, and developed a repertory of almost symphonic proportions. His task was not easy. The problems were compounded by the fact that the former leaders often took their music with them when they left. Most of Francis Scala's and Schneider's better scores and arrangements were gone when Sousa took over. He had to begin from nearly nothing.

Sousa was only twenty-six when he became leader of the Marine Band, considerably younger than most of the players. To give himself an image of authority he grew a square-trimmed black beard and dressed impeccably, always with clean white gloves and a sword hitched to his belt. Born in Washington, D.C., in 1854, he was the first to break the long line of foreign-born Marine Band leaders whose nationalities had encompassed Italy, Germany, France, Spain, and England. His Portuguese father, Antonio Sousa, had played in the band, and John Philip served in the fife and drum corps as a boy under Scala. In Washington he studied violin with John Esputa, harmony with G. F. Benkert (composer of Lincoln's inaugural song), and led a vaudeville orchestra. But it was Jacques Offenbach's orchestra in Philadelphia and Patrick Gilmore's famous band that influenced the great "March King" most directly. Ten operettas, twelve suites, over fifty songs, several fantasies, waltzes, a cantata, and a symphonic poem all came from Sousa's prolific pen. But his forte was the march. He wrote more than 100. Some of his most popular marches enjoyed today are "Semper Fidelis" (1888), "The Washington Post March" (1889), and "The Stars and Stripes Forever" (1897), that irresistible proud and perky bit of Americana that Harold Schonberg claims has made more friends for the United States than any piece of music one can think of.[36]

Sousa's first concern as leader was to soften the sound that hit the guests as they entered the White House. He felt the limited repertory was "too robust" for the confines of the mansion during the state dinners and receptions, and he outlined some specific plans for President and Mrs. Hayes's first New Year's Day reception:

> The first to enter are the ambassadors, then the cabinet, then the supreme court, then the officers of the army, navy

and marine corps stationed in Washington, the bureau chiefs
of the departments, winding up with the general public. As
the first-named arrived we played music of a subdued character,
eliminating the percussion instruments, so that the drums,
tympani and cymbals were largely squelched, all of which
did not please the drummers, who had from long usage believed
that they came not only to be seen, but to be heard. Then
as the guests came in greater numbers, light operas were
played, and when the general public arrived, I ran into marches,
polkas, hornpipes and music of the liveliest character. I think
my method gave the President a chance to shake hands with
double the number of people he could have met had I played
slow pieces. President Hayes's secretary told me it was a
splendid idea, that the President was less fatigued than he
had been after previous receptions. The President evidently
appreciated the work I was doing.[37]

There was also a Marine Orchestra at this time, though no reference
to string players or stringed instruments can be found in government
inventories of the period. In his autobiography Sousa states that "as
a band, we played in the ante-room which was an entrance to the
Portico; as an orchestra, beside the staircase between the East Room
and the reception rooms. When we had orders to play for the President
we assembled at the Marine Barracks and went to the White House
in a street car."[38] What orchestral works were played? Twenty selections
are listed under the category "Orchestral" in the catalogue compiled
by Sousa in 1885.[39] Among them are Mendelssohn's "Wedding March"
and Brahms's "Hungarian Dances." Since the orchestral versions of
Brahms's popular four-hand piano pieces were first published in 1872
and 1874, Sousa was indeed a pioneer in bringing the music of the
great German romanticist to America. President and Mrs. Benjamin
Harrison, moreover, were probably the first in America to hear portions
of Mascagni's *Cavalleria rusticana*, which was first produced in Rome
in 1890. Sousa conducted selections from the opera at the Harrisons'
New Year's reception in 1891, before the work had been given its
American premiere.

But Sousa cannot take credit for forming the first Marine Orchestra.
When President and Mrs. Hayes honored the Grand Duke Alexis at
the White House on April 19, 1877, "dinner was announced; right off
the grand Marine band commenced to play the Russian March; stringed
instruments, fifty of them, played all through dinner; they were so
far off the music was not deafening."[40] Orchestral sounds undoubtedly
permeated the White House on other festive occasions under the
Hayeses: at their Thanksgiving and Christmas celebrations, for the
first couple's twenty-fifth wedding anniversary, and for the wedding
in the Blue Room of Colonel Russell Hastings to Emily Platt, the
president's niece, on June 19, 1878. But it is reasonable to assume
that a small Marine Orchestra existed from the earliest days of the
White House. In both Europe and America the term "band" originally
denoted almost any combination of instruments, just as it did under
Lully, whose "24 violins du roy" was called "La Grande Bande," or

Photograph of the U.S. Marine Band taken in Albany, New York, in 1888. John Philip Sousa, the leader, appears second row, center. The Marine Band, America's oldest continuous musical ensemble, performed regularly throughout the nineteenth century for White House ceremonial and social events, as it does today.

Charles II, whose string ensemble comprised "The King's Private Band." For early White House dinners, and especially dances, wind players may have doubled on the strings, or supplementary musicians might have been borrowed from the local community, as is believed to have been the case during the Civil War.

While Sousa expanded the serious repertory of the Marine Band, it still comprised the works of mainly nineteenth-century European operatic composers, such as Offenbach, Rossini, Gounod, Glinka, Donizetti, Bellini, Halévy, Meyerbeer, Wagner, and Bizet, whose *Carmen* (1875) is represented by a medley. Eighteen operas of Giuseppe Verdi appear in Sousa's catalogue of 1885, as well as Haydn's "Surprise" and "Military" symphonies and Mozart's overture to *The Marriage of Figaro*. But while Sousa managed to enlarge the size of the band for its first national tour in 1891, its standard membership remained modest with thirty-eight players, less than Gilmore's band and other major concert bands in America at the time. "We had 10 B flat clarionets," explained solo cornetist Walter Smith, "one flute, two hautboys, two bassoons, one E flat clarionet, two saxiphones [*sic*], one second cornet, two trumpets, four French horns, four trombones, one B flat alto horn, one euphonium, two basses and the usual battery of drums, cymbals and triangles. . . . Nearly all the players are foreigners. There are three Americans and three Englishmen, but all the rest speak broken and some are unable to understand English at all, the number of Italians and Germans being about equal."[41] Smith himself was from Kalamazoo, Michigan.

Yet Sousa's reputation as a master musician continued to spread. "There is probably no band in the country that plays as heavy music as does the marine band," added Smith. "New music of the most difficult character is constantly being imported." When Sousa conducted Mendelssohn's *Ruy Blas* for President Arthur's New Year's reception in 1884, it was lauded by the press as a "rare effort for a military band . . . few have ever attempted it." And the reviewer added, "Professor Sousa's program was unusually fine. The selections have been made with care, and a glance will show the variety and elegance of the pieces."[42]

All well and good. But perennial problems persisted. The band versus The System remained a steadily widening fissure. Sousa had to cope with the loss of good players to better paying civilian jobs. Despite the fact that he personally scouted major American cities for potential bandsmen—and with luck found the fine second leader, Walter Smith—frustrations remained. "When the law of Congress was enacted creating the Band," Sousa wrote to the commandant, "music was scarcely recognized as a profession in this country and a musician's means of livelihood were precarious and uncertain, but with the progress of the country the art of Music has been elevated to a higher standard and as a natural result a greater demand for musical talent has been developed."[43] Sousa goes on to mention the competing music festivals, operas, concerts, and summer resort programs that paid four times the government wages and the fact that Washington was "not a good music centre." When the Marine Band plays there, he said, one-half the jobs are for charitable causes with no pay. "While the pride of organization keeps the Band up to a high standard of musical excellence and soldierly discipline," Sousa added, "I can not but feel that its esprit-du-corps will vanish, and that this Band with all its popularity and old associations will sink into oblivion, unless the fostering hand of the 'powers that be' come to its rescue."

"The powers that be" somehow rallied to the cause once again, and the band did not sink into oblivion. Sousa managed to maintain his high standards in the midst of all the obstacles—including not a penny increase in the bandsmen's pay. But at least they were able to retain their monthly $4 streetcar allowance!

James Garfield held office for only six months, from March 4 to September 19, 1881, when he died of an assassin's bullet. A devotee of literature, languages, and fine arts, the congenial Garfield liked to make up tunes for favorite poems by Tennyson and Longfellow and made certain his daughter Mollie and her four brothers all had music and dancing lessons.[44] Hal, aged seventeen when the close-knit family occupied the White House, was a gifted pianist, and the president often slipped upstairs to hear his eldest son play on the Bradbury upright still in the Oval Room. President Garfield's successor, Vice-President Chester Arthur, was, according to Colonel Crook, a long-time White House aide, "a different type of man from any who had preceded him during my experience there, and he was accustomed to light-heartedness and effervescence which has long distinguished social life in New York City. The new president was a large, heavy, tall man, strikingly handsome and possessing the Chesterfieldian manner. He delighted to entertain his friends; he wanted the best of everything, and wanted it served in the best manner."[45]

Arthur's wife, Ellen Lewis Herndon, had died only a year and one-half before Arthur took office, and Mary McElroy, the president's youngest sister, became the ranking lady of his administration. Arthur especially enjoyed music and must have had a special affinity with vocal music, particularly opera, judging from the number of noted singers who visited the White House during his administration. To Arthur opera was undoubtedly theater at its grandest, a true edification of the Gilded Age in which it was socially ensconced. Then, too, Arthur, like Lyndon Johnson who followed the arts-loving Kennedys, may have tried to keep alive some of the musical ambience that the Hayeses had brought to the White House.

Ellen Arthur had had a fine contralto voice that her husband appreciated and enjoyed. She was a member of the noted Mendelssohn Glee Club of New York City, which sang at her funeral on January 14, 1880.[46] Several items in the Chester A. Arthur Papers—receipts for theater tickets, piano tuning, "Music at the Home" ($2.00), piano rental for Chester Arthur, Jr., for the summer, and even banjo strings at $1.50 each—attest to the family's lively interests in music as a creative pastime.[47] A receipt dated May 22, 1884, from Nell H. Arthur to "Miss D. Clare, Dr.," indicates payment of $60 for twenty music lessons for the Arthurs' daughter with the added notation that "Nell takes a lesson every day."

It was Arthur and his desire for "the best" that reaped felicitous benefits for the White House—the first East Room concert for specially invited guests. Indeed, the program provided a prophetic glimpse of the dinner/musicale tradition of the twentieth-century White House. The gala event took place on February 23, 1883, in the newly renovated East Room that some thought resembled the Gold Salon of the Operá in Paris. But the concert did not feature Adelina Patti, as Esther Singleton and others, probably following her lead, have claimed. The famous Patti was singing with the Mapleson troupe in Washington at the time, but was ill when Arthur heard Rossini's *William Tell* at the National Theater on February 20. Records indicate that instead of Patti, the famous Canadian soprano, Emma Albani, sang for the president. Possessing a voice of rare beauty and warmth, she had sung many of the great Wagnerian roles at Covent Garden and would appear in the Metropolitan Opera premiere of Verdi's *Otello* in 1894. Before she sang for the president, she had performed for Johannes Brahms, Queen Victoria, and Czar Alexander II.

During his stay in Washington, Henry Mapleson, venturous impresario of Her Majesty's Opera Company, offered to bring several leading members of his troupe to the White House, indicating to the president that he would be pleased to pay him the compliment of a private concert. While Arthur's musical reception was private, it was hardly intimate. He opened the East Room to 100 guests who had been "invited informally."

> The grand piano was removed from the upper main corridor to the southeast corner of the improvised concert room, which had been decorated with palms and other growing plants for the occasion, and seated with rows of chairs facing southward. A collation was provided in the state dining room, consisting of cold meats and numerous dainties, with champagne.
>
> The hour was fixed at half-past ten, and guests began to arrive at that time, but the concert did not begin till twelve. All the leading ladies except Madame Patti and M'lle Dotti were present, and in fine voice. The applause was reached when Albani sang "Robin Adair." All the ladies present were in full evening dress, and the east parlor presented a novel and brilliant appearance.[48]

With the exception of the final number, "Robin Adair," the program was entirely operatic. It included two arias from Mozart's *Le nozze di Figaro*; "Tacea la notte" from Verdi's *Il trovatore* sung by the French soprano Emma Fursch-Madi; the popular "Abendstern" from Wagner's *Tannhäuser* sung in Italian by Guiseppe Frapolli; and "Nobil Signor" from Meyerbeer's *Les Huguenots* performed by Sofia Salchi.[49] But for the widower Arthur, the last song was the evening's crowning glory, and perhaps was even sung at his request. He was clearly moved by Albani's fluid performance of his long-time favorite, "Robin Adair." His late wife Ellen had sung the popular Irish ballad often before they were married, and time and again he had asked her to sing the song. Albani's interpretation—with its long, sustained phrases, even tone quality, and well-executed ornaments—must have conjured up memories for the lonely president.[50]

The following month the East Room was opened to Swedish soprano Christine Nilsson, for whom the president held a dinner and reception especially in her honor. The exact date of her White House program is not certain, but between March 27 and 30, 1883, she was captivating Washington with her performance at Lincoln Hall. The press raved: "Nothing could exceed the felicity of gesture, facial expression and dramatic warmth of delivery with which the 'Queen of Song' rendered each of her selections."[51] On the arm of the president, the graceful diva was escorted to the East Room for the large reception after the dinner. She then sat down at the Knabe grand piano moved in for the event and sang to her own accompaniment "The Last Rose of Summer" and Stephen Foster's "Way Down upon the Swanee River." Whether

Swedish soprano Christine Nilsson as Marguérite in Gounod's *Faust,* the role she sang at the opening of the Metropolitan Opera in New York. Her concert for Chester Arthur was one of the first to be presented in the East Room.

The Fisk Jubilee Singers during the 1880s, when they sang for President Chester Arthur at the White House.

or not the soprano included the great "Jewel Song" from Gounod's *Faust*, we do not know. But soon she would make operatic history. On October 22, 1883, Nilsson sang the role of Marguérite in *Faust* for the grand opening of the Metropolitan Opera in New York.

One of the most remarkable vocal programs of the century was held at the mansion during Arthur's term. The Jubilee Singers from Fisk University were the first in a long line of black choirs and ensembles to perform in the White House. Their hybrid art combined the lonely message of the blues, the rhythmic vitality of the minstrel song, and the diatonic harmonic structure of the European hymn. But the African roots and prejazz characteristics of the Jubilee Singers' style, such as syncopation and call-and-response patterns, must have created a distinctive sound for the audience. Writing in 1880, James Trotter says:

> The songs they sang were generally of a religious character,— "slave spirituals" . . . which had sprung spontaneously, so to speak, from souls naturally musical; and formed, as one eminent writer puts it "the only native American music." The strange, weird melody of these songs which burst upon the Northern States, and parts of Europe, as a revelation in vocal music most thrillingly sweet and soul-touching, sprang then, strange to say, from a state of slavery. . . .
>
> The rendering of the Jubilee Singers, it is true, was not always strictly in accordance with artistic forms. The songs did not require this; for they possessed in themselves a peculiar power, a plaintive, emotional beauty, and other characteristics which seemed entirely independent of artistic embellishment.[52]

The Jubilee Singers' program at the Congregational church in Washington on February 16, 1882, was received with high acclaim. Several members of Congress were in the audience. But with all their success the twelve-member group had problems being accepted in the city's hotels: "At the concert given by the colored jubilee singers at the Congregational church in this city last night, the Rev. Dr. Rankin stated to the audience that the members of the troupe, after having been everywhere courteously received, were last night denied admission to every hotel in Washington and did not succeed until after midnight in finding a place to sleep. In most cases a want of room was assigned as a reason for refusing them hotel accomodations, but in three instances the refusal was put upon the ground of color and race."[53]

Yet the Jubilee Singers could sing for the president in the White House the next night and gently draw from him a response only the powers of music could elicit: "By appointment the colored Fisk Jubilee Singers accompanied by Rev. Dr. Rankin, called yesterday to pay their respects to President Arthur, and while there sang several melodies among them 'Safe in the Arms of Jesus,' which actually moved the President to tears. 'I never saw a man so deeply moved,' said Rev. Rankin, speaking of the incident last night, 'and I shall always believe President Arthur to be a truly good man.' The President frankly informed his visitors after hearing them that he had never before been guilty of so impulsive an exhibition of his feelings."[54]

Arthur made certain that the White House walls reverberated with the type of music that he wanted to hear. But it was not always serious. Sousa was somewhat taken aback when the president, who Sousa felt had an aura of the "effete aristocracy of the Old World" about him, asked for a dance, the cachucha, made famous by Fanny Elssler when Arthur was a young man:

> A young lady wanted to do a Spanish dance to that tune. When I explained that we had not the music with us, but would be glad to include it on our next program, the President looked surprised, and said, "Why, Sousa, I thought you could play anything. I'm sure you can. Now give us the *Cachuca* [*sic*]."
>
> This placed me in a predicament, as I did not wish the President to believe that the band was not at all times able to respond to his wishes. Fortunately one of the bandsmen remembered the melody and played it over softly to me on his cornet. I hastily wrote out several parts for the leading instruments and told the rest of the band to "vamp."
>
> We played the *Cachuca* [*sic*] to the satisfaction of Mr. Arthur, who came to the door and said "I knew you could play it."[55]

One talent common to all Marine Band leaders was the ability to take orders—especially from the one in supreme command. Sousa was no exception, and his autobiography reveals that President Arthur often had specific ideas about the music. "What piece did you play when we went into dinner?" the president once asked Sousa.

> "Hail to the Chief, Mr. President."
>
> "Do you consider it a suitable air?"
>
> "No, sir," I answered. "It was selected long ago on account of its name, and not on account of its character. It is a boat song, and lacks modern military character either for reception or a parade."
>
> "Then change it!" said he, and walked away.
>
> I wrote the *Presidential Polonaise* for White House indoor affairs, and the *Semper Fidelis* March for review purposes outdoors. The latter became one of my most popular marches.[56]

But Sousa forgot to mention that "Hail to the Chief" remained, too.

During the 1880s and 1890s the banjo had assumed a role not unlike the parlor piano, but with an attraction for both sexes (the piano's appeal had been mainly to women). Chester Arthur played the banjo quite well. "President Arthur is no mean banjo player and can make the banjo do some lively humming when so disposed," said the *Star*. "His son is conceded to be an excellent player."[57] And Arthur and his son were not alone. "Washington players comprise some of our best people—Senator Bayard and his daughter Kate, Miss Beale, Miss Eustis, grand-daughter of W. W. Corcoran," and many others.[58]

What tunes might President Arthur and his friends have played on this newly fashionable instrument? "The comic operas of Gilbert and Sullivan are pleasant," noted the press. But the Dime Music Company's all-inclusive catalogue at the Library of Congress, *Sheet Music for the Banjo* (1881), boasts on its title page "a choice selection of over 8000 Songs, Jigs, Clogs, Duets, Polkas, Waltzes, Schottisches, Hornpipes, Galops, Galopades, Walk-arounds, Marches, Breakdowns, Hymns, Solos, Square Dances, Dirges, Dead Marches, Jubilee Hymns, Plantation Melodies, Mazurkas, Redowas, Cotillons, Quadrilles, Irish Jigs, Minor Jigs, Army Calls, Swell Songs," and on and on. And if this list is not sufficient lure for the player, the cost most certainly is— each piece, ten cents, or "three for 25."

Banjos even went Ivy League. Glee and Banjo Clubs sprang up in the most prestigious American colleges and universities, including Columbia, Princeton, and Yale. Young Franklin D. Roosevelt was a member of Harvard's thriving club, which toured several American cities. But it was the Yale Glee and Banjo Club that sang for President and Mrs. Harrison in the East Room on April 22, 1889.[59] Did it really matter that Yale's famous baseball team had just been "whitewashed"? After all, "the nine" had been invited to the White House on that day, too.

Still for all of its new image within social circles, the banjo remained the spirit and heart of blacks. This was no doubt sensed when twenty-one-year-old Frances Folsom heard Sam Weston playing during her train trip to Washington: "The sweet strains reached her ear," noted the *Star*, "and she requested the porter to open the doors of the cars so that she might hear distinctly. Weston's wife sang two Negro tunes, which brought faint sounds of applause from the secluded car."[60] But soon Miss Folsom would hear music of quite a different kind, the marches and airs that would celebrate her marriage to Grover Cleveland—the only president in history to be married in the White House.

CHAPTER 7

FAMILIAR TUNES
WITH A NEW MESSAGE

Cleveland, Harrison, McKinley

The President said a vacation he'd take;
Said he to himself, said he. . . .
And my friends who belong to the real estate ring
Have promised a cottage to which I shall cling,
Said he to himself, said he.

> Digby Bell (sung to the tune of the Lord
> Chancellor's song from *Iolanthe*
> by Gilbert and Sullivan)

If the first administration of Grover Cleveland opened in the midst of the great Gilbert and Sullivan rage, the second ended in the shadow of "Smoky Mokes" and "Goo-Goo Eyes," which were drawing the nation exuberantly toward ragtime and jazz. Cleveland seemed to pay little attention to America's bouncy musical mosaics. He was a serious man who frankly admitted a distaste for the glitter of White House social life. A prominent upstate New York lawyer, Cleveland was the only president to serve two terms nonconsecutively, from 1885 to 1889 and from 1893 to 1897. "When I left my breakfast table and went to my office, it used to seem that a yoke was placed around my neck from which I could not escape," he once said.[1]

Guest performers were rare at the White House under Cleveland, but there were times when music managed to lighten the load for the president. Occasionally he enjoyed the theater, "but I do not think he has seen a play since he has been in the White House," commented Washington journalist Frank Carpenter. "He is said to enjoy comedies and farces and to like a minstrel troupe or comic opera better than grand opera or an oratorio."[2] But like just about everyone else, Cleveland was caught up in the veritable mania then sweeping the nation—the Gilbert and Sullivan craze. Triggered by the American premiere of *H.M.S. Pinafore* at the Boston Museum on November 25, 1878, the popularity of these operettas with their satirical impersonations of

English society continued to spread until about 1890. During Cleveland's first term, the city of Boston boasted 163 performances of the *Mikado*, and New York saw *Pinafore* produced by churches, black companies, twelve-year-olds, and Yiddish theaters. The president did not have to leave the White House to hear these jaunty tunes, however. The Marine Band played them often[3]—even at his wedding.

The marriage of long-time bachelor Grover Cleveland to the attractive young Frances Folsom on June 2, 1886, set tongues wagging. She was twenty-one, he forty-nine. The daughter of Cleveland's former law partner Oscar Folsom, Frances proved to be a charming first lady and a devoted wife and mother. The couple planned a quiet, private ceremony, despite the pleas of journalists who wanted to attend and cover the big event. Cleveland was the only president ever to be married in the White House. All Washington thronged outside the mansion, craning their necks to see and hear. Some even bribed John Philip Sousa to let them in as members of the band. Sousa refused. But a detailed review of the big day hints that there might have been some who ignored the rules. With a modicum of drollery and charm, a *Star* reporter managed to capture the spirit of the occasion and music's powers of communicaion simultaneously.

> The first visible evidence of the approaching ceremony was the arrival of some of the musicians of the Marine Band, gorgeous in their red uniforms. The members of the band came straggling along in such a manner that their number appeared much greater than it actually was. Some of the spectators declared that at least 150 men in red coats, with

The only president to be married in the White House, Grover Cleveland wed Frances Folsom on June 2, 1886; the Marine Band provided the music. *Harper's Weekly*, June 1886.

horns and trombones went into the mansion, and this gave rise to a report that the newspaper reporters had gone in disguise, like Nanki-Poo, as second trombones. ... The last guest had hardly disappeared before a stout woman attended by a thin man, who had a mass of hair and beard worthy of an anarchist, came out of the house and made their way out. "It is the music professor [Sousa]" said someone near the door, and word was passed along the line of spectators. Then in the same way word was sent through the crowd that the couple were French hairdressers who had just finished their part of the evening's preparations. This gave an added interest to the couple, who were stared at until they cleared the crowd and reached the open street beyond.

Then the members of the band at the window left their stations and appeared to be falling into place. A moment later the window shutters were closed and then the music of the band—the wedding march could be heard and the crowd knew that the hour had come. During all the evening the crowd kept account—or fancied they were keeping account of what was going on inside by noting the character of the music played and the intervals between the pieces. ... As it grew dark the brilliantly illuminated mansion made a handsome spectacle. Light streamed from nearly every window. The band, which was stationed in the vestibule, played at frequent intervals during the evening and afforded very pleasant entertainment for the outsiders, several hundred of whom remained until the last musician had gone home.[4]

What music was selected for the wedding? As the guests assembled in the East Room the Marine Band played "And He's Going to Marry Yum Yum" and other airs from the *Mikado.* Only three months earlier, the president had heard soprano Emma Abbott in the role of Yum Yum at the National Theater. His sister, Rose Elizabeth, who had served as White House hostess before his marriage, had invited the president and a small party for his birthday. Diva Emma was delighted. She not only had the honor of singing for the president, but also she and the cast were entertained by him earlier that same day at the White House.[5]

Gilbert and Sullivan tunes, however, had to share the wedding program with other selections, perhaps more appropriate: wedding marches by Mendelssohn and Wagner. Sousa and the Marine Band also played Mariana's "Io son la Rose," Weber's "Invitation to the Dance," Mendelssohn's "Spring Song," Robaudi's "Bright Star of Hope," and Sousa's "Student of Love" from his opera *Désirée.* This final selection gave the president problems. Could the bandmaster merely call this piece "Quartette"—and eliminate the reference to "student of love"? Sousa complied.

There may have been a quartet of a different kind among the wedding repertory for that day. Four eager young ladies of Washington, calling themselves the St. Cecilia Quartet, wrote to the president asking to sing Söderman's "Wedding March" at the White House ceremony, but we do not know whether they sang. Their letter with

The White House illuminated for a gala reception about the time of Grover Cleveland's first administration. Lithograph by C. Upham.

a publicity flyer is preserved in the National Archives, an early prototype of thousands that would come from aspiring White House entertainers as the century progressed.[6]

The popularity of Gilbert and Sullivan at this time gave journalists, political cartoonists, and even performers themselves incentive to find new ways of satirizing current American politics. The *Post* ran the following in the February 24, 1884, issue: "Mr. Gilbert in 'Iolanthe' makes an ingenious and effective argument against brains, and in favor of respectable stupidity in the house of peers. He shows that, during those periods in which the house of peers was least troubled with brains 'Britain won her proudest days.' It has occurred to us—and the impression has been deepened and broadened by recent events—that the Republican party has a similar theory with regard to our house of peers—the august body which assembles in the north end of the Capitol."

Four years later the *New York Times* featured a bit of froth on the front page called "A Joke of Digby Bell's Was Not Appreciated." Bell had been playing *Iolanthe* with the Duff Opera Company in Chicago to an audience that included "Prince" Russell Harrison, son of the incumbent of the White House. Apparently few in the theater knew about the distinguished visitor, and Digby Bell, who was famous for his improvised gags and music within Gilbert and Sullivan's famous score, had his quiet shot at Harrison. An uncompromising Democrat, Bell managed to belt:

> The President said a vacation he'd take;
> Said he to himself, said he.
> Down by the blue sea, where the high breakers break,
> Said he to himself, said he.
> For the place needs the boom that my presence will bring
> And my friends who belong to the real estate ring
> Have promised a cottage to which I shall cling,
> Said he to himself, said he.

"Prince" Russell coughed and scratched his head behind his ear, and the Lord Chancellor on the stage continued his merrymaking oblivious to the fact that "Benny's own" was in the audience.[7]

But the classic of all Gilbert and Sullivan parodies is the cartoon showing Cleveland as "Grover Pooh-Bah" on the front page of the *Washington Post* of February 7, 1892, in "An Episode from the *Mikado.*" He is singing ("with great effort") to three kimona-clad gentlemen (one of whom has "Hill" printed on his fan) words to the effect that he "can't talk to little girls like you"—an obvious take-off on the Tammany attempt to capture the Democratic convention in February.

When Grover and Frances Cleveland were married, they received a spectacular musical wedding gift. A fine Steinway grand piano

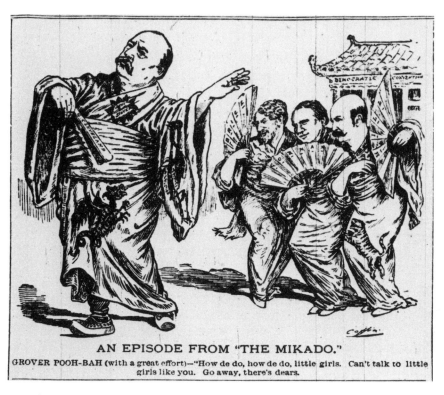

AN EPISODE FROM "THE MIKADO."

GROVER POOH-BAH (with a great effort)—"How de do, how de do, little girls. Can't talk to little girls like you. Go away, there's dears.

President Grover Cleveland as "Grover Pooh-Bah" before his second term. The caricature also illustrates the wide popularity of Gilbert and Sullivan operas, frequent sources of political satire at this time. *Washington Post*, February 7, 1892.

Frances Cleveland in the upstairs Sitting Hall of the White House with the grand piano presented to her and the president as a wedding gift by William Steinway. Photograph by Pirie MacDonald, 1893.

(#55,405) was presented to them on June 23, 1886, by William Steinway, head of the firm. William Steinway first met Grover Cleveland in Buffalo when Cleveland, a young lawyer, was settling the estate of Steinway's mother-in-law. Cleveland became governor of New York and twice president, and Steinway remained a close personal friend. He served as a delegate to the Democratic convention in 1888 and kept active in politics all his life.[8]

From photographs of the period, the Steinway grand was situated in the family's quarters upstairs during Cleveland's second term. How much it was used is hard to say. Neither the president nor Frances Cleveland was known to have played it. But Mrs. Cleveland was an aficionado of piano music, and artists great and lesser sometimes sent her scores and other musical mementos as a token of their respect.[9] After the first Cleveland term, the first lady received a copy of a piano piece composed by Leo Wheat, a now-forgotten Washington piano virtuoso, organist, composer, and teacher, whose scrapbook in the Library of Congress contains Mrs. Cleveland's photo and the following letter in her hand.[10]

Dear Mr. Wheat,

Please accept my cordial thanks for the copy of your new "Schottisch" which I have just received. To have it direct from you is the next best thing to hearing you play it.

Sincerely,

(signed) Frances F. Cleveland

143

If one wonders just who was Wheat that he should warrant such flattering attentions, then the comments of his close friend, that irrepressible music dealer E. H. Droop, penciled on the back of Wheat's photograph in the scrapbook, might shed more light on his apparently colorful career: " 'The Irresistable Virginian' as we call him! . . . rarely without a flower in his lapel in a little silver holder filled with water. Great gosh! How he *can play* the piano! He leans toward playing and interpreting the 'lighter' things in music! When he plays his own waltzes, etc. etc. the women flock about him as over a box of 'sweet chocolates'—poor old Leo! His life and career—a tragedy . . . potentially great pianism . . . gracious and with a courtesy of the highest order. I could write a book about him."

Droop's book about Wheat was never realized. But the image of the parlor pianist that he represents is reflected in hundreds of American pianists like him who studied in Europe and then tried to make their way on the American concert stage during this period. From notices in the newspapers, Wheat maintained an active concert life in Washington, but the extent of his performing history outside the city is not known. Perhaps one afternoon at the White House, the "Irresistable Virginian" himself tititlated the Steinway ivories with his perky "Schottisch" to the delight of the first lady.

Mrs. Cleveland's active interest in supporting young artists and aspiring musical organizations illustrates the important role that the performing arts were now playing in America. Both she and the president were honorary members of the Washington Choral Society, and they appear to be the first presidential couple to lend their names to the arts in this visible manner. From her correspondence in the Cleveland Papers, the young first lady showed a genuine concern for women who worked, and performing artists were no exception. She helped a struggling friend, who taught music to support herself, by obtaining several pupils for her. Through the sponsorship of Frances Cleveland, moreover, the young violinist Leonora Jackson went to Berlin to study with Joseph Joachim and walked off with the much-coveted Mendelssohn Stipendium—the first American to do so.[11]

One composer whose music the first lady especially enjoyed was Richard Wagner. Judging from the large Wagner repertory of the Marine Band at this time, the German giant must have been introduced to thousands of Americans via the popular "The President's Own." The rich orchestral scoring with prominent brass and wind passages offered fine possibilities for concert band transcriptions. John Philip Sousa once observed: "The President likes light music. . . . Mrs. Cleveland's favorite selection is the overture to Wagner's *Tannhäuser*."[12] He recalled seeing the Clevelands at the window during a band concert on the White House lawn. "The President stood up and held on to the window as though he were afraid it would get away from him," he said. "His pretty young wife sat down facing him, enthralled." The concert closed with a mosaic from Wagner's *Lohengrin*, which had been given its Metropolitan Opera premiere only the year before. A reviewer of the White House concert had some comments of his own: "Those who

Photograph of Frances Cleveland and her note thanking pianist Leo Wheat for his "Schottische," March 19, 1889.

Leo Wheat, called "The Southern Pianist" and "The Irresistible Virginian," played mainly "lighter music" with considerable dash and bravura.

weren't disciples of the 'music of the future' thought that King Ludwig was amply justified in going crazy, but there were many men who thought it was the best selection on the program."[13]

The most moving musical tribute to a nineteenth-century president was held in honor of Cleveland several months after his death. The concert at Carnegie Hall (which had opened in 1891) on March 18, 1909, would have taken place on Cleveland's seventy-second birthday. Walter Damrosch, conductor of the New York Symphony Orchestra, and the 150-voice Liederkranz Society presented a memorial program at which Mayor George B. McClellan of New York presided and President William Howard Taft gave an address. Correspondence between Mrs. Cleveland and Damrosch in the Cleveland Papers tells us how the musical program was arranged. Mrs. Cleveland had some decided opinions. The "Largo" from Handel's *Xerxes* should be sung instead of played, and lest the concert committee forget to include the music of Wagner, she felt the Funeral March from *Die Götterdämmerung* to be "appropriate to the dignity of the occasion."[14]

President Benjamin Harrison's term in office fell between the two administrations of Grover Cleveland. He served from March 4, 1889, to March 3, 1893. Before she married "Ben," when she was twenty-one and he twenty, Caroline Scott had taught in the music department of the Oxford Female Institute, later part of Miami University, Ohio, and at a girls' school in Carrollton, Kentucky. Mrs. Harrison, and later Florence Harding, were the only presidential wives who had been professional musicians. The Harrisons' daughter, Mary McKee, was also musically inclined and played the piano often in the White House where she lived with her two children.

In 1889 the Harrisons' son Russell gave his mother a gilt-incised Fisher upright piano as a Christmas present during the family's first year in the White House.[15] The instrument stood in the private hall upstairs, its lid piled high with the family collection of musical favorites. Many were pieces Caroline Harrison had saved from her teaching days. One in particular—a well-worn, pencil-marked copy of Louis Moreau Gottschalk's "The Last Hope," now in the Benjamin Harrison Home, Indianapolis—was characteristic of the music both mother and daughter enjoyed. Composed in 1854, the piece became a sort of "religious meditation" as Gottschalk called it, and was very popular in the last half of the nineteenth century. And if the Harrisons were like everyone else, they would have been intrigued by that highly fashionable poetic image—death, the "commercial literary staple" of the era. "To be so full of feeling, that you lose control of yourself," Arthur Loesser notes, "that you tremble or weep or faint or drop dead, was wonderful, was a blessing, a thing to live for, to boast about, to pretend to." Loesser's description of this type of music summarizes the cultural age in which the Harrisons' lived so marvelously that it deserves quoting at length. "*Last Hope* . . . consists of a sweet, slow, widely ranging melody; but this is decorated by a profusion of detached, rapid little tinkling twiddles in the high treble. Later on, longer ornamental runs and trills occur. To one of these the composer has appended the expression mark 'elegante,' to another 'scintillante,' and finally—toward the end—the word 'brilliante.' He cannot have intended these to represent the patient making a whirlwind finish; more likely they were a way of inducing the pianist to play those very high passages with great sparkle and thus to suggest the supernal refulgence of the heavenly next world."[16]

How "brilliante" or "scintillante" Caroline Harrison and her daughter played the piano, we do not know. But we do have records indicating that the president loved to dance and could kick up a pretty good "German." From the time of Nellie Grant's ball, only one dance was held in the White House before the turn of the century: Mrs. McKee's ball on April 23, 1890. Three hundred attended the brilliant event, and a canvas covering called "crash" was put down in the East Room to protect the floor. The *Post* entitled its review "Old Dreams Realized": "Such revelry by night has not been known at the White House for many a long year as filled the hearts of the elect brimful of joy last night. Mrs. McKee says that ever since the days that her father was in the senate and she used to hear the tantalizing waltzes that the Marine Band would play she has wanted to dance in the East Room. Last night her wish was fulfilled. . . . The Marine Band was stationed in the small hall, and when they played the waltz from 'The Brigands' at 10:00 Mr. and Mrs. McKee with a turn about the room started the ball." The dances were similar to the ones listed for President Andrew Johnson's ball twenty-two years earlier, except that, in addition to Johann Strauss, the composers included Jacques Offenbach, Emile Waldteufel, and John Philip Sousa—names familiar to every Marine Band devotee who had attended the popular White House receptions and outdoor concerts.[17]

One especially popular dance was the seemingly inelegant and controversial "German," which often fell under the designation waltz. In the eighteenth century this dance consisted of a series of ländlerlike passes, ending with "a tentative (not too close) embrace." During the 1880s the Army and Navy Assembly and German Club of Washington sponsored a series of dances "attended by the best society," including President Arthur. "The gaieties of the evening," according to Randolph Keim, "began with an assembly, with the ordinary round and square dances. The germans began after supper, at 12:00 and closed at 2:00 AM."[18] Critics objected to this "depraved" dance. *The Inland* made no pretensions about its views regarding President and Mrs. Harrison's reception in the White House "in which 'The German' was the most popular amusement":

> "The German" is a dance in full party snobocratic dress, where the hugging process is the chief ingredient. Chaplain Milburn, who has been conversant of life at the White House for many years, says that no such ridiculous performance has occurred at the President's mansion since the days of President Tyler.
>
> The "German" today is tabooed even in the most worldly

circles of society devotees. It is considered an offense to good taste, and the fringe or border on the cloak of lewd immorality. . . . In view of all the above, has not the christian [*sic*] people who supported him, and in whose christian integrity thus plighted their faith, a right to complain when he throws open the parlors of the Executive Mansion for a dance the depravity of which is found in the underground variety halls of the slums of the larger cities, and at his public dinners permits wine to flow as free as water? Have the christian people of the Nation been deceived in President Harrison or has he backslidden since he went to the "White House."[19]

One wonders what this reviewer would have said about the "Goo-Goo Eyes" two-step danced after the diplomatic dinner given by President and Mrs. William McKinley on Valentine's Day only a decade later.

But all was not mere social froth at the White House as the century drew to a close. The serious artists still came—the singers, flautists, child prodigies, string players, and chamber ensembles in oddly dichotomous combinations—all representing that wonderful potpourri that we might call "White House Musical Americana." For the president's home saw them all at one time or another. And this element of variety culminated in what appeared to be the first concert in the great mansion to use printed programs. "Mrs. Harrison's Musicale" was a kind of nineteenth-century mixed media that would become a prototype for many White House programs to the present. Indeed, variety has always been characteristic of the great mansion, where the curious melding of private and public, home and concert hall provides an endless source of fascination within the world of the performing arts.

While Chester Arthur was the first to hold concerts in the East Room, Caroline Harrison added her own special touch on April 18, 1890. Now the guests were given elegant commemorative programs. The selections were printed on nine-by-four inch, cream-colored satin ribbons with a gold presidential seal embossed at the top.[20] The whole affair was an ambitious undertaking: eleven selections performed by nine musicians for over 100 distinguished guests who came specifically to hear the music. The performers, mainly from the Washington area, played a variety of selections. Did it matter if Verdi and Handel were interposed among Metra and Pinsuti? The press did not think so. The program was "most pleasing," the artists "most charming," and the guests "very lovely" in their gowns of white silk or pearl-colored brocade, and the reporter did not miss a single flower. But of special interest to this study was the description of the piano used for the big event—the newly fashionable "baby grand." "The East Room had been specially decked for the occasion. A semi-circle of chairs was made to converge about the door to the red corridore [*sic*]. A Bradbury 'baby grand' piano was drawn up on one side of the door and by the other were set a clump of palms and a velvet divan. Here the President and Mrs. Harrison stood to receive their friends."[21]

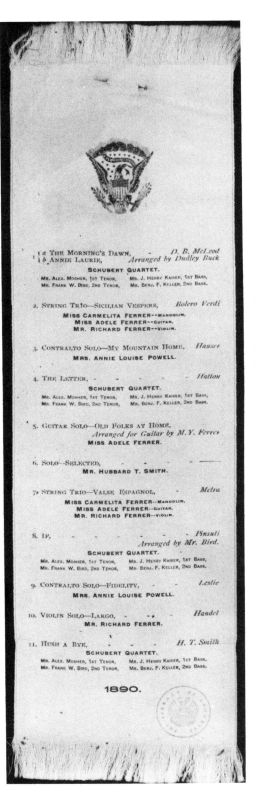

1 a THE MORNING'S DAWN, - D. B. McLeod
  b ANNIE LAURIE, Arranged by Dudley Buck
SCHUBERT QUARTET.
MR. ALEX. MOSHER, 1ST TENOR,   MR. J. HENRY KAISER, 1ST BASS,
MR. FRANK W. BIRD, 2ND TENOR,   MR. BENJ. F. KELLER, 2ND BASS.

2. STRING TRIO—SICILIAN VESPERS, Bolero Verdi
MISS CARMELITA FERRER--MANDOLIN.
MISS ADELE FERRER--GUITAR.
MR. RICHARD FERRER--VIOLIN.

3. CONTRALTO SOLO—MY MOUNTAIN HOME, Hauser
MRS. ANNIE LOUISE POWELL.

4. THE LETTER, - - - Hatton
SCHUBERT QUARTET.
MR. ALEX. MOSHER, 1ST TENOR,   MR. J. HENRY KAISER, 1ST BASS,
MR. FRANK W. BIRD, 2ND TENOR,   MR. BENJ. F. KELLER, 2ND BASS.

5. GUITAR SOLO—OLD FOLKS AT HOME,
Arranged for Guitar by M. Y. Ferrer
MISS ADELE FERRER.

6. SOLO—SELECTED, - - -
MR. HUBBARD T. SMITH.

7. STRING TRIO—VALSE ESPAGNOL, - Metra
MISS CARMELITA FERRER--MANDOLIN.
MISS ADELE FERRER--GUITAR.
MR. RICHARD FERRER--VIOLIN.

8. IF, - - - - Pinsuti
Arranged by Mr. Bird.
SCHUBERT QUARTET.
MR. ALEX. MOSHER, 1ST TENOR,   MR. J. HENRY KAISER, 1ST BASS,
MR. FRANK W. BIRD, 2ND TENOR,   MR. BENJ. F. KELLER, 2ND BASS.

9. CONTRALTO SOLO—FIDELITY, - Leslie
MRS. ANNIE LOUISE POWELL.

10. VIOLIN SOLO—LARGO, - - Handel
MR. RICHARD FERRER.

11. HUSH A BYE, - - - H. T. Smith
SCHUBERT QUARTET.
MR. ALEX. MOSHER, 1ST TENOR,   MR. J. HENRY KAISER, 1ST BASS,
MR. FRANK W. BIRD, 2ND TENOR,   MR. BENJ. F. KELLER, 2ND BASS.

1890.

The earliest preserved White House musicale program, 9 × 3½ inches, was printed on satin. The program on April 18, 1890, comprised the Schubert Quartet, contralto Annie Louise Powell, and a mandolin, guitar, violin trio.

Two other significant concerts took place during the Harrison years, both presented by opera singers (one black) who were achieving fame in Europe and America. The former, prima donna Laura Schirmer-Mapleson, offered her "soirée musicale" in the East Room on October 21, 1891. It was followed by a state dinner rather than light refreshments as the musicale the year before. After the dinner the newspapers indicated that the guests "returned to the East Room for more music." We do not have the details, but perhaps the Marine Band or Orchestra played while the guests had after-dinner coffee or cigars. Invited guests included members of the cabinet and diplomatic corps and their families, as well as some personal friends of Mrs. Harrison. The papers printed the entire program, and the Harrisons presented their guests with an elegant memento of the "soirée." While the original program is lost, a copy is preserved at the Martin Luther King Memorial Library in Washington, D.C. It appears to have been printed on a fine fabric, possibly brocade or moreen silk.

EXECUTIVE MANSION
WASHINGTON

Wednesday Evening, October 21st, 1891

SOIRÉE MUSICALE
MADAME
LAURA SCHIRMER-MAPLESON,

Royal and Imperial Court Singer,
Prima Donna of the Principal European Opera Houses,
Will Sing

The Mad Scene from "Lucia" Flute Obligato, Mr. Henry Jaeger	*Donizetti*
Songs (a) "Serenade" (b) "In der Fremde"	*Raff* *Taubert*
Air "Angels ever bright and fair"	*Handel*
Songs (a) "Marguerite" (b) "Ah! well a day"	*Henshaw* *Dana*
Serenade "Quand tu chantes" Flute Obligato, Mr. Henry Jaeger	*Gounod*
Song "Old Folks at Home"	*Foster*
Pianist	MR. HENRY XANDER.

Mme. Schirmer-Mapleson came to sing for the president in a special way. She had received a written invitation from President and Mrs. Harrison while she was in New York. She had not intended even to visit Washington, but she immediately left for the capital with her husband and manager, Henry Mapleson, who had brought the great Albani to President Arthur. The diva was a native Bostonian, a child prodigy who had been giving both piano and vocal concerts from the age of seven. In 1879 she made her operatic debut at the Globe Theater in Boston, then went to Europe where she became famous as one of the principal sopranos at the Imperial Opera House in Vienna. Her repertory was wide-ranging, and her varied East Room concert was received with great enthusiasm. Caroline Harrison herself had participated in choosing the music. The day after the concert, the *Washington Post* observed, "A feature of the entertainment was that the pieces were selected by Mrs. Harrison (one of which was the mad scene from *Lucia*), with the exception of 'Old Folks at Home' which was the choice of the President."[22] The Donizetti and Gounod arias were complemented by a brilliant flute obligato played by Henry Jaeger. Undoubtedly he brought along his solid gold flute, then the only one in existence.

Even more remarkable than this fine "soirée musicale" was the less formal and pretentious program presented by Sissieretta Jones. Called the "Black Patti" (after Adelina Patti), she also sang for William McKinley and Theodore Roosevelt, although we only have details for her program for the Harrisons. "Black Patti" was born Matilda S. Joyner in Portsmouth, Virginia, on January 5, 1869, the daughter of a former slave, and her early memories were those of a South burdened with social and economic problems. In 1876 she moved with her family to Rhode Island and began studies at the Providence Academy of Music at age fifteen, one year after her marriage to newspaper dealer and spendthrift, David Richard Jones.

Like Marie Selika (sometimes called the "Brown Patti"), who sang for President Hayes, Sissieretta Jones also went abroad to secure her reputation as a concert singer. In February 1882 President Harrison invited Jones to appear at a luncheon in the Blue Room of the White House, after which she sang Foster's "Swanee River," Bishop's "Home, Sweet Home," and the cavatina from Meyerbeer's *Robert le diable*. After the concert, Mrs. Harrison was so delighted that she presented her with a bouquet of White House orchids. Her voice, to judge from press accounts in her personal scrapbook, must have been extraordinary.[23] An undated *Washington Post* review is typical: "A Phenomenal Attraction ... the upper notes of her voice are clear and bell-like, reminding one of Parepa Rosa, and her low notes are rich and sensuous with a tropical contralto quality. ... In fact, the compass and quality of her registers surpass the usual limitations and seem to combine the height and depth of both soprano and contralto."

But for all the rave reviews and fame, Jones never realized her true ambition—to sing on the operatic stage. "I would like very much to sing in opera, but they tell me my color is against me," she told a *Detroit Tribune* reporter in 1893. Yielding to popular tastes of the time, from 1896 to 1916 Jones toured as the star of the Black Patti Troubadours, a company of about forty that combined elements of

Matilda S. Joyner, called "Black Patti" after the phenomenal Adelina Patti, sang for Benjamin Harrison, William McKinley, and Theodore Roosevelt.

minstrel show, vaudeville, musical revue, and grand opera. Amid this potpourri the singer managed to present her favorite operatic scenes with costumes and scenery from *Lucia*, *Il trovatore*, *Martha*, and Sousa's *El Capitan*. She died largely forgotten in 1933 at her home in Providence.

Before the time of the Harrisons, funeral ceremonies held inside the White House were brief and simple with no music. Two months before the Schubert Quartet sang for Mrs. Harrison's festive musicale in 1890, it had presented a program at the mansion for a much more solemn occasion—a double funeral. Early in February 1890 a fire broke out in the home of Benjamin F. Tracy, the secretary of the Navy, and his wife and daughter were both killed. On February 5 their funeral took place in the East Room, and the Schubert Quartet and the choir of St. John's Church provided the music. The choir, directed by William

H. Daniel, consisted of four basses, four tenors, and eighteen boys' voices divided into three upper parts. The piano moved into the East Room was played by the St. John's organist, F. E. Camp, and the small organ in the corridor by D. B. McLeod, the organist of St. Paul's Church. Shortly before 11:00 the Schubert Quartet entered the room by way of the private corridor. Standing inside the doorway they sang "I Cannot Always Trace the Way." After Secretary Tracy, his family and friends, President and Mrs. Harrison, and others had arrived,

> from out of the corridor, at its further end, came the sound of music. It came nearer and in a brief space of time the surpliced choir of St. John's Episcopal Church moved slowly into the room, singing "Lead, Kindly Light."
>
> . . . Beautiful, unintentionally so—was an effect produced by someone who thought one of the curtains on the north window was impeding ventillation. Just as Dr. Douglass prayed, "We humbly beseech thee to raise us from the death of sin to the life of rightousness," a curtain was drawn up to the top of a window, and a flood of light shot into the center of the previously gloomy room creating almost a transformation. The lilies on the two caskets looked dazzling white and the faces of the little choristers assumed cherubic attributes. It was a strangely fitting occurrence.
>
> In concert the clergymen and auditors repeated "The Lord's Prayer" and when that ended the choir sang "Abide with Me" as a recessional. During the singing of the first verse, Secretary Tracy stood up and watched the white-robed vocalists as they marched slowly around the remains of the dead and out into the corridor. The boyish trebles and altos, the pure tones of the tenors and the organ-like quality of the basses mingled and balanced perfectly in the most pathetic prayer ever put to music. The effect as the voices died away in the distance was almost supernatural. Every one was controlled by its influence and eyes that had hitherto been dry were moistened with lachrymal sympathy.
>
> "I fear no foe, with Thee at hand to bless;
> Ills have no weight and tears no bitterness."
>
> sang the choir, and the Secretary's lips trembled beneath his grizzled mustache. The President was by his side in an instant and putting his right hand beneath the Secretary's left arm, supported his friend while tears rolled down his own cheeks as the two caskets were carried out.[24]

For all of its sentimental overtones, this poignant account is a moving reminder of the power of music upon the human spirit. For no matter who resides in or visits the White House—president, first lady, family, staff, kings, princes, diplomats, blacks, whites—music provides an essential bond, an image, a message like no other art form.

"Administrations come and go, but the band plays on forever," said an account of the Marine Band concerts on the White House grounds in 1891.[25] During the final decades of the nineteenth century, America was caught up in a tremendous band craze. Not only were military bands all the rage, but so were industrial bands, Salvation Army bands, circus bands, and school bands. In 1893 seventy-one different bands marched in Grover Cleveland's inaugural parade. Outdoor band concerts after the Civil War became more than just an institution—they were an active social force. Hardly an event could be properly observed without a band, and every village or town seemed to have one. Like the parlor piano rage, which reached its peak, then tapered off just as the automobile, phonograph, movies, and radio began to take hold, amateur bands were springing up all over America. If the piano was the "family hearth," the bandstand was the town rallying point—an image of community spirit unknown to our era of COBOL and Concordes. The Marine Band during the second half of the nineteenth century was more than just "The President's Own." It was the people's as well. And it linked the presidential family with the nation like no other social or cultural phenomenon of the period.

The Marine Band under William McKinley was more vital to the spirit of the mansion than ever before. President McKinley took office on March 4, 1897, following Grover Cleveland's second term. A dignified lawyer from Canton, Ohio, McKinley provided strong leadership during the Spanish-American War and his acquisition of overseas territories laid a stable foundation for the expansion of presidential power as the twentieth century opened. The modern presidency emerged with McKinley, as communication with the media and handling of news releases by the White House became systematized. Six months after the beginning of his second term in office, President McKinley was fatally shot by an anarchist at the Pan American Exposition in Buffalo. He died on September 14, 1901, and was succeeded by Vice-President Theodore Roosevelt.

By the beginning of McKinley's era, White House receptions had deteriorated to "vulgar mobs," as one reporter bluntly put it. If an officer had to raise his arm, he could not put it down again. "One officer had his arm over a lady's shoulder the better part of an hour and was simply unable to remove it. Another was so irresistibly pressed against a lady she nearly fainted, and he was powerless to relieve her. . . . Ladies have had their dresses torn off their backs." So described Col. T. A. Bingham, the president's fastidious blond, wax-mustachioed aide, who brought about sweeping, though simple reforms.[26] Instead of one invitation that covered the four official receptions—diplomatic, judiciary, congressional, and Army and Navy—separate invitations were sent for each function, thus reducing the number of guests and the bedlam. House servants were instructed never to be visible in their shirt sleeves, ushers had to present a neat appearance with smooth parts of the face clean shaven, and tan shoes were never to be worn between November 1 and May 1. Women guests were never to wear bonnets at an evening reception nor gentlemen anything but proper evening attire, such as the claw-hammer coat. Fortunately—or not so fortunately—the Marine Band was now stationed "among the tropical palms of the conservatory and in a tropically humid and fragrant atmosphere." And this "delightful innovation," according to the *Post*,

An Army and Navy reception at the White House illustrated by a lithograph dated November 20, 1893, during the early months of Grover Cleveland's second administration.

"made the great space devoted to floral culture a pleasant rendezvous for the young lovers."[27]

But the efficacious Colonel Bingham had other ideas, too. With the mammoth McKinley dinners that seated sixty to eighty in the vestibule, where could the orchestra be placed? He tried the Blue Room but the music was lost there. "It would be better to have the full Marine Band at these dinners instead of the orchestra," he said. "They would then be well heard."[28] But how about not one band, but two? For the reception for President and Mrs. Sanford Ballard Dole of Hawaii, "the interior of the historic old mansion was more beautifully decorated than at any time this season. . . . The famous Marine band, fifty strong, was placed in the conservatory, while the band of the Sixth Cavalry, U.S.A. stationed at Fort Myer, was placed in the corridor dividing the lobby from the East Room, where their brilliant trappings of cavalry yellow added to the gay picture, which delighted all present."[29] The practice of having two bands play alternately at large receptions continued into Theodore Roosevelt's administration. Sometimes the Marine Band was divided into two units; at other times bands from local military organizations were employed, such as the 11th Infantry Band on New Year's Day, 1901. "The President's Own" now had some competition!

The Marine Band concerts held outdoors on the White House lawn also took on new proportions under McKinley, as up to 5,000 people attended. The tradition, begun by President Tyler, was so well established by the 1890s that one reviewer was convinced that people attended habitually, having been "inoculated with it in infancy," the babies in their carriages forming a "most entertaining part of these audiences."

> All kinds and conditions of men are apt to be found in the crowds, from clerks to millionaires, and there is music enough to stir all their souls. There is generally a good deal more music than there are seats to accommodate a tithe of those who could listen best if they could be comfortably seated. As a rule you will find the old folks sitting around, and a big, fat black "mammy" is frequently a conspicuous ornament of one settee all by herself. Her generous equipment of starched skirts adds largely to her ample width, and it would be a courageous soul who would dare to offer to share the bench with her. There are oftentimes quite lively battles of words over who shall occupy a bench, and one afternoon last summer two reputable citizens got so excited over their respective rights that they almost came to blows, until a wary policeman whispered a word of warning.[30]

The only thing the Capitol concerts had that the White House lacked was the sound of thousands of feet as they pounded the asphalt in time to the infectious martial rhythms.

The bandstand during the Lincoln and Johnson years had been much farther from the mansion than it was toward the end of the century. It was then "a green and white circular structure situated about midway between the hills at the lower part of the grounds, near the walk." By 1891 the bandstand was a low platform, which could be moved about at will. There were often flower beds on each side of the stand, and the entire area was fenced off with two policemen inside "who would not even let a lady-bug come inside unless he was down on the program for an aria."[31] The earlier custom was for the president to promenade around with some lady whom he wanted to honor on his arm, while his wife selected some gentleman to escort her, as the Grants had commonly done. By Grover Cleveland's time, the presidential entourage enjoyed the music from the mansion balcony and did not come down among the people at all. But President McKinley, whose fine bass voice attracted attention during Sunday church services, sometimes joined the concerts, humming along as he recognized the tune.

During McKinley's administration the band had the greatest re-organization of its history. On March 3, 1899, the president signed an act into law that doubled the band's membership and increased its salaries. Regular Marine Orchestra concerts were held as early as 1893 at the enlarged Marine Barracks music hall, but by 1900 under the leadership of William Santelmann, the orchestra received special focus at the White House as a concert, rather than merely a social ensemble. The repertory of both the orchestra and the band, however, was very similar. Chopin arrangements began to be included now as well as a variety of what were called "descriptives," a concept somewhere between a Richard Strauss tone poem and a D. W. Griffith silent film score. This was music that carried one to far away places. The audience loved it. Especially popular was Santelmann's creatively orchestrated "Voyage in a Troopship" and Francisco Fanciulli's "Voyage Comique— A Trip to Mars." Or if one wanted to stay closer to home there was the latter's "A Trip to Manhattan Beach," replete with daybreak, boat rides, gambling, dancing sea nymphs, fireworks, and an exhausted "Home, Sweet Home."[32]

When John Philip Sousa left the Marine Band on July 30, 1892, he was succeeded by Francisco Fanciulli. A fine musician, Fanciulli had a hard act to follow as Sousa's successor. There were those who, preferring Sousa's "El Capitain" March, complained that his taste was "too classical and did not have the necessary swing and snap." Indeed, one of his superiors accused the corps of being afflicted with a "chop step." Enraged, Fanciulli let loose some strong defensive language and practically wound up in jail. He was defended by Assistant Secretary of the Navy Theodore Roosevelt, no less. His record cleared, Fanciulli was honorably discharged on October 31, 1897.[33] His successor, Leipzig Conservatory–trained William Santelmann, by contrast, remained leader for twenty-nine years, the longest service in Marine Band history. Santelmann's son (also William) later served as leader for fifteen years (1940–55). Both father and son left the Marine Band in a blaze of glory with honors and accolades from across the nation.

Anyone who attends a White House state dinner today will watch the president and first lady come down the stairs and pause while "Ruffles and Flourishes" and "Hail to the Chief" are played by the Marine Band. While we know "Hail to the Chief" was formally associated with the president at the White House as far back as Tyler, there is no indication it was preceded by the short drum rolls (ruffles) and two-note bugle call (flourishes) until President McKinley's administration. The custom of announcing the arrival of royalty and heads of state with a fanfare of trumpets or drum rolls existed in England and was practiced by the colonists to honor high-ranking military officers during the Revolutionary War.[34]

In 1893 a regulation established that the chief executive would receive four ruffles and flourishes, but not until the state dinner for the president of Costa Rica on November 29, 1898, do we find that "four trumpeters were on hand to play the President's march, followed by 'Hail to the Chief' by the orchestra." In haste Bingham undoubtedly wrote the word "march" here when he meant bugle "call." His report on the dinner for President Dole of Hawaii on February 1 of this same year provides yet another version: "The Presidential party marched down the private stairs (The band playing 'Hail to the Chief,' the President's march on the bugle being omitted)." Finally, in describing the dinner for Admiral George Dewey, hero of the Spanish-American War, Bingham offers an account that seems to indicate the presidential honors we know today: "The Presidential party proceeded down the main staircase in the usual manner, the Band playing 'The President's Call' and 'Hail to the Chief.' "[35]

For most of the White House social events, the first lady received her guests while she was seated. Frail and infirm, Ida Saxton McKinley fought epilepsy and other illnesses most of her life. Santelmann's musical tribute to her offers a glimpse of the music she enjoyed. The maestro's "Timely Thoughts," first performed at the cabinet dinner on January 2, 1901, is a medly of her "beloved airs": the "Intermezzo" from Mascagni's *Cavalleria rusticana*, Stephen Foster's "Swanee River," and that indomitable symbol of Imperial Vienna, Strauss's "Blue Danube Waltz."[36] But the first lady also greatly enjoyed the few guest artists that came to perform at the White House during this period, especially her niece Mabel McKinley, a professional singer, and several string players.

While Florizel Reuter, a nine-year-old violin virtuoso, played on September 8, 1899, the remarkable young black violinist, Joseph Douglass, performed not only for McKinley but also later for President Taft. Grandson of orator and statesman Frederick Douglass, Joseph was born in 1869 in Washington, D.C., and studied in that city and at Boston's New England Conservatory. Thereafter he went to Europe to further his career. Returning to Washington, his many recitals were reputed to have been an inspiration to other black youths to study the violin seriously. Douglass even performed in Washington with "Black Patti" on March 5, 1893, during the inaugural week of Grover Cleveland. He was also the first Negro violinist to make recordings for the Victor Talking Machine Company of Camden, New Jersey (now RCA Victor). Called "a thorough master of his instrument" by the Washington press, Douglass later taught at Howard University and at the Music Settlement School in New York City.[37]

But the most important string program of this period will be remembered not for the performers, but for the way in which their music became a vital part of the occasion. The McKinleys, drawing from past traditions, set the stage for the state dinner/musicale pattern that would become the focal point for modern entertaining at the White House. They had invited about seventy people for their Supreme Court dinner on February 8, 1898. After the elaborate meal with tables spread into the vestibule, the guests gathered in the East Room, where a grand piano had been placed, and enjoyed music by Mr. and Mrs. Ernest Lent, violinist and pianist, with Joseph O. Cadek, cellist.[38] The trio had been touring cities east of the Mississippi and, after their successful Baltimore appearance, received an invitation to play at the

Joseph Douglass, grandson of statesman Frederick Douglass, performed for President William McKinley at the White House and for many years taught violin and gave concerts in Washington.

White House. For the Supreme Court dignitaries, the McKinleys chose a serious opener indeed: a piano trio, the first to be performed at the mansion. Chamber music concerts were still relatively rare in America, and rarer still in the nation's capital. Ernest Lent's Piano Trio in B Major was a lyrical four-movement work in the Schumann-Brahms tradition, not unlike the style Americans such as George Whitefield Chadwick were composing at this time, and for their White House appearance the performers selected the expressive finale. To commemorate the concert, the McKinleys printed the program on six-by-four inch cream-colored cards with blue lettering and a gold-scalloped border.[39]

A piano trio in the East Room, and still no piano regularly situated in the spacious parlor? Even so, the White House could now boast

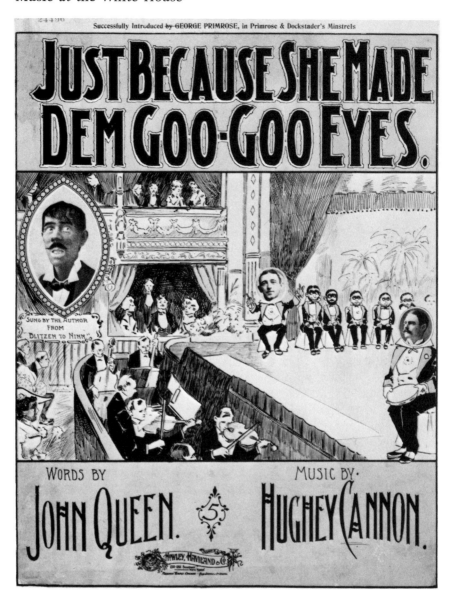

"Goo-Goo Eyes" (1900), one of the popular new two-steps on the McKinleys' dance program for Valentine's Day, 1901, illustrates the merging of ragtime and social dance as the century turned.

three grand pianos and an upright among its furnishings. The old Knabe of Arthur's time was still in the Green Room; the Bradbury baby grand from the Harrisons had been moved to the oval library upstairs; a fine A. B. Chase upright graced the other private family apartments;[40] but for the Supreme Court concert, the new Kimball grand most likely would have been the instrument chosen. The agent for the flourishing midwestern Kimball Company, Edwin S. Conway, was a great supporter of Ohio-born McKinley. As an inaugural gift he placed in the Blue Room a fine mahogany grand (#22091) with a blue-trimmed "scarf and stool to match."[41]

As the century drew to a close, the White House could count every variety of piano within its historic furnishings—small and wing-shaped pianofortes, massive squares, grands, uprights, and baby grands. One style was missing, however, that joyous icon of musical gadgetry—the player piano. But the mansion had had some offers. Hawlett Davis wanted to donate to the White House one of his "advanced electro-mechanical Pianophones," which was "built like a phonograph, has bearings like a bicycle and will last a lifetime."[42] And E. H. Droop, still on the White House musical scene as Washington dealer for Steinway and other makers, wrote to McKinley on April 24, 1901, with his bid. He asked if the president would like an upright piano and an "Angelus" (pneumatic attachment) placed in his private railroad car. Both offers were politely declined.[43] Apparently the White House had not yet succumbed to the persuasion of American advertisers that it was more enjoyable to pump pedals than to push keys.

The White House, however, did succumb to the fine art of dancing. Shortly after the turn of the century, before the president began his ill-starred second term, the McKinleys held a dance on Valentine's Day, 1901. It took place in the state dining room after a diplomatic dinner, and a protective cover ("crash") was laid over the fine carpets. Once again, the Marine Band was moved into the conservatory with the plants and flowers. The program for the dancing was broken into two separate categories. Gone were the European designations var-sovienne, esmeralda, polka redowa, and the like. In their place was a new category, the two-step—an American original. Like everywhere else in the nation, the White House was caught up in the great ragtime craze of the turn of the century. The McKinleys were right in style. A sample of their choice of music reflects the synthesis of cakewalk, ragtime, march, and dance typical of an emerging new popular art.[44]

TWO-STEPS

Whistling Rufus	*Mills*
Black America	*Dickel*
Bunch o' Blackberries	*Holdman* [sic *Holzmann*]
Hail to the Spirit of Liberty	*Sousa*
Admiral Dewey	*Santelman[n]*
Lanciers "Foxy Quiller"	*DeKoven*

WALTZES

Hydropaten	*Gungl*
"I Can't Tell Why I Love You"	*Chattoway*
Floradora	*Stuart*
Blue Danube	*Strauss*
The Fortune Teller	*Herbert*

Also included on the list of two-steps was Faust's "Galop St. Petersburg," appearing somewhat anomalous among the other titles. But while America may have "galoped" its way through the gay 1890s, it "trotted" through the early decades of the twentieth century to a new syncopated ragtime beat. For the fox-trot, "fish walk," and "bunny hug" heralded a new age. When the McKinley Legion rushed into the room carrying a pie six feet in diameter during the Gridiron Club Dinner on March 27, 1897, vaudeville star George O'Connor belted out his old-time minstrel songs for the president: "My Gal's a Highborn Lady" and "Mammy's Little Alabama Coon." A decade later he would sing tunes from George M. Cohan's "45 Minutes from Broadway." Times were changing. An era was emerging. Presidential power was reactivating. Unlike a tired dancer from the Gilded Age, the enfeebled office of the late nineteenth-century presidency refused to "just sit this one out." Stature, strength, and dynamism lay just around the corner. And the new steps would be bellowed vigorously from the "bully pulpit."

PART THREE

★ ★ ★

1901–61

WHEN THEODORE ROOSEVELT became president in 1901, he brought
to the nation a fresh image of vigor and excitement and strengthened
the office of the presidency through a broader use of executive power.
Roosevelt not only steered the United States more actively into world
politics, favoring a strong foreign policy, but he also energetically led
the nation toward progressive reforms. As one historian noted, "He
was the first influential man of his time to see clearly that the United
States was no longer a rural nation, but an industrial giant run amok."
To be sure, great things had been achieved by the turn of the century
in industry and agriculture. But many Americans believed that numerous
economic, social, political, and moral situations were unsatisfactory
in their "land of the free." Ralph Chaplin's "Solidarity Forever" and
Joe Hill's "Workers of the World, Unite" struck responsive chords.

The United States in 1912 consisted of forty-eight states with a
population of 90 million. Between 1900 and 1912, moreover, the number
of European immigrants, now primarily from Italy, Russia, and Poland,
increased to more than 8.8 million. One of Roosevelt's missions was
to alter the way in which immigrants were viewed as pools of cheap
labor. He improved the conditions of workers, forced the dissolution
of great railroad combinations through his vigorous "trust busting,"
and crusaded endlessly for conservation, establishing the first U.S.
Bureau of Forestry and numerous giant irrigation projects. President
Roosevelt's successor, William Howard Taft, continued these reforms,
and during Woodrow Wilson's presidency, voting rights were extended
to all women. Thus, from the great epics of Theodore Dreiser to the
western themes of Frederic Remington, from gigantic steel-built bridges
to robust Model Ts, from the illusions of the newly developing film
industry to the scholarship of the flourishing universities, America
in 1914 looked back with self-confidence and pride on the strong
achievements of a democracy.

But in that same year World War I broke out in Europe, and the
United States was not able to maintain its neutrality. On April 2,

1917, President Wilson asked Congress to declare war on Germany. With incredible speed the American war industry escalated, producing an abundance of modern weapons, and soon every school, park, and community center across the nation reverberated with morale-building war songs, such as George M. Cohan's "Over There." The spell of the German classical tradition on American culture was breaking, and the war and postwar years prompted a new awareness of America's own musical resources. In November 1918 Germany signed the Armistice. But the Versailles Treaty, which included the Covenant of the League of Nations, failed ratification in the Senate, and the United States turned inward.

Thus during the 1920s, under Presidents Warren Harding, Calvin Coolidge, and Herbert Hoover, America remained basically conservative in its domestic policies and isolationist in foreign affairs. Tariffs were high, and all sectors of the national economy produced huge quantities of goods. Consumer spending soared, and the "roaring twenties" brought wealth and prosperity to many people. However, the decade ended on a grim note, with the collapse of the stock market on "Black Friday," October 24, 1929. In three months one-half of the nation's total industrial capacity was idled. By 1931 the panic had spread to Europe, and soon the Great Depression engulfed the whole world.

In November 1932 Franklin D. Roosevelt was elected to the first of four terms as president. He took office the following March armed with a sweeping program that he called the "New Deal," with which he hoped to bring relief to the unemployed and to those in danger of losing their farms and homes. From 1935 to 1941 Roosevelt's Federal Music Project not only employed thousands of musicians but also brought symphonic and folk music to people who had never before heard these styles. But bellicose threats to peace from Germany, Italy, and Japan increasingly drew America's attention to foreign affairs. On December 7, 1941, Japanese aircraft attacked U.S. warships in Pearl Harbor, and America entered World War II.

The year 1945 was a monumental one—bringing both the end of one era and the beginning of another. Germany and Japan collapsed and were forced to accept unconditional surrender; the first atomic bomb was dropped; and a mighty new instrument of peace—the United Nations—was launched in San Francisco. On April 12 President Roosevelt died in office and was succeeded by Harry S. Truman, whose Marshall Plan of 1947 aided war-torn Western Europe and stimulated its vital economic recovery. Yet Truman faced another war, too, as the Communist government of North Korea attacked South Korea in June 1950, initiating a long, discouraging struggle that lasted until a peace agreement was signed in 1953 under President Dwight Eisenhower.

The Russians soon claimed construction of their own atomic and hydrogen bombs and quickly attained parity with America in the field of military armaments. In 1957 Soviet scientists launched the first Sputnik. Not only had the Cold War begun, but also the "Arms Race" as well, and both themes formed an ominous counterpoint within a drama whose peroration has yet to be realized. Not only America but also the entire world shared grave concerns for peace and for the future of all humankind—a future that President Eisenhower sought to ensure by turning to the arts to ease tensions between the Free World and Communist countries. The president's cultural exchange programs provided a solid, aesthetic bridge between the United States and the Union of Soviet Socialist Republics, allowing performers to gain international prestige and nations to communicate on new levels of understanding.

CHAPTER 8

THE MUSICALE TRADITION

Theodore Roosevelt, Taft, Wilson

> Paderewski outdid himself, though he
> was a little cold at first. By the time
> he got to the Polonaise . . . I think it
> may have been better than hearing
> Chopin himself.
>
> Cecilia Beaux
> The White House, April 3, 1902

The musical life of the White House during the energetic terms of
Theodore Roosevelt was richer, more diversified, and more representative of the American cultural scene than any other previous era.
It picked up the traditions and new concepts in musical entertainment
enjoyed by the Harrisons and McKinleys, added its own special touch,
then passed on this legacy to succeeding administrations, notably the
Tafts and Wilsons. During President and Mrs. Roosevelt's two terms
(1901–9), the White House blossomed as the nation's social center.
The first lady now had her own private secretary, Isabella Hagner,
and nine social aides instead of only three as in previous administrations.[1] Association with Steinway & Sons, dating as far back as Grover
Cleveland, now became firmly established. Joseph Burr Tiffany and
Henry Junge served as musical liaisons with the Executive Mansion.
They not only advised the first lady but also carried out her personal
wishes regarding the artists and musical selections to be performed
for the numerous distinguished White House guests. Music for "the
home" was becoming music for "the people." And the presidential
family became increasingly cognizant of the important role that this
elusive, yet powerful art form played in the life of the nation.
     When President William McKinley died on September 14, 1901,
Roosevelt assumed his new duties as chief executive with characteristic
flamboyance and flair. The youngest man ever to reach the presidency,
Roosevelt at forty-two captured public admiration with his vivid personality and multifaceted background as author, naturalist, explorer,

soldier, and statesman. He had served as assistant secretary of the Navy, commander of the Rough Riders in Cuba, and governor of New York before becoming president. But there always seemed to be an aura of glamour about him—a legendary vigor that resulted in policies that added greatly to the international reputation of America. When he left the presidency in 1909, the United States was admired, even feared, among world powers, and its favor sought and respected.

After Mrs. McKinley, whose severe headaches and nervous seizures kept her from an active social life, Edith Kermit Roosevelt seemed a unique White House hostess possessing élan, energy, and superb executive skills. But the president, too, had special talents in entertaining: "Mr. Roosevelt entertains not occasionally but constantly, not exclusively but democratically, not meagerly, but lavishly. ... He has a multitude of guests to luncheon, to dine, to hear music or to take part in various kinds of 'drawing rooms' and levees."[2] And music? For the first time in White House history the musical events became a major, regularly scheduled feature of the great mansion's social life.

Neither President nor Mrs. Roosevelt was especially musically inclined or talented, although they often enjoyed the Victor Herbert operettas at Washington theaters. According to Mabel P. Daggett, the president preferred ragtime to Chopin, but dutifully attended the musicales and supported Mrs. Roosevelt's endeavors. "Sometimes he gets to shifting uneasily in his seat, his gaze wanders, and before he knows it he is bowing his teeth to acquaintances across the room."[3] But the president, author of the multi-volume *Winning of the West*, was especially attracted to the simple western ballad. A handwritten note printed on an opening page of John Lomax's *Cowboy Songs* reveals his support of this new aspect of research in the field of indigenous American music.[4]

Dear Mr. Lomax,

You have done a work emphatically worth doing and one which should appeal to the people of all our country, but particularly to the people of the west and southwest. ... There is something very curious in the reproductions here on this new continent of essentially the conditions of ballad-growth which was obtained in medieval England; including, by the way, sympathy for the outlaw, Jesse James taking the place of Robin Hood. Under modern conditions however, the native ballad is speedily killed by competition with the music hall songs; the cowboy becoming ashamed to sing the crude homespun ballads in view of what Owen Winter calls the "ill-smelling saloon cleverness" of the far less interesting composition of the music hall singers. It is therefore a work of real importance to preserve permanently the back country and the frontier.

As for hymns, the president confided to his military aide, Archie Butt, that while one day his favorite could be "Abide with Me," on another it might be "The Son of God Goes Forth to War."[5] His favorite "battle music" was "Dixie," but one afternoon while riding on horseback with Captain Butt, he voiced his opinions about "The Battle Hymn of the Republic" by Julia Ward Howe: "The line 'As he died to make men holy, let us die to make men free' is universal, catholic, as true a hundred years ago as it is now, equally true of Anglo-Saxon or Hindu. Yes, that hymn ought to be our national hymn, but how can we bring it about? . . . I have it. I will write to Joel Chandler Harris, Uncle Remus, you know, and get him to start the movement in the [Atlanta] *Constitution.* Then I will write to others in the West and get them to take it up. . . . Would it not be fine to have a hymn that this great nation could sing in unison?"[6] In spite of the combined efforts of the president and his friends, the proposal was never realized, for fear of offending Jewish people who might object to the word "Christ" in their national hymn. As we shall see later, Franklin Roosevelt had his problems with this song, too.

The Roosevelts held five large receptions and three state dinners during the social season, and Mrs. Roosevelt had additional elegant teas, garden parties, and luncheons. But the striking innovations during this period were the "musicales," as the first lady called her important dinner-concert functions. These took place usually in the evening, though sometimes they were held in the afternoon—providing they did not interfere with the president's horseback riding. On the average, there were eight musicales each year with four comprising a series during the month of January. If a dinner began at 8:oo, the musicale would start at 10:oo, last about one hour, and add many more guests to the smaller number invited for the dinner. From 400 to 600 were invited to the musicales, which were held in the East Room, although about 350 usually attended. Each person received a card invitation that was checked before he or she entered the mansion—very similar to the state dinner entertainment plan at the White House today.[7]

The most striking aspect of the music of the Theodore Roosevelt administration was the number of "firsts" brought to the White House: the first full concert by a noted pianist; the first musicale devoted to a single opera; the first performance on a clavichord; and the first East Room piano—a fine concert grand from Steinway & Sons. Famous instrumental ensembles now played complete Haydn and Schumann quartets; fine singers programmed Mozart arias, Brahms and Schubert lieder, and the songs of the modern French composers André Messager, Cécile Chaminade, and Charles Koechlin (Claude Debussy was not included on a printed program until Frances Alda sang for Taft on April 21, 1911). American-born artists performed John Alden Carpenter, George Chadwick, Arthur Foote, and Amy Cheney Beach. Probably more Edward MacDowell was played in the White House during the Roosevelt administration than anywhere in America at this time, and the accent on American music and artists was a conspicuous philosophy of both Mrs. Roosevelt and the Steinway company, whose staff assisted in the arrangements.[8]

Joseph Burr Tiffany, head of the fine arts department of Steinway & Sons, was not only an expert in decorative arts, but knowledgeable in the field of music as well. Correspondence in the presidential papers indicates that his associations with the White House began as early as the McKinley period and continued until Tiffany's death on April 3, 1917. It is interesting that Tiffany wrote to George B. Cortelyou, secretary to President Roosevelt, on November 9, 1901, more than one year before the first state Steinway was presented to the presidential mansion, suggesting that a piano be placed in the White House: "Steinway and Sons are now informed by their Washington representatives, Messrs. E. F. Droop and Sons, that you have called on them and told them that President Roosevelt is now ready to receive the upright piano. Before sending a piano from here accordingly, I would suggest that perhaps a grand piano would be more suitable to Mrs. Roosevelt, and the kindness to ask her whether or not perhaps a Steinway parlor grand in mahogany case, such as was bought by New York State for the Executive Mansion in Albany when Mr. Roosevelt was Governor, would better answer her requirements than an upright piano?"

While there is no record of a mahogany piano being presented to the White House at this time, a gold grand was placed in the East Room in January 1903. Steinway honored the president with its 100,000th piano. Its case was covered with dull gold leaf and decorated with the coat of arms of the thirteen original states linked together with scrolls of acanthus. The painting under the lid, executed by Thomas Wilmer Dewing, represented the nine muses being received by the young republic America. While Tiffany was a member of the advisory committee, the actual design of the case was the work of R. D. Hunt and J. H. Hunt. "On behalf of the nation," wrote President Roosevelt to Steinway on March 2, 1903, "I accept with pleasure and thank you heartily for the beautiful piano which you recently placed in the White House."[9] The fine instrument graced the East Room, becoming the artistic medium of hundreds of pianists, until it was replaced by a new state Steinway during the administration of Franklin Roosevelt.[10]

At the turn of the century, Steinway & Sons had reached a point of maturity, prosperity, and preoccupation with the arts that brought them distinction as makers of "the Instrument of the Immortals." The Steinway round table at Luchow's restaurant on 14th Street became a meeting place for musicians from all over the world.[11] At the same time the entertaining prowess of the Roosevelts had spread, and artists began writing to the president and first lady asking to perform in the White House. Embassies, too, put in their bids for foreign artists. Thus the Steinway company served as a sort of clearinghouse—auditioning unknown performers, selecting the best, and securing the famous for appearances at the White House. Most of these impresarial tasks were assigned to Tiffany, but an intellectual, dapper gentleman with droll wit and European charm assisted him, becoming official White House arts liaison in 1911 under President Taft: German-born Henry Junge was a violinist trained at the Hanover Conservatory of Music, and his dedication to the cause of fine music at the White House lasted until his death in 1939.[12]

(Below) Grand piano made by Steinway & Sons, New York, and presented to the White House in 1903. (Above) Inside the lid is a painting by noted American artist Thomas Wilmer Dewing showing the elegant female figures characteristic of his style. Josef Hofmann, Ferruccio Busoni, and Sergei Rachmaninoff were among the great pianists to play this instrument.

With Steinway on the scene, the great pianists came—Paderewski, Busoni, Hofmann, Samaroff, Friedman, Zeisler, and a host of others. Even before the gold concert grand made its White House appearance, the legendary Paderewski, at the height of his fame, played his own Steinway brought in for the occasion. Through President Roosevelt's personal request to Tiffany, the famed Polish artist and composer played for the president, first lady, and about 400 guests on April 3, 1902. A glamorous yet dignified showman, Paderewski would play in the White House nine more times for six presidents. But for his first program he selected Beethoven's Sonata op. 27, no. 2; a Chopin group— Nocturne in G Major, op. 37, no. 2, Etude in G-flat, op. 10, no. 5, Valse in A-flat, op. 42, and Polonaise, op. 53; two of his own compositions; and Liszt's Hungarian Rhapsody no. 2. One of the guests at the musicale, portrait painter Cecilia Beaux, commented: "The yellow head of the Lion shone gloriously against the satin of the Blue Room. . . . It is a thrilling moment when the Sovereigns come in, and we all rise, if we had been seated, an act which would turn the head of any ordinary civilian. . . . Paderewski outdid himself, though he was a little cold at first. By the time he got to the [Military] Polonaise . . . I think it may have been better than hearing Chopin himself."[13]

Paderewski had played Chopin's heroic Polonaise at his first solo recital in Washington on February 5, 1892. Unlike the mixed audience of luminaries at the White House, however, the public concert crowd consisted mostly of women, who made the hirsute-headed pianist a victim of the greatest display of female adulation since the days of Franz Liszt. But the Polonaise itself created quite a stir according to the *Evening Star* of February 6, 1892:

> The Polonaise, a mass of technical difficulties, he played in the stately and majestic polonaise tempo and with wonderful breadth and a colossal tone. After the terrific left-hand octave work of the second part of this piece, at the point where this theme is about ended and the first to be taken up again, at the point where nine out of ten great pianists want to stop from sheer exhaustion, Paderewski introduces a semi-romantic cadenza in octaves for the right hand, and suddenly, like a flash of lightning, with apparently no effort, crashes his powerful arm down on the first chords of the opening motive, or "Hauptsatz" of the composition, producing a tone quality never before attained by any pianist.

And Theodore Roosevelt's reaction? Paderewski himself summed it up: "The President listened with charming interest and applauded vociferously and always shouted out 'Bravo! Bravo! Fine! Splendid!— even during the performance."[14]

Another legendary artist who performed for the Roosevelts was the Italian Ferruccio Busoni, the first of the great modern pianists. A program by Busoni during his early years of touring America would have been considered avant-garde by most critics. For Busoni cherished the *idea,* rather than the technical display of his Romantic predecessors.

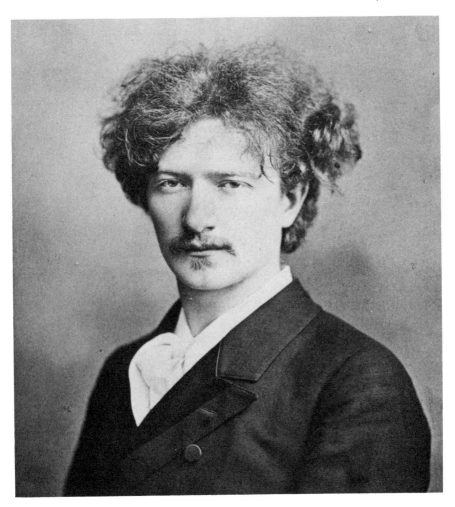

Ignacy Jan Paderewski, the famous Polish pianist, composer, and statesman, performed at the White House many times over four decades.

He was intellectual, an artist with a burning message, a fascinating genius whose White House program of three composers—Beethoven, Chopin, and Liszt—epitomized his epochal philosophies. Opening with the complete "Appassionata" of Beethoven was no frothy settling-in exercise. Busoni himself admitted that "one could never put enough passion into the 'Appassionata.' . . . When I play Beethoven, I try to approach the *liberté, nervosité* and *humanité* which are the signature of his compositions, in contrast to his predecessors."[15]

It is hard to fathom Signor Busoni agreeing to share a program with another artist. But apparently Mrs. Roosevelt considered this coupling for his program on January 29, 1904. "Paderewski is the only one who has ever had an entire evening at the White House," she said. She also considered having Fanny Bloomfield Zeisler play on this date instead of Busoni. Zeisler had just appeared in Washington as soloist with the symphony, but the president's secretary, William

Loeb, wrote to Tiffany that "from what we hear we do not care to arrange for her."[16] By January 23, however, Busoni had been secured.

> Mrs. Roosevelt has decided that it will be better to give Mr. Busoni the entire evening and will be glad to have him make up a program that will interest a very miscellaneous audience. Of course she wishes the best music, classical music if necessary, but feels sure the pianist can from his repertoire make selections that will hold the attention of such an assembly as you have seen on these occasions.
>
> Would it not be well to include something from "Parsifal," now that the opera is so much talked of?
>
> Please send me the program as soon as possible so that there may be opportunity for changes if any are desired.[17]

While Busoni did not include Wagner on his program, the operatic paraphrase was nonetheless represented by Liszt's *Rigoletto Fantasie.* But the reference in Loeb's letter to Wagner's *Parsifal* is particularly interesting. Wagner transcriptions were very much in vogue at this time and were found frequently on White House programs that featured technically gifted pianists especially. Albert Lockwood played Bressin's thundering arrangement of the "Ride of the Valkyries" on January 23, 1903. Texas-born Olga Samaroff played the same piece transcribed by her teacher Ernest Hutcheson for President Taft on February 11, 1910. (Her program also included Scriabin's Nocturne for the Left Hand Alone, composed in 1894.) And there were the perennial "Liebestods," "Fire Musics," "Senta's Ballads," and "Prize Songs." Liszt's virtuosic arrangement of the latter was a particular favorite at the White House. Like the medium of the concert band, the piano disseminated to the world the joys of opera at the turn of the century, just as it had in the previous decades.

But Wagner was also brought to the public through one of the finest contraltos of the era, Mme. Ernestine Schumann-Heink. Possessing a rich voice of extraordinary warmth and beauty, Mme. Schumann-Heink retired in 1932 at the age of seventy-one, having just sung the demanding role of Erda in Wagner's *Siegfried.* Her repertory, which featured Wagner, consisted of over 150 roles. Having acquired American citizenship in 1908, Mme. Schumann-Heink remained a devoted patriot and sang for numerous events during World War I, such as liberty bond drives, war rallies, and Red Cross benefits. Her program presented with the German Liederkranz and Arion Singing Societies of New York in the White House on February 24, 1903, was a milestone in the history of the presidential mansion. Alternating with the German choral works sung by the Liederkranz, she sang lieder of Schubert, Schumann, and Brahms.[18] The printed invitations for this concert were among the most beautiful musical mementos ever issued from the White House. Measuring 7 × 9 1/2 inches, they consisted of nine heavy cardboard pages bound with pink satin ribbon. The cover showed the White House with the West Wing as it was added in 1902, and page one bore cameolike images of President and Mrs. Roosevelt. But especially striking was the page showing portions

Ernestine Schumann-Heink, the great Austrian-born contralto who became an American citizen in 1908.

of the music itself, artistically arranged and decorated with graceful boughs. The texts for all the songs were also included with this attractive program, preserved in the T. A. Bingham Papers at the Library of Congress.

The newspapers now were beginning to feature White House musical events in a manner unparalleled since the time of Rutherford Hayes. "Singers Capture City" flashed the headline of an article in the *Washington Post*, May 7, 1906, entitled "Famed Austrian Society Gives White House Concert." The Washington Saengerbund served as host for its Austrian brothers, members of the Wiener Männergesangverein (Male Singing Society of Vienna), and the stir created reveals the power this type of music still held in America. The Austrian group, directed by Eduard Kremser, had come to the United States specifically to sing before the president. A long procession of carriages waited at the depot for the visiting singers. It bore the leader of the Washington Saengerbund and members of the society, wearing identifying badges of red, white, and blue ribbon fastened on conspicuously with Teddy Bear stickpins.

Guests and choristers crowded into the East Room and undoubtedly overflowed into the corridor. The papers indicated 500 people in attendance at the concert. After President Roosevelt had bowed to the president of the society, the program began with Schubert's setting of the Twenty-third Psalm conducted by Richard Heuberger, a professor at the Vienna Conservatory. "Each voice was perfectly modulated and blended with every other . . . as though a single instrument was being performed upon," said a critic. "The succeeding numbers were sung without accompaniment. The second, 'Alt niederdeutsches Lied,' by Heuberger, was written in modern style with harmonies of the advanced

Concert

Tendered by the

German Liederkranz and Arion

Singing Societies of New York

To the

President of the United States

And Mrs. Roosevelt

At the

White House, Washington, D. C.

February 24th, 1903

school of composition, many modulations and refreshing originality. The two songs by Kremser, in which he directed, were 'Niederlaendisches Volkslied' and 'Im Winter.' They were in folk song style, charmingly given and the programme concluded with Heuberger's 'Tirolis Nachtwache,' which according to President Roosevelt's request was sung a second time."[19]

Perhaps the Washington Saengerbund's president found the real key to the afternoon's success when he said, "The German lied—it has been our steady companion as we left our old home across the water and as the most beautiful gift in our possession, we have proffered it to this, the land of our choice." A large crowd accompanied the singers as they left.

> There was a long wait at the station and the Marine Band aroused the patriotic sensibilities of the guests and their entertainers alike by playing twice over the Austrian hymn and the "Star Spangled Banner" in which the voices of Americans and Viennese were blended with a bass accompaniment of engine snorts. . . . The Marine Band continued to keep the current of feeling warm with "Maryland, My Maryland," "Dixie," "Hail Columbia," "America," and "Yankee Doodle" . . . the visitors entered thoroughly into the spirit of Friedman's "Kaiser Friederich March," and "How Can I Bear to Leave Thee?"—a college song for us, but also a German folk song.[20]

As the train slowly pulled away, the American hosts ebulliently sang the tune in English while the visitors sang the same song in German. Thus the "lied"—the "song"—became a binding force between two cultures long after the train moved out of sight.

While America was just beginning to recognize the genre of serious chamber music in the concert halls, it still viewed with suspicion the esoteric music of the Baroque and Renaissance periods. French-born Arnold Dolmetsch was a pioneer in the revival of early instrumental music, a fine scholar who built and performed on the viol, lute, recorder, harpsichord, clavichord, and related instruments within his large collection. Dolmetsch wrote to the president in 1908 and on December 14 received the following reply from Roosevelt: "Indeed it would give Mrs. Roosevelt and myself great pleasure if you could come to the White House on Wednesday, at 2:30, and let us hear the clavichord. It is most kind of you to make the offer. I heard much of you thru Sir Harry Johnston, and of course entirely independently know about your work in introducing the harpsichord and clavichord, at least to the American world of music."[21] Apparently the president, although concerned with the pending election, enjoyed the music of this intimate little keyboard instrument "with the voice of a mosquito," as Dolmetsch once described it.[22] The instrument was brought to the White House

Opposite, three pages from the 8- × 9½-inch program for a concert presented by the German Liederkranz and Arion Singing Societies with Mme. Schumann-Heink at the White House. Images of President Theodore Roosevelt and Edith Kermit Roosevelt decorate the program.

for Roosevelt during the period when Dolmetsch made some of his finest clavichords under the aegis of Boston's Chickering and Sons.

Instrumental programs at the White House reached new heights during Roosevelt's administration. The celebrated Kneisel Quartet performed in the White House first on January 22, 1907, and later for Taft in 1911. Their program in 1907 opened with Haydn's four-movement Quartet in F Major, op. 41, no. 2, and included shorter works of Dvorak, Glazunoff, and Tchaikovsky. On April 25, 1904, the Arbós Quartet played Tchaikovsky's Quartet in D Major, op. 11, for His Imperial Highness Prince Lun of China and his large suite, who were given front seats on the left-hand side of the center aisle in the East Room. And when Alice Roosevelt, the president's daughter by his first marriage, celebrated her twenty-first birthday on February 12, 1906, a string quartet from the Boston Symphony Orchestra played Beethoven, Lalo, and J. S. Bach—a new name on White House programs. Only two weeks earlier twenty-one members from the six-year-old Philadelphia Symphony Orchestra, under the direction of Fritz Scheel, performed Richard Strauss's Serenade in E-flat Major, op. 7, as well as shorter works for various combinations of strings and winds. Even the new Washington Symphony Orchestra, conducted by Reginald de Koven, played in February 1903. But the largest musical ensemble to appear during this period was the forty-one member Marine Band Orchestra. Under the direction of William Santelmann, the orchestra played a full concert on the lawn for tea February 1, 1907, which included Humperdinck's *Hänsel und Gretel* Fantasia and two movements from Goltermann's Concerto in A Minor for cello. Santelmann, a Leipzig-trained violinist, had formed a symphony orchestra in Washington that presented an early performance of Rachmaninoff's Second Piano Concerto with Dutch pianist Martinus Sieveking.

The most distinctive program historically, however, was not an ensemble, but a solo recital. On January 15, 1904, twenty-eight-year-old cellist Pablo Casals shared a White House concert with Myron Whitney, Jr., a fine young baritone who traveled regularly with Nellie Melba and Lillian Nordica. Casals played a Boccherini sonata, Saint-Saëns's "Le Cygne," and "Spanish Dance" by the talented Czech cellist David Popper. Casals, who would later perform for John F. Kennedy, found President Roosevelt had an "infectious joviality. . . . He put his arm around my shoulder after the concert and led me around among the guests, introducing me to everyone and talking all the time. I felt that in a sense he personified the American nation, with all his energy, strength and confidence. It was not hard to picture him galloping on a horse or hunting big game, as he was so fond of doing."[23]

All of this music was undoubtedly heavy-going for some White House guests—a point made blatantly by one member of the audience:

Those invited are the Four Hundred of Washington and the personal and political friends of the President. Last year the president had some of his old hunter and trapper friends from Maine and the West at one of the musicales. One of these

Spanish cellist Pablo Casals, a few years after his performance for Theodore Roosevelt.

was Capt. Seth Bullock, a famous officer of Deadwood in the bad days of that town.

At the close of the music programme performed by well-known artists, someone asked Bullock how he liked the music. "It's most too far up the gulch for me," answered Bullock in true Western style. The President overheard the remark and was immensely tickled. "All I've been afraid of," said Mr. Roosevelt, "was that Bullock might draw his guns and begin shooting the fiddlers."[24]

If Captain Bullock was looking for music which was a bit more "down home," melodies that would perhaps speak more directly to the American people, he would find it on many other occasions in the White House. Irish, Welsh, and Dutch folksongs were programmed by various artists, but American music, both art and folk varieties, was especially popular. On January 8, 1904, two American-born artists, Metropolitan Opera singer David Bispham and pianist Katherine Heyman, performed. Bispham, an ardent exponent of American music, featured a group of songs by six living American composers: Henry Hadley, Edward MacDowell, Arthur Foote, George Chadwick, Max Bendix, and Hermann Wetzler. The noted baritone had visited the White House several times during Roosevelt's administration on public or private occasions, but his recital at the mansion was the crowning glory of his career:

> I was honored by being asked to give a program of American songs coupled with a group of ditties familiar to everybody. Accordingly I rendered Mendelssohn's "On Wings of Music [*sic*]," followed by my favorite Irish, Scotch, and English ballads, not forgetting North American Indian and Southern negro melodies.
>
> But the principal group, used as a climax to the occasion, included the work of six living American composers, which I was glad to present before the many foreign representatives present in their official and diplomatic capacity. Again I was asked, as in Albany, by my hostess not to include the harrowing "Danny Deever"; but it was demanded by the guests. Its conclusion brought the President upstanding to his feet, and with hands outstretched he came forward, saying, "By Jove, Mr. Bispham that was bully! With such a song as that you could lead a nation into battle!"[25]

Mrs. Roosevelt tried to keep the concert as American as possible. Shortly before Bispham's program Loeb wrote to Tiffany: "Referring to our telephone conversation of the other day, I beg to state that I have consulted Mrs. Roosevelt and she wishes you would confer with Bispham about . . . a strictly American evening."[26] But the evening did not turn out to be "strictly American." Among her other selections, twenty-six-year-old Californian Katherine Heyman played a flamboyant transcription of the "Liebestod" from Wagner's *Tristan und Isolde*. Mixing and melding, after all, was part of White House life—a way to relate to the heterogeneous guest lists of diplomats, poets, labor leaders, naturalists, or prize fighters under the Roosevelts. Did it really matter that Czech art songs and American ethnic ballads were on the same program? Not when such talented artists as Bohemian baritone Bogea Oumaroff and American soprano Mary Leech shared the stage for the opening musicale in February 1903. Oumaroff sang Dvorak's "Kduz mne siara matka" and Novak's "Slovenska pizen" while Leech rendered her own "Is dat you" and "Jus' a Little Nigger."

Incipient jazz styles had already come to the White House during the McKinleys, whose dance program of 1901 illustrated the close links among ragtime, two-step, and marching band styles. It is no surprise then that Scott Joplin's celebrated "Maple Leaf Rag" (1899) was first played at the White House by the Marine Band, which often seemed quite willing to experiment with new music. But there were times when some persuasion was in order, however. Alice Roosevelt had been pleading for new dance music at the Executive Mansion for quite awhile. On one occasion the engaging and impetuous "Princess Alice," as she was called, handed the genial bandmaster a "wallop that staggered his musical ideals," wrote the ever-observant bandsman and cartoonist, Ole May, in 1915.

> The band was playing for a diplomatic reception at the White House one evening about ten years ago, when Miss Roosevelt came up and said, "Oh, Mr. Santelmann, do play the 'Maple Leaf Rag' for me. . . . "The 'Maple Leaf Rag?' " he gasped in astonishment. "Indeed, Miss Roosevelt, I've never heard of such a composition, and I'm sure it is not in our library." "Now, now, Mr. Santelmann," laughed Alice, "don't tell me that. The band boys have played it for me time and again when Mr. Smith or Mr. Vanpoucke was conducting, and I'll wager they all know it without the music."[27]

They knew it all right—and Miss Roosevelt got her music. It has never left the Marine Band repertory.

Christmas in the White House was always a time when music was important. All five younger Roosevelt children—Ethel, Kermit, Theodore, Jr., Archibald, and Quentin—were present when Mrs. Roosevelt held her Christmas party on December 26, 1903. The Benjamin Harrisons often had Christmas parties for fifty to sixty children, but at the Roosevelt gala about 400 boys and girls between the ages of six and sixteen heard the Roney Boys Concert Company in the East Room and danced afterward to the music of the Marine Band. Mr. Roney's boys must have been amazingly versatile and talented, as well as adept at quick costume changes. They opened the program with a Pinsuti quartet dressed in military uniform, sang Christmas carols "in cotta and cossack," songs by Foster and Distin in college gowns, "Tenting Tonight on the Old Camp Ground" in patriotic costume, and concluded with Henry B. Roney's own "Merry Christmas" in Highland Scottish costumes. Mendelssohn's Violin Concerto in E Minor and Schubert's Serenade for violin, flute, and piano were also interposed within the program. Finally, "My Country Tis of Thee" was sung by the audience, standing, led by the boys with voices,

Exterior View.

Cartoonist/bandsman Ole May's interpretation of the crowded White House receptions under Theodore Roosevelt. Lower drawing shows both the "Marine Band" (right) and the "Sub Marine Band" (left) playing behind the president. To hurry the crowds through the receiving line, President Roosevelt asks to have leader Santelmannn "play 'Garry Owen' again and whoop 'er up." The song became identified with the U.S. Seventh Cavalry before the Civil War, and Roosevelt undoubtedly knew it from his days as commander of the Rough Riders during the Spanish-American War. *Pittsburgh Gazette Times*, January 2, 1908.

violins, flute, and organ chimes—ambitious fare for five boys from Chicago![28]

During the last years of this administration's distinguished and brilliant musical life, two dramatic events took place that brought the Roosevelt era to a close with a dash of creativity and charm. On April 23, 1907, the Indianist opera *Poia* by Arthur Nevin with libretto by Randolph Hartley was presented in an illustrated lecture at the piano. *Poia* reflected America's concern at the turn of the century for its native music. As Arthur Farwell claimed, America must "cease to see everything through German spectacles." Thus a number of Indianist composers, such as Nevin, Charles Wakefield Cadman, and Charles Skilton, were attracted to an indigenous cultural form out of which they believed a truly representative American music could be built. Ironically, Nevin, who had spent many months on a Montana reservation studying Indian music, was unable to secure a performance for his *Poia* in America; the opera was given its world premiere at the Berlin State Opera in 1910.[29] Three years earlier, however, *Poia* had been presented at the White House—and by the president himself, who arranged to give it publicity.

Theodore Roosevelt's concern for the welfare of the American Indian is well known. When the Indian Bureau in Washington was directed to destroy all things pertaining to the civilization of the Indian people, Roosevelt did everything he could to preserve Indian music and art. "It fits in with all my policies of conservation," he said. "I don't know anything about Indian music, but the translation of Indian song poems shows them to be of rare value." When the president learned that government agents were punishing Indians who talked or sang in their native tongue, he set about to have all such legislation revoked. He even arranged to have a Cheyenne victory song performed during a cabinet luncheon during which the Indian question was being discussed. "These songs," he said, "cast a wholly new light on the depth and dignity of Indian thought—the strange charm, the charm of a vanished elder world of Indian poetry."[30]

One can imagine how the president must have enjoyed *Poia*. Attractive programs had been printed for this event, complete with illustrations, a listing of the cast of eleven characters, and a detailed synopsis.[31] In the East Room Nevin described the opera and played portions on the piano. Walter McClintock, who had been to the West on a forestry expedition with Gifford Pinchot and had lived with the Blackfoot tribe, then spoke about the folklore and music that formed the motif for Nevin's opera. Assisting was an aide from the War Department Signal Corps Office, who had rigged up a large canvas at the north end of the East Room and "had successfully operated the stereopticon outfit by use of White House electricity which obviated some of the difficulties encountered heretofore in the use of gas."[32]

But the triumph of this era was the elegant enterprise held on the White House lawn not long before the presidency passed into the hands of William Howard Taft. There were no famous concert artists, no gilded state piano, and the quaint musical score arranged and conducted by W. H. Humiston is forgotten today. But the impact of the two children's musical plays produced in costume on October 16 and 17, 1908, remains a segment of history all its own. The *Post* considered the event "one of the most notable performances ever seen in Washington." About 4,000 people attended, having purchased tickets at $1 for adults and twenty-five cents for children beforehand to benefit the Washington Playgrounds Association. According to the *Star,* "The big throng included those who are, those who want to be and those who didn't care a fig, but just had the old one-dollar bill to enable them to edge inside the gates and put their complexions somewhere near the firing line with the elite. . . . They came in open carriages, closed carriages, broughams and buggies, in automobiles, in locomobiles, on legomobiles and some on mares' shanks. But every type of the curious and the ambitious sides of Washington life was on hand."[33]

Under the direction of the Ben Greet Players—a noted Shakespearean group with whom Dolmetsch had worked—two tales of Nathanial Hawthorne were presented, *Pandora and the Mischief Box* and *Midas and the Golden Touch.* Local children joined the professional players in these gentle and tender reminiscences of Olympian days, which employed singing, dancing, and processions. The *Star* noted something of the qualities of the old morality plays of Elizabethan days—something of the flavor of *Everyman* that the Ben Greet Players were the first to revive.

As for the musical score, we know only that it consisted of harps, flutes, and cymbals. The Marine Band, conducted by Santelmann, was divided into two sections—one as an ensemble furnishing music for the plays, the other as a band playing patriotic music before the performance, between the acts, and at the conclusion.[34] The stage was improvised, and there was no curtain. "From the rear," said the *Washington Herald,* "through the dense shrubbery, came the players, and when they made their exits they just vanished amid the foliage into the shade." The idyllic natural setting, cast amid the golden fall colors of the president's garden, impressed several reviewers. The *Herald* added that "we were returning to the ways of old, to the methods of the Greeks—and it seemed that in our modern theaters with their garish lights and tinsel scenery, we have not gained so much with the passage of the years."[35]

Many ambassadors and distinguished members of the embassies and legations were present in full uniform (with "blue and gold lace"), which heightened the "smartness" of the scene, said the press. Twelve boxes were provided with six green wicker chairs placed in each. The president and his party occupied the center box, which bore a handsome silk seal of the United States and two silk flags and was draped in green garland. As he returned to the White House after the program, President Roosevelt met a number of the boys who had taken part in the performance and were on their way back to their dressing room in the White House corridor. "They halted in single file, and as the President passed he grasped the hand of each, and said something that caused the blushes to appear beneath all the paint and powder."[36]

SYNOPSIS

of the

DIAN GRAND OPERA

POÏA

Described and Rendered by the Composer
MR. ARTHUR NEVIN

THE WHITE HOUSE
WASHINGTON

Tuesday, April Twenty-third
nineteen hundred and seven

Pages from program for Arthur Nevin's opera *Poïa*, presented at the White House, unstaged, with commentary in 1907.

What did he say? The assiduous showman probably just had a bit of his own drama to add to the festive scene.

The Theodore Roosevelts placed primary importance on the White House musicale, but the Tafts and Wilsons molded it into a well-established tradition. The William Howard Taft administration, from 1909 to 1913, began the concept of the "Lenten Musicale" series that continued throughout the Franklin Roosevelt years. These programs, from four to six in number, featured classical artists and were held between February and April of each year. They were usually preceded by small dinner parties with the Marine Orchestra or newly formed Marine String Quartet playing in the background. The Lenten Musicales were organized as a double bill. Mrs. Taft's first series held in 1910 illustrates the high quality of the artists, whose musical selections were generally stylistically compatible and tastefully juxtaposed:

Lenten Musicale Series for 1910

February 11   Olga Samaroff, pianist; F. ver Treese
               Pollack, tenor

February 21   Hess-Schroeder Quartet of the Boston Symphony
               Orchestra with Ernest Hutchinson, pianist

March 11   Carl Jörn, tenor; Yolanda Merö, pianist

April 15   Fritz Kreisler, violinist; Fannie Bloomfield
               Zeisler, pianist

Helen Taft was known to have selected most of the artists for her musicales. A fine amateur pianist, she had studied music as a young girl in Cincinnati and retained a fondness for music all her life. She was the founder and first president of the Cincinnati Symphony Orchestra, and soon after she moved to the White House, the Baldwin Piano Company of Cincinnati gave her a style B parlor grand in empire design with ivory finish. The piano was trimmed in gold to match the motifs in the Blue Room, called at this time Mrs. Taft's "Music Room." When illness restricted her social activities, the first lady found time to practice in this room, which occupied a special place in her life. Even the president had his own corner of the new music room. He installed one of the "finest of the enclosed-horn or concealed-horn types of phonographs, with a liberal library of those records of grand operatic selections of which the President is so fond," said the papers.[37]

As a pianist, Mrs. Taft seemed to favor for her musicales the top women pianists of the day. In reviewing the list of major pianists who performed in the White House during the Taft years, nine of the eleven were women. There were the fiery, independent Olga Samaroff (née

Olga Hickenlooper), who married Leopold Stokowski the year after her White House concert, and the twenty-three-year-old Hungarian-American Yolanda Merö, who played in the White House just four months after making her American debut in New York City. Fannie Bloomfield Zeisler was considered the most technically gifted woman pianist of her era with a staggering repertory. Others, important but less notable, were Augusta Cottlow, Estella Neuhaus, and Ellen Ballon. All came to the White House at a time when, according to Texas-born Olga Samaroff, "men pianists and women pianists were as rigorously separated in the managerial mind as the congregation of a Quaker meeting . . . and [women] received lower fees than a man with the same degree of success and reputation."[38]

The greatest pianist to appear at this time, however, was Josef Hofmann—a legendary figure and without a doubt one of the most remarkable talents in the annals of music. Hofmann represented the legacy of Busoni rather than of Paderewski: he fought the mannerisms of arch-Romanticism, perceived his music from a large-scale vantage point, and played with flawless elegance and purity. Born in Krakow on January 20, 1876, Hofmann made his spectacular American debut at age ten, electrifying his audiences with the Beethoven C Major Concerto at the packed Metropolitan Opera House. He toured all over the country and gave forty-two concerts until the Society for the Prevention of Cruelty to Children claimed his rare talents were being exploited.

At the turn of the century when pianists sported heads of hair á la Paderewski and Grainger, Hofmann wore his neatly cut. He was modern in appearance, short in stature, but a titan nevertheless. "His playing had a degree of spontaneity, of 'lift,' of dash, daring, and subtle rhythm that was unparalleled," said Harold Schonberg, a critic with the *New York Times*. "Nobody so made the piano sing."[39] On Friday, April 7, 1911, after an elegant state dinner, Hofmann played the following program for President and Mrs. Taft, the Netherlands minister and his wife, and about 400 guests. Gone now is the showy operatic paraphrase; preferred by Hofmann is a modern Russian group, which included Liadow's imaginative miniature, "Music Box" (Tabatière à musique), written in 1893 and Scriabin's "Poème," composed in either 1903 or 1905.[40]

While the Tafts focused upon piano music, they also selected vocal artists of renown and distinction. Baritone Alexander Heinemann and the great Johanna Gadski, leading dramatic soprano with the Metropolitan Opera, sang German lieder, and lyric soprano Frances Alda featured works of Debussy, Mussorgsky, Rachmaninoff, and Borodin on her program for the Tafts. Choirs, too, came to the White House: the Mormon Tabernacle Choir of 210 voices, as well as the New York Mozart Society that performed Ethelbert Nevin's popular "The Rosary" at Mrs. Taft's garden party on May 12, 1911. State dinners honoring foreign dignitaries often featured performers who reflected America's territorial expansion. William Taft, former governor of the Philippines, managed to transplant to the United States some

of the Philippine culture he loved when he invited the Philippine Constabulary Band to play at his inauguration on March 4, 1909. This colorful group from Manila also attracted attention when they entertained at the dinner for Japanese commissioners Wada and Sakai one month later at the White House. The following year a quartet of Hawaiians performed a series of "melodious and mysterious songs and renditions on stringed instruments" for His Imperial Highness, Prince Tsai Tao of China on April 28, 1910.[41]

When Steinway & Sons arranged the White House appearances of concert artists and singers, they usually paid their travel and other expenses, but the artists received no monetary remuneration for their performances. Appearing before the president was an honor and a highly sought-after experience—as it is today. Mrs. Hayes used to give women artists a bouquet of orchids from her conservatory. Theodore Roosevelt offered copies of his *Rough Riders* or an autographed photo in a silver frame. Mrs. Taft, however, initiated a gift of small gold medals for the artists, a custom the Woodrow Wilsons continued. On March 22, 1911, she purchased ten medals for $250 from Tiffany and Company in New York.[42] The medals measured 55 × 108 millimeters, bore the presidential seal on the front and a personalized inscription

Double bill at the White House under President William Howard Taft: Violinist Fritz Kreisler and pianist Fannie Bloomfield Zeisler.

on the back, and were decorated with a red, white, and blue ribbon. Their first presentation was made on March 24, 1911, when Alexander Heinemann and Lilla Ormond sang: "Prior to the reception of the guests for the Musicale, the President and Mrs. Taft entered the Red Room where the musical artists were presented to them by Major Butt. . . . As each artist was presented to Mrs. Taft, she had Major Butt present one of these decorations [medals] to each artist. It is a custom which she desires to be continued at The White House . . . at the special request of the President, Miss Ormond, after the classical numbers of the program, sang 'Home, Sweet Home,' 'Way Down upon the Swanee River' and 'Robin Adair.' "[43]

Does this last comment give us an idea of President Taft's tastes in music? Perhaps, but Ormond's encores seem somewhat sedate and old-fashioned compared with the new Tin Pan Alley songs coming from the president's graphanola at this time—Irving Berlin's "Alexander's Ragtime Band" (1911) and Lewis Muir's "Waitin' for the Robert E. Lee" (1912). Mrs. Taft bought all the latest records for the president, she said, to keep his mind off his troubles.[44] While the first lady avoided dancing because of her stroke, the president liked to dance and was known to have "waltzed most beautifully."[45]

The president also showed classical leanings, judging from his requests for encores during the musicales. He was fond of grand opera and once asked Fritz Kreisler to play the "Prize Song" from Wagner's *Die Meistersinger* after the famous violinist's concert at the White House on April 15, 1910. Without the score, Kreisler's accompanist could not play the piece. Some of the aides, however, rushed over to the house of Nicholas Longworth, violinist as well as congressman, who happened to have the score. Within eight minutes Kreisler was playing the elebrated "Prize Song" for Taft.[46] And why the "Prize Song" especially? Perhaps the president took a liking to it when Carl Jörn sang it in the East Room one month before. But it became a popular item at the White House. Tenor H. Evans Williams sang it on December 16, and violinist Efrem Zimbalist played it on April 12, 1912. Perhaps even pianists played it before Taft left the White House.

On January 14, 1910, President and Mrs. Taft heard John Mc-Cormack and Luisa Tetrazzini sing in Donizetti's *Daughter of the Regiment* at Washington's Belasco Theater. ("The only difference between us is that she is on one stage and I on another," said Taft.) But according to an aide, the president especially enjoyed Enrico Caruso whom he heard for the first time in Ponchielli's *La Gioconda* the following month in Baltimore. Taft often liked to unwind to Caruso's recording of *La bohème:*

> He went into his sitting room humming "Musetta's Waltz Song." . . . It was minutes after the President put the graphanola record on and the passionate voice of Enrico Caruso poured forth Rodolpho's "Che gelida manina, se la lasci riscaldar" that Maggie ventured a look. The door between the presidential bedroom and sitting room was wide open. Through it, she could see Taft overflowing in his favorite leather lounge chair. He was in her direct line of vision, and she in his. Fortunately, his eyes were closed. Enthralled with the music? Or asleep?
> Maggie didn't wait to find out.[47]

Performing artists were often prone to size up presidential tastes in music. One president, whom both David Bispham and Paderewski felt was especially musically inclined, was Woodrow Wilson. "President Wilson," said Bispham, "is devoted to music and something of a singer himself, with a tenor voice of considerable power and sweetness." Paderewski—who was so nervous when he played for President Wilson that he had to soak his hands in warm water beforehand—viewed the president as an "all-around, highly-educated man who recognized intellectually that music was a part of human progress . . . but he had little time for anything that was in the sphere of dreams."[48]

Woodrow Wilson's "sphere of dreams" had come earlier. Both he and his brother, Joseph, Jr., played the violin as boys, and Woodrow kept on playing, apparently casually, for many years as a young adult. Wilson sang tenor in the Princeton University Glee Club and later in

Woodrow Wilson with his first wife, Ellen Axson Wilson, and their daughters. Margaret Woodrow Wilson (left) sang several times in formal White House concerts.

the Johns Hopkins University Glee Club that he helped to organize. He also belonged to the College Chapel Choir and never really lost his interest in music. As president he had a way of thrilling his listeners by achieving and holding the high note at the end of "The Star-Spangled Banner" falsetto, à la John McCormack, some said. During the devastating years of World War I, Wilson was known to have asserted, "Music, now more than ever before, is a national need."[49]

President Wilson made music a vital part of White House life, but he entertained only during the first of his two terms in office. The presidential years from 1913 to 1921 were beset with problems— the illness and death of Wilson's first wife, Ellen Louise Axon, on August 6, 1914; the four grim years of the war that began the same year; and finally the stroke that incapacitated him for the last seventeen months of his presidency. But he was a dedicated leader who achieved unparalleled heights in domestic policy and who worked toward world peace.

Wilson's second wife, Edith Bolling Galt, whom the President married in a quiet ceremony at her home on December 18, 1915, was solace for the troubled leader. She was a handsome, strong-willed woman, and accomplished in the field of music, which she had studied at Martha Washington College. Margaret Wilson, another talented family member, was twenty-seven years old when her father became president and had studied singing at the Peabody Conservatory in Baltimore. She "sang with confidence," said a *New York Times* critic, but failed to attract the notices she had hoped for during the pursuit of her professional career. During the war she donated her services to the Red Cross and in 1915 made a recording of "The Star-Spangled Banner" for the benefit of the International Board of Relief. Her career ended shortly after the Armistice.[50]

First with her mother, Ellen, then later with Edith Wilson, Margaret arranged most of the White House musicales that were scheduled regularly until April 1916.[51] Thereafter formal programs appeared rarely until President Warren Harding took office on March 4, 1921. Probably because of her vocal interests, and perhaps her father's, Margaret planned a large percentage of programs that featured singers. Among these vocal luminaries, who usually shared their recital with an instrumentalist, were Alice Nielsen, Elena Kirmes, Louise Llewellyn (singing songs in Hungarian language and costume), Julia Culp, Louis Graveure, Vernon Stiles, Mary Jordan, and Ernestine Schumann-Heink. The latter artist was the only singer to present a recital (February 8, 1916) in which she alone was the soloist.

Margaret herself appeared in at least three formal musicales. Her recital on May 27, 1914, with harpist Melville Clark is especially interesting because an enlarged printed program, tied with red, white, and blue satin ribbons, included the texts of all the songs. A similar format had been followed for the Russian Cathedral Choir, which sang on February 28, 1914. In this case extensive program notes were included. Consisting of thirty-five men and boys from the St. Nicholas Cathedral in New York, the choir had been brought to Washington by Charles R. Crane, at one time nominated as ambassador to Russia. The music was described as "vocal without accompaniment and very remarkable in its Oriental character. . . . The musical genius of Russia has found fine interpreters on American soil . . . but hitherto there has been no opportunity to hear the Russian church music, with examples of the complete range of its historical development. . . . This concert—through the musical gems of Kastalsky, Arkhangelsky, Tchesnokoff, Lvorsky and others—will introduce to the hearers the very spirit and essence of Russian Church singing."[52] The concert was conducted by I. T. Gorokhoff, director of the Holy Synod Choir of Moscow.

On March 7, 1916, the distinguished Spanish composer Enrique Granados played a Scarlatti sonata and his own "Danza Valenciana," among other works, for the Wilsons. Granados had just enjoyed excellent success with the premiere in New York of his opera *Goyescas*, which was based upon the paintings of Goya. Two weeks after his White House appearance, he died at sea on his return voyage to Europe. And then there was Percy Grainger—that indefatigable, eccentric Australian! A health faddist with a wild thicket of wiry hair (bright orange in his youth), Grainger rarely wore an overcoat even in the most tempestuous weather. He played the piano with equal dash and vigor, and his

The celebrated Australian pianist and composer Percy Grainger played several of his own compositions for Woodrow Wilson and his family on March 28, 1916.

folksong interpretations displayed an effortless brilliance. Grainger's program rendered on the East Room gold piano March 28, 1916, featured three of his own compositions: "The Shepherd's Hey," "Colonial Song," and "March-Jig: Maguire's Kick." Concerning the middle selection Grainger stated in the printed program: "No traditional tunes of any kind are made use of in this piece, in which I have wished to express feelings aroused by the scenery of my native country Australia." But for all his popularity as a composer of "fripperies," as he called these charming little pieces, Grainger died a forgotten and isolated figure— an original musical spirit whose large-scale works have yet to be recognized.[53]

How many of these concerts did the president actually hear? Assuming he attended most of them as the gracious White House host the president must be, how many of them did he really enjoy? There must have been times when this music became a comforting sort of therapy—a calming way to forget, to capture, perhaps, that old "sphere of dreams," if only for a moment. Harpist Melville Clark recalled just this incident following the concert he shared with singer Margaret Wilson:

A velvety soft moonlit night, May 27, 1914, stands forth, cameo-like, among my otherwise nebulous recollections of 4,000 harp recitals I have given. . . .

The moonlight was so brilliant and all-pervading that night, out there on the portico at the rear of the White House, that I could distinctly see all the strings of my instrument. The historic pillars were sharply etched and wrapped in a phosphorescent glow; and from the shrubbery there peeped the secret service men—35 of them, I was later told—comprising the only audience for this extraordinary and, until now, unpublicized recital. . . .

Many who have thus far witnessed the motion picture, "Wilson," probably were surprised at scenes suggesting his fondness and his talent for singing, but I have known all these years that Woodrow Wilson had a remarkably fine light lyric tenor voice.

Yet, when I went to the White House for the concert that night, I little dreamed of the thrill that was in store for me. The storm clouds of World War I were gathering over Europe and the President had found it expedient to divide the annual diplomatic dinner into two parts. The first was for the Allied Nations, diplomats and their attaches, and the entertainment was featured by the playing of Paderewski.

The second diplomatic dinner, at which I had been invited to play the harp, was for representatives of the Central Powers— Germany, Austria, Turkey, and Bulgaria.

When the last distinguished guest had departed, the President asked me to take the harp and go with him to the rear portico of the White House. It afterward became plain that he was gravely worried over the possibilities of war between the United States and the countries of the diplomats he had just entertained; and sought to relieve the tension by singing.

I was counting it a great privilege, as well as a pleasure, to be able to give the President a lift at a time when he was burdened perhaps with the melancholy thought that his guests, that evening, might soon be his mortal enemies. But I assumed he wished merely to sit a while in the soft Maytime air and listen to the harp.

He asked me if I could play "Drink to Me Only with Thine Eyes," and I bent eagerly over the harp and began softly the familiar melody. Then I was surprised, most pleasantly, when the President began to sing the song in a clear, lyric tenor voice.

He suggested one song after another—Scotch and Irish songs, and those of Stephen Foster. He sang easily and with faultless diction, and it was nearly midnight when he stood up. And now, it pleased me to note, he was amazingly buoyant, relaxed, and unworried.[54]

But there was yet another White House "performer" that possessed an uncanny ability to distract and to sooth—the Victrola! Edith Wilson tells in her *Memoir* how the electric piano was turned on when she and the president were too tired to work: "We sat in the firelight and listened to some of the music from operas."[55] But for pure delight there was nothing like the Victrola. "Frequently at night we would go to the Oval Room upstairs after dinner," she wrote, "and he [the President] would put a record on the Victrola and say: 'Now, I'll show you how to do a jig step.' He was light on his feet and often said he envied Primrose the minstrel dancer and wished he could exchange jobs."[56]

CHAPTER 9

WHITE HOUSE JESTERS —MAKING THE PRESIDENTS LAUGH

Harding, Coolidge, Hoover

Saloon, saloon, saloon . . . it runs through my brain like a tune.
I don't like cafe, and I hate cabaret
But just mention saloon and my cares fade away
For it brings back a fond recollection of a little old low-
  ceiling room, with a bar and a rail
And a dime and a pail: saloon, saloon, saloon.

Ernest R. Ball, 1921

"Let the rest of them appeal to the finer, nobler things of life," said vaudeville's Irene Ricardo. "If I can keep my audience laughing, either with me or at me, I am satisfied." Ricardo, a comedian from the Earl Carroll Vanities, entertained President and Mrs. Calvin Coolidge with her act "Whoa, Pagliacci" at Keith's Theater on April 9, 1925. Watching "Silent Cal" throw back his head and laugh out loud must have brought the comedian pleasure indeed. For President Coolidge was better known for his quiet, remote ways and for his frugality in verbal, as well as political, matters. Seated in the same flag-draped box that was formerly used by Woodrow Wilson, the Coolidges enjoyed the various acts, which were part of the national vaudeville artists' annual celebration to benefit the sick and insurance fund. Along with Ricardo, who managed to "out-Brice Fannie Brice," according to the *Post* of April 25, 1925, the program featured lightweight champion Benny Leonard; the Royal Siamese Entertainers—dancers, musicians, and crack takrow players by permission of the Siamese government; Jim McWilliams, "the pianutist"; and the Brazilian wonder, Miacahua, the only woman in the world who walked on wire without the aid of a pole or umbrella. The Coolidges "applauded every act and did not leave until the moving picture ending the bill had been nearly completed," said the *New York Times* the next day.

The Keith Theater extravaganza was the first vaudeville Coolidge had attended since he had become president on August 23, 1923, after the sudden death of Warren Harding. But he enjoyed other theatrical events before leaving the presidency in March 1929. Some of these concerned the opening of theaters in Washington and New York. On April 13, 1923, for example, the president opened the new Guild Theater on West 52nd Street by giving a signal that raised the curtain on George Bernard Shaw's *Caesar and Cleopatra.* He accomplished this novel technological feat from the White House by pushing a button that, over a specially leased wire, rang a bell on the stage of the Guild Theater in New York City.

One of the most spectacular theater openings of the 1920s, however, was that of the Fox in Washington on September 19, 1927. Besides richly gowned and bejeweled society women and prominent theatrical producers, President and Mrs. Coolidge were there, accompanied by various diplomats and members of Congress and the cabinet, including Secretary of Commerce Herbert Hoover. As the soft lights began to dim slowly, the organ sank into its pit allowing the fifty-piece concert orchestra to rise up and take its place. Victor Herbert's "American Fantasy" was played, and on the stage was a replica of old Fort McHenry with the bay in the foreground, the inspiration for "The Star-Spangled Banner." The elaborate stage presentation ended with "Gamby" and her ballet pirouetting to the strains of "Glow Worm" while hundreds of fireflies flashed brilliantly. Even with this effulgent grand finale, the motion picture *Paid to Love* starring George O'Brian and Virginia Valli captured the evening's limelight, and President and Mrs. Coolidge remained until the final curtain closed on the new Fox Theater's gala christening.[1]

America in the 1920s saw many of these stage show/motion picture combos. They seemed to keep alive the dying vaudeville art, which tottered precariously when standing alone as a straight show. By the mid-1920s vaudeville's original vitality was waning drastically in the face of competition from radio, movies, and electrical recordings, as well as from musical comedy. And Movietones, raged James Caesar Petrillo, president of the Chicago Federation of Musicians, threatened to put most of the nation's musicians out of employment.[2] Music was rapidly becoming an industry.[3] Technology dispersed popular musical forms to an eager public, which could never have been reached otherwise. The Original Dixieland Jazz Band made the first jazz recordings in 1917, linking this important art form and the nation as a whole. In 1921 radio station KDKA began the first regular broadcasting service, and by 1925 radio's plugging of new songs brought millions to the music counters.[4] *The Jazz Singer* of 1927 starring Al Jolson was released as the first talking motion picture in which the sound track was on the film itself.

If the 1920s came in roaring "Yes, We Have No Bananas" from the seat of its madcap motor car, it left whimpering "Brother, Can You Spare a Dime?" in the throes of the Great Depression. The noisy, hot jazz of this decade seemed a musical counterpart to F. Scott Fitzgerald's dazzling lifestyle. But like no other decade, the 1920s could laugh—at least until late 1929.

Warren G. Harding took office on March 4, 1921, and served as president until his death in August 1923. Harding greatly enjoyed vaudeville, musical comedy, and especially the buoyant, brassy sounds of the concert band. As a student at Ohio Central College he played in the Iberia Brass Band. Later in Marion, Ohio, he admitted playing every instrument but the trombone and the E-flat cornet. He even won the third prize of $200 while playing in an important band competition in Findlay. He also organized the Citizens' Cornet Band of Marion, which played for both Democratic and Republican rallies. He once joined the Huber Band, playing tenor horn, B-flat cornet, or the huge helicon bass that encircled his head and sturdy shoulder like a life-preserver. Harding's love for bands did not end when he became president; he was known to have picked up an instrument occasionally and joined the Marine Band during its rehearsals at the White House.[5]

President Harding was also an avid fan of singer George O'Connor. But this was nothing new for a president. O'Connor entertained every chief executive from Cleveland to FDR. Called the "White House Jester," the red-faced, chunky little man had sung his way into the hearts of the administrations to such an extent that mail was addressed to him at the Executive Mansion. Between 1914 and 1918 he had recorded many of his most popular songs for Columbia Records, two of these at the insistence of Margaret Wilson, who enjoyed hearing the blue-eyed bard at the White House. Some of his renditions even appeared on the opposite side of recordings by Al Jolson, another blackfaced minstrel singer and native Washingtonian.

O'Connor was a prominent lawyer and president of the District Title Insurance Company. But with his rare talent and generous spirit he managed to keep alive an outmoded art form until he died on September 28, 1946, at the age of seventy-two. His minstrel pieces, ragtime melodies, and dialect songs "brought tears of laughter even to the faces of men so dignified they could be suspected of wearing their silk hats under the shower bath," said the press.[6] "President Coolidge laughed so hard one night that he followed it up with an after-dinner speech that would have made Chauncey Depew envious. Those who heard it say it was the best after-dinner speech ever delivered in Washington; and it was a song by George O'Connor, accompanied by Matt Horne, which hit the President just right and caused him to lean back and laugh very, very loud. This may change the viewpoint that Mr. Coolidge was lacking in humor."[7] The song that drew such attention was O'Connor's rendition of "Gasoline Gus in His Jitney Bus"—a ditty that celebrated the birth of the taxicab in 1915 and its ride for a nickel or a "jitney."

The president's troubadour derived most of his fame from entertaining for Washington banquets and parties such as the Gridiron Club, Alfalfa Club, Knights of Columbus, and White House Correspondents' functions. At these dinners, the chief executive could relax and enjoy himself. White House aide Archie Butt tells the story of

Warren Harding playing the sousaphone with members of the town band, Marion, Ohio.

President Taft who had spent the entire day listening to "brain-killing banalities" in his office. When O'Connor sang "My Cousin Caruso" and "A Warbling Rose" at a Gridiron dinner, the whole room began to shake and President Taft's smile became an "audible and vibrating laugh."[8] O'Connor tells a little tale of his own regarding Taft, who was certain he would be defeated in the November 1912 election.

> "George," he said, "I'm on good terms with the people who make Victrolas and Victor records, because I've installed a 'Victrola corner' here in the White House, and they've given it wide publicity. So I want you to go down to Camden and make two Victor records specially for me. They'll be glad to record them when you tell them they're for President Taft."
> "What are the songs, Mr. President?" I asked, and Taft's fat sides shook as if he would explode when he said:
> "They're two of your favorite coon songs. One is 'Tain' No Disgrace to Run When You're Skeered' and the other is 'If He Comes In, I'm Going' Out!' "[9]

So he went out—and Wilson came in.

Both Presidents Wilson and Harding were especially fond of "My Cousin Caruso," an Italian dialect song written by Gus Edwards and Ed Madden in 1909 through which the "Ridi, Pagliaccio" theme from Leoncavallo's opera had been cleverly woven. But Coolidge preferred a 1916 Irving Berlin hit that O'Connor often featured called "Cohen Owes Me 97 Dollars." The song told of an aged Jewish merchant instructing his son to collect from all their creditors so that the old gentleman could "die mit a smile upon my face." After the money was collected, papa got well because "when business is so good, it's no time for a business man to die." O'Connor thought that Coolidge's fondness for this song had to do with his New England appreciation of thrift and frugality.

Many who knew Herbert Hoover as president felt that his sense of humor was subjugated to the concerns of the Great Depression. He rarely took part in social functions outside the White House. On March 8, 1930, however, he was to have been guest of honor at the White House Correspondents' Dinner, but he had to cancel at the last minute because of the death of former President Taft. The program called "Hovering with Hoover, or Life under the Handout System," featured George O'Connor, Jane and Ginger Rogers, opera star James Melton, and other luminaries from radio and film. Also on the program were comedians Amos and Andy, who had visited the president at the White House earlier that day.[10]

In the O'Connor Archives are several notes to the singer from President Franklin Roosevelt: "Dear George, Like special vintage wine, you improve with age. More years to you! FDR" and "Dear George, At the next dinner [White House Correspondents] will you sing Father O'Flynn?" O'Connor, a devout Roman Catholic, obliged, and FDR in his rich baritone voice joined in the chorus of this spoof on the Irish clergy. But FDR's favorite was *not* "Home on the Range," as so often claimed ("George, if you ever sound off on that blankety-blanked piece, I'll kill you!"). Rather it was "Saloon," written in 1921 by Ernest R. Ball (under the name Roland E. Llab), and an O'Connor staple. Composer of such genteel parlor numbers as "Mother Machree" and "When Irish Eyes Are Smiling," Ernest Ball, in "Saloon," praises the glories of the old-fashioned bar that was supposed to have been killed by prohibition. The song was the joy of FDR, who had advocated prohibition repeal in his 1932 campaign, and also the hit of Coolidge and Hoover, who may have viewed its haunting tune as both an elegy of days gone by and a prayer for their return. Its lyrics by George Whiting run:

> Saloon, saloon, saloon . . . it runs through my brain like a tune.
> I don't like cafe, and I hate cabaret
> But just mention saloon and my cares fade away
> For it brings back a fond recollection of a little old low-
>   ceiling room, with a bar and a rail
> And a dime and a pail; saloon, saloon, saloon.[11]

Tin Pan Alley and the American musical theater were in a great state of verve and vitality in the period between the two world wars, and the Coolidges' interest in this dynamic sphere of entertainment was reflected in the White House guest lists of this period. Glamorous Ziegfeld soprano Mary Lewis visited the Coolidges from time to time and informally sang show tunes for them. Lewis was a beautiful star

Grace and Calvin Coolidge and various Hollywood stars at the White House in 1924. Immediately to the right of the president is Al Jolson.

of the roaring 1920s who catapulted to fame only to fall by the wayside after a brief career at the Metropolitan Opera and in movies.

In 1924 Coolidge invited legendary showman Al Jolson to help him launch his election campaign at a White House pancake breakfast. A group of forty stage stars, including Jolson, John Drew, the Dolly Sisters, Hal Ford, Raymond Hitchcock, Charlotte Greenwood, and Ray Miller's Jazz Band, staged impromptu entertainment in the rear grounds. In his characteristic style, Jolson told a few "presidential jokes" before singing his "Keep Cool with Coolidge." Mrs. Coolidge also joined in the singing. "Some note!" Jolson exclaimed approvingly as the first lady's clear soprano voice caught his attention. "Let's have it again!" And the song was sung half a dozen times more. Though the lyrics were notoriously bad, the president was delighted, and Jolson was successful in his threat to make the president "laugh out loud."[12]

Jolson later sang for FDR and Harry Truman, but the first president to invite him to the White House was Woodrow Wilson. "I've heard some of your records and I've read all about your great success on Broadway," said Wilson, "but haven't been able to see you perform." For the great Jolson this was the perfect cue. "Wait a minute—you ain't heard nothin' yet." And he sang "You Made Me Love You." The president smiled—and continued eating his breakfast.[13]

The famous songwriter, producer, and actor George M. Cohan first visited the White House on July 29, 1931, to present President Hoover with the premiere copy of his "Father of the Land We Love." He wrote the song for the George Washington Bicentennial Commission, and according to Sol Bloom, associate director of the commission, the song was predicted to achieve even greater success than Cohan's enduring "Over There," written shortly after the United States entered World War I. Although the piece had been copyrighted, no copies were ever sold, and the famous song and dance man's contribution to the George Washington celebration never reached the popularity expected.[14]

The 1920s was also a dancing decade. The fox trot and its many derivatives were replacing the two-step and cakewalk, and the new Latin beat gave rise to such innovative steps as the tango, rumba, and Charleston. The older waltz was quite passé, but the ubiquitous "Blue Danube" was played by the Marine Band for White House dances well into the century. Usually it was the final dance of the evening as it was on January 3, 1902, when Alice Roosevelt made her debut. Almost twenty years later President Harding continued to enjoy the great Strauss favorite—especially at Mrs. Harding's garden party on June 1, 1921, when not the Marines but the two-year-old Navy Yard Band played it: "When the Marine Band brought its concert to a close just at 7 P.M., President and Mrs. Harding returned to the White House where they joined the dancers in the East Room for the last number—

George M. Cohan, with Sol Bloom (right), presents his song "Father of the Land We Love" to President Herbert Hoover.

Jazz Band from the U.S. Navy Yard Band, founded in 1919, played for President Warren Harding's garden party in 1921.

not the jazz of the earlier hours—but the "Blue Danube" played by the Navy Yard Band which the President was unable to resist."[15]

The next day, however, the *Times* scoffed at "certain critics who would feel that it is not quite in accord with his high office for a President of the United States to waltz with other dancers in the East Room of the White House. . . . After all," the *Times* added, "it is well that we have a President who knows that his dignity does not require the constant maintenance of solemnity and a long face, and President Harding has been wise so soon to impress upon the whole country, as he has, that he is distinctly 'human' and not afraid of showing it." President Harding's "long face" would come later with the scandals that closed his last days as chief executive. But his terpsichorean pleasures fared at least better with the press than Benjamin Harrison's fondness for the German Dance—a "depraved" waltz where the "hugging process is the chief ingredient."

"Doesn't Herbert Hoover ever play?" was a common question around the Republican presidential nominee's personal headquarters in 1928. "His only hobby is having no hobbies," observed the press. Hoover, in truth, was an avid reader, but did not especially enjoy outdoor sports, playing cards, listening to music, or dancing. In illustration of the last point, a prominent Washington woman told the following story concerning an evening of music after dinner at the White House. The lady had been seated between the Reverend John J. Burke, head of the National Catholic Welfare Council, and Herbert Hoover, then secretary of commerce: " 'I cannot dance because of my cloth,' Father Burke told her when he noticed that the first number

was listed as a waltz. 'I shall have to leave the pleasure to Mr. Hoover.'
'I cannot dance because of both my faith and my ignorance,' responded
Hoover."[16]

But the age that could laugh and kick up its heels also saw major
new developments in the sphere of serious composition and performance.
Between the end of World War I and the economic collapse of 1929,
youthful American symphonic composers moved ahead with the dynamic progressive currents, while older composers were gaining reputation as inheritors of the American cultivated tradition. Contemporary
American music became an "organized movement," according to Aaron
Copland, and several societies were founded to give concerts of new
music, such as the League of Composers and the International Composers' Guild. It was a prosperous era and a time when the American
people were growing increasingly aware of the potential of their own
musical life. "Music is the art directly representative of democracy,"
wrote President Coolidge in a lengthy article for *The Musician* in
September 1923. "If the best music is brought to the people, there
need be no fear about their ability to appreciate it." Each administration
of the decade—Harding, Coolidge, and Hoover—showed a special
concern for the arts and a deepened interest in support, patronage,
and responsibility within the field of music.

A striking manifestation of the president's links with his people
through music was the great "human wheel" formed by 50,000 school-
children for the most impressive community sing the nation had ever
known. The event could be considered a culmination of the old presidential serenade tradition of the previous century where music became
an effective form of communication to convince, protest, or honor.
On June 3, 1921, at the Ellipse, a grand, gala tribute was sung to
President Warren Harding for his support of National Music Week.
Through an aisle lined with high-school cadets, the President and
Mrs. Harding walked to the hub of the "wheel" where a great eight-
foot floral lyre marked the throne of the Goddess of Music. There
they waved greetings not only to the massive body of children but
also to the thousands of parents, dignitaries, and other onlookers who
lined the rim of the Ellipse. Five bands, including the Marine Band,
played while the children sang "America," "The Star-Spangled Banner,"
and other patriotic songs under the direction of Robert Lawrence. The
conductor must have had a major task just starting the singing, let
alone keeping the young voices from straying into polytonal complexities. Scattered throughout the vast assembly, however, were separate cornetists who provided assistance by giving the signals upon
cue from the central stand.

Visibly moved by the tribute, the president stepped to the edge
of the platform and addressed the children: "I may say that in the
closing of Music Week you and your associates have brought to me
the most remarkable climax I have ever known in music. I have heard
the croon of the young mother to her hopeful in the cradle, the great

choruses with their trained voices, the great bands and orchestras, but I have never heard such music as from the sparkling voices of the children of the capital city. It is the supreme music of all my life."[17]

Between Taft and Hoover, the ceremonial status of "Hail to the Chief" suffered minor setbacks but "The Star-Spangled Banner" scored a plus. Like Grover Cleveland, who would become almost profane when he heard the presidential march, Taft had grown so tired of it he placed a ban on it for the duration of his term. Back it came with the Wilsons—but out it went with the Coolidges, who ordered the Marine Band to avoid all patriotic tunes when foreign guests were present. It was too much of a nuisance to be saluting and standing at attention all the time, the president claimed. Hoover felt differently. Not only was the age-old president's march restored, but on March 8, 1929, a joint resolution of Congress approved "The Star-Spangled Banner" as the "National Anthem of the United States of America."[18] Even this famous tune, so beloved to countless Americans, met with opposition. Some citizens thought it "unfit for children to sing," or "too warlike," or "not American enough in its origins from an old English drinking song," or just "not a very good tune." John Philip Sousa's "Stars and Stripes Forever" was suggested as a better choice. One man wrote an entire book entitled *The U.S. National Anthem: Its Problems and Solutions*, published it himself, and sent it to the president. His solution? His own composition. But on March 3, 1931, President Hoover signed the act making the "Banner" America's official anthem. And thus it has remained, despite the fact that millions have to struggle with the melody's wide range.

Each of the first ladies of this period was important in fostering and sustaining the nation's cultural life, and the unusually high quality of programs in the White House during this decade can be attributed mainly to their efforts. Of the three, Florence Kling Harding was the only professionally oriented musician, having studied at the Cincinnati Conservatory of Music. Her music sustained her, both emotionally and economically, through the difficult years prior to her divorce from Henry De Wolfe in 1886; she gave piano lessons to the neighborhood children and especially enjoyed playing Chopin for pleasure. She was known to have practiced an hour daily while in the White House. Shortly after moving to the mansion, a mahogany Baldwin grand piano was shipped to her and appears in photographs of the second-floor oval room of this time.[19]

Florence Harding's support of the young pianist is reflected in eleven-year-old Shura Cherkassy's White House recital on May 17, 1923. The young Russian-born prodigy was a student of his mother, a protege of Sergei Rachmaninoff. Mrs. Harding was deeply impressed with the child's playing. Judging from his Washington recital at the time, her opinions were justified. The ambitious program included major works of Handel, J. S. Bach, Beethoven-Busoni, von Weber, Mendelssohn, Chopin, Grieg, Scriabin, Rachmaninoff, and the dazzling Strauss-Schutt "Fledermaus" paraphrase as a rousing finale.[20]

Grace Coolidge came from a background that fostered the love of music through what she called the "family orchestra." As first lady she attended concerts in Washington frequently and once evoked a comment from the president, "I don't see why you have to go out to get your music. There are four pianos in the White House."[21] Mrs. Coolidge was honorary chair of the World Fellowship through Music Convention, which featured the first Washington performance of J. S. Bach's B-Minor Mass on April 16, 1925. The 250-voice Bach Choir of Bethlehem, Pennsylvania, as well as a section of sixteen Moravian trumpeters, performed with the Philadelphia Orchestra, and Mrs. Coolidge later received the choir at the White House.[22] She also attended the Washington Opera Company and supported the National Symphony and the New York Philharmonic of which the president was an honorary associate member. On April 6, 1925, Mrs. Coolidge brought to the White House the noted Dutch conductor Elizabeth Kuyper who came to the United States to found the Professional Woman's Symphony Orchestra of America. Mme. Kuyper was also the first woman to win the coveted Mendelssohn Prize for composition.

"A Lady in every sense of the word, Lou Henry Hoover was equally at home with royalty as with the little Girl Scouts camping out under the tall redwoods," recounts Helen White, the substitute secretary at the White House during the summer of 1930.[23] Mrs. Hoover, who served as national president of the Girl Scouts, believed thoroughly in the value of teaching young people group singing. At Christmas time she usually led a group of caroling Scouts carrying lighted candles through the darkened halls of the White House, and each Easter Monday they presented a program of national and international dances on the south grounds. Lou Hoover's interest in our nation's musical heritage also led her to furnish the White House with a pianoforte made by Astor and Company of London between 1799 and 1815. Realizing the little square resembled an Astor of the same period that James Monroe purchased while minister to England, she borrowed the instrument from the Smithsonian and placed it in what she called her "Monroe Room" (today's Treaty Room). Thus, the White House captured a charming segment of its early musical ambience—if only for a few years.[24]

The most interesting musical side of Mrs. Hoover, however, was recognized shortly after she and the president left the White House and resided at Stanford in California. Mrs. Hoover was a good friend of the noted arts patron Elizabeth Sprague Coolidge, who came for lunch from time to time at the White House.[25] On August 10, 1937, Lou Hoover invited a few interested friends to meet Mrs. Coolidge and consider her offer to share expenses to begin a series of chamber music programs at Stanford University. Thus, the Friends of Music was born with the Roth Quartet providing the first concerts during the summer of 1938. Mrs. Hoover assisted with the wording and layout of the society's constitution and also served as its first chair, underwriting many of the programs herself. Famous musicians who were brought to Stanford by the Friends of Music included Nicholas Goldschmidt, the Pro Arte Quartet, Darius Milhaud, Bela Bartok, Alice

Square pianoforte made by Astor and Company, London, 1799–1815. In 1932 Lou Henry Hoover borrowed the instrument for the White House from the Smithsonian Institution.

Ehlers, William Primrose, the London String Quartet, and Ralph Kirkpatrick. The former first lady took a continuing interest in the organization until her death in January 1944, and her influence upon the development of music at Stanford and within the community as a whole was felt for many years thereafter.[26]

During the 1920s the garden parties, musicales, state dinners, and other social functions at the White House, which had been discontinued when the United States entered World War I, were revived. The season of 1921–22 lists four state dinners and five receptions, and the Easter egg-rolling and outdoor Marine Band concerts were also resumed. The next season was very quiet due to Mrs. Harding's illness, and in the summer of 1923 President Harding died of a heart attack. The Coolidges retained an entertainment plan similar to the Hardings' first year in office, but when the Hoovers took charge of the White House in 1929, they did away with the public band concerts and the old New Year's receptions, by now an assembly line of thousands. The population was growing too large, and there now were other ways for the public to see and hear the president—radio and motion picture. The social life of the Hoovers was remarkably elegant, despite the nation's suffering from a steadily worsening economic depression, but the Hoovers paid for their own small staff and used their own private funds for White House entertaining.

The entire period from Taft through Hoover can well be considered the "Golden Age" of the White House musicale. It was a time when the quality of artists and coordination of programming were finely tuned, and the seasons always had a classical aura about them. During the 1920s the White House became established as a performing arts center with the world's finest artists in a highly honored spotlight. Missing from these programs, however, were the newest currents of the 1920s and early 1930s—the music of Varese, Cowell, Ives, and Stravinsky. Not even the new jazz-oriented sounds of Gershwin, Copland, or Berlin appear on the printed programs of this period. The selections artists chose to perform for the president often had an encore flavor, drawn from the more traditional, shorter nineteenth-century repertories.

But there were some notable exceptions. On March 22, 1928, the Pro Arte Quartet, famous for its promotion of modern music in both Europe and America, played Claude Debussy's String Quartet in G Minor, Op. 10 (1893). The four-movement work followed a performance of "Two Indiscretions" composed and dedicated to the Pro Arte in 1922 by Louis Gruenberg the year before he organized the League of Composers. Gruenberg was one of the earliest American composers to incorporate jazz rhythms in large symphonic works. And for Mrs. Coolidge's second Lenten Musicale on March 17, 1924, the eminent harpist and composer Carlos Salzedo played works by Pierné, Debussy, and his own intricate "Whirlwind," as well as some dances of Couperin and Rameau. With Edgard Varese, Salzedo founded the International Composers' Guild in New York, which introduced many important contemporary works to American audiences.

The Coolidges continued the tradition of Lenten musicales begun during the Taft administration. There were two to four of these programs, and, in addition, a musicale after each of the state dinners: cabinet, diplomatic, Supreme Court, and Speaker's. The Lenten musicales were usually held on Monday afternoons and were followed by tea, with the audience numbering from 300 to 400. Mrs. Coolidge generally received guests in the Green Room, and the recitals were held in the East Room. The invitations, sent out in Mrs. Coolidge's name, reflected the personal rather than official character of these programs. During the month of March 1924, Sergei Rachmaninoff, Salzedo, Greta Torpadie, Marguerite D'Alvarez, John Barclay, John Charles Thomas, and the twenty-year-old violinist Erica Morini all appeared on the Lenten musicale series.[27]

Sergei Rachmaninoff played in the White House three times during the Coolidge administration, enough to make the papers comment that he had become a "White House tradition." Besides his 1924 program he played on January 16, 1925, and again on March 30, 1927. His programs, in general, focused on the shorter classic and Romantic repertory, rather than the big works for which he was famous, such as Schumann's *Carnaval* or Liszt's Sonata in B Minor. True to his style, however, a Chopin group appeared on all three White House concerts. And like other virtuosos of the Romantic tradition, he liked to conclude his programs with Liszt's Hungarian Rhapsody no. 2. This he did on March 10, 1924, adding a special flourish with his own cadenza. Also on this program was his own Prelude in C-sharp Minor which, Harold Schonberg said, "followed him around wherever he went. . . . Just as Hofmann was the great colorist," Schonberg added,

Sergei Rachmaninoff, the great Russian pianist and composer, and the first of three programs Rachmaninoff played in the White House during the Coolidge administration (original measurement: 4 × 6 inches).

Mr. SERGEI RACHMANINOFF

PROGRAM

Rondo Capriccioso . . . . *Mendelssohn*

(*a*) Nocturne
(*b*) Valse } . . . . *Chopin*
(*c*) Scherzo

(*a*) Prelude in C sharp minor . . . *Rachmaninoff*
(*b*) Minuet . . . . *Bizet-Rachmaninoff*
(*c*) Hopak . . . . *Moussorgsky-Rachmaninoff*

(*a*) Liebestraum . . . . *Liszt*
(*b*) Rhapsodie No. 2.
(Cadenza by Rachmaninoff) . . *Liszt*

Monday, March 10, 1924
THE WHITE HOUSE

"so Rachmaninoff was the great pianistic builder of his day ... his marvelous, infallible hands created bronzlike sonorities ... with a musical elegance in which phrases were shaped with exquisite finish."[28]

Rachmaninoff took America by storm and rapidly became a legend. He did not like touring, however, and commented in a letter to Somov on January 15, 1925, "Now I sit in Washington. My concert here was yesterday, and if I sit one more day, it's only because I am to play for the President at the White House. And then begins the *Perpetuum mobile* until April 1st."[29] In 1909 Rachmaninoff wrote about America, "You know, in this accursed country, you're surrounded by nothing but Americans and the 'business, business,' they are forever doing, clutching you from all sides."[30] Twenty years later, his opinions were considerably mollified: "I have had ample opportunity of convincing myself of the great progress made by American audiences both in their power of assimilation and in their musical taste. ... They have used every means in their power and have not spared any money in their effort to surpass Europe in this respect. They have succeeded. No man will dare to dispute the fact."[31] For certain the dour, unsmiling genius succeeded in captivating the friendship and respect of Mrs. Coolidge, who commented, "Dr. Rachmaninoff came and played again for me a week ago. I had about three hundred in for the music and tea. As Mrs. (Adolphus) Andrews, wife of the Captain of the *Mayflower* says, 'He looks like a convict and plays like an angel.' " Then the first lady added, "I do hear lots of wonderful music."[32] How right she was!

But there were fine artists who never made it to the White House—Paul Robeson, for example. President Coolidge felt that an appearance by the great black American bass might offend the southerners and turned down Robeson's offer to sing. Many others were invited, however, including singers Richard Crooks, Maria Jeritza, and John McCormack; the Flonzaley String Quartet; and pianist Myra Hess and violinist Joseph Szigeti. Hess and Szigeti formed a sensational double billing when they played after the Supreme Court dinner for Chief Justice Taft and other guests on January 26, 1928. Interestingly, Dame Hess's selections—Brahms waltzes, Chopin etudes, and pieces by Albeniz and De Falla—reflected her earlier programming tendencies. By the late 1920s the great English pianist preferred Beethoven, Schumann, and the sonatas of Schubert and Brahms—the "roast beef" as she said, rather than merely the "shrimp cocktail." Like Szigeti, she was admired for her classical precision and warm poetic imagination.

Perhaps the most elegant and unique program to appear in the White House at this time was given on December 15, 1927, after a diplomatic dinner. The Cappella, a stringed orchestra of fourteen players, consisted of the Lenox, New York, and Vertchamp quartets with bassists Paville Ouglitchy and Max Pfeiffer. Assembled and directed by Dr. Thaddeus Rich, the chamber orchestra represented "the type of musical entertainment customary at the courts or in the salons where such cappellas were maintained," according to Olga Samaroff's explanatory notes.[33] But the program also made musicological history because works by Thomas Tomkins (1572–1656), William Byrd (1543–1623),

Dramatic soprano Maria Jeritza sang at the White House for the Coolidges shortly after her debut with the Metropolitan Opera in New York.

Dame Myra Hess, the great English pianist, played Brahms, Chopin, Albeniz, and De Falla for members of the Supreme Court at the White House in 1928.

and Domenico Scarlatti (1685–1757) received important modern revivals. In the spring of 1927, Edmund Fellowes, eminent Byrd scholar, had transcribed and edited the great English composer's *Pavane and Galliard* from the Bodleian Library manuscript especially for the Cappella, and earlier that same year Gian Francesco Malipiero had prepared an edition of Scarlatti's *Concerto per archi e organo da una Sonata.* While a portative organ was used for the Scarlatti concerto, rare Stradivarius, Amati, and Guadagnini instruments from the Rodman Wanamaker private collection comprised the ensemble. The strings were of a somewhat later period than the Byrd and Tomkins works, but the whole evening was ambitious and noble, done at a time when concerts of early music were still rare in America. For an evening, the White House had become America's most prestigious "royal court."

Music of the Renaissance and Baroque played on authentic period instruments was not new to the White House. Arnold Dolmetsch had played the clavichord for President Theodore Roosevelt, and in February 1927 harpsichordist Lewis Richards performed John Bull's "Dr. Bull's Myselfe" from the Fitzwilliam Virginal Collection and works by Rameau researched from manuscripts in the Library of the Society of Ancient Instruments of Paris. During Hoover's administration Paul Shirley gave what is no doubt the only solo performance on the viola d'amore in the White House's history. His program included selections by Gluck, Marcello, Gaillard, and "Unknown Masters of the XVIIth and XVIIIth Centuries."[34]

Choirs had been singing in the White House from the time of James Buchanan, but under Coolidge they came much more frequently. The president saw these musical ensembles as a direct link with the nation's universities, religious organizations, and diverse population. The University of Missouri, University of Wisconsin, Furman University, the Arion Singing Society, the Bethlehem Bach Choir, and the president's alma mater, Amherst College, all sent their choruses. From Rome came the Vatican Choir, bridging nations as well as states. Famous for allowing himself to be photographed, President Coolidge posed with each of the choirs on the White House grounds. But the budding new broadcast media was quite another matter. Fearing a precedent would be set, he refused a request to broadcast the Amherst Glee Club musicale. As his aide, Edward T. Clark, said, "I think probably arrangements could be made to broadcast the concerts, but I frankly doubt the propriety of broadcasting what is really a private entertainment given by the wife of the President."[35]

The roster of prominent artists who performed for Hoover at the end of the 1920s and into the early 1930s reads like several seasons at Carnegie Hall. With the exception of the Aguilar Spanish Lute Quartet of Madrid and the Gordon String Quartet, the musicales presented mainly soloists, including Margaret Matzenauer, Claire Dux, Vladimir Horowitz, Rosa Ponselle, Efrem Zimbalist, Gregor Piatigorsky, Grace Moore, Carlos Salzedo, and Ossip Gabrilowitsch. Jascha Heifetz, who made his Carnegie Hall debut at age sixteen in 1917, was enjoying international triumphs when he played for President and Mrs. Hoover,

THE CAPPELLA

Formed by RODMAN WANAMAKER
in honor of the master Luthiers of the
XVI, XVII, and XVIII Centuries

THADDEUS RICH
Conductor

SOLOIST:
OLGA SAMAROFF
Pianist

CHARLES M. COURBOIN
At the Organ

Thursday, December 15, 1927
THE WHITE HOUSE

RARE ITALIAN INSTRUMENTS
USED AT
WHITE HOUSE MUSICALE
December 15, 1927

VIOLINS

Antonius Stradivarius, The "Joachim," 1723
Antonius Stradivarius, The "Dancla," 1710
Antonius Stradivarius, The "Comte de la
    Chesnaie," 1687
Jean Baptiste Guadagnini, 1752
Jean Baptiste Guadagnini, 1760
Jean Baptiste Guadagnini, 1761

VIOLAS

Jean Baptiste Guadagnini, 1774
Jean Baptiste Guadagnini, 1775
Jean Baptiste Guadagnini, 1784

'CELLOS

Domenicus Montagnana, 1721
Jean Baptiste Guadagnini, 1754
Mateo Gofriller, 1696

BASSES

Nicola Amati, 1684
Pietro Giacomo Rugeri, 1730

Unique courtly entertainment for President and Mrs. Coolidge included Baroque chamber music on rare eighteenth-century instruments and pianist Olga Samaroff playing J. S. Bach's Concerto in D Minor for piano and strings. Two pages from the seven-page program. Original measures 3½ × 5 inches folded.

President and Mrs. Coolidge with choir from Amherst College, the president's alma mater. The Coolidges were the first to allow themselves to be photographed with musical artists at the White House.

and his program included his famous transcription of the whirlwind "Hora Staccato" by Romanian composer Grigoras Dinicu.

When Lawrence Tibbett presented a program of four groups of songs in the East Room, his audience consisted of a large aggregation of Metropolitan Opera stars and their spouses, whom Mrs. Hoover had invited for luncheon. The gala affair took place shortly after the Hoovers moved to the White House; the next day the President and Mrs. Hoover heard Tibbett sing *Pagliacci* with the Metropolitan at Poli's. Thirty-three-year-old Tibbett, born in Bakersfield, California, was then one of the Metropolitan Opera's most successful singers. How did he react when singing for the president? Social Secretary Mildred Hall Campbell recalls wandering into the Green Room where the great baritone was waiting before the concert. "He must have been a little nervous," she said, "because he admitted his hands were cold!"[36]

Ignacy Jan Paderewski was just about becoming the "White House pianist" at this time, in the same vein that George O'Connor was nicknamed "White House Jester." The great Polish pianist/statesman usually resided in his private railroad car when he visited Washington, but the Hoovers gave him the elegant Rose Bedroom (now called the Queen's Bedroom because so many royal guests have slept there), and he kept his Steinway with him in that room. Paderewski was an old friend of the Hoovers.[37] Mrs. Hoover sponsored his concert at Constitution Hall on January 25, 1932, to benefit the Unemployment Fund of the American Red Cross, as well as several other recitals he gave to show his appreciation for America's aid to his country during and after World War I.

Paderewski played his last concert at the White House on November 25, 1930; six weeks later the twenty-seven-year-old Vladimir Horowitz played his first. The young Russian pianist, who already possessed one of the most dazzling techniques of the century, had astounded audiences at his American debut four years earlier. Henry Junge had arranged for Horowitz to perform for President and Mrs. Hoover at a diplomatic dinner on January 8, 1931, and the pianist was more concerned about conversing with the guests in his broken English than about his program. Junge gave him some pointers on the train to Washington. Just say "I am delighted" and nothing more when passing through the receiving line, Junge advised. Horowitz took the suggestion to heart and voiced ebulliently to each of the solemn dignitaries in the line: "I am delightful, I am delightful!" No one seemed to mind the error. They probably agreed.[38] Horowitz had just played a superb program of Bach-Busoni, Hummel, Dohnanyi, a Chopin group, and closed with the sparkling, vertiginous "Carmen" paraphrase that later became his signature piece. The selections were representative of his early concert fare, but the "Carmen" would reappear when the great Russian master played for President Jimmy Carter—and the world— in the first White House concert to be publicly telecast.

Visiting heads of state were still rare in America at this time (only eighteen came during the Theodore Roosevelt–Hoover era, a period of thirty years), and when they were invited to dinner at the White House, the Marine Band rather than a guest artist usually entertained. Twenty-eight-year-old Russian soprano, Nina Koshetz, sang after a state dinner for President-elect Pedro Nel Ospina of Columbia under Harding, but the first artist to entertain a head of state was harpist Mildred Dilling, who played for King Phra Pok Klao Prajadhipok of Siam on April 29, 1931. Dilling was a close friend of Mrs. Hoover and played in the White House three times during this administration as well as once for President Coolidge and twice for Franklin Roosevelt. Her links with Lou Hoover's final years and death are poignantly retold by her personal secretary, Mildred Campbell: "Mrs. Hoover was so delighted with her [Dilling] that she asked to have her for the music after the dinner for the King and Queen of Siam. She even asked her to wear the lilac-colored dress which she had worn previously, and the flowers in the East Room were lavendar lilacs. Apparently Mrs. Hoover was so fond of her that she went to a concert that Miss Dilling gave in New York in January 1944. She walked back to the Waldorf Astoria with Bunny Miller (Mr. Hoover's secretary) after the concert, went up to their apartment, had a word with Mr. Hoover and some guests, went into her room—and died suddenly of a heart attack."[39]

Steinway & Sons served as liaison for the White House guest soloists, but bands and choral groups were usually invited through correspondence from the social secretary directly to the group. Three

Horowitz

Among the numerous great artists who performed for President and Mrs. Herbert Hoover and their guests were pianist Vladimir Horowitz, soprano Rosa Ponselle, and harpist Mildred Dilling. Dilling was the first to entertain a head of state at the White House.

such organizations succeeded in appearing before President Hoover. The manager of the Washington bureau of the Music Trades, Alfred T. Marks, for example, wrote to aide George Akerson on June 10, 1929, asking that the Philadelphia Harmonica Band of sixty boys ranging in age from twelve to seventeen "be accorded the privilege of playing for the President and Mrs. Hoover." The band played at the White House on July 3, at 12:45 P.M. Judging from their standard repertory, which included such sophisticated arrangements as the Sextette from *Lucia*, Brahms's Hungarian Dances, Schubert's "Unfinished" Symphony, and Sousa's "Stars and Stripes Forever," they measured up to their nickname "Harmonica Wizards."[40]

Both the Hampton and the Tuskegee choirs were the first all-black organizations to sing in the White House since the Fisk Jubilee Singers. The Hampton Institute Choir, led by the distinguished American composer R. Nathaniel Dett, was on its way to New York, preparatory to going abroad "to counteract some of the unfortunate impressions that have been made over there by certain vaudeville and jazz performers during the last few years." The trip was underwritten by John D. Rockefeller, George Peabody, and Arthur James. The choir sang two numbers on the south grounds on April 21, 1930.[41] En route to New York for an engagement at the opening of Radio City Music Hall in early 1933, the Tuskegee Institute Choir asked to sing some "new and unusual arrangements in a semi-formal setting" at the White House, and Mrs. Hoover complied.[42]

As the 1930s began, unemployment continued to be a grave national concern. Just before the stock market crash of 1929, 60 percent of U.S. citizens had annual incomes of less than $2,000, the bare minimum to supply the basic necessities of life. By January 7, 1931, unemployment was estimated at between 4 and 5 million, and while President Hoover tried desperately to stem the floodtide of the Depression, his programs were never realized. The voters insisted upon a change and elected Franklin D. Roosevelt. Hundreds of songs—many whose lyrics were depressingly moving—were composed by ordinary Americans in the early 1930s and sent to the president. It was as if the bread lines seemed shorter if one could sing, or perhaps political chaos was less unsettling if one hummed through its storms, as Jerome Kern once said.[43]

The marked increase in the number of offers to perform in the Executive Mansion during the decade of the 1920s is noted in a memo indicating that "requests for artists to appear at the White House almost equals the request for appointments in this office."[44] Both Paul Whiteman and Meyer Davis with their orchestras offered to play for the Coolidges, but their offers were politely declined. Letters during the Hoover administration often reflected the sober moods of artists feeling the pinch of the Depression, as well as a characteristic view of Americana: dulcimer players, folk singers, "Peaceful Bear" who studied at Juilliard, and even a prize-winning billiard exhibition backed by a congressman's letter. Performers young and old wrote to the president asking to play in the White House for the prestige it would accord. Members of the Aeolian French Horn Quartet were earning money "to help their parents in hard times," they said. Some of these requests were referred to Henry Junge for auditioning and appraisal; others were turned down graciously.[45] Few made it to the White House.

The last formal musicales to be presented during the Hoover administration were held on February 11 and 21, 1933, after a somewhat curtailed winter social season due to President Coolidge's death. The concerts were prophetic. They seemed to foreshadow features of the Franklin Roosevelt programs—multiple artists in one evening, black choirs, Indian and ethnic music—a tendency to reach out to more varied aspects of the American musical spirit. President and Mrs. Hoover, while differing from the Roosevelts in their musical tastes, undoubtedly felt the need to link the White House programs to the American people more closely as the Depression intensified. Sometimes the "triple bill" resulted in some rather puzzling juxtapositions. The appearance of Mary Garden, a celebrated operatic singer, with Mildred Dilling at the diplomatic dinner on February 11, 1933, does not seem too incongruous—until an American Indian singer, Chief Yowlache of the Yakima Tribe of Washington, is added to the program.

Closer examination of this program, however, makes one wonder whether the individual selections are so widely disparate as they might seem. Nature—serene, contemplative, elegiac, and impressionistic—becomes a connecting link, bridging eras and nations, and elegant art music with humble chants. Thus, twentieth-century French composer Hahn's "The Boat" complements the American Indians' "Canoe Song"; Claude Debussy's "Clair de lune" idealizes moonlight while the Zuni Tribe's "Invocation" worships the Sun god. Russian steppes, Scotch highlands, and American eagles and hills are all part of the same world. For music, like nature, has the uncanny power of speaking directly to the people. And that is precisely what Franklin D. Roosevelt felt to be the special communicative power of this art form during the twelve years he served as president.

CHAPTER 10

NEW MUSIC FOR A NEW DEAL

Franklin D. Roosevelt

You never know the people
Or what the people bring;
You never know the nation
Till you hear the people sing.

Angela Morgan
The People's Chorus of New York
The White House, March 18, 1936

Franklin Roosevelt heard his people sing. He heard balladist Joe Glazer sing, "When a fellow's out of a job," and a ragged Texan sharecropper cry, "Work all week, / Don't make enough, / To pay my board, / And buy my snuff." He heard massed choruses bellow "Onward Christian Soldiers" at the Atlantic Conference before the United States went to war, and the single, poignant voice of Marian Anderson in "My Country 'Tis of Thee" on the steps of the Lincoln Memorial, after she was denied an appearance in Constitution Hall because she was black. He heard the sounds of symphony orchestras from Brooklyn to Cedarburg, Wisconsin, playing to millions a form of music they had never heard before; and he felt the beat of "Rosie the Riveter" as 6.5 million women entered the labor force during World War II. From the Great Depression to the great war, America's musical voices were native, human, eager, and alive. Franklin Roosevelt heard them all—and listened.

He was known by many as the "people's president" because he seemed to reach the masses in the same spirit with which he touched his neighbors at Hyde Park. His paralysis appeared to forge a bond between him and the truly forsaken—the "forgotten man" as he called the lonely, depressed American. But he also related to the people in a new, intimate way. He was the nation's first media president. His legendary Fireside Chats brought his voice directly to the American home via radio, a form of communication he claimed restored contact between the "masses and their chosen leaders." During Roosevelt's terms in office, from March 4, 1933, to April 13, 1945, the mass media came of age. Not only radio, but also motion pictures, newspapers, and picture magazines, wire service photographs, and even television transformed the way America viewed its presidency and the world. Speaking as a friend to listeners and viewers of all classes, FDR was "at the center of that era's great social dialogue."[1] It is not surprising, then, that music, with its dynamic powers of imagery, was also a form of communication to FDR—a vital artistic medium that should speak directly to the people. Through the New Deal's dedication to social values, the music world entered into a relationship with the public as never before in America.

The FDR years began grimly. Sobered by the impact of the Great Depression, America's concert music in the 1930s was less innovative and exuberant than it had been during the 1920s. But with a new conservatism in musical attitudes came a trend toward historical and regional Americanism and a reaching out to broader audiences through the "simplest possible terms," as Aaron Copland admitted about his works of the 1930s. But America's musical moods during the Roosevelt era were also in a constant state of flux, shifting and melding like a kaleidoscope. The budding, brassy jazz sounds of the 1920s flowered into swing—and exploded into bop. Irving Berlin, Richard Rodgers, Cole Porter, Frank Loesser, and George Gershwin composed music reflecting a society not so much torn by war as buried in escapism. For the Hollywoood sound film and the New York musical stage became entertaining ways to forget the nation's problems. It was an era of "the Great Entertainer," and Leopold Stokowski, Jose Iturbi, and Arturo Toscanini were placed as high upon the gleaming public pedestal as were Kate Smith, Eddie Cantor, and Tony Martin. But within all these moods was one which seemed to persist, undaunted, untainted by despair—the spirit of optimism engendered by the New Deal, which spread into every gloomy corner of America.

Repercussions of the New Deal policy and ideology were felt within all areas of musical experience—composition, performance, and listening. While the Federal Music Project made no direct grants or commissions for composers, it provided a valuable service in furnishing them positions and affording opportunities for awards or premieres of their works. But one of the major philospohies of the Federal Music Project was that the musical life of a community depends to a large extent on the musicality of the public as a whole. Thus music in the home, the school, and the church is just as important as that heard in the concert hall. Music now found a new, grass-roots audience. Stripped of its mysticism, it reached out to all—rich, poor, young, old, the man-on-the-street. It touched rural as well as urban America and proved that there was an enormous audience for serious music, if the trouble were taken to bring music to this audience.

President Roosevelt's concern for art was social, but behind this pragmatism lay a more intimate, personal vision. Roosevelt had always shown keen interest in Hollywood, the legitimate stage, and radio; there was always a touch of the showman in him, perhaps stemming from his youthful love of music and theater. Like many families during the final decades of the century, Franklin's parents, Sarah and James Roosevelt, and their children enjoyed gathering around the family piano for evening "sings."[2] Sarah played quite well, and her diaries indicate a particular fondness for opera, especially Wagner productions, which she attended often in New York and Europe. Between February 1899 and February 1900, she saw two performances of *Die Walküre*, as well as *Les Huguenots, Siegfried, Götterdämmerung, Roméo et Juliette, Tannhäuser, Don Pasquale, Tristan und Isolde,* and *Cavalleria rusticana* with stellar artists such as Marcella Sembrich, Emma Calvé, and Lillian Nordica. When Franklin was fourteen, she took him to *Die Walküre,* and together they "read over the story of the day's performance" beforehand.[3]

From 1896 until his graduation in 1900, Franklin sang regularly in the choir and performed in various school plays at Groton. His letters to his mother during this period indicate an active interest in singing, first as soprano then tenor, finally baritone in college: "Today I got somewhat banged to pieces [at football] receiving a crack on the head, a wrench of the knee. . . . What do you think! I am going to take singing lessons! A Miss Reid comes up here once a week and gives lessons in either singing or declaiming. However, singing should come before speaking so I have decided to take one lesson a week, as they are not very expensive."[4] Franklin was seventeen years old when he took singing lessons, and in March of this same year he wrote that he was playing the small reed organ at some of the little neighborhood mission houses near Groton: "You know I wrote to you on Thursday that I had become an organ player. Well, on Thursday night in the midst of a blinding snowstorm four of us left in a two seated wagon. . . . I drummed the organ for all I was worth and drowned out the singers. I had to pump, play and use the swells all at the same time."[5]

At Harvard FDR was member and secretary of the Freshman Glee Club ("I have rowed every day and had three Glee Club rehearsals this week"). Much to his disappointment, he did not make the University Chorus, but he remained active in the Harvard Glee, Mandolin, and Banjo clubs, which toured around Boston rendering such frothy delights as "Ghosts Patrol," "Colored Tea Party," "Frog Song," and "Koonville Koonlets."[6]

As an adult FDR loved songs that conjured up images and feelings of America—unpaved country roads, the open West "where the skies are not cloudy all day," and always the sea. From his earliest childhood, Roosevelt loved the sea and considered water an emotional as well as physical therapy. "The water put me where I am," he once said of his paralysis, "and the water has to bring me back." He served as assistant secretary of the Navy under President Woodrow Wilson in 1913 and throughout World War I. His interesting collection of sheet music on nautical themes reflects not only a pastime but also an awareness of history told through song. For in these choruses, dances, and descriptive piano and guitar pieces are recounted great naval battles, historic ocean voyages, and personalities relating to the sea. Most of the pieces comprise the period ca. 1800 to 1875, and many have beautifully lithographed covers, some in color. Records indicate that Roosevelt purchased certain pieces in 1917 for $3.50 each from Max Williams of New York City; others were acquired during the early part of his presidency.[7]

In a memo by Stephen Early, assistant secretary to the president, FDR's favorite pieces of music are listed as "The Yellow Rose of Texas," "Anchors Aweigh," "Home on the Range," "Fire Music from Wagner," and "My Wild Irish Rose." The last song was sung at the president's request by John McCormack as a birthday tribute in 1934.[8] Preference for the great closing music from Wagner's *Die Walküre* was probably rooted in the president's early memories of his mother and his boyhood days. From Groton he wrote home once that the "new Aeolian player piano, the rage of the school . . . played *Die Walküre* and *Siegfried*, which seem quite familiar to me."[9] Camille Robert's one-step march, "Madelon," was also a favorite with FDR and appears often on the Marine Band repertory lists of the era.

Opera for FDR had to reach out and touch everyone. Both he and Mrs. Roosevelt were honorary sponsors of the Metropolitan Opera Guild, formed in 1935. On January 31, 1940, the president wrote to David Sarnoff, chairman of the Met's Radio Division, a message that was read during Saturday afternoon's opera:

> I want you to count me among the thousands of radio listeners throughout the nation who wish the Metropolitan Opera to continue, and to go on to greater glory. Very often, on Saturday afternoons, when my work is done I have listened to the opera broadcasts and have enjoyed the music which this modern miracle has brought into my study in Washington.
>
> Grand opera has now become in a real sense, the people's opera rather than the possession of only a privileged few. I know that all our citizens for whom this field of entertainment and culture has taken on a new democratic significance wish the Metropolitan to continue to maintain its leadership. In some countries, opera is subsidized by the government; here it depends only upon those who have love for immortal music.[10]

Among FDR's favorite hymns were "All Hail, the Power of Jesus's Name," "Oh, Master, Let Me Walk with Thee," and "Be Strong" by Dr. D. Babcock, a relatively unfamiliar hymn that is in the hymnals of several denominations. Its text seemed especially suited to the times—

> Be strong!
> We are not here to play, to dream, to drift.
> We have hard work to do and loads to lift.
> Shun not the struggle, face it, 'tis God's gift.
> Be strong![11]

—words ironically close to those of the speech the president was writing shortly before he died: "The only limit to our realization of tomorrow will be our doubts of today. Let us move forward with strong and active faith."

For the memorable Thanksgiving Day service at the White House during Roosevelt's third term, the president chose "Onward Christian Soldiers," "Faith of our Fathers," "Eternal Father Strong to Save," and "Battle Hymn of the Republic." While all the hymns, except the last, appear on the printed program in their entirety, only stanzas 1, 2, and 5 are given for "Battle Hymn." FDR admitted that the South still objected to some of the words of Julia Ward Howe's immortal hymn, and he wished that "somebody could eliminate those verses and substitute something else."[12] In general the hymns he preferred were those of various denominations, as his eldest son James verifies: "None of us was bashful about opening our mouths and singing, particularly in church, though Father, whose robust voice ranged between baritone and tenor, sometimes sang so loudly that we children were just a little embarrassed. Though Episcopalian, Father particularly enjoyed hearing and singing the rousing Methodist and Baptist hymns, and occasionally attended churches of those denominations for that reason. 'I love to sing with the Methodys!' he would reply if anyone took him to task for deserting his own church."[13]

Through her sensitivity to the needs of the underprivileged of all races, creeds, and nations, Anna Eleanor Roosevelt transformed the role of first lady when she came to the White House. She broke precedents by holding press conferences, traveling, lecturing, and expressing her opinions candidly in her daily syndicated newspaper column, "My Day." "She was an extraordinary woman," claimed contralto Marian Anderson. "She will never really be understood. She left an example behind her which influenced even those who have not yet lived." Her appearance? "To me she was beautiful, because in her one sees much more than just the physical. She radiated a beauty as big as life itself. And with all of this one was aware that she was shy— there was always a sadness in her eyes."[14]

To Mrs. Roosevelt music was an international language: "People," she said, "can get together and understand each other while making music in a way that would be impossible were they doing anything else in the world." She was as touched by a group of undernourished children responding to a young teacher's guitar in a deprived community as she was when the People's Chorus came to sing in the White House: "it was brought home to me very forcibly what it meant to young and old in the great city of New York to have an interest of this kind to occupy one's leisure time. . . . I wonder as we develop a greater understanding of music if it will not help us to a better international understanding. I remember during the World War that we banished German music from our stages. I never could see why, if Wagner's operas were beautiful and uplifting before the War, the mere fact that we had gone to war with Germany would make them taboo. . . . Music, when it is great, belongs to the world."[15]

Mrs. Roosevelt was an especially warm, thoughtful, and congenial hostess. As first lady she brought to the White House a new touch of élan and informality. The wide variety of musical styles and performers more closely resembled the White House of Theodore Roosevelt than any of the later administrations, but there were some significant new developments. While operatic and concert artists still outnumbered other types of performers, the Franklin Roosevelts brought professional dancers to the mansion for the first time; monologists (the "diseuse"); a large percentage of black vocal artists; various WPA choruses; the first staged opera—*Hänsel und Gretel* produced by the National Music League; women's organizations, such as the New York Women's Trio with Antonia Brico and the National League of American Penwomen with Mrs. H. H. A. (Amy Cheney) Beach; ethnic groups from Pan America, China, Russia, and Spain; and finally an array of American folk singers and players as never before seen in the White House.

How was all of this accomplished? Mainly through a voluminous amount of correspondence between Edith Helm, social secretary to Mrs. Roosevelt, and Henry Junge of Steinway & Sons in New York. Through his long association with Steinway, Junge knew just about every prominent artist in the world. John Steinway recalls: "Eleanor Roosevelt was an old friend of my parents [Theodore Steinway], and she and Henry Junge were great friends. He would spend a great deal of time discussing the entire season. He was almost blind shortly before he died—I remember helping him up and down the stairs. Eleanor kept him on just because she was so fond of him. They would sit upstairs and have tea together."[16]

Junge died on July 16, 1939, after more than thirty-five years of service to the White House. He was succeeded by Alexander Greiner, also of Steinway & Sons. "I know you must have a feeling of great personal satisfaction in having done so well what must have been at times a difficult and trying task," wrote President Roosevelt to Junge, concerning his many years of arranging entertainments for the first families. The FBI was not as flattering. An anonymous letter received by the bureau on June 21, 1938, charged that Junge was using his position to introduce German musicians at the White House musical performances for espionage purposes. J. Edgar Hoover submitted a fourteen-page report five months later indicating that there was no evidence obtained to substantiate the allegations in the letter, signed merely "a former FBI man."[17] Hoover's report, moreover, verified that German-born Junge had graduated from the Hanover Conservatory of Music, taught violin in England, and came to America to work for Thomas Edison, after having demonstrated Edison's new invention— the phonograph—at the Paris Exposition of 1900. Junge's association with Steinway began in 1903. But the report maintained that Junge was definitely an American citizen and a registered voter. Where was he on November 8, 1938, when he could not be reached for questioning? Infirm and almost blind, he had left his small farm in Newburgh on the Hudson River to vote.

Offers to perform at the White House came in at the rate of 250 per season during the 1930s. Aspiring artists felt a personal tie with the Roosevelts from hearing the president's voice on radio and reading

Eleanor's "My Day" column. The latter, wrote Henry Junge to Mrs. Roosevelt, "seems to be devoured daily by your admirers, creating a unique interest in performing at the mansion not existing before."[18] People with dreams scratched their simple, polite notes on cheap writing paper: a woman whose husband earns $3.50 per week wants her little girl to dance for the president; a young baritone with infantile paralysis asks to sing in the White House; Hickey, the "Cowboy Caruso" sings "The Star-Spangled Banner"; a young man demonstrates the "Theremin Wave—a scientific musical mystery"; a woman plays the piano wearing mittens; a black mother's family of nine plays by ear, with baby of eighteen months directing in perfect time; a man and his little niece want to play "My Country 'Tis of Thee" on their violins for the president and at "every capital of the 48 states." None ever made his way to the White House.

But others did. As Mrs. Roosevelt said on her radio broadcast of March 22, 1935, "There are so many artists who are kind enough to offer to play at the White House and so many people who enjoy hearing them that we have decided to increase these opportunities this year." The established artists were usually sought after and invited by Mrs. Roosevelt via Junge. Invitations were often delivered personally by messenger to Washington area residents. Mrs. Roosevelt kept actively involved, making suggestions, approving artists, and indicating the type of music she and the president preferred. Seasons' lists of performers often had scrawled across the top in Mrs. Helm's hand, "OKed by the President."[19]

Included among those who offered to perform were young Nathan Milstein, the Andrews Sisters, and the fifteen-year-old radio star, Deanna Durbin; a memo dated February 16, 1934, indicates that Duke Ellington offered to play for the president while he was in Washington. However, due to the Roosevelts' busy schedules none of these artists performed in the mansion during this period. Igor Stravinsky and violinist Samuel Dushkin asked to pay their respects to the president during Stravinsky's second American tour, and an appointment was made for lunch on April 9, 1935. The invitaion was withdrawn when Mrs. Roosevelt had to go to New York for a funeral.

Remarkably, each offer to perform was answered graciously by Edith Helm, who regularly referred the more promising unknowns to Henry Junge. The elderly impresario would then "placate these artists generally with a dose of ingenious platitudes where necessary, and encourage others who possess merits," as he wrote to Mrs. Helm in his usual prosaic manner.[20] Auditions for the White House were sometimes very grueling. It was an all-day session at Steinway Hall when the program "Det Norske Folkedanselag" for the crown prince of Norway's visit to Hyde Park was approved. Twenty-four costumed dancers, six fiddlers, and three singers were found by Junge to be "attractive and gay, with dancing couples colorfully draped, their gestures most graceful and their singing in chorus of mellow quality and remarkably in unison." Another group recommended after a three-hour audition was Alexander Haas and his Budapest Gypsy Ensemble of eight to ten pieces, "who play ravishingly. They are dressed in scarlet coats and their Vienna Valses are so deucedly seductive that they would awaken Rip Van Winkle to dance the 'Blue Danube' all the way from 'Krum Elbow' to Washington, D.C."[21]

Combing the performers at the beginning of the season, worrying about which artists would come for dinner, who would need a stage and simple props, what selections were appropriate, and whether or not sufficient American artists were represented were some of the responsibilities facing Helm and Junge during the entertainment seasons of the busy early years. A few of Mrs. Helm's comments follow.[22]

> October 2, 1937: "I have sorted out the infant prodigies, snake swallowers and others who have applied this year."
>
> October 26, 1934: "Here is another of our rising young musicians. I sometimes wish they would stop rising and stay put."
>
> November 10, 1934: "I know nothing about this lady and remembering a long diseuse of last year, I say 'heaven defend us from any more.'"
>
> January 17, 1935: "The diplomatic dinner is a very large one and space is at a premium. Of course we would have to ask Madame ———, but I hope that she will feel that she can't eat and dance. Will you let me know if she should come and if she has a husband, which I hope she hasn't."
>
> January 21, 1935: "I have taken off the 'Star-Spangled Banner' which is really not appropriate for a musicale. Mrs. Roosevelt felt that it would be better to omit it also. . . . Just for your ear, I think they [a Viennese choir] are extremely silly to put in a negro spiritual and 'Dixie.' I do not see why people do not keep to the songs of their own country."
>
> January 18, 1935: "I have several letters from her asking to perform. She sounds to me mentally unbalanced, but after several years at the White House, I am beginning to think everyone is—myself included."

Silver-haired Junge had some candid views of his own, too. On February 22, 1936, he wrote to Malvina Schneider, secretary to Mrs. Roosevelt: "I wonder whether my 'weekly dozen' of letters to Mrs. Helm do not bore her with the many details, which necessarily enter into our correspondence? However, once in a while Mrs. Helm and I indulge in riotous, competitive revelry, who of us can dress the 'naked truth' in a most becoming verbal gown to fit the artists, who think that the Ermine of self importance is the only garment to wear?"[23]

Rarely, however, were the artists anything but extremely gracious, humbled by the awesome experience of performing for the president of the United States. They received $25 for travel, a room at the Mayflower Hotel, and local transportation—courtesies of Steinway & Sons. Following their performance, they were sent autographed photos of the president and first lady. The president's bore a bronze presidential seal, and both frames, made at Mrs. Roosevelt's Val Kill factory, were inscribed: "This wood was part of the White House roof erected in 1817 and removed in 1927." After the famed Metropolitan Opera baritone, Lawrence Tibbett, sang in the East Room for the king and queen of England, he wrote to the Roosevelts on July 7, 1939: "You will never know how surprised and delighted I was to find your photographs waiting for me when I got back from Calfornia. I am deeply touched by your kindness and thoughtfulness and shall always treasure the pictures. Again may I tell you how greatly honored I felt at having been asked to participate in the entertainment on such a great and thrilling occasion."[24]

Certain artists had restrictions placed upon them, as in the case of pianist Jose Iturbi who wrote to Mrs. Roosevelt on November 10, 1934: "I received your kind invitation through Mr. Younger [*sic*] of the Steinway Co. to play at the White House. It would be a great pleasure and honor but owing to my contract with the Baldwin Piano Co. I am not permitted to play any other piano than the Baldwin. Naturally there would be no preoccupation for the White House to place the piano because Baldwin would attend to all arrangements. I trust you understand my situation. Will you please convey my respects to the President and I remain most cordially yours."[25]

Junge was quite perturbed by the reference to Mrs. Roosevelt's "invitation," when in fact he had only casually suggested at the Lotos Club that Iturbi might one day play at the White House. When the subject of the piano restrictions was raised, Junge considered the matter closed. Iturbi apparently did not.

With the innovative features of White House musical entertainment—such as the large number of black performers and the dancers and the dramatic artists who required staging—came new concerns for those making the arrangements. To Mrs. Roosevelt music knew no racial or ethnic boundaries. Not all agreed with her. When word spread that Marian Anderson and the North Carolina Spiritual Singers were to sing in the East Room for the king and queen of England, "a staunch Democrat from Miami" protested: "It is an insult to the British King and Queen who are caucasians to present a negro vocalist for their entertainment. Do you want to engender racial hatred which might lead to serious consequences in the entire South?" Mrs. Helm calmly replied: "Mrs. Roosevelt asks me to acknowledge your telegram and to tell you that she is trying to give the King and Queen a picture of all American music. As the colored people are outstanding in a musical way, Mrs. Roosevelt feels that they should be presented with the others who will appear here."[26]

Thus the White House resounded with the rich, moving voices of black singers and choirs from all over America in a way that was never heard before in the mansion. The Sedalia Quartet from South Carolina sang on May 17, 1933; Arenia Mallory appeared with six black singers from the Industrial and Literary School of Lexington, Mississippi, on September 27, 1938. The Golden Gate Quartet, the Colored Group of Detroit, and the Hampton Choir sang, and the

Spirituals Society of Charleston, South Carolina, sang in a modification of the Gullah tongue, a strange corruption of English spoken by the lowcountry Negroes and chanted by the slaves around their cabins.[27]

But there had been no black opera singer at the White House since Black Patti sang at the turn of the century. Lillian Evans Tibbs of Washington, D.C., was a young black lyric soprano who changed her name to Lillian Evanti and managed a successful career, even though her color created problems for her both abroad and at home. She was the first black to appear with an organized European opera company, the Nice Opera, in 1926.[28] On February 9, 1934, Evanti sang for the Roosevelts, who were delighted with the brilliant young singer. The next year they invited Dorothy Maynor and baritone Todd Duncan. Maynor, a twenty-five-year-old black soprano with a soaring bell-like voice, was to make her New York debut four years after her concert at the White House; she would eventually achieve international fame. She and Duncan presented a program for the Roosevelts on March 8, 1935, that consisted of groups of arias alternating with selections by the Trade School Singers of Hampton Institute, of which Maynor was a graduate. "My uncle entertains high hopes for the colored baritone Mr. Duncan, and he wonders if you liked the little soprano," wrote Junge's niece, Dorothy, to Mrs. Helm. "Mrs. Roosevelt wishes me to tell you Miss Maynor's voice is very lovely, as well as Mr. Duncan's," Helm answered. "Altogether it was one of the nicest musicales we have ever had."[29]

From Duncan's standpoint, there were some reactions that night that provoked his ire. He was miffed by the mild applause Maynor received after her aria "Depuis le jour" from Charpentier's *Louise*. "It was so weak, polite and antiseptic," he said. "She was so great—these people just didn't understand opera. So when I stepped up to sing 'Vision fugitive' from Massenet's *Hérodiade*, I told them that here was a man who was tormented and asking for love; he was losing his wife, child and sight all at the same time. At the end of the aria there was a storm of applause. I was just honest enough to do what I believed was right—and it paid off."[30]

That same evening Duncan sang Cecil Cohen's "Death of an Old Seaman" because he knew the president loved the sea. "I can see him beaming right now," Duncan said. "How he loved that song! He beckoned me to come down and shake his hand after I sang it, and then I went back and sang the next song. All evening the President never stopped looking and never stopped listening. I never lost him for one minute." Duncan sang at the White House three more times during the Roosevelt administration. He had created the role of Porgy in George Gershwin's *Porgy and Bess* when it first opened in Boston on September 30, 1935. When he sang "I Got Plenty of Nothin' " on March 31, 1937, and the dramatic "Buzzard Song" on May 6, 1940, he brought to the White House a totally new operatic experience— and a truly American one.

Marian Anderson, whose powerful, compelling, contralto voice Arturo Toscanini found "comes once in a hundred years," sang in-

Scene from the New York premiere of George Gershwin's *Porgy and Bess*, 1935, with Todd Duncan (left) and J. Rosamond Johnson. Duncan sang selections from the opera for the Roosevelts in 1937 and 1940.

Dorothy Maynor, a twenty-five-year-old soprano, shared a program of arias with baritone Todd Duncan for the Roosevelt's concert in the East Room on March 8, 1935.

formally in the Monroe Room on February 19, 1936, one month after her Carnegie Hall debut. There were no printed programs. "I sensed a bit of fear—awe is a better word," she said, "even though there was such warmth in the atmosphere."[31] The charming Monroe Drawing Room, to the left of the oval room on the second floor, had been decorated with Monroe period furnishings by Lou Hoover. During FDR's time, it became an intimate rendezvous for musical artists, such as Irving Berlin, who played and sang there at 11:50 P.M. after a Fireside Chat party in 1941. Three years after Anderson sang in 1936, she would sing again at the White House, this time for the king and queen of England in the East Room.

Dancing of all varieties made its way to the White House during the 1930s with unprecedented vitality. For America at this time was truly—to use *Variety's* phrase—"hoof nutty." In vogue was the new swing style, and the dance bands of Benny Goodman, Glen Miller, Guy Lombardo, Louis Armstrong, Fats Waller, and others were all the rage. Pseudo-foreign dances, such as the rumba, the carioca, and the continental were attracting attention—the latter two popularized by Fred Astaire and Ginger Rogers. But more serious dance was beginning to take firm hold in America, proven by the Ballet Russe de Monte Carlo's smash hit of 1936, *L'après midi d'un faune.* Balanchine's School of American Ballet, which opened in New York in 1934, gave rise to the production of ballets on American subjects. Aaron Copland's *Billy the Kid*, for example, was staged in 1938 by Ballet Caravan. In 1941 the Martha Graham School was founded in New York, creating a seminal, energetic focus for modern dance in America.

To the White House musicales came the nation's tangos, waltzes, and mazurkas, as danced by two couples from the Arthur Murray Studio, January 8, 1941. Another team, Chaney and Fox, danced on three separate occasions, each time featuring pieces dedicated to their close friend, Eleanor Roosevelt. There was the "Eleanor Glide," the "Eleanor Walk," and the "Eleanor Waltz—Tea for Two," called a "musical comedy dance." The latter, accompanied by the fourteen-piece Marine Band, appeared on the same program as the Aguilars Spanish Lute Quartet, which featured fifteenth-century troubador songs. Even the Spanish dancers were placed in anomolous surroundings. Carola Goya, in her galaxy of bright costumes, shared the program after a diplomatic dinner with the renowned cellist Gregor Piatigorsky and a Vienna State Opera contralto, Enid Szantho—"an aristocratic combination," claimed Junge, "which would appeal to the less musically-inclined." La Argentina presented her fiery "impressions of a bull fight," followed by the Vienna Choir Boys' serene interpretation of "Silent Night." Perhaps the oddest combination of all was the program for Governor and Mrs. Herbert H. Lehman of New York on May 17,

Eleanor Roosevelt with contralto Marian Anderson during Mrs. Roosevelt's visit to Japan in 1953.

1934. The brilliant young American, Paul Haakon, who had danced beside Pavlova, came after an old-timers' group that featured eighty-two-year-old Betty Smith fiddling away "Hell Broke Loose in Georgia."

But it was Martha Graham who made artistic history at the White House. Not only was she the most important dancer to appear there before the Kennedy era, but she also opened the door to fresh, artistic approaches at the mansion. The leading modern dancer of her generation, Graham was obsessed with a desire for freedom, for bursting the binding icons of the past, and the powerful ballets she created proved her to be a pioneer in a new, expressive style. On February 26, 1937, at Mrs. Roosevelt's request, she performed *Frontier*, the controversial dance that had premiered two years earlier at the Guild Theater in New York. The critics were still baffled. Shouldn't dance be "pretty"? Where were the mountains and prairies? Graham's *Frontier* was devoid of a lyrical pictorial image—but not of the Puritan blood and bone that were her entire being.

Shortly before her program at the White House, Graham inquired about the space, lighting, and especially the floor surface of the East Room:

> Miss Hawkins, my manager, has just come back from Washington where she talked with Mr. Crim [the chief usher]. He showed her the room where the party for Mrs. Morgenthau is to be held. Miss Hawkins tells me that it has a highly polished parquet floor. Even though I have wanted very much to dance at the party and have been looking forward to it. . . . I am afraid of slipping and injuring an ankle which was hurt last season . . . rosin is no solution because I dance barefoot.
>
> If when I return from the tour you would like me to dance, I should be delighted to have the opportunity.

Edith Helm wrote immediately that a stage could be put up and that Mrs. Roosevelt had not meant for her to dance on the floor itself. "It was simply an idea that the window would furnish a charming background for you." Frances Hawkins wired: "Martha Graham delighted stage will make it possible for her to dance," and she listed the dancer's numbers as *Sarabande* (music by Lehman Engel), *Frontier* (music by Louis Horst), *Imperial Gesture* (music by Lehman Engel), and *Harlequinade* (music by Ernest Toch).[32] Louis Horst, Graham's accompanist, would later conduct the premiere of Copland's *Appalachian Spring*, one of the great achievements in American music. The ballet was written for Martha Graham and first performed in the new Coolidge Auditorium at the Library of Congress on October 30, 1944.

Stages, props, and lighting were new aspects of entertaining with which the president's graceful home had to contend during this period. If the requests were too complicated and unreasonable, they were turned over to the chief usher, who politely dealt with the situation. One monologist asked for six pieces of furniture "harmonious in design and color," an easily accessible dressing room with seven wall hooks, red, white and blue lights, a pink spot light, a "black-out" system to

Martha Graham, noted innovator in modern dance, as the young bride in Aaron Copland's *Appalachian Spring*.

eliminate afternoon sun, and a stage curtain of neutral color. Another artist offered his "Peace Music Drama" for the White House, and Junge replied that "the production of such an opus, where *mise en scène*, curtain rising and lowering, and a chorus are essential, are not within the compass of White House performances: a production of this kind really needs a fully equipped theater."[33]

Crim made the following outline to aid Alexander Greiner, who took over as liaison for the musicales in 1939.

White House Musicales: General Information about the East Room

Dimensions: Entire length 80 feet; width 40 feet.

Current: AC, 2 floor outlets, 3 chandeliers.

Seating capacity: 300.

Platform: 17 inches from floor; 2 sections—12 feet and 21 each; 1 section 252 sq. feet; 2nd section 504 sq. feet; total; 756 sq. feet.

Garden parties: Special platform.

Stage: Accommodates about 30 persons without piano, 20 with piano.

In an accompanying letter Crim added, "We do have a curtain which can be used before the stage. However, it is made of discarded material, is extremely heavy and is not as beautiful as it probably should be. It requires about three or four men to run it back and forth between scenes."[34] The not-so-beautiful curtain did come in handy, though, when Humperdinck's *Hänsel und Gretel* was staged in the East Room by the National Music League on March 30, 1935. The three-act production had only six characters, ranging from eighteen to twenty-five years of age, and simple scenery, but it was the first opera to be staged in the White House.

One highly beneficial facility that allowed the musicales to run more smoothly was the donation of a new state piano by Steinway & Sons. The Gold Piano, which the firm had installed during Theodore Roosevelt's first term, was showing signs of wear. Junge had written to Helm on June 6, 1934, offering to remove the action and replace it with the latest improved action invented by Frederick Vietor, a director of the company. Apparently this was never realized. On December 12, 1936, Junge wrote to President Roosevelt that the piano #100,000 was now thirty-four years old and that Steinway would like to build another grand for the White House when it reached serial number 300,000 in about two years.[35]

Presented to the nation on December 10, 1938, the new 9'7" instrument replaced the old one, which was donated to the Smithsonian Institution. It was designed by New York architect Eric Gugler. The case of Honduras mahogany was decorated in gold leaf by Dunbar Beck and the giant supporting eagles, also covered with gold leaf, were modeled by the sculptor Albert Stewart. The paintings on the case represented five forms of American music: the Virginia reel; the Indian ceremonial dance; the New England barn dance; black folk music;

"HAENSEL und GRETEL"
Opera by Humperdinck
Produced by the National Music League Inc.,
New York City

CAST OF CHARACTERS
(In order of appearance)

Haensel	*Selma Bojalad*
Gretel	*Cecile Sherman*
Gertrude, their Mother	*Marion Selee*
Peter, a broom-maker, their Father . .	*. John Gurney*
The Sand Man ⎱ The Dew Fairy ⎰	*Dorothy Orton*
The Witch Who Eats Little Children .	*. Marion Selee*

PROGRAM

ACT I
The Cottage

ACT II
The Magic Forest

ACT III
The Witch's House

Mr. RUDOLPH THOMAS
at the Piano

Saturday, March 30, 1935
THE WHITE HOUSE

Scene from Humperdinck's *Hänsel und Gretel* as staged in the East Room by the National Music League, with its accompanying program.

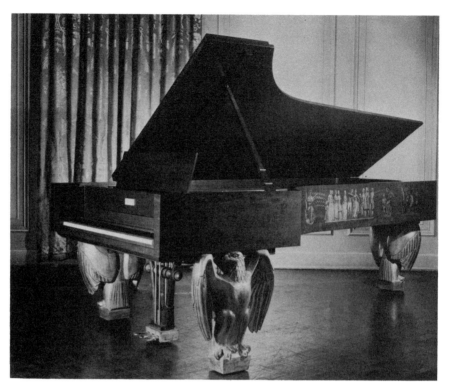

Mahogany Steinway concert grand piano, with supporting eagles of gold leaf, was presented to the White House by Steinway & Sons in 1938 and remains in the East Room today.

and the cowboy song. Last renovated in 1981 during the Carter administration, the historic piano remains in the East Room today.

The designs for the piano went through several changes as they were being formulated and codifed. The Commission of Fine Arts, which served as consultant for the project, first presented a cream-colored piano with a gilt panel, an idea promptly discarded. At one point Theodore Steinway suggested two plans for decoration under the lid: (1) the frigate *Constitution* in full sail with Aeolus, Orpheus, and other heavenly personalities furnishing the wind or (2) a legendary figure of America or Columbia welcoming the music of all foreign countries. These highly allegorical schemes were also never realized, and the lid remained plain. But the press latched on to President Roosevelt's keen interests in the piano and the new red drapes in the East Room. A little parody called "White House Decorative Interlude" appeared in the *Philadelphia Inquirer* of February 15, 1937:

> Mrs. Roosevelt.—Alice [Roosevelt Longworth] hears everything and I understand she's boiling. It's the first time anything in the East Room has been changed since she had the run of the White House.
>
> The President.—The piano should have been thrown out years

ago. It was all dented up from Theodore banging his fist on it to emphasize his points. What color is the new one?

Mrs. Roosevelt.—Gold.

The President (thoughtfully).—Silver would have been better. What did the Fine Arts Commission have to say about that?

Mrs. Roosevelt.—They've approved the piano. It's the red draperies that bother them. They think the red's too red.

The President.—Too red for what?

Mrs. Roosevelt.—Oh, I suppose they see some political significance. One of the boys said something about Moscow.

The President.—For goodness sake! Don't tell me there is still a commission left under my Administration with a Republican on it!

In the afternoon of May 29, 1938, Theodore Steinway, his son John, Eric Gugler, and Junge met with the president at Hyde Park to elicit his approval of the piano designs. "We brought scale models in three enormous suitcases," John Steinway recalled, "and I think the President made his selection rapidly so he could talk stamp collecting with my father."[36] While the completed piano was described as "modernistic" by the press, its case more closely resembled that of a harpsichord. Shortly after Josef Hofmann performed three Chopin selections at the White House presentation program, American pianist Stell Anderson played the new piano at a musicale. Her reaction?—an excellent concert grand but the keyboard has the appearance of being boxed, and the hands of the pianist are not visible to the audience. "The question remains," said the *Times*, "how many pianists will bash their knuckles before realizing this piano offers no scope for the grand manner?"—in gesture, at least.[37]

Often between Christmas and New Year's, the Roosevelts invited special entertainers for the younger children and their friends—a custom dating back at least to Theodore Roosevelt's terms. There were the usual magicians, puppeteers, and Lee Pearson with his wonder dog Grease Ball. But by far the most distinctive and creative performer was Wendy Marshall, "The Toy Lady," who entertained on December 26, 1933, Franklin Roosevelt's first Christmas as president. Having studied voice at Juilliard, Marshall was one of the first specialists in juvenile song and was among the first children's performers to appear on television. In the 1920s, when singing for children in costume was unique, Marshall appeared in a variety of elaborate changes, which she would don before the children at their requests. For "The Icicle," which she sang at the White House, she had a brick wall with long icicles and a sunburst on her head. As the sun melted the icicles, the song followed along with the words, "drip, drip, drip." At one time she was "The Toy Balloon," at another "The Cookie Bush" or "The Little Yellow Dog." The children were delighted, but even more so was Marshall. She described her adventure singing for the party for the Roosevelt's grandchildren, Sistie and Buzie Dall, as follows:

I was so thrilled . . . Mr. Junge called me again as Mrs. Roosevelt wanted to be sure the date of December 26 would not interfere with my Christmas. She was always so considerate of others . . . We decorated the East Room with balloons for the first time in its history. President Roosevelt attended the entertainment and afterwards I was presented to him. He was most courteous, complimentary and gracious. He asked if I had had any ice cream, and when I said Mrs. Roosevelt had invited us to stay for tea, he said, "That's good. That's taken care of." He was always the perfect host.[38]

Many brilliant concert and operatic artists performed for President and Mrs. Roosevelt: Percy Grainger, Josef Hofmann, Jascha Heifetz, Ruggiero Ricci (aged fifteen), Ray Lev, John Charles Thomas, the Curtis String Quartet, Kathryn Meisle, Frederick Jagel, Guiomar Novaes, Lotte Lehmann, Giovanni Martinelli, Antonia Brico, Lauritz Melchior, Bidu Sayao, Eugene List, William Masselos, and Elizabeth Schumann are only some. Schumann, a soprano, sang a group of German lieder that President Roosevelt specifically mentioned he had enjoyed. There was also the Russian princess, Dagmar Renina-Troubetskoi. And during this era duo-pianists appeared at the White House for the first time: Edwin and Bethany Hughes, Guy Maier and Lee Pattison, Ethel Bartlett and Rae Robinson. Washington's Steinway dealer, E. H. Droop, supplied the second pianos. Lily Pons sang Jerome Kern's "I Dream Too Much" from her recent RKO movie, bringing popular contemporary sounds to the formal White House musicale. Appearing with violinist Roman Totenberg and Cornelia Otis Skinner on January 2, 1936, Pons closed the program with her legendary interpretation of the "Bell Song" from Delibes's *Lakmé*. Petite and glamorous, Pons was *the* coloratura of the era. Her revealing costume for the Met's *Lakmé* broke at the rib cage and resumed at the hips. Momentarily America forgot that these were the grim years of depression and war.

To FDR the music that spoke most directly to the people, however, was the folk music—"the voices of miners, farmers, lumberjacks, workers of all kinds, their wives and children . . . a tide of music rich and strange but vital and undeniably American," as the distinctive program notes for the June 8, 1939, White House concert read. President Roosevelt recognized that in this music was "a national fabric of beauty and strength," and he encouraged the country to "keep the original fibres so intact that the fineness of each will show in the completed handiwork."[39] America was just beginning to recognize this heritage, and scholars with a special interest in folk music, such as John and Alan Lomax and Charles Seeger, contributed positively to its preservation.

Eleanor Roosevelt enjoyed the American traditional dances, especially the Virginia reel, which she danced at the White House newspapermen's parties. The president often served as caller. Most of the folk singers and players were brought to the White House through Mrs. Roosevelt's avid encouragement. Their simple art was somewhat too undignified for genteel Henry Junge, who told Edith Helm that

Eleanor Roosevelt and the famous German soprano, Lotte Lehmann, shortly after her Metropolitan Opera debut in 1934.

"a little of Kentucky ballads, like a bottle of fine Kentucky Whiskey, goes a long way with me." However, he always accommodated the first lady by auditioning the performers if necessary and making the arrangements.

When Kentucky balladist Iva Roberts asked to play at the mansion, Mrs. Roosevelt responded "Perfectly splendid!" and expressed a warm interest in the singer's creative revival of American balladry. "She accompanies herself on a quaint old instrument, called I think, a dulcimer, which she places on her knees like a lap dog," wrote Junge. "However, it does not bark nor bite and when the strings are gently agitated by the fingers of the singer, a rather plaintive, but not unpleasant sound, is emitted." John Jacob Niles also played the dulcimer. "It can be played at the supper table if you like," he wrote to Mrs. Roosevelt, who had invited him for dinner at the White House on April 15, 1934.[40] Niles wanted to sing a song about Mrs. Roosevelt that ran something like: "Have you heard about Frank Roosevelt's woman; Have you heard about Frank Roosevelt's wife; How she clum up White

American conductor Antonia Brico brought members of her New York Women's Symphony to perform Mozart at the White House in 1935. Eleanor Roosevelt, always sympathetic to the plight of women struggling for identities in fields dominated by men, invited Brico shortly after she had been the object of cynicism for conducting the Berlin Philharmonic overseas.

Top Mountain; At the peril of her sweet life; She come and give us a present; She give us a five dollar bill." Junge quickly expunged the song from the program.

The most ambitious program presented at the Executive Mansion to date was the elaborate production honoring their Britannic Majesties Queen Elizabeth and King George VI on June 8, 1939. Remaining in the country for five days, the king and queen were the first British sovereigns to visit the United States. The logistics of amassing from various parts of the country square dancers, cowboys, black spiritual singers, and opera and popular singers into a coordinated whole for an "Evening of American Music" were staggering. They involved Edith Helm, the perennial Mr. Junge, Charles Seeger, pioneer ethnomusicologist and deputy director of the Federal Music Project, and Adrian Dornbush, head of the Special Skills Division of the Resettlement Administration, as well as President and Mrs. Roosevelt. Dornbush managed the folk portion in consultation with Seeger, Junge procured the concert artists and established the format of the program, while Mrs. Helm passed on all developments to the Roosevelts for their final approval. And it all managed to gel—ultimately. "The committee who is always hanging around to manage things at the White House managed to filter in some things that were out of key, but it was the folk music that gained the evening," affirmed Seeger.[41]

It was the folk music that was striking, innovative, and courageous—"a step forward for American music, as significant in its way as other progressive policies of the Roosevelt administration," said folklorist Alan Lomax. "Out of key" perhaps were Kate Smith, Marian Anderson, and Lawrence Tibbett who represented the second part of the program. But to Junge, it was Seeger and Dornbush who were out of step: "the simple material which Mr. Dornbush seems to have at his disposal appears to be somewhat *bucolic*, or let us call it *pastoral*. . . . May I say, with all deep respect, dear Mrs. Roosevelt, that such a scene would be, to say it midly, very incongruous."[42]

Another incompatibility, according to Mrs. Helm, was that black and white performers would have to appear on the same night. Memos indicate that there were to have been two "evenings of American music," but one had to be canceled due to a British embassy dinner. Mrs. Helm felt that the white performers would then have to be told they would be performing with blacks, and plans for a dinner beforehand were discarded: "It might be rather difficult to have a white person invited to dinner and leave out the other one," she mused.[43] Americans,

Traditional musicians play for Franklin D. Roosevelt and daughter Anna at Warm Springs, Georgia, 1933.

The Roosevelts with King George VI and Queen Elizabeth of England in 1939, the first visit of a reigning British monarch to America.

it seemed, could sing together, but breaking bread together was yet another matter.

The president was enthusiastic about all the arrangements except the cost. On April 13, 1939, Edith Helm wrote to Dornbush: "I have been over the question of entertainment with the President. He feels that sixty-six people are too many for the East Room in the negro chorus. He thinks thirty as many as can sing in that room to have it pleasant. . . . The Coon Creek Girls, he thinks are all right [there were four], but the cowboys are very expensive."[44] As a result, the western music was represented only by Alan Lomax and his guitar. Lily Pons wrote and asked to sing on the program for the king and queen but was politely advised that only American-born artists were performing that evening.

The order of the program and the selections themselves were revised several times. Right up to the last, Junge juggled singers and dancers. At one point he had folk and classical musicians alternating, then finally decided on a two-part program, with folk music first and then the concert singers. He was perpetually worried about the twenty-one dancers who would be cramped for space. Since they wore heavy clogs, the platform would have to be reinforced "or I am afraid they might crash through the floor." He also noted that high jumps were dangerous and should be avoided "inasmuch as the chandelier leaves only a headroom of six feet one inch." And at the last minute Tibbett and Anderson—perhaps judiciously—omitted their operatic arias. "It was a hectic day," Junge admitted right before the big event—a rare admission from this devoted, patient servant.[45] Five weeks later, at the age of eighty-one, he was dead.

Heterogeneous as it was, the concert was a success. But like other innovative gestures, its message was not to be fully heard or appreciated until decades later. Its beautiful printed program booklet of eleven pages effectively described each folk selection and its significance with a note about the performers.[46] The North Carolina Spiritual Singers were a community activity group under the direction of the North Carolina Federal Music Project. Twenty-two-year-old Alan Lomax, assistant in charge of the Archive of American Folk Song at the Library of Congress, sang "Whoopee, Ti Yi Yo, Git Along Little Dogies" and "The Old Chisholm Trail." The Coon Creek Girls from Kentucky played and sang, among other tunes, "Cindy—a 'cracker-jack' party tune with countless verses, probably of part Southern Mountain white and part Negro origin." And the Soco Gap Square-Dance Team, rural people from the mountains of western North Carolina, were directed by Bascom Lamar Lunsford, a lawyer and farmer from Leicester known as "The Minstrel of the Appalachians."

Representing the popular and art music of America, Kate Smith chose "These Foolish Things," Macmurrough's "Macushla," and her own "When the Moon Comes over the Mountain." The last song became her trademark. Marian Anderson sang Schubert's "Ave Maria"— which had moved to tears the 75,000 at the Lincoln Memorial fourteen months earlier[47]—and the spiritual "My Soul's Been Anchored in the Lord." The young Metropolitan Opera baritone, Lawrence Tibbett, closed the program with "The Pilgrim's Song" by Tchaikovsky, Oley Speaks's "Sylvia," and Marx's "If Love Hath Entered Thy Heart." There were no compositions by Irving Berlin, Cole Porter, Aaron Copland, George Gershwin, or Virgil Thomson. Oddly, "These Foolish Things" was listed as merely "an old time popular tune." The song in fact was written by Strachey, Link, and Marvell and became the first big hit of Benny Goodman's band in 1936.

The concert spoke a direct language, in the precise spirit the Roosevelts wanted. But did it reach the king and queen? In just as direct and homespun a style, Coon Creek Girl Lily Ledford gave her answer:

> There were 89 guests, the cream of Washington society. Then I began to gather my wits about me, Lord! right there in the front row, about five feet from the stage, sat the King and Queen and the Roosevelts! I like to dropped a stitch or two on my banjo, but recovered and went on and tried not to stare, though I was able to size them up from the corner of my eye. Our spirits rose as we realized that the Queen and Mrs. Roosevelt were smiling as well as Mr. Roosevelt; but the King, with rather a long-faced, dour, dead-pan look, worried me a little. Then as I glanced down I caught him patting his foot, ever so little, and I knew we had him![48]

The popular singer Kate Smith entertained the king and queen of England at the invitation of the Roosevelts.

On Sunday, December 7, 1941, the Marine bandsman responsible for keeping the logs wrote: "White House at 1:00 P.M. Orchestra. Formal luncheon. Special full dress uniform. Leader in charge, 18 men. President did not join guests. At 2:25 Leader was informed by Mr. Searles, Assistant Usher, that Japan was making an air raid on Hawaii. Luncheon finished at 2:45 P.M."[49] The following day Congress voted for war against Japan, and a fearful nation responded with a single-minded unity.

In comparison with earlier major wars in which America had been involved, World War II produced few songs. Charles Hamm attributes this phenomenon to the urbanization of American popular song, which, emanating mainly from New York, had become more sophisticated and less absorbent of the social and political issues of the day.[50] On July 29, 1942, 300 song writers met at the Park Central Hotel in New York and bemoaned the failure of present-day music "to send America marching off to war . . . with the best damn songs in the world." Roosevelt wired Sigmund Romberg, president of the Song Writers' Protective Association, that "particularly do we need the sustaining power of song as an inspiration to our fighting forces and to strengthen the hearts and hopes and aspirations of those who carry on at home."[51]

The war in Europe cast its shadow over the capital's traditionally brilliant social season. Nineteen events are listed under "Musical" in the index for the scrapbook "White House Social Entertainment, 1933–1934," and twenty-three are listed for the following season (four Lenten Musicales were added). But by the 1937–38 season only eight "musical" events are indicated. Five of these followed state dinners and utilized a total of twenty-five performers, fifteen of whom were American. The next season, surprisingly, lists twenty-one events, but 1939–40 and 1940–41 have only eight once again. After this time there are only four musical entertainments indicated before April 1945: the Hampton Institute Choir, the Mongolia High School Choir, the Priority Ramblers of the United Federal Workers of America, and the Winged Victory Chorus, which was featured on April 2, 1945, two weeks before the president died. However, the lists do not include all the musical programs for Christmas parties and the numerous dances, receptions, and informal functions involving the Marine Band.

By far the most significant musicale of the early 1940s was "A Program of American Songs for American Soldiers," presented on February 17, 1941. Designed by Alan Lomax and Mrs. Roosevelt herself, the unusual program was printed on brown construction paper, creating a rough-hewn burlap effect. A reproduction of the 1846 *Crockett Almanac* frontispiece appeared on the cover with the words "arranged entirely on the Davy Crockett or Go Ahead Principle." Inside, the contents were described as: "Songs made by men who would rather hear a wild bull roar in a canyon than three choirs in a concert hall. Tunes made by men who like to begin their dances Saturday night

Also on the program for the king and queen of England was Lawrence Tibbett, a young Metropolitan Opera baritone from Bakersfield, California.

and knock off again Monday week. Accompaniments devised by men who like to whip a fiddle, a guitar or a five string banjo right down to a plank."

The performers included folk, spiritual, and ballad singers, such as J. M. Hunt, Wade Mainer, Burl Ives, and Joshua White, as well as enlisted men from posts nearby Washington. But the program was far more than an evening of "hillbilly" music. It was a new concept, a conscientious effort to relate American traditional music to the armed services at a critical period in the nation's history. This rationale is described by Alan Lomax:

> Archie MacLeish, who was then the Librarian of Congress, and I were talking about what kind of music program we ought to have in the armed services. I felt that facilities for Americans who like to make their own music could be set up in the training camps. We would then get together a literature of songs against fascism and songs about soldier experience, and marching songs, and so on. These would add enormously to the morale of America's struggle in World War II. He thought it was a good idea so he went to Mrs. Roosevelt with it. She decided to have a White House concert and a conference at the same time, including all the people in agencies in Washington concerned with morale.

Lomax was pleased with the concert and was congratulated by Mrs. Roosevelt, but "we did not get our program of folk music into the camps," he said. "The Pentagon considered the morale of the armed forces a strictly military matter. I believe that's a mistaken idea. Morale, like culture, is everybody's creation. Both belong to the people."[52]

Even under wartime conditions the arts flourished, and symphonic societies, ballet groups, and opera houses sprang up all over the United States. Entertainment-hungry civilians and service personnel were offered romantic, escapist music, and the "dream" became all-pervasive with hits such as Irving Berlin's "White Christmas" of 1943. FDR had great rapport with the entertainment world and celebrities often wrote to him during the war years. Many performed for him and Mrs. Roosevelt at birthdays, inaugurals, and charitable functions. Their letters reflect the national political and cultural scene as well as the warm personal associations and high esteem in which the Roosevelts were held.[53]

Eddie Cantor, who founded the March of Dimes infantile paralysis benefit, wrote to FDR suggesting that U.S. families adopt 10,000 Christian and Jewish refugee children. Leopold Stokowski discussed his plans for forming a National Youth Orchestra in 1940–41. Arturo Toscanini, whose NBC Symphony had performed for infantile paralysis benefits, expressed his devotion to the cause of liberty—"the only orthodoxy within the limits of which Art may express itself and flourish freely." Lily Pons asked to sing for the servicemen overseas. Correspondence between Roosevelt and Clark Gable includes a telegram from the president expressing his condolences in the death of thirty-two-year-old Carole Lombard, Gable's wife who was killed in a plane

A PROGRAM OF
AMERICAN SONGS
FOR
AMERICAN SOLDIERS

arranged entirely on
THE DAVY CROCKETT
or
go ahead PRINCIPLE

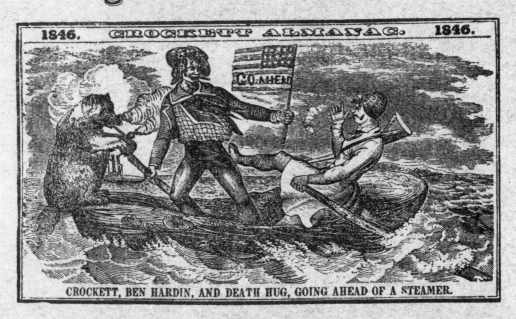

CROCKETT, BEN HARDIN, AND DEATH HUG, GOING AHEAD OF A STEAMER.

The White House
Monday, February Seventeenth
Nine P. M.

Burl Ives and other folk singers participated in Eleanor Roosevelt's innovative program for the armed services at the White House in 1941. The program cover was designed by Mrs. Roosevelt and Alan Lomax.

crash while returning from a war bond drive in Indianapolis. And Ellin and Irving Berlin wrote after the president's broadcast on March 15, 1941: "We were among the millions who heard you last night, and we are grateful because you express so magnificently what we all feel."

On May 1, 1940, President Roosevelt presented George M. Cohan with a gold medal for his songs "You're a Grand Old Flag" (1906) and "Over There" (1917), two years before the famed vaudevillian died. In 1941 Mrs. Roosevelt honored Ignacy Jan Paderewski on the golden anniversary of his American debut. FDR was the last of seven presidents whom Paderewski knew or entertained. When Paderewski died on June 29, 1941, at eighty-two, the president ordered his state interment at the Arlington National Cemetery.

Perhaps the real "unsung hero" of the FDR White House was the ubiquitous Marine Band. It played for every important state dinner, reception, birthday, debut, anniversary, and holiday celebration at the White House and for numerous ceremonies within the capital and beyond. When an extra band was needed at the White House, the Navy Band was called upon. Taylor Branson had served as Marine Band leader from 1927 until William Santelmann (son of the earlier Santelmann) took over on April 3, 1940, and remained the director into Dwight Eisenhower's term. The basic ceremonial traditions established over the years were retained from one president to the next—so much so that the military aide at President Roosevelt's first reception at the White House announced blatantly, "The President and Mrs. Hoover!"—just as President and Mrs. Roosevelt had stopped at the established spot on the carpet and "Ruffles" was played. "I broke into 'Hail to the Chief' as fast as I could and tried to drown him out!" said the flustered Santelmann, who was second leader at the time. "I don't know what ever happened to that gentleman, but I know we never saw him at the White House again."[54]

The Marine Band in various instrumental combinations often accompanied the guest artists. But moments were rare, indeed, when the artist was the first lady herself—and she cannot sing. Colonel Santelmann tells the tale of Mrs. Roosevelt's part in the Gridiron Widows' skit at the White House:

> The skit was set to the tune of "I've Been Working on the Railroad" and Mrs. Roosevelt and Mrs. Morgenthau were to sing. We started the composition in the key of D. We found it didn't suit Mrs. Roosevelt's voice so we dropped a half tone. We tried again. No, that wasn't it. We dropped a tone. No. Again we went down ... all the way to A flat when finally the great lady said:
> "You know, I don't think I can sing at all. Suppose you have your musicians play it. I'll just recite the words."
> And that was the way we finally presented it.[55]

The White House repertory of the band and orchestra at this time was generally conservative. Waltzes, marches, and the show tunes of Sigmund Romberg and Vincent Youmans served as pleasant background

Graham Jackson plays the accordion as the casket departs after Franklin D. Roosevelt's funeral service at Warm Springs, Georgia.

music for dining and conversation. Newly composed works were rarely selected, although Taylor Branson played a medley from *Girl Crazy* for the king and queen of Siam the year Gershwin's hit was produced in 1930. The presidents' favorites were always on the list. At his White House homecoming on November 7, 1940, after the election, the band played "Happy Days Are Here Again," "The Franklin D. Roosevelt March," and "FDR Jones." Designed for a concert audience, the programs presented outside the White House were more ambitious and occasionally included works by Igor Stravinsky, such as the "Danse Infernal" from his *Firebird*. But to the president "American" music meant Stephen Foster medleys, Sousa marches, and historic patriotic pieces, such as "The Battle Hymn of the Republic." Accompanied by the Marine Band, FDR and Winston Churchill bellowed out the great "Hymn" on the White House lawn, May 20, 1943, when the prime minister was in the capital for the momentous war conference—in the pouring rain.

Usually twenty-five to thirty motion picture stars were invited to the White House for luncheon the day after they participated in the annual presidential birthday ball held in New York to benefit the Infantile Paralysis Foundation. The small Marine orchestral unit often played for these luncheons, and the full band played for the large war rallies, such as the one on August 31, 1942. Riding in jeeps behind the band as it marched along Pennsylvania Avenue were Edward Arnold, Dinah Shore, Virginia Gilmore, Kay Kayser, Ann Rutherford, Walter Abel, Hedy Lamar, James Cagney, Greer Garson, Martha Scott, Irene Dunne, Bing Crosby, Bud Abbott, and Lou Costello.[56]

But for dancing at the White House, the Roosevelts had to have an up-to-date swing orchestra. Ruby Newman reported, "The family members are all good dancers. . . . They do not particularly care whether it be sweet music or modern swing, but they enjoy the new styles."[57] Dance bands were brought to the White House for the first time during the FDR terms, mostly before 1941, whereas earlier administrations relied on the Marine or Navy bands for their dances. The new swing style was "terrible and disgusting," according to the band member who kept the logs in 1934 and must have watched Sidney Sideman's band playing the jitterbug for the Roosevelt boys. Other bands that appeared at this time in the president's home were those of Eddie Duchin, Joe Moses, Meyer Davis, and Eddie Peabody, who sometimes played the banjo during dinner.[58]

The Marine Band served to underpin nearly every mood at the White House—humorous, heroic, lyric, melancholy, exhilarating, poignant. But it also shared supreme moments of mourning. The band logs for April 14, 1945, show the word "cancelled" scrawled across all events for that day—except one: "Marine Band to head funeral procession for the late President Franklin Roosevelt. Leader, Second Leader and Drum Major with 81 men. Dress Blues with white caps. Band played at cadence of 100–110."

Franklin Roosevelt died on April 12 at Warm Springs, Georgia, on the eighty-third day of his fourth term. There was no music or dancing at New York's famous clubs the following day. A pall gripped Broadway as news of the president's death swept the great amusement belt. The burial service was simple and austere; the Army Band from West Point intoned Chopin's "Funeral March," "Nearer My God to Thee," and "Now the Laborer's Task Is Done."[59] But FDR's legacy to Americans for decades to come would be found in the hymn he especially loved: "Shun not the struggle, face it. . . . Be strong!"

CHAPTER 11

A STUDY IN CONTRASTS

Truman and Eisenhower

It gets lonely in the White House when your cares begin
And the White House is a big place to be lonely in

. . .

When they come around for favors, and you start to turn them down
You become the loneliest man in town.

Irving Berlin, 1948

"I don't dare think of facing the next two months let alone two years," Harry S. Truman wrote to his mother and sister shortly after he became president. He was spending an evening alone in the White House and seemed especially aware of the array of clocks all chiming the hour at once—the little one that, "like most small people, has a big voice"; the ship's clock with its "crazy sailor count of bells"; and the old grandpa clock in the hall, a high-pitched "fat tenor." "It is rather lonesome here in this old barn without anyone," admitted the new chief of state, ". . . but I get a lot of work done."[1]

From the time Truman was chosen as vice-presidential nominee on the ticket with Franklin Roosevelt in the summer of 1944, he knew that FDR was very ill. Nevertheless, the news of Roosevelt's death on April 12, 1945, was a shock, as Truman wrote: "When I arrived at the Pennsylvania entrance to the most famous house in America a couple of ushers met me, bowed and scraped and took my hat; . . . Mrs. Roosevelt put her arm on my shoulder and said, 'Harry, the president is dead.' It was the only time in my life, I think, that I ever felt like I'd had a real shock. I had hurried to the White House to see the President and when I arrived I found *I* was the President. No one in the history of our country ever had it happen to him just that way."[2]

Truman met the sudden, almost overwhelming, challenges of world leadership with courage, honesty, and a zestful, no-nonsense philosophy that he characteristically called "horse sense." His first year in office was monumental. Germany and Japan collapsed, and between the two surrenders Truman met with Joseph Stalin and Winston Churchill at Potsdam. On August 6 the first atomic bomb was dropped—a dramatic event that changed the entire world. "It was a terrible decision," Truman wrote to his sister Mary three years later. "But I made it. And I'd made it to save 250,000 boys from the United States, and I'd make it again under similar circumstances. It stopped the Jap war."[3] No one could say this as directly and effectively as Truman.

President Truman's intense love of music is lengendary, and he admitted that his tastes were conservative. He preferred music with a recognizable melodic line to the more avant-garde sonorities ("I've heard the Enesco *Rhapsody* over the radio a couple of times. He's not a noise composer—thank goodness").[4] But even though Truman hoped and expected that his daughter Margaret would some day sing with the Metropolitan Opera, he never became an opera buff. When he was a young man, some friends took him to a performance of Wagner's *Parsifal* in Kansas City: "I haven't recovered from that seige of grand opera yet," he wrote to Bess Wallace before they were married. "Perhaps if they had given me small doses I might have been trained because I do love music. I can even appreciate Chopin when he is played on the piano. But when it comes to a lot of would be actors and actresses running around over the stage and spouting song and hugging and killing each other promiscuously why I had rather go to the Orpheum. Perhaps if I could understand Dutch and Dago I could appreciate it better for I did hear an opera in English once that sounded real good. They say though it isn't good form to appreciate singing in English. I am sorry."[5]

When he was president, Truman had a radio by his bedside and a piano by his desk. "It seemed hard for him to pass a piano anywhere without sitting down and playing, even for a minute or two," Rex Scouten recalls. Scouten, who became White House chief usher in 1969, was Truman's Secret Service agent during the presidential interim at Blair House and remembers that Truman would often go in and play the Steinway grand all by himself "because he enjoyed doing it— sometimes an hour or so."[6]

But Truman also played often and unabashedly in public. He played for world leaders (Stalin and Churchill), for U.S. presidents (John F. Kennedy), for concert artists (Eugene List), for movie stars (Lauren Bacall), for painters (Grandma Moses), and for some 30 million Americans during his televised tour of the newly remodeled White House in the spring of 1952. "He simply loved it," said Margaret, who performed herself as a professional singer. There was no attempt to provide the world with an image. He was just too candid for that. Perhaps "the fingers wouldn't work" on all the pieces he knew, but he would play them anyway. He was once asked if he sang tenor or baritone and replied, "I *Never* sing. I'm like Artemus Ward. 'I'm saddest when I sing and so are those that listen to me' "[7]

This election-year cartoon by John Collins depicts the beleaguered Truman, score in hand, hurriedly abandoning the White House piano.

Encouraged by his musical mother, Truman studied piano from age eight to about sixteen. He was a quiet boy with thick spectacles and a music roll tucked under one arm—who could nevertheless wallop a good baseball, according to his brother Vivian.[8] He never had to be coerced to practice, which he always claimed was "pleasure and not work," adding that the only reason he missed being a musician was because he "was not good enough."[9] He loved the music of Mozart, Chopin, Liszt, Mendelssohn, and Debussy, and also enjoyed Strauss waltzes, Gershwin's *Rhapsody in Blue*, J. S. Bach's Preludes and Fugues from *The Well-Tempered Clavier*, Mary Walsh's "Black Hawk Waltz," Stephen Foster's songs, and that musty old Broadway smash of the early years of the century, *Floradora*, by Owen Hall and Leslie Stuart. But the piece that most certainly bored him was the ubiquitous "Missouri Waltz": "I don't give a damn about it. But I can't say that out loud, because it's the song of Missouri. It's as bad as The Star-Spangled Banner so far as music is concerned."[10] He was also irked by that "peculiar American complex," which seems to want to know "what the President eats, how he sleeps, when he gets up," and so forth. "They want to know my favorite songs and when I say 'Pilgrim's

Chorus' from *Parsifal* or 'Toreador' from *Carmen* or 'Hinky Dinky Parlez Vous' or 'Dirty Gerty from Bizerte,' they are not sure whether I'm on the beam or not."[11]

The large collection of music in the Harry S. Truman Library at Independence is perhaps reminiscent of that found in anyone's grandmother's—or great-grandmother's—piano bench, with a singular exception: several pieces bear the autograph "Harry S. Truman." Among these are Chopin's Valse, op. 42 in A-flat Major and Nocturne no. 4 in F Major (both published by Schirmer); Tchaikovsky's Barcarolle, op. 37, no. 6 (Schubert); Paderewski's Minuet, op. 14, no. 1 (B. F. Wood); and Ralph Jackson's Second Valse-Caprice (Schirmer). And, of course, somewhere within these archives must lie a well-worn copy of Mozart's Sonata no. 9 in A Major (K331)—a perennial Truman joy that he memorized from beginning to end shortly before he became a U.S. senator in 1934.[12]

A number of pieces in the Truman collection bear the initials "GMW" and probably belonged to Truman's piano teacher, Mrs. Edwin C. (Grace Matthews) White, Sr., a pupil of Theodor Leschetizky and Fanny Bloomfield Zeisler. Under Mrs. White, Truman learned Clementi's *Gradus ad Parnassum*, several of Mendelssohn's "Songs without Words," works by J. S. Bach, Beethoven, and MacDowell, and two flashy escapades by von Weber, *Rondo Brillante* (La gaité) and *Polacca Brillante* (L'hilarité), as well as some pieces bearing his autograph. All this was a large and rather weighty repertory for a boy in his early teens.[13]

During his years as president, Truman's "thirst for good music sometimes drew him out of the White House," as Margaret Truman observed in her book *Harry S. Truman*.[14] He attended outdoor concerts at Watergate and with Bess Truman heard Lauritz Melchior sing at Constitution Hall on the twenty-fifth anniversary of his American operatic debut. The Trumans also attended several musical plays in historic Gadsby's Tavern in Alexandria, Virginia, one of which was a production of the Gay/Pepusch *Beggar's Opera* of 1728. Both President and Mrs. Truman were great supporters of the National Symphony and good friends of the conductor, Howard Mitchell. "Just don't play that modern stuff," said Truman. But he went anyway, bringing along Prime Minister Ferenc Nagy of Hungary in June 1946 for a program of Bartok and Stravinsky. "I just couldn't believe it," said Mitchell.[15]

The president also saw William Warfield and an all-black cast in a new touring production of *Porgy and Bess* at the National Theater on August 5, 1952, and shook hands with members of the cast backstage. Only five years earlier he attended a performance of Sigmund Romberg's operetta *Blossom Time* while the same theater was being picketed in protest against the policy of refusing admission to blacks. Concerning the new *Porgy and Bess* production the *New York Times* announced: "The purpose of the tour is to show central Europeans that . . . Negro players are not debased or oppressed as the Communist line says."[16]

If there were no musical programs of interest in town, Truman

President and Mrs. Truman with pianist Jose Iturbi, Drucie Snyder, and Margaret Truman before Iturbi's concert at Constitution Hall, Washington, on January 6, 1948.

would conjure up his own. Sometimes this took the form of a "phonographic concert" like the one he held in his vacation cottage for the White House staff. He played and discussed various recordings of Chopin, comparing the interpretations of Brailowsky, Horowitz, Rosenthal, Paderewski, Lhévinne, and other great artists that he had heard in concert as a young man. "Josef Lhévinne is my favorite—the greatest pianist since Liszt," he said. The *New York Times*, commenting on the sophistication of this endeavor, noted that "some members of the President's staff listened loyally but others fled to Key West night spots to hear a different kind of music."[17]

That Truman held only one series of concerts in the White House during his period in office may seem ironic, since he was the most musical of all U.S. presidents and had a daughter who was a professional singer. But the Trumans had to contend with the frugal postwar years, as well as a residence that was slowly crumbling and deteriorating. The upper floor of the White House had become so perilously weak that Margaret's Steinway grand, given to her by her father when she was a child, cracked through the surface. And when Eugene List played in the East Room on February 11, 1947, he noticed a large space left under the chandelier. The president explained that the house was just not safe and if the audience were to be seated under the giant crystal fixture, someone could be killed if it fell. In November 1948 the Truman family moved to Blair House where they lived for almost four years during the White House renovations.

The Truman musicales consisted of six programs held after the state dinners during the administration's only social season of 1946–47. These programs were arranged through the assistance of Steinway & Sons and Alexander Greiner, who succeeded Henry Junge as White House arts liaison in 1939. Greiner had joined Steinway as manager of its concert department in 1928 and helped the artists select pianos for their concerts both in the United States and abroad. A graduate of the Moscow Imperial Conservatory of Music, Greiner served in the czar's army during World War I, then fled to the Orient after 1917, where he worked for the American Red Cross. He was fluent in seven languages. In 1958 Greiner was succeeded by John Steinway, secretary of the firm, who began helping with the programs during the Truman period. "They are very nice people and delightful to deal with," Edith Helm wrote to Mrs. Truman shortly before the social season began.[18] The Truman musicales had none of FDR's dichotomous mixture of artists and styles, due largely to the classic tastes of the Trumans themselves. The president's letter to Margaret shows how the program planning became a family affair under the Trumans:

> We are doing all sorts of things in the musical line while you are away—cat's away, you know! As you see, your father had first choice on the pianists; then your mother and I took over the violinists and they have been marked, leaving the vocalists for you. Would you mind marking your first, second, third, and so on, choice? Mr. Greiner, of Steinway & Sons, tries to find out if the concert and other engagements of the artists will allow them to come to the White House. A great many of them have concert tours arranged and cannot make it on our dates, so that is the reason for the various choices. Will you help me and let me have this back soon please, so that I can send on the list to Mr. Greiner? We are saying nothing about the music after the dinners, which is to be for only a half hour and no outside guests invited.[19]

The musicales, all held on Tuesdays, followed white-tie state dinners and the final schedule appeared as follows:

Nov. 26, 1946	Sylvia Zaremba, Pianist	Diplomatic Dinner
Dec. 3, 1946	Lawrence Tibbett, Baritone Edward Harris, Accompanist	Diplomatic Dinner
Dec. 17, 1946	Helen Traubel, Soprano Coenraad V. Bos, Accompanist	Cabinet Dinner
Jan. 14, 1947	Oscar Levant, Pianist	Dinner for Chief Justice & Supreme Court
Jan. 28, 1947	Frederick Jagel, Tenor Collins Smith, Accompanist	Dinner for President pro tempore of Senate

Feb. 11, 1947   Carroll Glenn, Violinist   Speakers dinner
                 Eugene List, Pianist
                 Joseph Wolman, Accompanist

The Trumans always invited the artists to the state dinners before their programs, although many did not want to eat before performing. John Steinway often arranged with Chief Usher Howell Crim to have a "small something" for the performer after the program. "These little suppers were usually quite private and were held in the family dining room just around the elevator before you get to the State Dining Room," he said. "I remember Margaret, Freddie Jagel and I were sitting there after his program and in came the President. He sat down and no word was said, but immediately one of the waiters came in and placed a double bourbon in front of him," Steinway chuckled. "A charming, wonderful man! I adored Harry Truman. He was one of our truly great Presidents."[20] Truman enjoyed Jagel's singing very much according to his letter to "Mamma and Mary" two days after the concert. He enclosed one of the programs and commented, "He is a little man with a lovely voice but he makes terrible faces when he sings. Also he was scared. They all seem to get a fit of nerves when they sing in the East Room. I don't know why. I'm not such a terrible person."[21]

Each of the artists performed at least one favorite Truman piece on his or her program. With Truman's broad tastes, it was not hard to do. Lawrence Tibbett closed with the "Toreador Song" from *Carmen*. Helen Traubel, the great dramatic soprano who coached Margaret Truman, sang Schubert and Beethoven lieder. Oscar Levant, a bundle of nerves according to Margaret, played the opening movement of Beethoven's "Moonlight" Sonata among his eight selections and closed with an improvisation on Gershwin's *Rhapsody in Blue*. Both Levant and Eugene List played Chopin's Waltz in A-flat, op. 42. Only fifteen-year-old Sylvia Zaremba tried something new for the president—a piece by Aaron Copland, a composer unfamiliar to Truman (and to the White House). But after all, who could go wrong with "The Cat and the Mouse"?

Eugene List, who had played in the White House for FDR in 1941, was a great favorite and friend of the Truman family. A brilliant young pianist, at sixteen List had presented the American premiere of Shostakovich's Piano Concerto no. 1 with the Philadelphia Symphony Orchestra. Truman knew of List's fame and not only brought the young Army sergeant to Potsdam to play for the Big Three on July 19, 1945, but even turned pages for him. Years later List recounted his impressions of the historic occasion:

> If you can imagine, here was Stalin puffing on his pipe and Churchill with his cigar sort of leaning on the piano. And then I played. I tried to play some Russian music and some American and British, as well as some Chopin for President Truman. Churchill was not a music lover, which surprised me because he was a great writer, orator, and liked to paint.

I played the theme of the Tchaikovsky Piano Concerto and Stalin sprang to his feet and said "I want to propose a toast to the sergeant." I couldn't believe it! I was about twenty-two years old. I didn't know what to do. I was rooted to the spot. The President beckoned to me to come forward to the center of the floor and somebody stuck a glass of Vodka in my hand—it was so unbelievable![22]

The next night List played again, and Stalin had sent to Moscow for some samplings of his version of Russian artistry. A quartet of two pianists and two violinists played Tchaikovsky, Liszt, and Ukrainian folk dances. "I never heard better," said Truman. "Since I'd had America's No. 1 pianist to play for Uncle Joe at my dinner, he had to go me one better. I had one and one—and he had two of each." Then he added, "They had dirty faces though, and the gals were rather fat."[23]

List's White House concert in February 1947 was the last formal program at the mansion before the Trumans moved to Blair House. However, before they left there had been several informal events: the 100-piece Army Air Force Band had played on the south lawn, the U.S. Naval Academy Choir sang in the East Room, and the vaudeville team of John Olsen and Harold Johnson entertained the White House staff. So did Hildegarde, popular night club comedian, who sang several off-color songs, which Eben Ayers, assistant press secretary, said "left something of a bad taste with some of us." That she succeeded in getting the president to play a portion of Paderewski's "Minuet" was "the best part of the entertainment," added Ayers.[24] In addition, Robert Merrill and Risë Stevens sang for Bess Truman's birthday party. On February 7, 1946, the first dance to be held in the White House since 1938 was given by Margaret Truman for a friend who was getting married. "The music was wonderful," said a young woman who obviously had enjoyed herself. "It was the Marine Band and they played sambas and rumbas like I've never heard them played before. And the President was there . . . Mrs. Truman was there when we came in, standing with Margaret to welcome us."[25]

Unlike the other musical White House Margaret (President Wilson's daughter) Harry Truman's Margaret never presented a formal program in the White House. Her much publicized debut as a coloratura opera and concert singer took place on March 16, 1947, when she sang with the Detroit Symphony Orchestra for a radio audience of 15 million. Following this concert she performed in the Hollywood Bowl, toured across the nation, and appeared several times on television as a comedian with Jimmy Durante and other stars. But she was always the child of Harry Truman—talented, sensitive, resolute—and of Bess, a sincere, quietly charming first lady who seemed to leave the spotlight to her more politically and artistically inclined family.[26] President Truman, who gave Margaret her first music lessons as a child, was a constant source of encouragement to his daughter. Her intense love of music mirrored his own. They were two of a kind. "Of course if that is what you want—that is what I want you to have," the president told her.

The noted American soprano Helen Traubel with her pupil Margaret Truman before Margaret's concert with the St. Louis symphony in 1949.

"It seems to me you have gone about your career in the right way. . . . Your Daddy will support you to the end in whatever it takes to make these trials. But daughter don't fool yourself. You know what it takes."[27]

Many critics admired Margaret's warm presence and lithe, lyric voice that soared within a range of nearly three octaves. Others were less complimentary. After Margaret's Constitution Hall concert in December 1950, critic Paul Hume of the *Washington Post* wrote what became the most talked-about review in the annals of music criticism. "Miss Truman cannot sing very well. . . . She is flat a good deal of the time. . . . There are a few moments during her recital when one can relax and feel confident that she will make her goal, which is the end of the song." Bristling, the president dashed off a vitriolic note to Hume on White House memo paper calling the hostile critic "an eight-ulcer man on four-ulcer pay. . . . Some day I hope to meet you," lambasted Truman, "and when that happens you'll need a new nose, some beef steak for black eyes and perhaps a supporter below!"[28]

Sergeant Eugene List presenting President Harry Truman with an autographed copy of the Chopin score that he played at the Potsdam Conference.

The incident did not deter Margaret from her career. Letters poured in from all over the country expressing indignation over Hume's harsh diatribe. The nation, it seemed, rallied to the support of the talented young woman from Missouri whose father happened to be the president of the United States. And the folks "down home" cared just as much as the top brass. "Mr. Truman Dear President!" began a letter from a member of the "Arkansaw Travelers Band" from Emporia, Kansas. "Mutch obliged for telling that ignorant hillbilly off. . . . I say Margaret has what it takes, and I wish Margaret would form her a good orchestra of her own and sing our modern songs. She can sing with the Arkansaw Travelers Band anytime as we think she is tops."[29]

Two years later Truman had another run-in with the *Post*—this time over pianist Gina Bachauer's recital, which he and Bess attended at Lisner Auditorium. The next day the president wrote to Philip Graham of the *Post* suggesting that Graham "retire this frustrated old fuddy-duddy and hire a reviewer . . . who knows what it's all about." Of course, the reference here was to none other than Paul Hume, whose review this time Truman called a "disgraceful piece of poppycock." Attached to the letter was Hume's review with the president's candid comments penciled in: "She depends upon the soft pedal more than custom and Haydn require . . . [Bunk!] . . . showed little knowledge of Bach, the adagios should remain quiet throughout

Senator Harry S. Truman playing the piano with his daughter Margaret during the senatorial campaign of 1940.

. . . [How does he know? Bach is dead!] . . . the slow waltzes were badly misshapen . . . [More lousy bunk!]." Enclosed with Hume's review was a glowing one by Dillard Gunn of the *Star*. The president obviously was still convinced that Hume had no place in the world of music.[30]

Like earlier presidents, Truman was bombarded with mail from all over the country on topics consequential and frivolous, from people great and small. And entertainers were no exception. Pianists led the ranks. The "Liberettes" and every other Liberace fan club imaginable asked if their idol could play in the White House. There were scores of mothers with their child prodigies—and the unique phenomenon, Cirederf Nipohc, a sixty-four-year-old parking attendant from New York City who claimed he could *sing* all the Chopin Nocturnes, complete with turns and other ornamentation. Perhaps he could. After all, he claimed he was "The Ghost of Chopin."

Duo-pianists—father and daughter, teacher and pupil, identical twins—all wanted to appear in the East Room after the president's televised tour of the recently renovated White House on May 3, 1952. During the nationwide broadcast, Truman played snatches of Mozart on each of the two fine concert grands in the East Room—the 1938 Steinway and, in the northwest corner, a sleek ebonized Baldwin, style D, which the firm donated to the White House on April 7, 1952. Thus, for a few short months, the White House could boast two state grands in the East Room. After his televised demonstration, the president said that he hoped there would now be duo-piano concerts in the White House. But they did not take place until he had left office. When Virginia Morley and Livingston Gearhart played on November 17, 1953, at the opening of the Eisenhower era, the famous team undoubtedly used two matching Steinways borrowed for the event. The Baldwin, in any case, had been moved to the White House library on the ground floor the day the Eisenhowers took residence in the mansion.[31]

Truman, like President Roosevelt, received numerous letters from film stars and various entertainers, many of whom attended his White House luncheon on January 30, 1946, in conjunction with the Roosevelt Birthday Ball. The Truman Library has these documents, as well as other significant telegrams and correspondence between the president and Perry Como, Harpo Marx, Humphrey Bogart, Jose Iturbi, George Burns, Gracie Allen, Douglas Fairbanks, Lawrence Tibbett, Vladimir Horowitz, Hans Kindler, and many others. But unique among presidential collections are the musical gifts presented to Harry S. Truman. Somehow they seem to symbolize and summarize his great love of music and keen attributes of leadership. No other president of the United States had been given so many autograph manuscripts, rare first editions, and fine facsimile scores by major artists and great world leaders.

The entertainment world was well represented among these gifts. On September 29, 1950, Duke Ellington presented to Truman portions of his manuscript "Portrait of New York Suite," which had been commissioned by Toscanini. Kate Smith brought the president her copy of "The Red Feather," which she had sung for the Community Chest Drive of 1946. Irving Berlin sent his new song, "It Gets Lonely in the White House," composed in 1948 and used later in his Broadway show *Mr. President* (1962), with a note congratulating Truman on his recent reelection. And Harpo Marx presented his book, *Harpo Speaks*, with the inscription: "From the man who says nothing to the man who always says the right thing."

Among the gifts of classical music were two books of songs by Franz Schubert, both first editions bearing the composer's signature, from the Austrian minister for foreign affairs, Bruno Kreisky.[32] On September 25, 1951, the prime minister of Italy, Alcide de Gasperi, sent Truman a photographic facsimile of the autograph manuscript of Verdi's *Falstaff* and a most intriguing, beautifully bound edition of excerpts from Giovanni Bononcini's *Il trionfo di Camilla* (1696). The opera, extremely popular in its day, was first performed in English at the Royal Theater, Drury Lane, London, in 1706. Truman's edition with its fine Dublin-style binding dates from this period. Appended to the end of the book are 216 handwritten pages of arias, cantatas, and minuets composed by Scarlatti, Caldara, Steffani, Mancini, Bononcini, and others—a valuable example of the spread of Italian vocal styles to the other side of the channel.[33] Perhaps the most fascinating group of items among the state gifts, however, are the photostatic

Film stars at White House luncheon before the Roosevelt Birthday Ball on January 28, 1946, with President Truman and his family. (Front, left to right): Ilene Woods, Diana Lynn, Margaret O'Brien, Constance Moore, Dorothy Kilgallen, and Eileen Barton. (Back, left to right): Jo Stafford, Eleanor Lambert, Angela Lansbury, Helen Sioussat, Eddie Bracken, Paul Henreid, Zachary Scott, Alexis Smith, Cesar Romero, Lucy Munroe, William Bendix, Reginald Gardiner, Sergeant Harvey Stone, and Charles Coburn.

copies of the original contracts made with several great composers, given to President Truman and Margaret by David L. Bazelon, assistant attorney general in 1949. During the war the Attorney General's Office vested the copyright interests of all designated foreign nationals where royalties were earned by the performance of their works in the United States. Handwritten in ink, the agreements specified the terms of presentation, royalty stipulations, and participations, and bear the signatures of the composers. Several French operas are represented among the contracts: Thomas's *Mignon*, Delibes's *Lakmé*, Debussy's *Pelléas et Mélisande*, Ravel's *L'heure Espagnole* and his ballet, *Bolero*, and a number of operas by Massenet. Interestingly, *Thaïs* was signed by both Massenet and Anatole France, upon whose novel the opera was based.[34]

But for Truman the elegant gold medal that he received from the City of Salzburg, Austria, on October 4, 1951, meant more to him perhaps than anything else. About five years after he was presented with the medal, he made his first post-presidential trip to Europe. Salzburg, birthplace of Mozart, was part of the itinerary, and Truman was in his glory. He played part of Mozart's Sonata in A Major (K331) on the 250-year-old organ at the Salzburg Cathedral, visited Mozart's home, played his pianoforte, and was entertained at a concert of Mozart's music at the former palace of the archbishop of Salzburg. "I've never attended a happier or more pleasing musical event," wrote Truman in his diary.[35] Austria felt just as warmly toward Truman. On the plaque accompanying the gold medal he received in 1951 was inscribed:

Mr. President:

On April 19, 1951 the city of Salzburg unanimously passed the resolutiion to present to you, Mr. President, the

GREAT GOLDEN MOZART MEDAL OF THE CITY OF SALZBURG,

the highest award of the city for outstanding service in the field of music.

The great name of Mozart, son of our city and dear to us all is attached to this decoration, which is only presented to those who promote the cultural aims of the Mozart City, and who have furthered its good cause. It is with deepest gratitude, Mr. President, that we remember the good deeds of the citizens of the United States of America, whose representative you are. Without this help the cultural life of our country would not have grown again so soon.

In 1952 Truman decided not to run for reelection and Dwight D. Eisenhower, hero of World War II, captured the nation with his prestige as commanding general of the victorious forces in Europe. Like Zachary Taylor and Ulysses Grant, Ike was a professional soldier who had never held a political office. The enormous popularity that carried Eisenhower into the White House on January 20, 1953, over his Democratic opponent, Adlai Stevenson, continued through his reelection in 1956. During his eight years in office, Eisenhower stopped the fighting in Korea, strengthened NATO, created the National Aeronautics and Space Administration, and, shortly before leaving office, welcomed America's forty-ninth and fiftieth states, Alaska and Hawaii.

Although the threat of Communism continued to trouble the world, Americans enjoyed unprecedented prosperity during the Eisenhower era. The arts were beginning to develop and thrive as never before, with increased sources of patronage, both public and private, and ever-expanding audiences. Arts centers, such as Lincoln Center in New York City, were being planned and built across the nation, providing fresh focus on musical performance and dance, while cultural exchange programs proved that the arts could also be a vital bridge between nations. And with the new long-playing microgroove recording, the music industry was booming.

In their personal cultural tastes Truman and Eisenhower were about as different as two people could be. Truman, "gentleman amateur" pianist, was overtly infatuated with classical music, while Eisenhower, who had little musical background, quietly preferred the sentimental popular styles of Lawrence Welk, Fred Waring, and certain Broadway shows. Ironically only one season of formal musical programs took place during Truman's nearly eight years as president, while the Eisenhowers enjoyed most of their seasons filled with music and entertainment. And while Truman's activities in the area of arts legislation were minimal (due mainly to pressing postwar concerns), Eisenhower's were significant. Both administrations, however, seemed to hold a common viewpoint: the latest innovative trends in American music at this time—bop, cool, jazz, and the new, explosive rock 'n' roll—had no place in the White House. This music made a social statement too strong, too controversial for after-dinner entertainment in the president's home. And electronic or other experimental music? There were segments of the American public who found political and subversive elements in *all* modern art, no matter what form it took.[36]

The Eisenhower era was heralded by a giant rally in Madison Square Garden on February 8, 1952. Entertainment luminaries such as Clark Gable, Lauren Bacall, Irving Berlin, Ethel Merman, Fred Waring, and Mary Martin urged the nation to support Ike in the upcoming presidential election. At the next rally in October, attendance doubled, and massed throngs bellowed "I Like Ike," which Irving Berlin had borrowed and rewritten from his Broadway show, *Call Me Madam*. But standing before thousands Eisenhower himself put into song the ideals he cherished most—"God Bless America." His voice, clear, true, warm, sang Berlin's patriotic classic with the crowds at the rally under the direction of Fred Waring.[37] For another musical prayer, Ike himself wrote the words: his 1953 inaugural message was set to music by Robert Rogers and performed by the National Symphony conducted by Howard Mitchell upon Ike's reelection. "Especially we pray that our concern shall be for the people regardless of station, race or calling," sang the all-black Howard University Choir on January 8, 1957.

While President Truman preferred classical instrumental music, General Eisenhower and "Mamie," as the first lady was affectionately called, were fond of sentimental ballads and current show tunes—"Banks of the Wabash," "I Believe," "Stardust," "Oh, What a Beautiful Morning," and many old-time hymns. Mary Jane McCaffree, social secretary under the Eisenhowers, recalls Mamie playing both the piano and the Hammond organ in the White House with Ike, family, and close friends gathering around to sing. "Mamie never had lessons. She played entirely by ear," Mrs. McCaffree said. "The Eisenhowers also enjoyed all the current Broadway shows. Once when the President had to give a speech in New York City, he went to a performance of *My Fair Lady* just because he was so fond of the song 'Get Me to the Church on Time.' He missed curtain time, but Mamie had saved a seat for him."[38] Both the Eisenhowers attended the National Symphony concerts on occasion, occupying the presidential box (number 13) at Constitution Hall. "Mr. President, what kind of music do you like?" Howard Mitchell asked, shortly after Eisenhower took office. "Do you know anything by Lawrence Welk?" Eisenhower responded, and then added, "I also like a good bass voice." Mitchell rallied to the request with the best American basso he could find—George London, who sang scenes from Musorgsky's *Boris Godunov* with the orchestra on October 21, 1953. "The President loved it," said Mitchell.[39]

Ironically, the person whose job it was to know the president's musical tastes, the director of the Marine Band, had the hardest time of anyone finding this out, as Colonel William Santelmann relates:

What *is* President Eisenhower's favorite musical selection? I tried to find out shortly before the inauguration in 1953. But my formal inquiry was answered by an aide to the effect that the President would take up the matter at a later date. However, another aide said the General's favorite was "Serenade" by Drigo. Another ventured the opinion that he liked military marches—the Sousa kind. From others I learned that the General liked "Beer Barrel Polka" when he was in Europe. From Navy Captain Butcher's book I discovered that when he and the General were in Algiers they shared a phonograph— and one record. If exposure to a few hundred playings of a tune could do it, said Captain Butcher, then "One Dozen Roses" was it.

I tried again after the President had been in office awhile. This time I decided to try a different approach. I listed over a hundred selections covering the entire range of music, both classical and popular. Would the President be kind enough to check his favorite? When I got the list back "One Dozen Roses" was checked. So was "Beer Barrel Polka"—and eighteen others![40]

The musical programs that followed the state dinners under the Eisenhowers especially reflected their fondness for Broadway and other popular styles. "Frankly," admitted Mary Jane McCaffree, "the Eisenhowers wanted to hear lighter music after a long, arduous day. They were not particularly concerned about what the public thought, and they felt their guests would enjoy this style of music, too." The Eisenhowers were also military people, and many concerts featured the newly formed musical groups and soloists from the Army, Navy, and Air Force in addition to "The President's Own" Marines. Before he turned the baton over to Albert Schoepper in 1954, Santelmann tried hard to keep the other service bands out of the White House.[41] He explained to Chief of Staff Sherman Adams, a former Marine, "We have a new president who is an Army man, and there are *those* who think he wants an *Army* band in the White House." Ike did, though not exclusively. But he also can be credited with recognizing the fine talent of the other service organizations and bringing their music to the White House. Military music was also less expensive; Steinway & Sons no longer paid the artists' expenses as they had done for fifty years of White House entertaining.

Solo piano recitals were presented from time to time by Staff Sergeant Thomas Redcay of the Marine Band, whose program on May 3, 1954, for the governor of Canada comprised works by Debussy, Chopin, and De Falla. Bands of the Air Force and Navy as well as the Army Chorus and Navy Sea Chanters offered varied programs after state dinners. And there were also the Singing Sergeants (Army), Singing Idlers (U.S. Coast Guard Academy), Singing Strings (Air Force), and Singing Violins, who were not military but a quartet of civilian women who called their program "Memories in Music." Formed in 1954, the Strolling Strings was an ensemble of twenty men from the U.S. Air Force Symphony Orchestra conducted by Colonel George S. Howard,

President Dwight D. Eisenhower and Mamie Dowd Eisenhower attending *My Fair Lady* at the Mark Hellinger Theater in New York.

who performed for King Saud of Saudi Arabia on January 30, 1957. The concept of the roving musicians, so vital to the ambience of state dinners, began under Eisenhower. This ensemble was the featured attraction of the evening, judging from its enlarged, 8 × 6 1/2-inch decorative program with an imprint of the White House on the cover.

By the time of the Eisenhowers, the musicales had become a structured event, and Alexander Greiner made out a five-page memo of instructions to insure careful coordination between the Steinway firm and the White House. Some sample comments:

—Musicales last from 25 to 30 minutes. Each group not longer than 10 or 11 minutes.

—Notify Mrs. McCaffree and Mr. Crim if platform is needed or any other paraphernalia, such as electric lighting, loud speakers, or any special wish by artist.

—No fee, artist pays all expenses including accompanist. President sends artists autographed photograph.

—Ask artist for exact program (be sure to get right spelling of titles and composers).

—No advance publicity. Publicity after.[42]

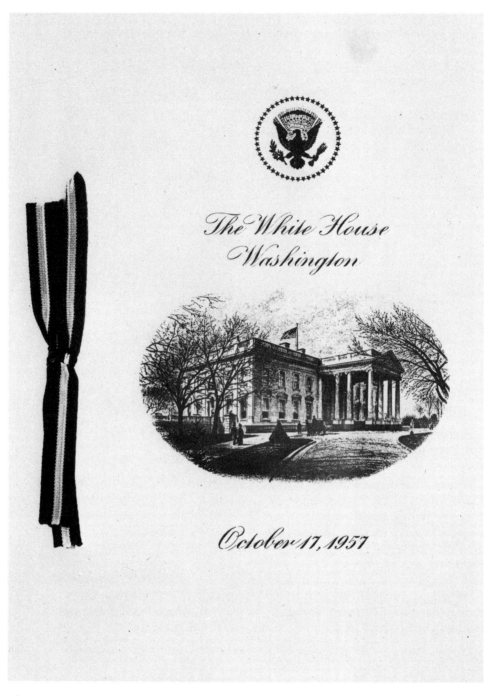

This special cover for the program presented by Fred Waring and his Pennsylvanians for Queen Elizabeth II and Prince Philip of England is decorated with an image of the White House and a red/white/blue ribbon. Under the Eisenhowers, after-dinner musical entertainment for visiting heads of state became an established tradition. Original measures 5 × 7 inches.

Greiner's "suggestions" for the 1954–55 season included a new category—"Special Attractions." On this list were the pianist Carmen Cavallero and several small vocal ensembles such as Les Compagnons de la Chanson, the Trapp Family Singers, the Carolers, and the Men of Song. The Eisenhowers, who liked quartets, selected the latter two groups, as well as the Deep River Boys and the Revelers. Toward the close of Eisenhower's second term, Carmen Cavallero played "Begin the Beguine," "Voodoo Moon," and "Warsaw Concerto" on the East Room Steinway—signature pieces of America in the 1950s with its mood music, its popular classics, its "background" recordings, and its music for eating, sleeping, or ironing shirts. It was music that relaxed, uplifted, spoofed, and always diverted.

But the Eisenhowers also brought to the White House noted popular orchestra leaders, many who were personal friends—Paul Whiteman, who featured Gershwin on his program, and Lawrence Welk, whose ensemble performed after the state dinner honoring Vice-President Richard Nixon on January 26, 1959. *Newsweek* picked up a frothy vignette about the event: "The President asked Welk, 'Don't you know 'The Yellow Rose of Texas?''' Replied Welk: 'Well, if we don't we can certainly make it up.' Then reports a White House aide, Welk and his band proceeded to do just that. No one could recognize the tune."[43]

Guy Lombardo's orchestra played for the king of Thailand, and his program illustrates how the concerts for heads of state were becoming more directly tailored to their interests. Sometimes this created problems. The king, for example, liked swing and other popular American styles, but not Rodgers and Hammerstein's current Broadway hit, *The King and I*. Lombardo had to eliminate his planned medley of songs from the show when he learned that the King felt the play treated his ancestors with too much frivolity. But of all the orchestra leaders, one moved the president more than any other: Fred Waring and his chorus of "Pennsylvanians." Waring performed three times in the White House during Eisenhower's terms in office. The most memorable to both the president and first lady was the program for Queen Elizabeth II and Prince Philip of Great Britain on October 17, 1957. Waring closed with his poignant arrangement of "Battle Hymn of the Republic." When he put down his baton and looked over at the president, both he and Mamie were weeping.[44]

The Eisenhowers' enjoyment of vocal music brought part of the great Mormon Tabernacle Choir to the East Room for members of the cabinet and other government officials on October 26, 1958. The famous ensemble was sponsored by the Mariott family and had first sung in the White House under William Howard Taft. Radio's "Voice of Firestone" with Risë Stevens, Brian Sullivan, and Oscar Shumsky performed for the Eisenhowers and President Arthur Frondizi of Argentina on January 20, 1959, the type of program they had made famous since their NBC debut in 1928—a little opera, some operetta, and a popular classic or two. Among the guests were Harvey Firestone and his wife Idabella, who composed the show's popular theme songs heard that evening, "If I Could Tell You" and "In a Garden."

But the show that was a very special delight to the Eisenhowers took place on May 8, 1958, for Chief Justice Earl Warren and about 150 after-dinner guests.[45] Nine stars of five Broadway musicals left their New York engagements for one evening to sing for the president and his guests:

"Steam Heat"	Pat Stanley
Pajama Game	Frank Derbas
	Peter Gennaro
"Balcony Scene"	Carol Lawrence
"Tonight"	Larry Kert
West Side Story	
"Trouble"	Eddie Hodges
"Gary, Indiana"	
Music Man	
"You're My Friend, Ain'tcha?"	Thelma Ritter
New Girl in Town	Cameron Prud'homme
"I Could Have Danced All Night"	Sally Ann Howes
"Show Me"	
My Fair Lady	

The evening was a White House first—the celebration of a great American musical form that would reappear at the mansion time and again to the present day.

Toward the end of the Eisenhower presidency, significant changes in the frequency and content of the after-dinner musicales began to take place. The Eisenhowers had the usual round of official dinners for the cabinet, Speaker of the House, the chief justice, the vice-president and the diplomatic corps, and in February 1958 the president added a new "science-military" dinner (after which some "indecorous" songs were rendered by Anna Russell). These dinners were usually followed by a short concert attended by the dinner guests numbering from thirty-five to sixty. Not until early 1958 were between 150 and 250 additional guests invited for many of the programs.[46] Social activities, it must be remembered, were limited considerably after the president's heart attack, especially from fall 1955 to about January 1957. At the same time, air transportation greatly increased the number of heads of state and foreign government leaders who visited the country. While not all were entertained with a dinner and musicale before 1959, after this date most were. Of the twenty-four dinner/musicales for heads of state held under Eisenhower, thirteen took place between January 1959 and October 1960.

With the increased number of concerts came the added responsibility of inviting more world-renowned artists to perform. America's cultural life was booming in the 1950s. By the Eisenhowers' 1957–58 social season, the press began to take an active interest in the

Dwight Eisenhower presents the composer Irving Berlin with a gold medal authorized by Congress in recognition of Berlin's patriotic songs. Secretary George Humphrey and Mrs. Berlin look on. February 18, 1955.

quality of the White House programs, and not merely in the flower arrangements. The drama critic with the *Washington Post and Times Herald* called the White House "one of the nation's worst show spots," and the *Star's* Betty Beale wondered why there was not more top American talent in the Executive Mansion, for example, Leonard Bernstein, Burl Ives, Bing Crosby, or Duke Ellington. She felt some of the problem lay in the increasingly busy White House staff, who could not possibly have their fingers on the pulse of the vast entertainment world, and she recommended that a committee of experts assist with the programs.[47]

Beale's article came out just about the time John H. Steinway was sparing little in his "campaign to get good musical artists into these White House dinners." His recommendation to Mrs. Eisenhower, who wanted to have one of the military bands play for the twenty-eight-year-old King Baudouin of Belgium, was fruitful: "I said, 'Look, this is a man whose grandmother, Queen Elisabeth, gives the most prestigious prize in the world of music. He has been brought up on good music. And incidentally, the first American to win the Queen's International Competition was a young pianist, Leon Fleisher. He's the one to invite.'"[48]

The concert, held on May 11, 1959, was a total success. For the first time in White House history music critics from major newspapers were invited to attend an after-dinner musical program—and it created a furor. The *Washington Post and Times Herald* published Paul Hume's review on the front page under a three-column banner. "His tone was notably sensitive, his fluency distinguished," reported Harry Truman's favorite critic. Fleisher played an hour-long program of works by J. S. Bach, Hess, Mendelssohn, Chopin, Debussy, and Ravel. Many of the papers applauded President Eisenhower's official recognition of America's standards of musical excellence, which they said marked a "turning point" for the White House. Did they forget, perhaps, that only two years earlier Artur Rubinstein had played for the Eisenhowers?

Rubinstein's historic program for the president of Vietnam, Ngo Dinh Diem, was unique. The legendary pianist played on May 8, 1957; it was his first and only concert in the White House. The program came as a surprise to the Steinways, since it had been arranged by the American National Theater and Academy (ANTA), of which Robert Dowling was the chairman. Rubinstein's only problem came when he wanted to use a different Steinway piano from the East Room grand renovated by Steinway & Sons in 1956. "I called Rubinstein and I told him that it was kind of a black eye to the piano presented to the nation," said Greiner, "to which Rubinstein replied that he had never thought of this angle, but that he wanted to do the very best for the president and found the state piano lacking in brilliance." Greiner arranged to have a fine ebony Steinway delivered to the White House via Campbell Music Company in Washington, however, and asked Chief Usher Crim to remove the state piano from the East Room: "Since it is not on casters and dreadfully heavy, it takes almost a regiment of men to carry it. I then called Mrs. McCaffree, who was, as always, very nice and she told me that she did not want to bother me, but that Mr. Rubinstein had made such an impression at his recital in Washington, that the President and Mrs. Eisenhower expressed the desire to have him for a Musicale."[49]

Rubinstein's performance in the White House was an isolated example of a serious instrumental program under the Eisenhowers before 1959. The first family enjoyed many fine singers from the time they took office until early 1955, including James Melton, Gladys Swarthout, Patrice Munsel, Jeanette MacDonald, and Marian Anderson, but great opera and concert stars had always been a White House staple. Brand new, however, was a solo cello recital. While Pablo Casals played for Theodore Roosevelt in 1904, he shared the program with basso Myron Whitney. On October 26, 1959, the great Russian cellist, Gregor Piatigorsky, presented an entire program for President Ahmed Sekou Touré of Guinea, and his international reputation was highlighted by a biographical sketch printed on the cover of the program.[50] Accompanied by Alexander Zakin, he played: Sonata in G Minor by Henry Eccles; Introduction and Rondo by Carl Maria von Weber; Habanera by Maurice Ravel; Allegro Appassionato by Camille Saint-Saëns; Prelude by George Gershwin; and Variations on a Paganini Theme by Gregor Piatigorsky.

Culminating the Eisenhower administration artistically was the program presented by Leonard Bernstein, the distinguished American conductor, composer, and lecturer. Bernstein not only conducted the New York Philharmonic, but also was the piano soloist. His White House debut on April 5, 1960, was not the first time a pianist had

Pianist Artur Rubinstein played his only concert at the White House in 1957 for the president of Vietnam. His program comprised Chopin's Polonaise in A-flat, op. 53, and Nocturne in F-sharp Major; Debussy's "La plus que lente"; and De Falla's "Fire Dance."

played a concerto with orchestra in the mansion, however. Olga Samaroff performed a J. S. Bach concerto with the Capella for Calvin Coolidge in 1927. A memo to Major John Eisenhower, assistant to the president, from Mary Jane McCaffree indicates how some of the larger groups of musicians made their way to the White House via military transport during this period:

> Leonard Bernstein has accepted our invitation to perform for the President of Columbia on April 5th and would like to bring 44 musicians (N.Y. Philharmonic) with him.
>
> *Question:* May we have the President's approval to transport musicians by plane from and to N.Y. as we have done in the past for Fred Waring (always on state occasions, of course). Col. Draper has no objection.
>
> As you know, Mr. Bernstein conducts the Philharmonic and is planning to do "Rhapsody in Blue" and a Mozart Concerto for our program on the fifth.

On the bottom of the memo is penciled in bold handwriting, "OK with DE." The president wrote to Leonard Bernstein afterward: "I am

At the age of twenty-four, Leon Fleisher was the first American to win the Queen Elisabeth International Competition in Brussels. The pianist was invited to play at the White House for President and Mrs. Dwight Eisenhower, the king of Brussels, and other important guests.

personally most grateful to you for contributing so much talent and time and effort to the affair. It was an occasion we shall all long remember."[51]

Dwight David Eisenhower did more for America's artistic life in terms of support and legislation than any previous president. True, there were some politics lurking. The Committee for Arts and Sciences for Eisenhower (CASE) was organized in July 1956 by a group of artists, scientists, and educators to back Eisenhower's reelection. The papers noted, a trifle sardonically, that now the Republican party had its "egghead" drive like the Democrats, who flocked to Adlai Stevenson's tailored banner in 1952. An interesting White House memo shows that Eisenhower had met with Harold Dodds, president of Princeton University, with the suggestion that a government commission on the arts be formed, as well as a "public building for the arts which he felt Washington needed," as early as January 1955.[52]

Even before this date, however, in 1954 the president sought $5 million for cultural exchange programs. "The exchange of artists is one of the most effective methods of strengthening world friendship," he said. The funds were promptly forthcoming. Thus, the *Porgy and Bess* company, the New York City Ballet, the Boston and Philadelphia Symphony Orchestras, Louis Armstrong, and other major artists toured Europe and the Soviet Union with the primary mission of easing tensions between the Free World and Communism.[53] The president's Music Committee of the People-to-People Program, chaired first by Eugene Ormandy and later by Mrs. Jouette Shouse, initiated the concept of American artists' participation in foreign competitions. As a result a twenty-three-year-old, strapping six-foot-four-inch Texan, Van Cliburn, was awarded first prize in the Soviet Union's International Tchaikovsky Competition by sixteen Moscow jurors—"an artistic bridge between the US and Russia," heralded the front page of the *New York Times*.

The president also signed a bill (H.R. 811) on August 1, 1956, granting a federal charter to the National Music Council, which represented all of the major voluntary musical organizations in the country. But his most significant achievement in the arts was the realization of the National Cultural Center. He signed the National Cultural Center Act on September 2, 1958 (Public Law 85-874), which also specified the formation of an Advisory Committee on the Arts for the center. With Robert Dowling as chairman, the thirty-four member committee consisted of such prominent individuals as Marian Anderson, Earl Moore, Martha Graham, George Murphy, Fred Waring, and John Brownlee. The giant complex—later to be renamed the John F. Kennedy Center for the Performing Arts—would radically alter the entire cultural life of Washington and provide a focal point for the finest performing arts groups from every corner of the nation.

The White House concerts during Eisenhower's second term, together with his visible encouragement of the nation's arts, link him more closely with his successor, John F. Kennedy, than with his predecessor, Harry Truman. In Eisenhower's ideology, "The development of American music, and the native development of any art, is the development of a national treasure." There is a prophetic ring to these words. Soon President John F. Kennedy and his artistic wife would add their own special flair to the American cultural scene. The nation was ready.

PART FOUR

★ ★ ★

1961–Present

JOHN F. KENNEDY was inaugurated president of the United States during an especially problematic era that challenged the intellect and administrative talents of the nation's youthful leader. In foreign policy Kennedy was met with civil wars in Laos and the Congo, continued Russian threats in Berlin, and a crisis brought about by the presence of Russian nuclear missile sites in Cuba. In October 1962 Kennedy imposed a quarantine on all offensive weapons bound for Cuba; at the brink of war the Soviets finally abandoned their Cuban project. And the test-ban treaty of 1963 did not end the threats to world peace. Kennedy had hopes and visions for his country, for its quality of life and the development of the potential of all its citizens, but these dreams were never realized. On November 22, 1963, in Dallas, Texas, he was assassinated.

Lyndon Baines Johnson, Kennedy's successor who served as president from 1963 to 1969, created Great Society programs to provide government help for education, urban renewal, Medicare, antidiscrimination, the development of depressed regions, and a wide-scale fight against crime and poverty. But two major crises in these years distracted America's attention. In the states with high black populations, race riots bordered on civil war, and battles between blacks and whites over civil rights culminated with the murder of the peace-loving advocate of civil rights, Martin Luther King, Jr. The other open sore that festered on the nation's body was the Vietnam War, opposed initially by students and pacifists who demanded the end of American involvement in Southeast Asia. "Make Love, Not War," promulgated the youth of America as they formed protest movements that began in California and stretched to the big cities of the East. Their messages gained momentum in the outspoken lyrics of Joan Baez, Bob Dylan, Paul Simon, and others.

The nation was divided by war overseas and turbulence in the cities when Richard Nixon took office in 1969. During his presidency Nixon ended American fighting in Vietnam. He also improved strained relationships with Japan and the Common Market countries. In 1972 he visited both Peking and Moscow, thus reducing tensions with China and Russia in his quest for world stability, and a general process of detente seemed to be underway. But the Watergate scandal at the beginning of President Nixon's second term curtailed his plans and led ultimately to his resignation in 1974.

The tasks that Gerald R. Ford faced when he took office seemed almost insuperable. In foreign affairs the governments of Cambodia and South Vietnam collapsed, and long-standing hatreds in the Middle East led to new crises. At home smoldering economic problems, racial tensions, and the oil crisis (with its resulting fuel shortage) impaired America's effectiveness as a once-undisputed leader. In January 1977 Jimmy Carter was inaugurated as president; he promised a return to America's traditional moral and humanitarian values, aspiring to make the government more "competent and compassionate." Carter created a new Department of Energy, and appointed record numbers of women, blacks, and Hispanics to government jobs. In foreign affairs he signed the controversial Panama Canal treaties, and in a "framework for peace" through the Camp David agreement of 1978 he helped bring amity between Egypt and Israel. But these accomplishments were not enough to offset problems of malaise, the Iranian hostage crisis, and continued high rates of inflation. Ronald Reagan was elected president in 1980.

"I was born in the USA!" belted Bruce Springsteen to an audience of 60,000 fans in Dallas in 1985. Rock boss Springsteen and other superstars reflected the resurgence of joy, confidence, and patriotism that has become the key image of the Reagan presidency. In many respects President Reagan restored what he called "the great, confident roar of American progress, growth and optimism." His conservative program called for the reduction of taxes and government spending to stimulate economic growth, curb inflation, and increase employment. Reagan also strove to insure national security by strengthening the armed forces.

And this aura of pride, so characteristic of the 1980s, also speaks eloquently of the unbroken vitality of American scientific achievements and cultural strength. For the United States has not only produced more Nobel Prize winners than any other nation but has made great contributions to human progress through its modern laboratories and research institutions. American literature is adorned with such names as Sinclair Lewis, John Steinbeck, Ernest Hemingway, and Pearl S. Buck; its music, by such talents as George Gershwin, Cole Porter, Aaron Copland, and Leonard Bernstein. Its film industry largely dominates the world market, and its modern art is exhibited at galleries from New York to Paris, from Tokyo to San Francisco.

Thus, this nation that "threw off the yoke of kings" over 200 years ago still fights for the ideals that give it birth—freedom, democracy, and the rights of humankind. But, as John F. Kennedy believed, "after the dust of centuries has passed over our cities," America will be remembered less for its economic and military achievements than for its culture—that compendium of pride, imagination, and humanity valued by every president from George Washington to Ronald Reagan. For it is the adventure and mystery of the arts that lie at the core of a nation's character. John Ruskin summarized this philosophy when he said, "Great nations write their autobiographies in three manuscripts—the book of their deeds, the book of their words, and the book of their art. Not one of these books can be understood unless we read the two others; but of the three, the only quite trustworthy one is the last. The acts of a nation may be triumphant by its good fortune; and its words mighty by the genius of a few of its children; but its art only by the general gifts and common sympathies of the race."

CHAPTER 12

THE VALUE OF
CULTURE FOR ALL

Kennedy and Lyndon Johnson

Ask every person if he's heard the story;
And tell it strong and clear if he has not;
That once there was a fleeting wisp of glory—
called Camelot.

Alan Jay Lerner and
Frederick Loewe, 1960.

He was a knight *extraordinaire*, possessing élan, elegance, courage, and wisdom; she was "Guinevere in a contentious Camelot," whose large eyes reflected an elegiac sophistication, sensitivity, and hint of shyness. John Fitzgerald Kennedy and Jacqueline Lee Bouvier brought to the White House fresh images of youth and vitality that appealed immediately to America's pride and sense of self-confidence. "I feel that I'm a part of this man's hopes," said gospel super-star Mahalia Jackson when Kennedy was inaugurated in January 1961. "He lifts my spirit and makes me feel a part of the land I live in."[1]

Taking a vigorous stand in the cause for equal rights, Kennedy's administration saw the rise of new hopes and visions for an America that would be remembered, as he said, "not for our victories or defeats in battle or in politics, but for our contribution to the human spirit."[2] In an era of burgeoning commerciality, Kennedy looked forward to a nation that would not be afraid of grace and beauty. "I am determined that we begin to grow again, and that there will be an American renaissance in which imagination, daring and the creative arts point the way."[3] But he saw only the beginning. He was killed by an assassin's bullet at the close of his third year in office while riding in a motorcade through Dallas, Texas—the youngest man to be elected president, and the youngest to die in office.

John and Jacqueline Kennedy's arrival upon the national scene at this time was a felicitous and dramatic coincidence in American cultural history. The United States was experiencing a wave of city living, advances in mass communication, and an awareness of education that provided fertile soil for artistic pursuits. But without the Kennedys to give these pursuits a clearly defined focus, they might have fallen on barren ground and progressed less vigorously. Leonard Bernstein summarized Kennedy's rare attitude toward the arts as stemming from "the reverence he had for the functions of the human mind in whatever form, whether as pure thinking or political thinking or creative functions of any sort, including [those of] art and literature."[4] August Heckscher, who was appointed by Kennedy as the first White House Cultural Coordinator in February 1962, noted that the president "wanted to move 'without fanfare' in a field new to the national government, and with awareness that it would always be the artists and creators themselves, along with support of private patrons, who would play the main role in the development of the nation's cultural life. I fully agreed with this approach. Yet as the popular reactions proved favorable and popular interest mounted, he seemed ready to give increasing support to activities in this area. Toward the end of his life President Kennedy came to feel, I think, that progress in the arts was intimately related to all that he wanted America to be. . . . In part it was because he was responding, as any sensitive and enlightened leader must, to currents that were stirring within the social order."[5]

The newspapers were full of America's great "cultural explosion" and the young president became a sort of mythical hero. In the words of Dore Schary, "When Kennedy endorses ballet, painting and the theater, the average man is bound to change his mind about such things as being effete."[6] Kennedy's brief administration did not allow much time for inaugurating and developing public policies in the arts, but the young president immediately surrounded himself with astute advisory talent—such as Press Secretary Pierre Salinger, Presidential Assistant Arthur Schlesinger, Secretary of Labor Arthur Goldberg, and August Heckscher, whose resignation as cultural liaison in June 1963 included a report that had seminal bearing on the formation of the National Endowment for the Arts. Heckscher stressed the need to consider our domestic cultural community now, as well as our international cultural relations, and he recommended a national arts foundation to provide grants in aid to states and institutions of the arts. To guide, encourage and sustain the arts, President Kennedy supported the dynamic development of the National Cultural Center plans and established by Executive Order the formation of a Federal Advisory Council on the Arts the month Heckscher resigned.

The real spotlight on the American cultural scene, however, fell on the White House itself—on the dramatic, cynosural array of musical entertainments that now had a positive mission: "to demonstrate that the White House could be an influence in encouraging public acceptance of the arts."[7] It was more than just a question of bringing the finest quality artists to the great mansion, however—fine opera stars, dancers, instrumentalists had performed there from the earliest years. It was the superb focus that the Kennedys managed to create. The White House became a deliberate showcase for America's leading performing arts organizations—the Metropolitan Opera Studio, Jerome Robbins Ballet, American Ballet Theater, Interlochen Arts Academy, American Shakespeare Festival, New York City Center Light Opera Company, Opera Society of Washington, Robert Joffrey Ballet, and others. Entire scenes were presented, tastefully staged with costumes and lighting. "My main concern," said Jacqueline Kennedy, "was to present the best in the arts, not necessarily what was popular at the time."[8]

New also were the youth concerts presented *by* young people and organized into a definite series. Chamber music programs included longer, more serious works, such as the complete forty-five-minute Schubert B-flat Trio performed as the evening's only selection by the famous Stern/Rose/Istomin Trio for French Cultural Minister André Malraux. Elizabethan music, elegantly underpinning poetry readings from this era, was played on authentic early instruments—viols, virginal, cittern, and lute.[9] Jazz, a long-time poor sister of the classical arts, was now listened to attentively for its own artistic merits rather than merely heard as a background for dancing. But the most significant innovation of the Kennedys involved the guest lists that included not only political and business leaders but also prominent performers, critics, composers, producers, and cultural luminaries from all over the nation. The press capitalized on the "Kennedy Command Performance," and an enchanted America followed every nuance and interpretative detail of the White House performing artists that the media offered. "In all those areas, it wasn't a matter of social entertainment in the White House at all," said Heckscher. "It became a matter of recognizing great talent, regarding great achievement in the cultural field."[10] And displaying these points to the nation with drama and imagination.

Culture was by no means new to the Kennedys when they came to the White House; their patronage was a natural extension of their accustomed way of life. A Harvard graduate, John F. Kennedy won the Pulitzer Prize in history for his *Profiles in Courage,* and his professional dealings with words and images are legend. Music, however, was another matter, and his tastes ranged from middlebrow to noncommittal. He studied piano as a child but, as one report indicated, "Anybody studying this boy's character when he was practicing scales would have said he'd never grow up to become President of the United States."[11] When Carl Sandburg's daughter Helga sent a query to the White House regarding Kennedy's favorite song, the president "wondered if Jackie might have a suggestion" for him, and the reply to Mrs. Sandburg was: "Greensleeves, a very old English song."[12] It was not only that he didn't particularly enjoy it [music], but I think it was really painful," August Heckscher noted:

> I don't mean only painful for him to sit because of his back for any length of time, I think it hurt his ears. I really don't think he liked music at all except a few things that he

knew. Other forms of art, however, he felt very differently about. Painting I think he looked on with a certain amount of good nature as any man would look upon something which his wife both practiced and appreciated. Ballet I think he looked upon the way any normally healthy man would, as something that was really quite beautiful and exciting to see. Poetry he liked very much. . . . So it was a shading, really, from music, which I think he found painful, into poetry, which for various reasons he found both challenging and quite fascinating.[13]

With Jacqueline Kennedy, the performing arts were quite a different matter, and there can be no doubt that the White House programs reflected her cultivated and intuitive tastes as well as her direct involvement in their planning. Jackie was educated at the finest private schools, wrote poems and stories for which she drew her own illustrations, and studied piano and ballet. During her junior year at Vassar she studied in France, and its culture left a mark upon her throughout her life. "Mrs. Kennedy was White House impresario," asserted Chief Usher Bernard West. "She knew all of the arts extremely well. When the ballet dancers rehearsed at the White House, she seemed to know even when they took a wrong step. . . . She often wrote to the artists herself inviting them to perform or even called them on the telephone. Can you imagine the performer's reaction to the first lady saying, 'Can you come and play for us at the White House?' "[14] But Mrs. Kennedy also had an astute advisor. "Pierre Salinger had been a child prodigy on the violin," she admitted, "and his great musical knowledge was enormously helpful in suggesting artists who might perform at the White House."[15]

It is significant, ironic perhaps, that it took almost ten months for the new White House image within the performing arts to take firm hold. As administrations change hands, there is always a transitional period of two to three months during which the musical entertainments are planned, scheduled, and realized along the lines of the new first family's tastes. With the Kennedys, however, there seemed to be an unusually long experimental period. Heckscher's words qualify this when he noted that everything President Kennedy did in regard to the field of the arts was a "trial step. . . . I don't think he ever had any grandiose—he would have hated the word 'grandiose'—any large plan from the beginning. So, when one hundred and fifty eight scholars, artists and creative individuals were invited to the inauguration. . . . I don't think he had any idea of the reverberations or the expectations that it would create in the mind of the artistic community itself. They all said, now the President has done this, what is he going to do next?"[16]

There is also indication that at first the Kennedys preferred small, private parties with informal entertainment to the large structured concerts held after the state dinners.[17] Mrs. Kennedy valued her privacy perhaps more than the nation realized. "I can't be away too much from the children," she once told Heckscher. "I can't be present at too many cultural events. After all, I'm not Mrs. Roosevelt," she said with a sort of smile.[18] But the big, spectacular parties came anyway—assembled with such skill and flair that they still managed to achieve the warmth and intimacy the first family so cherished. No better overview of this ambience and its engaging tribute to the nation's great artists can be found than that of Leonard Bernstein, who had last played at the White House under Dwight Eisenhower. At the Eisenhower dinner, Bernstein recalled,

> the food was ordinary, the wines were inferior, and you couldn't smoke. By the time I got to play I was a wreck. Compare that with the Casals dinner at the White House. . . . Dinner turns out to be not at a horseshoe table but many little tables, seating about ten people apiece, fires roaring in all the fireplaces, and these tables are laid in three adjacent rooms so that it's all like having dinner with friends. The food is marvelous, the wines are delicious, there are cigarettes on the table, people are laughing, *laughing out loud*, telling stories, jokes, enjoying themselves, glad to be there.
>
> I'll never forget the end of that evening when there was dancing. The Marine Band was playing waltzes or something, and Roy Harris and Walter Piston and people like that were kicking up their heels in the White House, a little high, just so delighted to be there, so glad that they had been asked, feeling that they had finally been recognized as honored artists of the Republic. You know, I've never seen so many happy artists in my life.[19]

Ironically, both the first and last major entertainment to be held at the White House by the Kennedys featured the bagpipes, the noble, haunting instruments that especially appealed to the president's Irish heritage. The Air Force Pipers and the Drum and Bugle Corps performed on the South Lawn after the first state dinner on May 3, 1961, for President Habib Bourguiba of Tunisia. The next function, for Mohammad Ayub Khan, the president of Pakistan, broke all tradition. It was the first White House state dinner to be held away from the mansion, in this case at historic Mt. Vernon. For the seventy-four-piece National Symphony Orchestra that played an outdoor program of Mozart, Debussy, Gershwin, and Morton Gould, a specially constructed shell-backdrop was provided by the chief usher and his crew—three hours before the guests were to arrive. Although the White House staff had to grapple with poison ivy, lack of electricity, and ways of concealing the portable toilets, the evening was a total success. The guests were transported to Mt. Vernon on boats floating down the Potomac with small orchestras on board. Somehow the whole concept had a regal flair that conjured up images of King George I's festive party reverberating with the music of George Frideric Handel from picturesque barges on the Thames. Indeed, the idea of holding the party at Mt. Vernon may have been inspired by the Kennedys' recent visit to France when President Charles de Gaulle entertained them with a dinner and ballet at Versailles.

But with the historic Pablo Casals concert of November 13, 1961, the White House dramatically displayed the way in which it wished to participate in the cultural life of the nation. Without question the Casals event was the most publicized of all White House concerts—perhaps of any concert in America—and it drew press attention from all over the world. It harked back to the great musicale tradition of Taft, Coolidge, and Hoover, but with the important distinction of being opened now for the world to enjoy. It was broadcast nationally by NBC and ABC radio (though turned down by CBS because the tape made by the Signal Corps did not meet the network's standards), and a recording was distibuted commercially by Columbia with four pages of notes, critiques, and photographs. "It is evident that the present first family has a proper appreciation of the relation of art to life," wrote critic and musicologist Paul Henry Lang in the *New York Herald Tribune* on November 14.

President Eisenhower had been attempting to do this sort of thing at the close of his administration, but it did not work as well as it did for the Kennedys. Among the 200 invited guests for the Casals evening, moreover, was an aggregation of the nation's most prominent composers: Samuel Barber, Elliott Carter, Aaron Copland, Henry Cowell, Normal Dello Joio, Howard Hanson, Roy Harris, Alan Hovhaness, Gian Carlo Menotti, Douglas Moore, Walter Piston, William Schuman, Roger Sessions, and Virgil Thomson. Included also was composer-conductor Leonard Bernstein and conductors Eugene Ormandy and Leopold Stokowski. It was perhaps the rarest chance in history for musicians, cabinet members, diplomats, and arts patrons to mix and meet at a single, very special, event.

The program was a serious one, lasting over an hour. To open, Casals chose Mendelssohn's flowing, virtuosic Trio in D Minor, op. 49, for which he was joined by pianist Mieczyslaw Horszowski and violinist Alexander Schneider. The remainder of the program consisted of Robert Schumann's Adagio and Allegro in A-flat Major, op. 70, for cello and piano, and a suite of five pieces by François Couperin. Critics lauded the eighty-four-year-old master's retention of the same power, variety of inflections, and muscular control that had made him famous when younger: "Even in a long, slow bow there was not the least waver at the tip," observed Lang.[20] But it was a simple encore that expressed Casals's feelings most eloquently and powerfully. He closed his program with a piece from his birthplace, which he claimed depicted the people's longing for freedom. "You might know this song," he said almost weeping as he grasped the hand of Marine Band musician, John Bourgeois, after the concert. "It's a Catalan folk song, 'The Song of the Birds'—but to me, it's the song of the exile."[21]

Casals, who had played in the White House for Theodore Roosevelt in 1904, ceased his American appearances in 1938 because the United States recognized the Franco dictatorship that he despised. His long, self-imposed exile from his native Spain led him to establish residence in Puerto Rico, and when he received a letter from President Kennedy inviting him to play for a state dinner honoring Governor Luis Muñoz-

Pablo Casals bows to a prestigious audience that included President and Mrs. John Kennedy, Governor and Mrs. Luis Muñoz-Marín of Puerto Rico, and luminaries from the arts world.

Marín of Puerto Rico, he accepted because of his admiration for Kennedy. Returning to Puerto Rico after his historic White House concert, he wrote Kennedy:

> I have received your letter of November 14th and again, I have been moved by your very generous words.
>
> Last Monday night I played with all my heart—and I feel that the results have been rewarding. I am grateful and happy if my humble tribute to you may have at the same time contributed to music and culture. That whole day of November 13th will always have a very special meaning for me. My visit and conversation with you have strengthened and confirmed my faith and hopes for our ideals of Peace and Freedom. Thank you, Mr. President.
>
> We are still re-living the wonderful moments spent at the White House. There was much more than the honor we received—we were enriched by your and Mrs. Kennedy's human warmth and kindness.
>
> May I repeat once more my respects and my affectionate wishes.[22]

Five months after the Casals concert another array of *cognoscenti* were invited to dine in the White House. The forty-nine Nobel prize winners included composers, scientists, authors, and artists, prompting the president to comment that it was the most "extraordinary collection of talent, of human knowledge that has ever been gathered together

President and Mrs. John Kennedy with Igor Stravinsky and his wife Vera at a White House dinner party honoring the composer's eightieth birthday.

at the White House with the possible exception of when Thomas Jefferson dined alone."[23] At another historic cultural event in the mansion, the dinner for André Malraux, Kennedy's comments to the distinguished group of artists carried overtones of his characteristic wit and charm: "This is becoming a sort of eating place for artists," he said. "But they never ask *us* out!"[24]

On January 19, 1962, along with other distinguished guests from the arts, eighty-year-old Russian-born composer Igor Stravinsky was fêted by the Kennedys. Mr. and Mrs. Leonard Bernstein were there, as well as Princess Lee Radziwill, Mrs. Kennedy's sister; Goddard Lieberson, president of Columbia Records and his ballerina wife, Zorina; Mr. and Mrs. Arthur Schlesinger, Jr.; the Parisian composer Nicholas Nabokov; and Robert Craft, musical associate of Stravinsky. "When I came into the room," recalls Leonard Bernstein, "there was a line greeting Stravinsky, and when he came to me, he kissed me on both cheeks in the Russian fashion, and I kissed him on both cheeks. There was all this Russian kissing and embracing going on when I suddenly heard a voice from the other corner of the room saying, 'Hey, how about me?' And it was the President. That's the sort of thing I mean: it's so endearing and so insanely unpresidential, and at the same time never losing dignity or that quality, I can't think of the word, but stateliness is the only thing I can think of, majestic presence."[25]

Programs for children throughout White House history had usually been given by adult entertainers and centered around holidays, such as Christmas and Easter. The Kennedys' inspired touch of offering a series called "Concerts for Young People by Young People" paid tribute to the nation's burgeoning talented youth groups and became a source of encouragement to young people everywhere. Presented mainly outdoors on the White House lawn, the programs were executed, in the words of the social secretary, Letitia (Tish) Baldridge, "on a minimum financial budget and a maximum blood-sweat-and-tears budget."[26] The Social Office in conjunction with the chief usher not only had to work with the carpenters and sound engineers on the acoustical shell and loudspeaker system, but also had to arrange for the housing and feeding of the visiting musicians and chaperones who numbered about 100. They usually stayed at Army barracks just outside of Washington. All progressed smoothly, but there was one accident when embassy teenagers representing sixty-nine countries crowded into the East Room for a ninety-minute production of Mozart's *Così fan tutte* sung in English by the young professionals of the Metropolitan Opera Studio: Stanley Kolk as Ferrando wore an exotic turban with a towering plume that caught fire from a burning candle sconce in the State Dining Room afterward.[27]

Other programs in the youth series were presented by the eighty-five-piece Transylvania Symphony Orchestra from the Brevard Music Center (August 22, 1961); the Greater Boston Youth Symphony with the Breckenridge Boys Choir from Texas (April 16, 1962); the National Music Camp Symphony Orchestra and Ballet (August 6, 1962); the Central Kentucky Youth Symphony Orchestra and Berea College Country Dancers (April 22, 1963); and the twenty-year-old Korean pianist Ton Il Han who played Scarlatti, Schubert, Chopin, and Liszt on the same program as the Paul Winter Jazz Sextet (November 19, 1962). All of the youth programs took place outdoors with the exception of the Mozart opera and the jazz sextet—the latter an especially important event, since it featured a jazz concert for the first time in White House history. While Paul Winter did not move on to become a major force in the development of jazz, he founded a talented combo of twenty-year-olds that had toured Central and South America under the Cultural Exchange Program shortly before they played in the White House. Their program for the mansion included several pieces in the newly emerging bossa nova style, which combined Brazilian and American jazz idioms. The group capped its tribute to Latin America with the excellent "Toccata" written for Dizzy Gillespie by the Argentinian pianist Lalo Schifrin. How did all of these foot-stomping nuances impress the audience of diplomatic children? "They applauded politely but sat placidly through the concert," noted the press.[28] More pronounced reaction to the innovations of jazz came from the president's daughter earlier in the year. The dynamic Jerome Robbins dancers wore deliberately understated white sweatshirts, black pants, and sneakers for their program for the shah of Iran. Six-year-old Caroline kept asking when they were going to put on their costumes.

Youth was honored once again when twenty-five-year-old Grace Bumbry from St. Louis made her American debut on February 20,

Final scene from Mozart's spirited comic opera, *Così fan tutte*, presented in the East Room by members of the Metropolitan Opera Studio. The Kennedys were the first to allow photographs of entertainment inside the White House.

1962, following a state dinner for Vice-President Lyndon Johnson, Speaker John McCormack, and Chief Justice Earl Warren. The black mezzo-soprano, a European sensation since her appearance with the Paris Opera as Amneris in 1960, drew raves from U.S. critics. Irving Lowens reported in the *Star*: "The Bumbry voice is astonishingly rich, flexible and powerful. . . . Americans can take pride in more than Astronaut Glenn's exciting achievement yesterday. They can also take pride in the fact that musicians such as Grace Bumbry can feel comfortable and at home in the President's house."[29] The singer's enthusiastically received program consisted of Gluck, Marcello, Strauss, Duparc, Copland, and Dawson. Henri Duparc's elegiac "L'invitation au voyage" seemed to be a favorite of Mrs. Kennedy, who leaned over toward the president and gently sang the words to him.[30]

More than any other administration to date, the Kennedys placed new emphasis and demands on the role of the social secretary. With the large productions, both inside the White House and on the lawn, came new problems that would have chilled the marrow of Henry Junge and the modest White House staff of the early years. "Fortunately, a kind of euphoria sets in," noted Tish Baldridge, "not the drug-induced kind, nor the starvation-induced kind of the far-Eastern monks. Ours was simply a White House Mania."[31]

With the Kennedys came the White House's first portable stage, a simple series of panels covered with rich red velours mounted on top of an eighteen-inch-high platform. The lighting, however, was completely inadequate, and Tish Baldridge called on Georgetown University's fine drama department to order the proper stage lights and manipulate them for each performance. "The Georgetown boys [all volunteers] saved our lives," she said. But for Baldridge it meant becoming embroiled in a dispute with one of the electrical labor unions shortly thereafter. Then she and Bernard West (nicknamed the "miracle maker of 1600 Pennsylvania Avenue") soon learned the hard way that their basement makeshift dressing rooms were not adequate: "We were to learn new lessons with each type of performer—actors, singers, dancers, and musicians ... we would soon have enough full-length mirrors for costume checks, enough hangers and enough chairs for performers to flop in, enough ironing boards and irons, and makeup mirrors with good strong lights."[32]

The Opera Society of Washington's *Magic Flute*, mounted during the company's regular 1961–62 season in the Auden-Kallman version, had to be brought indoors because of drenching rains. "This was an operation very much like pouring two quarts of milk into a one pint bottle," wrote Lowens in the *Star*. "The scenery would not fit ... there was no place for the orchestra. ... Mr. [Paul] Callaway stood with one foot in the East Room and one foot out," conducting the orchestra placed in the grand foyer. And then there was the problem of the costumes. Superbly rendered by Constance Mellon, they were caricatures of Indian dress that the State Department felt might offend the guest of honor, President Sarvespalli Radhakrishnan of India. Fortunately they were not changed, and the production came through as a well-presented, highly satisfying endeavor, despite all the harrowing circumstances. For Lowens the real unsung hero of the occasion was William Ramone, "who made the East Room sound like an opera house with his hidden microphones, loudspeakers and technicians—a brilliant acoustical achievement which surely should not go unnoticed."[33]

There were other brilliant feats of technology—and some less notable. For the New York City Center Light Opera Company's presentation of excerpts from Lerner and Loewe's *Brigadoon* for the king of Morocco, Baldridge used two tape recorders playing simultaneously (with only one turned up) in place of the usual live accompaniment of the Marine Band. While this managed to save precious space, it

John Kennedy introduces the Greater Boston Youth Symphony and Breckenridge Boys Choir, Texas, on the South Lawn of the White House before their performance for the congressional children.

evoked comment from the president: "He stopped by the rehearsal as he often did and asked with a worried frown, 'But what if the tape breaks?' " Tish pointed to the two recorders, explaining, and the President smiled, "Smart girl." But the evening was not yet over.

That night a rotating trooper light was installed by the Georgetown boys at the back of the room to give a very strong center spotlight. They had not used it at rehearsal. Toward the end of the first half of *Brigadoon*, they turned it on. Voila—the electrical circuits could not take it. Every fuse in our part of the mansion blew, plunging the East Room into total darkness. No lights, no music, no nothing. The Secret Servicemen sprang to all exits, guns drawn, fearing the worst.

The audience was shocked into silence, but I heard the President from the first row, saying in embarrassment, "Your Majesty, it's part of the show, you know."

It was the longest minute and a half I ever spent in my life. I half prayed in English, half swore in Italian, for those fuses to be fixed. Then the lights went on again, and the tape began to revolve. The dancers on stage had frozen in their stances, without a word, when the electricity failed. They began again exactly in step; they had not missed one beat. It was an incredible tribute to the dancers and to Agnes de Mille's training. It was also a tribute to the sanity of the Social Office that we all lived through it.[34]

One of the most important tasks the social secretary faces is communicating with the president about matters of taste and protocol. The Kennedy years were no exception. Some samples follow from the Baldridge files.

On applauding:

> The President had always had a little problem with classical music. He had been caught in the East Room on several occasions clapping at the wrong time and not being sure when the concert was finally over. Even following a program, the number of different movements within one composition confused him—as it does many people. We therefore worked out a code system for the Stern concert. As the last piece was almost finished, I was to open the central door of the East Room from the outside about two inches—enough for him to glimpse the prominent Baldridge nose structure in the crack. It worked beautifully that night and for all future concerts. When the President noticed the door slightly ajar, that

Members of American Ballet Theater, who had performed Aaron Copland's *Billy the Kid* in the East Room for the president of the Ivory Coast, are congratulated by President Kennedy.

meant the last piece was in progress. He would await the applause; then, clapping heartily, he would take Mrs. Kennedy by the arm, and escort the honored guests to the stage, to congratulate the musicians. Both Kennedys thought I was brilliantly sophisticated in music to be able to do this. What they did not know was that I knew less than they did about serious music. I simply made one of the Social Aides stay by me. He happened to be an accomplished musician who was familiar with all major classical compositions.[35]

On hurt feelings:

Sol Hurok was deeply hurt by The President's joke the night of the Roberta Peters–Jerome Hines concert when he stood up and said to the guests: "Miss Peters and Mr. Hines are here—courtesy of Arthur Goldberg." Although I tried to convince him that it was a jest and that every guest in The White House knew for sure that Sol Hurok had sent them to us, his Russian heart is bleeding. I think he needs a nice letter from The President subito. He has been out of pocket considerably in getting the artists down here, paying for their hotels, etc. Thanks a lot.[36]

On guest lists:

I have made up the list on the basis of fresh faces. . . . Supreme Court; Congress; White House Staff; Press (OK'd by Pierre); Negroes; Writers; Education; Music . . . Nadia Boulanger should have been invited to Casals from France; Theater; Ballet; Medicine and Science; Religion; Art; Big Contributors; Miscellaneous.[37]

On donating money to the symphony:

I found out that the Eisenhowers gave $25 in their check last year. Does the President wish to match or better it? Will you handle that? The amount of the check will not, of course, be publicized in any way. It's just the action of handing the check over to Diana Walker that counts.[38]

On the Harvard dinner:

3. Would you like a big cake with an "H.U." monogram on the icing?
(served with a light dessert?) ["yes" scrawled in the president's hand]

4. Would you like the Strolling Strings to come in at dessert time and the Marine Band to play in the hall? ["yes"]

5. Would you like the menus to have printed at the top: "Harvard Overseers Dinner" ["yes"]

6. Would you like a comedian to come in during coffee and liquers? ["no"].[39]

But Baldridge, always full of enthusiasm, would sometimes "get her ears pinned back a little bit," according to Heckscher: "I would see memoranda—Tish would sound up some idea to Mrs. Kennedy and Mrs. Kennedy would just write "no" with an exclamation point on it."[40] The first lady, in fact, vetoed ideas presented to her on several occasions. "Someone came up with the idea that the Marine Band should wear Lederhosen when they performed for German Chancellor Konrad Adenauer—but Mrs. Kennedy said 'no' after seeing me modeling mine," admitted John Bourgeois, a horn player who later was to become the leader of the Marine Band.[41]

The Kennedys expanded traditions in the area of military musical practices, both ceremonial and social. They added more dignity to the arrival ceremony for a state visitor by holding it now on the White House grounds rather than at the railroad station or airport where it had taken place formerly. They also formalized the position of director of ceremonies under the Military District of Washington, established in 1960 by President Eisenhower, and appointed Paul Miller. Under the Kennedys, moreover, the current practice of alternating the four service bands (Marine, Army, Navy, Air Force) for White House arrivals was established. The Kennedys also added pomp and historical flair in greeting their foreign dignitaries through both the Fife and Drum Corps in their Continental Army dress red uniforms and the U.S. Army's Herald Trumpets created under Eisenhower in 1959.

Inside the White House, however, the Marine Band held firmly to its tradition as "The President's Own." But it now fell more directly under the thumb of Mrs. Kennedy, who wanted "constant music— no dull moments."[42] As a consequence, the band formed more units and ensembles. Under the Eisenhowers, the guests entered the mansion and then mounted the long stairway into the East Room in silence, passing the red-coated musicians who sat "like so many mournful bellhops on a coffee break." Now "happy, peppy music by the Marine Band flooded the house the minute the guests began to arrive. The music was contagious. Everyone walked with a spring in his step, from footmen to dowagers."[43] But the new emphasis on the social scene prompted the presidential military aides to succumb to Tish Baldridge's "war plan"—a command they clearly were not used to: "My favorite young Marine captain came up to me one afternoon when a general had issued instructions counter to mine, and said, 'But Miss Baldridge, think of the predicament. You're a girl—and hell, I mean, excuse me, Ma'am, the General is my commanding officer here.' "[44]

With all their innovative finesse, the Kennedys, like other presidents and their wives, had their share of criticism. Objections were made to "twisting in the historic East Room" to the vigorous beat of Lester Lanin's orchestra. While the president did "NOT," as the press emphasized, dance the twist, he did go in to get a look at the new fad. Twenty-six-year-old Andrew Burden, who had the reputation of doing "the best Twist in New York Society," showed the president how it was done. Kennedy, however, preferred to dance the more conservative steps with his two dinner partners, Signora Gianni Agnelli, wife of the president of Fiat Company, and Chiquita Astor, wife of the Honorable

John Jacob Astor, son of Lady Astor.[45] There was more criticism of the "finger-snapping, sweatshirt-and-sneakers jazz ballet," performed in Jerome Robbins's *Ballets: USA*, however, than of any social dancing at the White House. Robert Prince's snappy *New York Export, Op. Jazz* was presented for the shah and empress of Iran after a state dinner, on April 11, 1962. A slightly flabbergasted reporter from the *Washington Star* wrote that the "hipswinging, torso-tossing" Robbins choreography "at times seemed rather strong stuff to be serving up to visiting royalty."[46]

The accusation by Republican Representative William E. Miller in October 1963 that "Sinatra types were infesting 1600 Pennsylvania Avenue" was mere mud-slinging, however. Frank Sinatra's intense loyalty in top political arenas is legend. Labeled "a skinny kid who looked like he still had milk on his chin," the crooner's first association with the presidency was in 1944, when he had tea at the White House with FDR. He also backed Truman and Adlai Stevenson and later Nixon and Reagan, but with his endorsement of John F. Kennedy's campaign in 1960 came real political power—or so it seemed. Sinatra participated generously in Kennedy's inaugural gala, the "super-benefit of all time" despite a snow storm that left rows of empty seats and forced Leonard Bernstein, who had been marooned in a stalled car with Bette Davis, to conduct his "Fanfare of Inauguration" in a shirt two sizes too big. But it was not long afterward that the Kennedys cooled in their attitude toward Sinatra, mainly because of his alleged Mafia connections, a rejection Sinatra never quite got over. He tried to produce a recording of the inaugural program for a price of $15 a copy which, he said, "should bring us some loot," but nothing came of it.[47] The White House was edgy that the notorious "Rat Pack" was making its nest in the great mansion. And while Sinatra attended a luncheon at the White House on September 18, 1961, which included Peter Lawford (the president's brother-in-law), Walter Pidgeon, Franchot Tone, and Henry Fonda, a White House memo of this date indicates a snub may have been more in order; "Frank Sinatra is also coming. Tish said there was no way she could keep from asking him as he was in Peter Lawford's room when she called him about the luncheon."[48]

On November 13, 1963, the famous Royal Highland Regiment, The Black Watch, presented a special program of piping, marching, and spirited dancing on the South Lawn. Guests for the afternoon were 1,700 children from childcare agencies served by the United Givers Fund, and they managed to devour over 10,000 cookies. "I don't know when I have seen the President enjoy himself more," wrote Mrs. Kennedy to Major W. M. Wingate-Gray. "The ceremony was one of the most stirring we have ever had at the White House."[49] Soon she would hear the pipers again. Jack would not. Ten days later the president was assassinated by Lee Harvey Oswald. At the White House nine pipers played once again "The Barren Rocks of Aden." But this time the hauntingly poignant march was rendered for the statesman's funeral cortege—and the whole world mourned.

Washington, London, Tokyo, Paris, Berlin, Nairobi—for a fleeting moment the world joined hands and with bowed heads turned to music to quell its grief and eulogize John Kennedy. There could be no other way. The majestic procession, touching the Capitol, the White House, St. Matthew's Catheral, and Arlington Cemetery, was followed by millions on the day of the funeral. And for a moment millions shared the hymns dear to America's only Roman Catholic president: "Holy God, We Praise Thy Name," "Ave Maria," the Gregorian "Subvenite," "O God of Loveliness," and "Holy, Holy, Holy." Millions also shared his love for Irish and Scottish melodies. On the north portico of the White House, the Naval Academy Catholic Choir sang "Above the Hills of Time the Cross Is Gleaming" (the "Londonderry Air"). The Royal Highland Regiment led the cortege from the White House to the Cathedral playing "The Badge of Scotland," and the Air Force Bagpipers rendered "Mist-Covered Mountain" as the coffin was moved to the burial site. All five service bands participated in the day's ceremonies and their selections included patriotic and religious memorial music chosen by the Kennedy family.[50]

But the most impressive use of music took place the day before the funeral. Twenty-four drummers, their instruments muffled and draped in black cloth, accompanied the caisson as it moved down Pennsylvania Avenue from the White House to the Capitol where the body would lie in state. It was Mrs. Kennedy's wish that there be no bands or choirs on that day, and the ponderous stately "dead march," paced to 100 beats per minute, reached back momentarily into the past—to the somber processions from the White House for Presidents Franklin Roosevelt, Garfield, Lincoln, and William Henry Harrison. It reached back further—to the year 1652, when John Evelyn described the "magnificent funeral" for Cromwell's son-in-law, General Ireton: "[He was] carried in pomp from Somerset House to Westminster accompanied with drums, regiments of soldiers, horse and foot. Thus in a grave pace, their drums covered with cloth . . . [they] proceeded through the streets in a very solemn manner."[51]

Musical artists, great and small, paid tribute in ways they knew best: a young Bosnian in Sarajevo, Yugoslavia, sang to his own accompaniment on the ancient single-stringed *gusla*, his lyrical epic:

> They know for certain John was gone.
> The caisson carries him
> With a white horse from the White House
> To the soldiers' grave of heroes.[52]

In New York Isaac Stern, Leonard Rose, and Eugene Istomin played on television the expressive slow movement from Schubert's B-flat Trio, which they had performed at the White House for André Malraux. Symphony orchestras all over the land paid their last respects with commemorative programs. One of the most hauntingly moving was the National Symphony's post-midnight performance to a completely empty Constitution Hall, a few blocks from the White House. "The orchestra of the presidents," as it had come to be called, was conducted by Howard Mitchell and played Debussy's *La mer* in memory of the president's love of the ocean and his valor as a naval officer; the "Adagio for Strings" by the American composer Samuel Barber, the last distinguished representative of the arts to be invited to the White House before the president's death; and the overture to Beethoven's *Fidelio*, a tribute to Mrs. Kennedy, described by Mitchell as a "true heroine" who "walked in tragic beauty" during her days of sorrow.[53]

In memory of the assassination, Igor Stravinsky composed a miniature for baritone (later revised for mezzo-soprano) and three clarinets called simply "Elegy for JFK" (1964.). The text by W. H. Auden consists of four stanzas of free haiku, and the atonal, transparent textures seem to feature an interplay between the diabolical tri-tone (G#-D) and the eternally hopeful perfect fifth (D#-A#)—the "oneness," perhaps, of both "sorrow and joy." Thus music, a vital part of the Kennedy White House years, offered its own special tribute to the new image, the fresh promises, and the bleak dawn.

> When a just man dies
> Lamentation and praise,
> Sorrow and joy are one.
>
> Why then? Why there?
> Why thus, we cry, did he die?
> The Heavens are silent.
>
> What he was, he was:
> What he is fated to become
> Depends on us.
>
> Remembering his death
> How we choose to live
> Will decide its meaning.[54]

On November 22, 1963, Vice-President Lyndon Baines Johnson became the nation's thirty-sixth president. He took the oath of office standing in the crowded presidential plane with his wife Claudia Taylor (Lady Bird) Johnson at his right side and Mrs. John F. Kennedy (her pink suit still stained with the blood of the assassinated president) at his left. Johnson was a man of great complexity. He was sensitive and ruthless, devious and candid, commanding and compassionate. In the words of Jack Valenti, Johnson's White House advisor and confidant, he was "a very human President."[55] The poverty of the Texas hill country, where Johnson was born, could not be easily forgotten as he grew up, and this link with the human spirit in its humblest as well as proudest form permeated his thinking on the arts. "Lyndon felt that the arts belonged to and came from all over the country," Mrs. Johnson once said, "and that they should not be concentrated in just the big cities. Early in his life his mother made him practice elocution, and he grew up in a sort of grass roots expression of the arts. His pleasure in sharing in the enjoyment and growth of the arts was very

Grand Duchess Charlotte of Luxembourg compliments Basil Rathbone and members of the Consort Players, who presented an evening of Elizabethan poetry and music for the Kennedys and their guests.

Violinist Isaac Stern chats with the Kennedys after his program with cellist Leonard Rose and pianist Eugene Istomin. The trio entertained President André Malraux of France on May 11, 1962.

In the main foyer of the White House Carol Channing dances with President Lyndon Johnson after portions of *Hello, Dolly!* were performed in the East Room. Among those watching are House Minority Leader Gerald Ford and his wife, Betty.

On the new portable stage given to the White House by the Rebekah Harkness Foundation, dancers from the Harkness Ballet perform Prokofiev's *Classical Symphony*. The stage, cleverly designed to match the decor of the East Room, was presented on September 29, 1965.

Four trumpeters from the Marine Band herald the arrival of President Richard M. Nixon before the state dinner for President Josip Broz Tito of Yugoslavia, October 28, 1971.

Special presidential accompaniment is provided for Pearl Bailey, as she sings for the Governors Reception, March 7, 1974.

President Gerald R. Ford awards the Medal of Freedom to pianist Artur Rubinstein, April 1, 1976.

Van Cliburn performs Chopin, Debussy, and Schumann for the emperor and empress of Japan on October 2, 1975.

Betty Ford, Martha Graham, and Cliburn converse after the pianist's concert.

President Jimmy Carter enjoys the Marine Band String Quartet in the foyer of the White House while a Secret Service man watches.

Agnes DeMille is a special guest of Jimmy and Rosalynn Carter during the American Dance Machine's performance on February 6, 1979. The program followed a state dinner for Prime Minister Khunyinng Virat Chomanan of Thailand (right) and his wife.

Ronald Reagan introduces his long-time friends, Frank Sinatra and Perry Como, before they sing for President Alessandro Pertini of Italy after a state dinner on March 25, 1982.

Nancy Reagan helps a small White House visitor explore the trumpet as guest conductor Keith Brion looks on. Brion, a Sousa scholar, dressed like the legendary bandmaster for the Marine Band concert for congressional children on the White House Lawn in July 1982.

The Reagans' first Christmas in the White House was celebrated by a concert in the foyer on December 17, 1981, presented by one of the many choirs that serenade the first family at Christmastime.

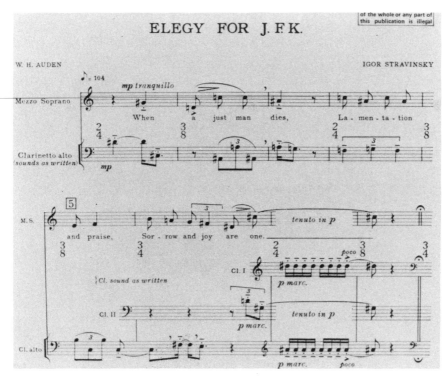

Opening of Igor Stravinsky's "Elegy for JFK," with text by W. H. Auden.
© 1964 by Boosey & Hawkes Music Publishers Ltd. Reprinted by permission.

great. This joy, in fact, was the genesis of the bill which created the National Foundation on the Arts and Humanities."[56]

The vital role that President Johnson played in developing the arts in America has been largely unsung, overshadowed by President Kennedy's image. Indeed, Kennedy's was a hard act to follow. August Heckscher might have spurred some action when he charged in March 1964 that the Johnson administration was failing to carry out the cultural arts programs of Kennedy. Two months later Johnson appointed Roger Stevens to the post of special assistant to the president on the arts, and on September 3, 1964, the president signed Public Law 88-579 establishing the National Council on the Arts, an advisory body of twenty-four distinguished citizens with Stevens named as chairman six months later. The dramatic outcome of the council's meetings was the establishment of the National Foundation for the Arts and Humanities, the first federal agency in our history designed specifically to support the growth of the arts in America. But President Johnson did more than just sign this law on September 29, 1965—he was personally and directly responsible for the foundation's existence. His firmness kept the bill from remaining in committee; he sent word to Speaker McCormack that consideration of the arts and humanities bill was a "must" even if the House had to be kept in session until early morning hours.[57]

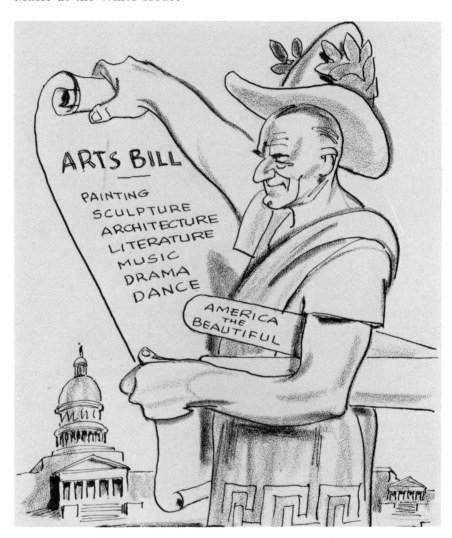

A caricature of President Lyndon Baines Johnson, who established the National Foundation for the Arts and Humanities in 1965.

The comments of renowned violinist Isaac Stern, a founder of the council and member for its first six years, add another dimension to the human picture of LBJ:

> When Johnson became President, Abe Fortas and I continued the conversations about the National Council on the Arts and conveyed the concept to President Johnson who thought it was a very good idea. In 1965, I went from Zürich to London, which is a short hour flight, and on to Washington for a 36-hour marathon just to come in for the inauguration of the Council. I remember Johnson saying . . . "I don't know a damn thing about music, but I know it is important, and I know it is necessary, and I know this is a good idea. The only thing I can promise you is that I'm going to keep my

cotton-pickin' hands off it. You people run it." Which was a wonderful way to put it and very important.[58]

Johnson's commitment to art as our "nation's most precious heritage" was more than mere words drafted by an astute speech writer. His administration gave major impetus to numerous other cultural programs, including the authorization of the John F. Kennedy Center in January 1964, the National Museum Act of 1966, and the federal acquisition of the Joseph H. Hirshhorn collection of 6,000 paintings, drawings, and sculpture. "One of the things that people don't realize about Johnson is . . . his extraordinary aesthetic sensibility," said Abe Fortas, one of the president's most intimate advisors and an enthusiastic music lover and amateur violinist. "It's untrained as far as music and art are concerned . . . he just has a kind of natural appreciation."[59] Another opinion—that of the Secretary of the Smithsonian S. Dillon Ripley—brings into focus more clearly Johnson's "grass roots" sensitivity. "The President had a friendly and genuine interest in the art with which he had grown up in the West. . . . He loved Western pictures that reminded him of the past, pictures of cowboys, Remington's paintings, local artists who painted around Fredericksburg, Texas, who transmitted some of the spirit of derring-do."[60] He liked western music, too—"Wagon Wheels," "Don't Fence Me In," "Navajo Trail," the songs from *Oklahoma!*, and, of course, "The Yellow Rose of Texas."[61]

The Johnsons claimed they did not consciously try to continue the type of musical programs held at the White House by the Kennedys, but there is no way they could have escaped their influence. Like the Kennedys, the Johnsons strove for the highest quality of talent, superb productions, and fresh ways in which the White House could publicly honor the performing arts of America. And they succeeded. During their five-plus years in office, November 22, 1963, to January 19, 1969, they arranged some of the most outstanding programs ever presented at the White House, especially in the areas of musical theater, youth programs, jazz, and the dance. The Johnsons, it seemed, went a step further than the Kennedys in their aim to reach out to all of America. They reached also to the West, not just as a geographical area, but to what it stood for—freedom, the wide-open spaces, the common man, sunshine and soil, the human side of the arts.

Coming right after the Kennedys' sophisticated tastes, these philosophies were not immediately grasped by the nation—and less so by the music critics. In retrospect, however, it was just as logical to hold the first state dinner, in this case for Chancellor Ludwig Erhard of Germany, at the Johnsons' Texas ranch in the hill country, settled by German families in the 1840s, as it was for the Kennedys to entertain the president of Pakistan at historic Mt. Vernon—perhaps even more logical. Mid barbecue, red-checkered tablecloths, and bales of hay, Van Cliburn, who was born in East Texas, performed on his elegant Steinway concert grand while Cactus Pryor courageously and masterfully held together the diverse program. This incongruous practice of mixing and melding national spirit, sensibilities, and styles was characteristic of the White House as it related to its honored guests. But it can become problematic aesthetically when the musical styles themselves are too disparate. Where else, for example, but at the White House (western or otherwise) would one find a world-famous concert pianist playing Beethoven after a nun had conducted her choir singing "Deep in the Heart of Texas"? The chancellor, nevertheless, was delighted, and after this touch of western froth he turned to Lady Bird and said, "We know that song in Germany too."[62] Another bridge between two nations had been built.

At their next state dinner, this time at the White House, the Johnsons juxtaposed contrasting musical *and* national elements. The first half of the program for President and Mrs. Antonio Segni of Italy on January 14, 1964, consisted of an Italian tribute—arias by Verdi and Rossini sung by the Metropolitan Opera tenor, Robert Merrill. The second part presented a sample of Americana with the ebullient New Christy Minstrels rendering "Walk the Road," "Ohio," and "Saturday Night," among other pieces. Via the Johnsons' informality and warmth, the American "Hootenanny" spirit with all its youthful vigor and joy made its way to the White House.

The program, however, was a "sharply-contrasted twin-bill," in the carefully chosen words of critic Irving Lowens.[63] It was reminiscent of FDR's musical White House, with the distinction that the Minstrels were "citybillies," not authentic folk singers, such as Alan Lomax and Charles Seeger. Their type of art had a show-biz flair, the kind that was enjoying great success on television at this time. Along with the Kingston Trio, invited to the White House later that summer by the Johnsons for the 121 young Presidential Scholars, the new Christy Minstrels were representative of an immensely popular, but short-lived, pseudo-folk phenomenon that died out in the mid-1960s as "Beatlemania" escalated. But while Paul Hume lauded Merrill's superb bravura interpretation of the Italian aria, he also felt that "it would have been wonderful if we had shown what we could do with the finest America music."[64] Another critic, Harold Schonberg of the *New York Times*, did not want to review the program at all because he felt some of the music was just too trivial. That was enough for LBJ. The president thereafter thought twice before inviting intellectuals, as he called Schonberg, to review concerts at the Executive Mansion.[65]

While this anomalous type of double-bill was not presented at the White House again, the Johnsons did invite back Merrill and the New Christy Minstrels as a nostalgic gesture right before they left the mansion. At their last state dinner, on December 11, 1968, they entertained the amir of Kuwait, Shaikh Sebah al-Salim al-Sabah. But apparently the foot-stomping rhythms baffled the amir. Looking nervously at Mrs. Hubert Humphrey on his left and Mrs. Johnson on his right, he patted his hands meekly to the strange sounds. President Johnson, however, bounced up and down in his chair with enthusiasm. He looked back to try to encourage a row of silent sheiks behind him—but it was hopeless.[66]

The new currents in American music were picked up by the Johnsons with caution, but those that did make their way to the White

Members of New Christy Minstrels chat with Lady Bird Johnson after their program in the East Room for President Antonio Segni of Italy.

House were significant. Jazz occupied a prime place in the mansion now. Dave Brubeck and his quartet played for jazz-fan King Hussein of Jordan, guitarist Charlie Byrd was invited for the king and queen of Nepal, and the excellent North Texas State University Lab Jazz Band performed for the king of Thailand. Other jazz artists to appear were Stan Getz for the College Student Leaders, the Gerry Mulligan Trio for the Presidential Scholars, and jazz flutist Herbie Mann for Princess Alexandra of Great Britain. But the jazz highpoint of the Johnson years was Duke Ellington's performance of his *Impressions of the Far East* (with William Strayhorn) and his tone statement on the Negro's plight in America, *Black, Brown and Beige* (1943), as the finale of the White House Festival of the Arts on June 14, 1965.

Occasionally folk, pop-folk, Baroque-pop, and night-club styles

(Tony Bennett, Tammy Grimes) had their place at the White House. "I remember Robert Goulet getting down on the floor with his microphone singing intimately into the rather flushed faces of the guests," Luci Johnson confided. "They weren't used to this in the White House."[67] But the Johnsons, with the assistance of Social Secretary Bess Abell, took great pains to program carefully and suitably for each occasion. Bess, according to Jack Valenti, "counted dullness as the original sin. If you were invited to an evening in the State Dining Room or East Room, then, by God, you weren't going to be starched with tedium. She worked at her job, although it was impossible to search out any signs of nervousness. She just simply went about her tasks with no minute wasted, pursuing every void until it was filled."[68] Bess Abell was assisted by Barbara Keehn and a memo from her dated November 16, 1964, indicates that she, too, had her tasks: "At Mrs. Carpenter's request, I would like to have FBI reports on the following entertainers—as quickly as possible." On Keehn's list were Carol Channing, Frank Sinatra, Lena Horne, Debbie Reynolds, Carol Burnett, Rudolf Nureyev, and Danny Kaye.[69]

Children and youth programs were important during the Johnson terms—always varied to include opera and symphonic music, as well as musical comedy and jazz. The Johnsons two daughters, Luci Baines and Lynda Bird, often sponsored these concerts, such as the thirty-six-member Boston Symphony Orchestra program conducted by Eric Leinsdorf for which both young women served as hostesses. The program was held in the East Room on March 31, 1964, and consisted of the orchestral suite by Richard Strauss written as incidental music for Molière's *La bourgeois gentilhomme*. Produced for 200 children of embassy families, the concert was broadcast on NBC television. Leinsdorf, whom Congressman Johnson had helped gain U.S. citizenship, was a long-time friend of the president. He was appointed by Johnson to the board of trustees of the Kennedy Center and to the Corporation for Public Broadcasting as an assistant director. "When there were musical and cultural things happening, the President used to turn to me sometimes for a little assistance," said the noted conductor. "I was, of course, very happy if I could be helpful. . . . I think the President was keenly aware of the enormous importance which music played in the creation of a better life for people."[70]

The Johnsons showed their commitment to the arts by several programs at the White House that honored talent and achievement, but also seemed to underscore how American attitudes had changed. On July 4, 1964, composer Aaron Copland and soprano Leontyne Price became the first musicians to receive the Presidential Medal of Freedom, created by John Kennedy shortly before he died to honor distinguished Americans from the fields of science, business, journalism, theology, and the arts.[71] Ironically, only a decade earlier, Copland's *A Lincoln Portrait* had been hastily removed from Dwight Eisenhower's inaugural concert program in 1953 because a member of Congress considered the composer a "Communist sympathizer." And on September 7,

1966, President and Mrs. Johnson saluted eleven young Americans who had won prizes in the recent Tchaikovsky International Music Competition in Moscow. Van Cliburn, the first American to win the contest (in 1958), served as master of ceremonies, but the evening was highlighted by the president's words: "I hope that history will record this example of how music has reached across the oceans, the walls, and the ideologies that separate us all, and has found response in the hearts of the Russian people."[72]

World-renowned concert and operatic artists also performed during this period—Leontyne Price, Walter Trampler (a violist who broke a string during his program for the president of Korea), André Watts, Richard Tucker, Patricia Brooks, Isaac Stern, Rudolf Serkin, and Jaime Laredo.

Two artists especially, Van Cliburn and Robert Merrill, had become close friends with the Johnsons. "We had a sort of parochial pride in Van Cliburn from Texas," admitted Mrs. Johnson. "And there was no more congenial, obliging, amusing person than Robert Merrill. He would pinch-hit whenever we needed him," she added.[73] Both artists had their ups and downs, however. Things did not always go as planned, even at the White House. For example, a few days after the assassination of Martin Luther King, Jr., Van Cliburn was to play for the chancellor of Austria. Washington was in an uproar. The dinner at the White House was delayed, so that when Cliburn arrived with John Steinway, he had time to warm up on the third floor piano. Steinway, who generally assisted with a concert only when it involved a Steinway artist, looked down the hall and said to the pianist:

> "Van, get your coat on quick. Here comes the President."
> Lyndon saw us and said, "Leave those coats where they are, boys." And he took off his own coat, put his feet up and talked with us for ten or fifteen minutes in the middle of the hall. He turned to Van and said, "Van, you know we are having a little trouble. But will you play for my guests?" Then he went back to his work apologizing for not being able to hear Van's program. After the concert, which had been considerably delayed, Van was hungry. It was midnight and he hadn't eaten any dinner. Nothing was open because of the rioting that had imposed a curfew on all of Washington. We went into the Red Room where a table had been set up and dinner was served to Van, after the kitchen was closed and the President and his family had gone to bed. There we were with one lone secret service man at 1:30 A.M.[74]

Robert Merrill had a near miss when he selected his program for Prime Minister Harold Wilson of Great Britain. The famous opera singer gave his list to Liz Carpenter, Mrs. Johnson's press secretary (the "merry warrior," according to Valenti), who promptly put out a press release. The reaction was instantaneous. "You must be out of your minds," exclaimed Walt Rostow, who, among others, did not see how Merrill could sing "On the Road to Mandalay" when Great

Britain had just pulled all their troops out of Suez. And he thought "I Got Plenty of Nothin' " was totally inappropriate since Great Britain had just devalued the pound. Liz Carpenter picks up the story.

> There was a brief flap among reporters and staff members, and Robert Merrill began pondering what to do about changing his program. In the meantime, I ran into the President and Prime Minister in the corridor. To my surprise, the President looked at me and winked and said, "Liz, do you know what the Prime Minister and I have been talking about the last two hours? We've been talking about songs!"
>
> The Prime Minister spoke up before I could utter a word. "Look," he said, "don't change those songs. I like them."
>
> So Robert Merrill sang them with fervor that evening, and then added another number: "It Ain't Necessarily So"— as a musical disclaimer.[75]

The newspapers had a grand time with the songs. One cartoon depicted Robert Merrill as a bloated baritone and President Johnson and Harold Wilson singing a dirge over the emancipated body of the British lion. But no one appreciated Merrill's talent and dedication more than LBJ. Merrill, the only opera singer on the gala program for Congress held at the State Department, shared the program with Mahalia Jackson, the Bitter End Singers, Anita Bryant, and other popular entertainers. The concert was opened by the president who stayed until the end, then set out for the hospital at midnight to be operated on the next morning. Not long afterward he wrote the following note to Merrill: "In my book, you are a Western man's Western singer! I know the Senate was equally as spellbound as I, not only by your top performance last night, but your versatility as well. It was so successful that your fans will probably demand 'Tumblin' Tumbleweed' at the Met. Mrs. Johnson joins me in appreciation of your time and talent. You made my hospital eve a happy send-off."[76]

The most striking feature of the musical programs presented at the White House by Lyndon and Lady Bird Johnson was the sheer magnitude of their scope. Most of the concerts combined several performers and groups, and many were staged with costumes, lighting, props, and sound amplification. The intensity, informality, and thorough attention to detail surpassed any previous administration. Many of the parties were held on the South Lawn for which a specially constructed sixty-four-foot stage was built. One of the most spectacular evenings was the first "Salute to Congress" on August 19, 1964. "You of the 88th Congress have made many of his [JFK's] hopes a reality," said the narrators. "Tonight a song is dedicated to YOU, the 88th! And hereby begins a tradition. As far as we know, no one before has ever sung a song to Congress—certainly not from the White House lawn."[77]

Narrated by Walter Cronkite, Howard K. Smith, and Nancy Dickerson, the gala utilized a production crew of twelve: a director, a set designer, an associate producer, musical directors, an art director, stage managers, and some others. "Our own costs have run up to $22,000 thus far," wrote Nat Greenblatt of *Life Magazine*, the organization

Metropolitan Opera baritone Robert Merrill, accompanied by Marion Merrill, sings for Prime Minister Harold Wilson of Great Britain on February 8, 1968.

sponsoring the show. Greenblatt hoped the White House would pick up the Department of Interior's bill amounting to $3,303.45 for lighting equipment, labor, and materials for the stage set, and he noted that it was "traditional for the White House to pick up the tab for the housing and meals for the cast and production team."[78] The cast of forty-five young singers and dancers in snappy costumes of red, white, and blue sang a compendium of campaign songs from 1810 to 1964, including "Fair and Free Elections" (1810), "Old Abe Came out of the Wilderness" (1860), and "Keep Cool and Keep Coolidge" (1924).

With Lincoln Center opening its new theaters during the Johnson years—and the Kennedy Center not yet completed—New York was the source for many of the big musical shows that came to the White House. For the Vice-President/Chief Justice/Speaker's parties, the Johnsons chose musical comedy and Broadway hits. On January 17, 1967, Carol Channing and a cast of twenty-five presented a thirty-minute segment from Act II of *Hello, Dolly*, the smash success that closed in 1970 after 2,844 performances. Called "Operation Big Daddy" by the ebullient Channing, the show had to be restructured by director Gower Champion to fit the East Room stage. The famous song "Hello, Dolly" brought back memories of the 1964 campaign when its words were changed to "Hello, Lyndon" and one more president was sung into office.

Other musical shows at the mansion were equally effective: scenes from Rodgers and Hammerstein's *Oklahoma!*; Carol Lawrence and

Gordon MacRae in portions of *I Do, I Do*; the New York City Opera Company's *Guys and Dolls* in 1967 and *Fiorello* in 1968; and the American Light Opera Company's scenes from *Peter Pan*. For the first time in White House history the same entertainment was held two nights running. The Manhattan School of Music staged "A Salute to the American Musical Theater" on June 1, 1967, for Prime Minster Harold Holt of Australia and on June 2 for Harold Wilson. Only one opera was presented during LBJ's terms—portions of Jacques Offenbach's fantasy, *Voyage to the Moon*. Presented by the Boston Opera Company and directed by Sarah Caldwell, the opera was replete with rocketships, a girl-in-the-moon, a "Dr. Blastoff," and all the whimsical science fiction of a bygone era. It was staged in the East Room on December 9, 1968, for 140 guests, who included the Apollo 7 and 8 astronauts. Some nearly got into the cast. "A man from NASA called," observed Bess Abell, "and suggested that some of the astronauts appear in one of the scenes."[79] But the idea fell rather flat.

The 1960s saw a great increase in the dance as an important national artistic medium, and the White House recognized these exciting new ventures by inviting the most prominent companies of the day: the Joffrey Ballet, American Ballet Theater, Harkness Ballet, National Ballet, Martha Graham Dance Company, and the Alvin Ailey Dancers. There was also a performance by Maria Tallchief with the National Symphony, and on another occasion Jose Limon danced in his moving set of variations on the theme of "Othello," *The Moor's Pavane*. For President Habib Bourguiba of Tunisia, Geoffrey Holder and Carmen deLavallade danced to the music of Villa-Lobos and Quincy Jones. "I especially loved the whole range of ballet performances we had," reminisces Mrs. Johnson. "The appreciation for that form of dance really entered my life during our White House years." Her reaction to the innovative Alvin Ailey Dancers shows her sensitivity to the new styles and her concern with beauty and beautification in America from every aspect. She felt that the program

> was a marvelous combination of spirituals and ballet, the numbers entitled "Pilgrim of Sorrow," "Take Me to the Water," and "Move, Members, Move." It was an absolutely stunning entertainment—exciting, moving, and beautiful. I don't re-member a more spellbound audience—one more in tune with what we had to offer. I think it was Isaac Stern sitting next to me who kept murmuring about a certain dancer, "How beautiful she is—how beautiful!" The costumes were varied, but there seems to be a certain style in ballet today for the dull earth colors—beige and gray and black. Some of them actually looked like the gunny sacks of my youth. When the dancing was over there was thunderous applause, and I could hear Lyndon leading it.
>
> It must have been past 7 when we went to the Blue Room and stood in line to meet our guests. I had worked happily on this guest list. In many ways it expressed my own pleasures of the past five years in the field of arts and entertainment.

Most of the members of the Arts Council in whose honor it
was given were there—Marian Anderson, Duke Ellington,
his long hair curling over his collar, O'Neil Ford, Larry Halprin,
Bob Merrill, and gentle kindly Rudolf Serkin.[80]

The major event that ultimately made dance more sophisticated
and comfortable at the White House was the donation of a portable
stage by the Rebekah Harkness Foundation. The historic presentation
took place on September 29, 1965, the day the president signed the
Arts and Humanities Foundation bill, and was celebrated with a program
by the Harkness dancers choreographed by Robert Scevers, George
Skibine, and Michael Smuin. The stage, designed by Jo Mielziner, a
New York scenic artist, is still used in the White House. It creates
the illusion, quite ingeniously, that it is an integral part of the room.
It has its own damask gold curtain, built-in lighting system, and
curved set of steps constructed into both sides of a semi-circular apron.
The stage elevation at maximum depth (36′ 3″) consists of thirty-eight
modular platforms that fold into a compact storage unit. With all its
improvements over the Kennedy makeshift stage, which was in essence
a platform, there were still complaints. Chief Usher Bernard West
called the East Room now "a stage with a room, rather than a room
with a stage," because it occupied about one-third of the room. And
Gregory Peck's solution to provide the back rows of the audience with
portable risers provoked a look of horror on the face of the Broadway
producer, Richard Adler, who assisted in arranging many of the big
programs. "They would ruin that beautiful floor," he said.[81]

For many of the Johnson productions, the orchestra of the Marine
Band (and sometimes the Air Force) played the accompaniment. It
also provided music for dancing, which often took place after dinner
in place of entertainment, and smaller units, especially the string
quartet, played in the foyer to greet arriving guests or provide background
music at luncheons. Johnson enjoyed the pageantry and elegance that
surrounded his official activities. The Marine Band not only played
for social occasions but also was often at the White House when the
president signed an act into law and on other business occasions.
"The President's Own" also played for Lynda Johnson's marriage to
Charles Robb at the White House on December 9, 1967. But shortly
after he took office, Johnson issued some orders for the Band to appear
at a staff party clad in the oddest attire of their long dignified career:
"At approximately 1625 this date Yeoman Cuff called to say that Capt
Shephard had a long distance conversation with the Social Secretary
who had talked to President Johnson. President Johnson is aware of
the feelings of General Shoup that he would prefer to have the Army
Band play the calypso music in calypso costume, but the President
said he didn't want the Army Band—he wanted the Marines—in
calypso dress. At 1635 General Greene was notified of this and said
to execute these wishes of the President.[82]

There were many social dances held at the White House during
this period. The Johnson daughters enjoyed the new rock-inspired

gyrations of the early 1960s—the frug, watusi, twist, freddy, swim, and the mashed potato. Lyndon Johnson, who genuinely loved to dance, preferred "Alexander's Ragtime Band," and the rating given him by his dancing partners ranged from "not bad" to "very good." Singer Edie Adams was more explicit: "He was a marvelous dancer, a strong lead. You don't find dancers like that anymore. Usually they're sort of Milquetoast fellows, but he knew exactly where he was going. . . . I thought, 'Gee, that's good. This is a strong man we've got up here running the country. I like that.' "[83] Johnson once danced with the great blues singer, Sarah Vaughan; Bess Abell later found her sobbing in her dressing room after the party for the prime minister of Japan. "What's the matter?" Bess asked her, distressed. "Nothing is the matter," Miss Vaughan said. "It's just that 20 years ago when I came to Washington, I couldn't even get a hotel room, and tonight I sang for the President of the United States in the White House— and then, he asked me to dance with him. It is more than I can stand."[84]

During his administration Lyndon Johnson named the first black Supreme Court justice and fought civil rights inequities and poverty. Americans spoke openly in protest against racial, intellectual, and human injustice. And music was becoming an especially powerful tool, an effective, sometimes acidulous, weapon for exposing sterile values. Reminiscent of the Hutchinsons of the 1840s, folk-rock musicians, led by Bob Dylan, belted out protest songs. While their music did not yet appear at the White House, their philosophies sometimes did. Black night-club singer Eartha Kitt found her own form of protest. When she rose at Lady Bird's Woman Doer's Luncheon on January 18, 1968, it was to lash out angrily against the war in Vietnam and Johnson's policies as the cause of ghetto crime. The subject of the luncheon was "Crime and What the Average Citizen Can Do to Stop It," and Kitt's diatribe came through as abrasive, ill-mannered, and rude. The stunned first lady, her voice trembling and eyes welling with tears, answered, "Because there is a war on . . . that still doesn't give us a free ticket *not* to try to work for better things, such as less crime in the streets, better education and better health for our people."[85] For days the nation let Mrs. Johnson know its feelings about the incident in a deluge of mail that poured into the White House. One sample follows.

Dear Mrs. Johnson:

Please know that the majority of the Negro race is ashamed of the way in which Mrs. Eartha Kitt conducted herself at your dinner. . . . Mr. Johnson has done more for the Negros than any other President. . . . Why would one *bite the hand that feeds them*?

Respectfully submitted,
A Group of Interested Citizens
in North Carolina[86]

314

Another *scena* took place when poet Robert Lowell refused an invitation to an all-day "White House Festival of the Arts" because of his distrust of the president's actions concerning U.S. foreign policy. The festival, held on June 14, 1965, was an ambitious extravaganza that presented exhibitions of paintings, sculpture, and photography; prose and poetry readings; music and ballet, both inside the White House and on the lawn. But as Liz Carpenter reported, instead of poetry, Lowell produced for this occasion "some blistering prose." By sending his telegram refusing the invitation to the press, a felicitous artistic event immediately became a political travesty. Twenty artists and writers backed Lowell publicly—eighteen of whom had not even been invited to the festival. One who had, Dwight MacDonald, disrupted the festival's ambience by circulating a petition that was, in effect, pro-Lowell and anti–Vietnam war. "I think most of the guests were embarrassed and confused by what occurred," said Barbaralee Diamonstein.

> Mr. McDonald arrived (I shall long remember his appearance because it was, I think, somewhat significant) red-faced, furious, racing around from guest to guest, with what he later described as not a petition but, I believe, a letter to the press.
> . . . no one stopped him from what he planned to do. He wore a widely striped shirt, as I recall, and a sport coat. He was quite obese and extemely untidy. The thing that I remember is that in his frenzy, the lower buttons of his shirt were open. The shirt was tucked into his trousers, and his bare stomach was exposed and no one even chose to point that out to him, let alone deter him from circulating this petition.[87]

President Johnson had made it clear earlier in his speech to the 400 guests, who included the nation's cultural and political leaders, that "art flourishes most abundantly when it is free—when the artist can speak as he wishes and describe the world as he sees it."

The tragedy of the event lay not in its content, which was expertly planned and presented, but in the way it was perceived. Buried among all the political rubble and the confusion over what President and Mrs. Johnson were trying to accomplish was an extraordinary cultural occasion—one of the most striking ever to be held at the White House. No one bothered to consider the adventuresome, creative touches: Duke Ellington, at age sixty-six, was making his long-overdue debut at the White House;[88] with an introductory narration by Gene Kelly, the Joffrey Ballet presented the American premiere of *Gamelon* to the music of Lou Harrison; scenes from five motion pictures recognized the U.S. film industry as an important art form. And not since Louis Gruenberg's "Two Indiscretions" was performed for Calvin Coolidge was an instrumental work of a serious contemporary American composer featured in a concert at the White House. At the festival Ned Rorem's *Studies for Eleven Players* (1959), which treats each of the players as virtuoso soloists, was presented by members of the Louisville Symphony

Orchestra. (In 1976 Rorem won the Pulitzer Prize for his composition, *Air Music*.) The great American flavor of the festival was underscored when pianist Rudolf Serkin declined an invitation to play because his current repertory included no American compositions. Serkin graciously offered a Brahms or Beethoven sonata, then admitted in his telegram (labeled "confidential") that regretfully he "may have been a poor choice."[89]

The festival was coordinated by Eric Goldman, special consultant to the president, with the assistance of Bess Abell, who maintained that the event "must have direction and pacing."

> Liz—yes, I see a *good many hitches.*
> [1] I would like the W. H. attached to it by calling the day "White House Festival of the Arts."
> [2] The programming needs to be revised for bounce. Ellington may not play Cole Porter and I'm not sure he should ... I think we ought to save the Cole Porter for a special evening honoring American composers. ...
> [3] Duke Ellington should *not* play background music during dinner ... a great composer and international figure does *not* play background music at the White House. ...
> [4] Another thing that perhaps needs a bit more explanation: all of the afternoon will be American. For example, Roberta Peters will sing an aria from *Candide* by Leonard Bernstein and the Louisville Orchestra will perform works by American composers.[90]

Grass-roots philosophies? Perhaps. For over the entire day loomed the imposing figure of LBJ. The president had scrawled his approval earlier across a memo from Goldman describing the ideology of the festival: "I like this. Ask Bill M. and Jack to see me about it before I take final action."[91] It was, after all, a Texas-size event for the White House, in keeping with his thinking. As he told the artists during the festival, "Your art is not a political weapon. Yet much of what you do is profoundly political. For you seek out the common pleasures and visions, terrors and cruelties of man's day on this planet. You help dissolve the barriers of hatred and ignorance which are the source of so much pain and danger. In this way you work toward peace—not the peace which is simply the absence of war—but the peace which liberates man to reach for the finest fulfillment of his spirit."[92]

CHAPTER 13

EVENINGS AT
THE WHITE HOUSE

Nixon and Ford

What is truth?
Can you blame the voice of youth
for asking, "What is truth?"

Johnny Cash
The White House, 1970

On August 8, 1974, facing almost certain impeachment, Richard Nixon became the first president to resign from office, leaving an administration embattled over the political scandal known as Watergate. There was something Wagnerian about the whole drama—the rivalry between truth and power, dignity and corruption. President Nixon, although he denied any personal involvement, left office to end the scandal; one month after Nixon resigned, his successor, Gerald Ford, granted him an unqualified pardon.

Nixon's strengths as president lay mainly in the area of foreign policy and in his dedicated quest for world stability, for a peace that had "healing in its wings" as he said in his 1969 inaugural address. He eventually succeeded in ending American fighting in Vietnam and southeast Asia, and reduced tensions with the People's Republic of China and the Union of Soviet Socialist Republics. In 1972 he became the first president to visit China, and during this same year he signed a treaty with Chairman Leonid Brezhnev of the Soviet Union to limit the nuclear arms race.

Ceremonial flourishes proliferated during Nixon's administration. The chief of state clearly enjoyed the pageantry that went with his office, causing some press people to call his administration "The Imperial Presidency." "I think," said Paul Miller, director of ceremonies for the Military District of Washington, "that this 'Imperial Presidency' business came about because Nixon was trying to upgrade the White House ceremonial guards. He gave them new uniforms with 'student prince' caps that some thought rather foolish-looking. I think this is why the media gave him a hard time about the Imperial Presidency. In reality, he was no more ceremonial than his predecessors."[1]

President Nixon did add an extra ruffle or two to the basic flourish, however. He continued the Kennedy and Johnson traditions for state arrival ceremonies, stationing on the south balcony the fourteen trumpeters, two drummers, and leader, known as the U.S. Army Herald Trumpets. Their instruments ranged from E-flat to G bass and were draped with the red, white, and blue heraldic tabards that symbolized the army. Founded by Gilbert Mitchell and Bramwell Smith, the Herald Trumpets had their premier performance in July 1959, when Queen Elizabeth II and Prince Philip were welcomed to Chicago for the opening of the St. Lawrence Seaway. The ensemble's links with England go back at least to the sixteenth century when trumpeters were used to herald the troops and convey orders. Even a fanfare by British composer Arthur Bliss ("Master of the Queen's Music") is played today at the White House as the honored guest leaves the ceremony and enters the White House. President Nixon took the Herald Trumpet concept a step further by bringing it indoors. He used four trumpeters from the U.S. Marine Band to herald his arrival as he walked into the East Room to greet his guests at receptions. They played a specially composed "Presidental Fanfare" that lasted fifteen to twenty seconds, sounding a majestic, or at least an attention-getting, entry.[2]

Like Harry Truman, Richard Nixon gravitated toward the piano whenever he had a chance. He studied piano and violin as a boy, claiming to have enjoyed music very much: "As a child I spent hours sitting at the piano picking out tunes. ... During my high school years, I played the piano for various church services each week. ... Although only a freshman at Whittier College, I was elected the first President of the Orthogonians, and I wrote our constitution and our song."[3] President Nixon played simple, popular fare on the piano for birthdays, at Christmas parties, and sometimes alone on the second floor of the mansion. Rex Scouten, who took over as chief usher when Bernard West retired early in Nixon's first term, recalls: "I was with him as secret service agent and when we'd go out of town and stay in a hotel suite, he'd have a piano there. I remember he'd play for one-half hour or so. He was really very good. That was when he was vice-president and had more time."[4]

Nixon himself tells of the importance of music in his memoirs: "Playing the piano is a way of expressing oneself that is perhaps even more fulfilling than writing or speaking. In fact, I have always had two great—and still unfulfilled—ambitions: to direct a symphony orchestra and to play an organ in a cathedral. I think that to create great music is one of the highest aspirations man can set for himself."[5]

The President's enjoyment of recorded music led First Lady Patricia Nixon to propose her plan for a White House record library to the Committee for the Preservation of the White House. In 1973 the Nixons received a collection of 2,000 long-play albums and a variety of hi-fi stereo components as a gift to the White House from the

Recording Industry Association of America. The president personally selected many of the components, and the wide variety of recordings were chosen by a committee under the leadership of Willis Conover, jazz broadcaster for Voice of America.[6]

Throughout Nixon's years as president, the media repeatedly criticized his "mundane" artistic tastes and his attitude of "benevolent indifference" toward the arts. Frank Getlein of the *New York Times* charged: "The Nixon taste is, in a word, deplorable. Or in a couple of words, there isn't any."[7] But there was no "benevolent indifference" when Nancy Hanks, chairman of the National Endowment for the Arts, received the president's approval for a big increase—almost double—in the annual budget for the endowment in 1971, and double again for 1972, bringing the total arts and humanities money to $61.2 million. "Nixon really perceived the arts as non-political," said jazz master Billy Taylor, who served for six years on Nixon's National Council for the Arts. "He saw the arts as something which should be encouraged and nurtured and in which the government should be the junior partner. He was extremely supportive of jazz and made me feel most comfortable—and I'm a registered Democrat!"[8]

The media lashed out against the Nixon White House entertainment, too. It was either too "bland" ("Writing about the Nixon Administration," said Art Buchwald, "is about as exciting as covering the Prudential Life Insurance Company");[9] or it was too filled with Hollywood entertainers and night club acts. But an overview of the state entertainment from March 24, 1969, to March 7, 1974, reveals a variety of styles, overlooked by a press perhaps still charmed by the spectacular Kennedy/Johnson decade: twenty-four popular and night club performers; nineteen classical artists; six jazz programs; three dance; three country music; one musical theater. With its special focus on American styles—jazz, country, and popular—the Nixon White House repertory was broader than any of its predecessors. "Pat and I looked forward to the evenings of entertainment at the White House as much as any of our guests," the president said. "We felt that performers invited to entertain after state dinners should reflect the whole spectrum of American tastes—and, incidentally, our own eclectic preferences."[10] But unlike the Johnsons, the Nixons avoided big productions. "The logistics are just very difficult," said Connie Stuart, Mrs. Nixon's staff director. "It takes twelve hours to put up the stage. This is not just a theater," she added. "It's a house. A very alive, vital house. Everything does not come to a grinding halt because we're producing a show."[11]

During 1973 especially, Paul Keyes, a former writer for the Jack Paar show and a long-time friend of the president, helped in the selection of performers. "He just kind of took over," recalled a White House staff member.[12] He lined up performers for the White House from his Los Angeles office; at times his choices were not known by even White House members until a few days before the event. Keyes also rarely consulted the embassies about the musical preferences of the foreign dignitaries as the social secretaries under Kennedy and Johnson had, but he managed to produce a stellar array of entertainers. For the first half of 1973 the White House could boast appearances by Frank Sinatra, Johnny Mathis, Tony Martin, Vic Damone, Sammy Davis, Jr., Bob Hope, Phyllis Diller, John Wayne, Edgar Bergen, and Irving Berlin. The latter seven performers appeared together on the spectacular program for the returned Vietnam prisoners of war in May 1973.

There was nothing "bland" about the way Nixon perceived his entertainment nor his own role in its structure and imagery. He personally made the decisions on the performers. "You wouldn't believe the detail he got into on social stuff," commented Dwight Chapin, the president's appointment secretary: ". . . the wines, where the receiving line should be, entertainment, what musical numbers will be played. He loves to know all that."[13] The president's picture also appeared frequently with various artists on the front page of the newspapers—including the *New York Times*. The accompanying text often carried: ". . . the President invited . . .," or "President Nixon is having" such and such a musical program. The White House printed programs, moreover, reflected the increased importance attached to the entertainment. Many contained fairly extensive biographical data about the artists. Several were enlarged and realized in brilliant colors, rather than the traditional plain white, and decorated with colorful braid and tassels such as emerald green satin-finish with gold tassel for the Shannon Castle Irish Entertainers; purple with orchid tassel for Patricia McBride, who danced for Indira Gandhi; gray with red border and green tassel when pianist Garrick Ohlsson played for Prime Minister Edward Heath of the United Kingdom. But always on the cover by itself was the gold presidential seal.

In January 1970 a short piece in the *New York Times* announced the president's intentions of holding a series of programs called "Evenings at the White House." The series would "bring in stars from the whole range of the lively arts" and were to be somewhat more informal than the white-tie state dinners. The president even thought about experimenting with "theater in the round" in the East Room, but this did not materialize.[14] The programs ended up being mainly popular entertainment. Starting usually at 8:00, they lasted about one hour and were followed by a reception (without a receiving line) and sometimes dancing. The programs were more frequent during the first year and no "Evenings" seem to have taken place during 1972 or 1974. The following list comprised the series

1970	January 29	Red Skelton
	February 22	Broadway musical, *1776* (complete)
	March 19	Nicol Williamson, backed by the World's Greatest Jazz Band
	April 17	Johnny Cash
	December 18	David Frost, Billy Taylor, and the U. S. Army Chorus

President Richard Nixon chats with rock 'n' roll balladeer Elvis Presley in the Oval Office in 1970.

1971	February 2	Beverly Sills
	March 16	Shannon Castle Entertainers from Ireland
	November 2	Richard Tucker
1973	March 3	Sammy Davis, Jr.
	March 16	Merle Haggard
	April 17	Frank Sinatra

Last to perform on the "Evenings at the White House" series was the legendary crooner, Frank Sinatra. During his two and one-half years of retirement, Sinatra presented his only concert when he sang for President Giulio Andreotti of Italy at the White House. His selections included "The House I Live in," "Moonlight in Vermont," and "I've Got the Whole World on a String." The president told the 200 guests, who included Vice-President Spiro Agnew, National Security Advisor Henry Kissinger, cabinet members, union leaders, businessmen, and members of Congress (many of them Italian-Americans): "This house is honored to have a man whose parents were born in Italy, but yet from humble beginnings went to the very top in entertainment."[15] Sinatra ended the evening emotionally in tears. About ten months earlier he had appeared before a House committee investigating Mafia infiltration into horse racing, and only a few weeks before the White House concert he had loudly cursed a *Washington Post* columnist, Maxine Cheshire. But for one important evening Ol' Blue Eyes worked his ineffable magic on the White House.

Music was so vital to the Nixons that hardly a national holiday, family birthday, White House church service, or important world event took place without some form of musical expression at the mansion.[16] Pat Nixon's birthday, March 16, was celebrated with a party that usually had an Irish theme because of its proximity to St. Patrick's Day as well as the first lady's heritage. The Shannon Castle Entertainers, ten singers and seven dancers, performed for the Irish Prime Minister John Lynch on March 16, 1971. The program of Irish ballads, "Galway Bay," "Danny Boy," and others, was part birthday celebration and part continuation of the "Evenings at the White House" series. (It also served to announce the engagement of Tricia Nixon to Edward Cox.)

Another famous birthday celebration was the party for Duke Ellington, who turned seventy on April 29, 1969. The president honored Edward Kennedy Ellington ("The Duke") with the Medal of Freedom and a round of "Happy Birthday," which he played later on the East Room state Steinway. The guest list for the event was as impressive as the array of performers. It included Dizzy Gillespie, Harold Arlen (composer of "That Old Black Magic" and "Stormy Weather"), Benny Goodman, Cab Calloway, Billy Eckstein, Richard Rodgers, and Mahalia Jackson. The event was one of the greatest aggregations of jazz luminaries ever assembled in one place. Performing were pianists Dave Brubeck, Earl "Fatha" Hines, Hank Jones, and Billy Taylor; singers Jo Williams and Mary Mayo; and instrumentalists Gerry Mulligan, Clark Terry, Urbie Green, Paul Desmond, and others. But this was just a start.

After the formal program, which included an all-Ellington sample from the master's numerous compositions, a massive jam session took place. Some of the audience rose to join in—including Vice-President Spiro Agnew, who surprised everyone with his interpretation of "Sophisticated Lady." The president went over to the Duke and led him to the piano. "The room was hushed as he sat quietly for a moment," Nixon recalled. "Then he said he would improvise a melody. 'I shall pick a name—gentle, graceful—something like Patricia,' he said. And when he started to play, it was lyrical, delicate, and beautiful—like Pat."[17] "The whole evening was one of the nicest, most relaxed parties I had ever been to at the White House or anywhere else," noted Billy Taylor.[18] The president thought so too. "We can tell the next day if the boss had fun," commented Dwight Chapin. "He was in great spirits the morning after the Bob Hope dinner. After the Duke Ellington party, he was ecstatic."[19]

Richard Nixon was the first president to acknowledge important world events with a major commemorative musical tribute. Three of

Duke Ellington at the White House birthday dinner given in his honor by President Nixon on April 29, 1969.

these occasions stand out for their originality and enterprise: the gala for the Apollo 11 astronauts; the dinner honoring the twenty-fifth anniversary of the United Nations; and the celebrations for the returned Vietnam prisoners of war. On July 20, 1969, the Apollo 11 mission—Neil Armstrong, Edwin Aldrin, and Michael Collins—landed on the moon. The nation went wild. Hundreds of millions all over the world watched on television. President Nixon held a state dinner on August 13 in the ballroom of the Century Plaza Hotel in Los Angeles, which was large enough to accommodate the 1,500 invited guests, who included the governors of all but six states, nearly every cabinet member and congressional leader, prominent executives of the aerospace industry, and a bevy of Hollywood stars. Flown in from Washington to provide the dinner music were the fifty-eight-member combined Armed Forces Strolling Strings, thirty-two members of the Marine Band Orchestra, sixteen members of the Army Herald Trumpets, the thirty-two members of the Army Chorus, and forty-eight members of the Marine Drum and Bugle Corps. The music hardly ceased all evening, with "the President clasping and unclasping his hands in cadence."[20] A special choral piece was written for the occasion by Ron Harris and sung by the Army Chorus with Richard Stillwell, soloist.[21] Astronaut Neil Armstrong had provided the opening lyrics when he first stepped upon the barren lunar surface and made his famous statement: "One small step for a man; one giant leap for mankind." For centuries song lyrics had been composed *about* the moon. Now they were written *on* the moon.

Just as spectacular was the banquet for the 600 former Vietnam prisoners of war, held on May 24, 1973. Bob Hope was master of ceremonies. (The press, in its sometimes vitriolic style, called the bash a counteroffensive to shift focus from the bitter Watergate episode.) The Nixons had to build special outdoor facilities on the South Lawn for the musical program, which featured Phyllis Diller, Edgar Bergen, Irving Berlin, and others. "We constructed a large stage with built-in lighting, a huge tent for the dinner, another for the dressing rooms and a third where the performers could relax and have a cup of coffee," Rex Scouten said. Then it rained. "It was the only time in my life that I had ever seen them mopping the grass at the White House with a regular floor mop," recalled Nelson Pierce, Scouten's assistant.[22]

On Saturday, October 24, 1970, the Nixons held a state dinner to celebrate the twenty-fifth anniversary of the United Nations. For the concert in the East Room afterward, Metropolitan Opera stars James McCracken and Sandra Warfield sang arias from *Fidelio, Cavalleria rusticana, Turandot,* and *Carmen* and concluded with the duet from Act II of *Samson and Delilah.* It was a brilliant program, typical of the couple's concert repertory and sensational singing. "The idea that we were married and that we represented mid-America [they were from the Midwest] Nixon seemed to like," said the noted tenor. The McCrackens were also told by the Social Office that more heads of state would be at the White House for this concert than ever before. "We really didn't need to know this; we were nervous enough just knowing that we'd be singing for the Nixons," related McCracken. "The East Room is not a very big room, and unlike a darkened theater, we could see everybody who was there. A few feet from us in the lighted room sat Haile Selassie, Golda Meir, Prime Minister Heath, and so many other dignitaries it was all we could do to keep our minds on the music."[23]

These great opera singers were by no means unique to the Nixon White House. Roberta Peters, Jerome Hines, Anna Moffo, Birgit Nilsson, and Beverly Sills all sang for the President and Mrs. Nixon and their guests. All but Nilsson, the famed Swedish-born Wagnerian soprano, were Americans by birth. Their programs ran about one-half hour (except Sills, who sang on the "Evenings" series) and generally consisted of lighter works with a familiar aria or two. Nilsson sang Grieg's "I Love Thee," Samuel Barber's "The Daisies," Sieczynski's "Vienna, City of My Dreams," in addition to "O babbino caro" from Puccini's *Gianni Schicchi.*

The great pianists were also represented on the White House programs of this era: Rudolf Serkin,[24] André Watts, Van Cliburn, Eugene List, Grant Johannesen, Whittemore and Lowe, and Garrick Ohlsson, who had just won the 1970 Chopin competition in Warsaw. List, who had played for Roosevelt, Truman, and Kennedy, featured American works on his program: Alexander Reinagle's Sonata in D Major and three pieces by Louis Moreau Gottschalk. For the final number List played Gottschalk's piano duet "Creole Eyes" with a talented former pupil, Harry Scaggiari, who was at that time a member of the Marine Band. "In the middle of the piece," said List, "we played the Whittier College Song and really surprised the President. He was so delighted. He got up after we had finished and told us why this song was so special, why it had a character very different from the usual college song. Whittier College was a Quaker school whose founders were missionaries from Hawaii. The song, in fact, was originally Hawaiian."[25]

While the visiting string quartet performing in the White House seemed to have gone out of fashion with Calvin Coolidge—not to be reinstated until Jimmy Carter's administration—the virtuoso violinist was a major event in the mansion during every administration. Isaac Stern (who played for seven presidents) performed Mozart and Bloch with Leonard Bernstein during the state visit of Israeli Prime Minister Golda Meir. Israeli Foreign Minister Abba Eban told President Nixon that Stern had once played Bloch's *Nigun* (which has heavily religious overtones for Jews) in Russia—"a courageous thing to do."[26] The hauntingly expressive piece moved the seventy-one-year-old leader of embattled Israel to tears. But then the great violinist had a way of making the Bloch an emotional experience for everyone who heard it.

Leonard Bernstein played on a new Baldwin concert grand that had been moved into the White House for the occasion. Most of the artists, however, used the state Steinway in the East Room, and for these programs John Steinway was on hand, as he wrote to Eugene List: "I have arranged for a lot of these, as you well know, and will do my best to get down there for this one. I will not be a guest at the dinner but will be working the backstage area as your personal manager."[27] And manager he was. He often had to oversee the placement of the piano, assist the artists with the security of their instruments, and check details for the artists' comfort and other particulars. Zara Nelsova, for example, needed a linoleum mat for the pointed support on her cello. "Naturally she does not wish to put that spike into your beautiful parquet floor," wrote Steinway to Scouten.[28] And though the social secretary, Lucy Winchester, was concerned about the room looking "tidy," Steinway had to convince her that the piano had to be placed in a way the artists could see each other while playing.

Security can pose special problems for the White House when several trunks of costumes and cases of instruments have to come into the mansion. Everything has to be checked. "I remember the case of Nelsova who was to play with her husband Grant Johanneson," said Steinway. "Her cello was insured for $180,000 and could never

Violinist Isaac Stern and composer/conductor Leonard Bernstein with the Nixons in the East Room after their concert for Prime Minister Golda Meir of Israel.

leave her side. A problem arose when we had to leave the hotel to rehearse. I called the White House and alerted them to the situation, so out in front of the hotel at which we were staying a secret service man arrived promptly in a station wagon with driver. The cello was slid into the wagon and we rode to the White House and back again to the hotel. I said to the men assigned to us, 'The cello stays right there!' And it did. They really take care of the people. . . . it's really superb."[29]

It could only happen in the White House. But it could also happen that tourists passing through the mansion by the thousands each day tended to steal the handles or "pulls" on the state Steinway lid. "Dear Mr. Steinway," began Scouten, "I regret to inform you that after all of these years, someone has taken one of the pulls from our Grand piano. We would prefer not to have any publicity on this matter as the millions of people who visit the White House are in the main most respectful of its property and furnishings.[30]

It's good they were; perhaps they were more so than the president himself who to the surprise of Steinway & Sons donated the second floor Steinway (#290,498) to the Harry Truman Library. It was a generous gift on the part of President Nixon—especially since he did not own the piano. It had been loaned to the White House by Steinway in December 1937 during the administration of Franklin D. Roosevelt. "Now it's on loan to the Harry Truman Library from the Steinway firm," added John Steinway with a smile.[31]

Music at the Nixon White House reflected the music of the late 1960s and early 1970s all over America. Magnified by explosive tones, provocative lyrics, and the all-pervasive power of mass media, popular music made a social statement so intense that there were times when not even the presidential estate could escape its message. We were a nation suffering from a massive ego trip, from rebellion and unrest manifest in nearly every aspect of American life from hippies to hemlines. Gigantic rock festivals and other musical trends vividly told the story, while the lone hip-gyrating balladeer, Elvis Presley, became a nostalgic hero. But all had their messages—sometimes oddly poignant ones.

> We don't smoke marijuana in Muskogee
> We don't take our trips on LSD
> We don't burn our draft cards down on Main Street
> We like living right and being free

Thus sang Merle Haggard, legendary country and western singer on March 16, 1973, as part of the "Evenings at the White House" series. Along with "Okie from Muskogee," he sang "Walkin' on the Fightin' Side of Me." "Okie" and "Welfare Cadilac" (spelled with one l) were Nixon favorites that the president had requested Johnny Cash sing in his 1970 White House appearance. Cash told the White House staff that he would prefer not to sing these songs and substituted "A Boy Named Sue," another Nixon favorite, and "What Is Truth?" The husky singer, dressed in his black frock coat, ruffled shirt, and riverboat gambler's vest, judiciously avoided the derisive message of "Cadilac":

> They tell me this new President has put in a whole new
>   poverty plan
> He's gonna send us poor folks money, man;
> They say we're gonna get it out here in stacks
> In fact my wife is already shopping round for her Cadilac.

Some singers were not as concerned about offensive lyrics as Cash. White House or not, they belted out their messages. The Guess Who, a rock group famous for its anti-American music, performed "American Woman" at the dinner dance for Prince Charles and Princess Anne of England in July 1970. The satirical song pictures the United States as an overpainted "broad" who is "no good for me"—sort of a "Welfare Cadilac" in reverse, mused one top record-industry source. Then there was the Carol Feraci incident. During her White House performance, the thirty-year-old singer unfurled a blue banner from her bosom that read "Stop the killing." Staged as a protest against the Vietnam War, the act shocked the Nixons' distinguished audience. "Stop bombing human beings, animals and vegetation," cried Feraci in the middle of a choral number directed by Ray Coniff. "If Jesus Christ were here tonight, you would not dare to drop another bomb." How to prevent such incidents? "I don't know," said Lucy Winchester. She recalled a cartoon that Bess Abel had placed on her desk along with a vase of flowers when she first took over as social secretary. It showed a concert pianist in his white tie and tails with a piano in the background. He was saying, "Before I begin my concert, I would like to make a foreign policy statement."[32]

The appearance and dress of some of the White House performers during these years raised eyebrows. The press, perennially prone to latch on to an unbuttoned shirt (Tony Bennett's "strip tease" act for LBJ), or a "cleavage down to here" (Metropolitan Opera singer Anna Moffo's "slipped moorings"), or just the crass headline, "Topless at the White House," which referred to opera star Beverly Sills's gown that came unzipped (luckily, in back) while she was singing Donizetti. "I threw my velvet evening coat over my shoulders just in the nick of time," she said.[33] Male performers fared no better. A young, long-haired violinist and member of the faculty of the Chicago Musical College was led away by a White House guard until the social secretary rescued him and verified that he was part of the program inside. Bill Schustick, a leading expert on nautical songs and lore, had other problems. He was to accompany New York City ballet star Edward Villella with several sea chanties during the program for Prime Minister Indira Gandhi on November 4, 1971. His problems began the minute he arrived from New York.

> A young man with a beard, long hair, leather fringed vest and a Civil War hat got off the plane at National Airport Wednesday afternoon and walked over to a Marine officer standing beside a White House limousine. "Hi," he said. "Are you here to meet someone?" "Yes," replied the officer. "I'm here to meet two people who will perform tomorrow night at the White House." "Well," said the young man, "I'm one of them." The Marine looked him up and down, then broke into a big grin. "Boy," he said, "they're not going to believe this at the barracks."[34]

Then Schustick had his program cut and was asked to wear black tie instead of his green blousy shirt and leather vest, which he called "a sort of minstrel outfit." After arguing that all he had was a tuxedo that was "too tight under the arms and chest to perform in," he was allowed to keep his original costume. An artist-in-residence at Dartmouth University teaching American folk lore, Schustick would perhaps have been more at home in the FDR White House. Sea chanties rang prolifically in the mansion's great halls then. "This country has negated a lot of its cultural background," said Schustick. "That's why I'm really tickled to take a gut-busting sea chanty to the White House and sing it for heads of state, because what I'm saying is this is really us and in spite of my politics I really hope Nixon digs it. But I feel a little funny singing for him after all the things I've said about him."[35]

There were performers who refused to come to the White House as Watergate became more intense. Yale's famous Whiffenpoofs turned down an invitation to sing Christmas carols. "We were afraid our appearance might imply we support President Nixon—and we don't."[36] The last few months of 1973 and the first ones of 1974 were grim socially—"White House Tomb" the press called the president's home. "I really don't know how Nixon stood up," said pianist Eugene List, who played at the summit meeting in Moscow a few weeks before Nixon left the White House. "Everybody knew it was the end. And Mrs. Nixon must have been under terrible pressure. She was such a lovely, noble lady. I remember her wearing a very beautiful gown that day."[37]

There was no way to escape Watergate. But there was a way to hide momentarily. "Mrs. Nixon disclosed that the President has taken to playing the piano late at night in the family quarters of the White House," the *New York Times* reported. Then on March 7, 1974, the nation's governors were treated to one of the liveliest White House after-dinner shows in years when Pearl Bailey and the president collaborated in an impromptu performance. The great blues singer coaxed the president into playing, pointing out that he could choose anything he wanted. But when he began "Home on the Range," Bailey smiled and complained, "Mr. President, I want to sing a song, not ride a horse." And then they had problems finding the same key at the same time. "I don't know whether I'm finding him, or he's finding me," Bailey quipped. Vice-President Gerald Ford said he had never laughed so hard in his life. The president added, "I just want to say to our distinguished guests that this piano will never be the same again, and neither will I."[38]

Shortly before Nixon resigned from office, mobs lined the White House gates chanting their eerie permutation of a time-honored tune— "Jail to the Chief!" On August 9, 1974, Vice-President Ford was sworn in as the nation's new leader. The curtain descended on the final scene. The drama was over.

Gerald and Betty Ford continued the diversity of entertainment that the Nixons had enjoyed, but their tastes leaned even more toward the popular and night-club styles. While President Nixon had been the overseer of White House programming, the weight shifted back to the first lady under the brief years of the Ford administration. Ford was not particularly fond of music. "I'm so envious of talent," Ford once said, "Betty says I can't even listen on key." Paul Miltich, Ford's long-time press secretary on Capitol Hill, commented: "As long as I've known him, he's never been interested in painting or sculpture or anything of that kind. He doesn't understand classical music. It just doesn't mean anything to him."[39]

With First Lady Betty Ford the arts were quite a different matter.

She loved the theater, especially all forms of dance. "I think she's got every book ever written on ballet," said Nancy Howe, Mrs. Ford's close confidant and personal assistant at the White House.[40] Betty Bloomer Ford studied dance at Bennington College in Vermont. Deciding to make her career in dance, she then became a member of Martha Graham's company in New York City. "She was a very dedicated student and the central member of a group of girls I had at that time," recalls Martha Graham.[41] She danced in Graham's "American Document" at Carnegie Hall on October 9, 1938, and on Christmas Day of that year at the Alvin Theater. After she was married, she kept up her dancing lessons until a pinched nerve compelled her to stop.

The Ford White House entertainment was marked by relaxation and spontaneity. President and Mrs. Ford seemed to enjoy their parties. Of the thirty-four state dinners, twenty-eight featured light entertainment, and, unlike the Nixons, dancing was often a focal point of the evening. "Jerry likes to dance to old Glen Miller–style numbers like 'In the Mood'," Mrs. Ford related in her book, *The Times of My Life*. "Some members of the press have written that he does the same two-step no matter what the music is." Mrs. Ford went on to explain how the president was once very unhappy about the impulsive modern sounds coming from the band. "If they won't play some music I can dance to, I'm just not going to come to these things any more," he said. "I'm the President of the United States and I should be able to have some music I can dance to."[42]

For the dinner for President Walter Scheel of Germany, Mrs. Ford had read that trumpeter Harry James was appearing at Wolf Trap and invited him to come over after his show. The Fords were entertaining with a spirited after-dinner show staged by Tennessee Ernie Ford and the Opryland Singers. When Scheel had left and the Fords stepped inside the Grand Foyer after bidding him farewell, the president swung his wife around the dance floor upon a momentary whim. Soon both had separated and were spinning around with different partners. Harry James, in turn, sat in as trumpeter with the Marine Band combo. "That was really something," recalls Mrs. Ford, ". . . Harry James playing 'Sheik of Araby,' Helen O'Connell singing a duet of 'Hey, Good Lookin'' with Tennessee Ernie, and Jerry calling out a request for 'Hello, Dolly.'" Thus it went on long after midnight with James's mellow trumpet rising clear and sweet above the songs.[43]

Betty Ford danced with everybody. Even if they did not dance, she danced with them. Sometimes it seemed to her more like jogging than dancing, however, as in the case of her partner President Urho Kekkonen of Finland. Her greatest disappointment was being turned down by Fred Astaire. "I'd dreamed all my life of spinning around the floor with Fred Astaire while people stood back watching us," she admitted. "He said he just wasn't a ballroom dancer and had to have a routine."[44] During the Ford's first state dinner on August 16, 1974, for King Hussein of Jordan, dancing was held in the East Room to the music of Howard Devron. One of the featured numbers of the evening was "You've Got to Be a Football Hero," in honor of Ford, a former

President Gerald Ford dances with Queen Elizabeth II of England during her visit to the White House in 1974.

member of the University of Michigan team. On another occasion the *hora* was danced in the marble foyer. Betty Ford took part in the traditional Israeli circle dance during the festivities for Prime Minister Yitzhak Rabin of Israel on September 12, 1974. And, of course, there were dances for the younger set. Susan Ford, for example, danced the bump at one of her White House shindigs—just as the two Nixon girls before her had tripped to the tunes of The Turtles and The Temptations.

For advice in the development of her White House entertainment, Mrs. Ford had the assistance of Mrs. Nixon's social secretary, Lucy Winchester, until October 1975. Then Maria Downes took over as social secretary. Mrs. Ford also depended on Scouten for guidance, too. "When they get to talking about certain things, I'm going to try and catch your eye and I'll expect you to tell me whether the plan under discussion is the right plan or the wrong plan to go ahead with," she told him during one of her weekly staff meetings.[45] Her guest lists read like tools of internal relations, some said. They allowed the president to pay political debts, lobby for congressional votes, recognize campaign contributors, and honor various segments of society from science and business to sports and the arts. They also served to "heal wounds, invite back those political forces who were left out in the cold, and perhaps neutralize old animosities."[46] All this through the music of Ann-Margret, Vikki Carr, Wayne Newton, Carol Burnett, Helen Reddy, Tony Orlando and Dawn, and a host of others.

One of the most important musical evenings under the Fords was the Bicentennial diplomatic reception on July 20, 1976. The gala White House celebration of America's independence was realized through the efforts of Broadcast Music Incorporated's Russell Sanjek, which perhaps explains the focus on America's more commercially oriented creative output. Representing country music were Tammy Wynette and Roger Miller; also on the program were Ella Fitzgerald, The Jordanaires, and The World's Greatest Jazz Band, featuring Yank Lawson and Bob Haggart. It was essentially an overview of conservative, mainstream popular music, very well performed from all accounts.

But the state dinners were the feature of the Ford entertaining. In 1975, for example, there were fourteen state dinners representing thirteen different nations. Following the custom of the Nixons, the Fords preferred colored printed programs with the honored guests' names on the covers and biographical details of the performers inside, although their selections, curiously, were not always indicated. President and Mrs. Ford were especially successful in matching the musical programs to the interests of the state visitors, by this period a major factor in selecting the entertainment. It is a study in itself to peruse the artistic preferences of foreign heads of state while they are guests in this country. For example, Betty Ford learned that Chancellor Helmut Schmidt of West Germany loved opera, so she invited Phyllis Curtin to sing; for France's blues-loving, piano-playing Giscard d'Estaing, Earl Hines performed; and the extraordinary blind jazz genius George Shearing satisfied the request of President Kekkonen of Finland. Ann-Margret sang and danced for the shah of Iran "because the Shah likes pretty girls," according to the president. As her costume grew briefer while her act grew longer, there were undoubtedly others who felt the same way.

For President Giovanni Leone of Italy, the White House offered its first ragtime evening on September 25, 1974. Composer and jazz historian Gunther Schuller brought his New England Conservatory Ragtime Ensemble for a program of the music of Scott Joplin, harking back to the time "The Maple Leaf Rag" was played by the Marine Band in Theodore Roosevelt's White House. One year later Johnny Cash was asked to perform for President Anwar Sadat of Egypt, a great fan of western music. But at the last minute he could not come, and Pearl Bailey substituted for him. The outgoing, ebullient singer summoned an embarrassed Sadat to dance on stage with her. Her characteristic warm informality "had helped bring our two nations together," said President Ford. So did Van Cliburn's sweeping interpretation of Chopin, Schumann, and Debussy during the first White House entertainment for a reigning Japanese emperor. The great American pianist opened his concert with a majestic interpretation of the Japanese national anthem.

The most effective use of music as a binding force between two nations during this period, however, is recounted by jazz composer and pianist Billy Taylor. Taylor and his trio played on February 5, 1974, for Prime Minister Begum Bhutto of Pakistan. "The audience clapped so loud and long that we finally thought we should play an encore. So I said to President Nixon and the Prime Minister, 'We had not planned anything at this point, but since we have the opportunity, I'd like to show you how much we admire the music of *your* country.' And we improvised on a *raga*. It was a smash and they loved it. Bhutto came over and gave us high praise and invited us to a program the next night in which Pakistani musicians were to play. Those few days were very exciting ones for us."[47]

The White House, with its unique melding of music, politics, and protocol, has been perennially prone to mishaps and infelicities of coordination. The Captain and Tennille's big hit "Love Will Keep Us Together" was an appropriate theme song for the two nations, England and America, during their program for Queen Elizabeth II and Prince Philip on July 7, 1976. Their "Muskrat Love Song" was not, however. According to some guests, the gentle little song's cutesy, suggestive lyrics—punctuated with animal love gurgles from the ARP synthesizer— were unsuitable fare for royalty. The applause was unusually weak for lyrics like:

> Now he's ticklin' her fancy, rubbin' her toes
> Muzzle to muzzle now anything goes
> As they wiggle, Sue starts to giggle
> They whirl and they twirl and they tangle.[48]

Queen Elizabeth II received another ill-timed tribute when, purely by accident, the Marine Band struck up "The Lady Is a Tramp" just as she started to dance. "We took the piece immediately out of our repertoire," said Marine Band Leader Colonel John Bourgeois, recalling the incident.

There were no such accidents in the cases of the concert and operatic artists who performed at the White House during this time, however. Two brilliant young artists played at different state dinners: Violinist Eugene Fodor, who won the 1974 Tchaikovsky Competition in Moscow (and was the first noncitizen of the Soviet Union ever to place in the violin division); and James Tocco, the first American pianist to win the Munich International Piano Competition the year before. Other artists who performed for the Fords were Gil Morgenstern, Beverly Sills, Roberta Peters, Phyllis Curtin, and Sherrill Milnes. Edward Villella and Violet Verdy from the New York City Ballet danced, without Bill Schustick this time, and the Claude Kipnis Mime Theater rounded off its interesting program with "Circus Parade" to Stravinsky's Suite no. 2 for chamber orchestra.

On three occasions President Ford bestowed the Medal of Freedom on distinguished Americans in the fields of science, humanities, and the arts. Artur Rubinstein was the first recipient, on April 1, 1976. The eighty-nine-year-old pianist had played only once in the White

House, for Dwight Eisenhower in 1957, and although he had been decorated by fifteen other countries, the United States had never recognized him. "Artur Rubinstein has given something more than the joy of music—he has given the joy of life itself," remarked Ford at the opening of the ceremony. "His country, the United States of America, is proud to proclaim him as a giant among artists and men."[49] Rubinstein, a native of Russia, bowed to the president and said, "I blush orally, because my old age doesn't allow me to blush on my face. I am touched deeply . . . due to the second World War I brought my wife and children with me [to America] and have never left the country since. And this country began to spoil me—to love me, to give me such long, long years of affection. I cannot express it in words, really. Millions of people are my friends. Well, my feeling toward the United States is one of *great* gratitude and the continuation of a long, beautiful love affair. Thank you, Mr. President, for giving me the best sign of anything I could receive in this country."[50]

Later that year eighty-two-year-old iconoclastic dancer and choreographer Martha Graham also received the distinguished Medal of Freedom. Betty Ford's former teacher became the first to be honored in the field of dance on October 14, 1976. Upon acceptance of the medal she commented that the honor was "not a recognition of me but of a new attitude toward the arts and dance," adding that dance had had an uphill struggle in acquiring acceptance in the United States because of its European heritage.[51] After the ceremony, a program was presented by Janet Eilber, a member of the Martha Graham Dance company. Finally, on January 10, 1977, President Ford awarded twenty-two more Medals of Freedom. Included among the illustrious recipients were Irving Berlin, Arthur Fiedler, and arts patron Catherine Filene Shouse.

The press was particularly critical of entertainment during the Nixon and Ford years. White House tastes were either too "dismal" (George Will) or "establishment" (Charlie McCollum) or just plain "lowbrow" (Betty Beale). "Indeed," continued Beale, "any singer who won't perform without clutching a mike shouldn't be there."[52] Other critics recommended more exploration of the riches of our culture by bringing to the White House segments of the current Folk Life Festival in Washington; performances from the John F. Kennedy Center (which opened in 1971 with Bernstein's controversial *Mass*); artist groups from across the country encouraged by grants from the National Council on the Arts; and, for the first time, that wayward son of American socio-musical life—rock, "distinguished" rock that is.

How about Paul Simon in the White House, recommended Charlie McCollum of the *Star*, or Linda Ronstadt, The Eagles, Bobby Short (who, McCollum forgot, *did* play for the Nixons in 1970), folk singer Woodie Guthrie and "such 'outlaws'" as Bob Dylan?[53] McCollum may have had a point. But the mere fact that rock groups were now considered respectable at the White House tells us something about American tastes of the later 1970s—a time less innovative than inventive, less radical than romantic. It was a period for reworking, reconsidering, and the drive to protest society's ills unabashedly in song was less urgent. "I just wonder what establishment Washington is going to think if Jimmy Carter gets elected and has Bob Dylan and the Allman Brothers play his first state dinner? mused McCollum He was in for some surprises.

CHAPTER 14

MUSIC, MASS MEDIA, AND THE MODERN WHITE HOUSE

Carter and Reagan

> We are trying to do at the White House
> what Leontyne Price has always done:
> to prove that opera is not just a luxury
> for the few, but a thing of beauty for all.
>
> Jimmy Carter
> PBS Telecast, October 8, 1978

There was little warmth in the filtered sun, and the wind whipped unmercifully about President James Earl Carter, Jr., as he smiled and waved to the throngs nearby. Dramatically departing from tradition, the new president and his family walked from the Capitol to the White House following the inauguration on January 20, 1977. During his vigorous campaign to capture the Democratic nomination and the presidency, Jimmy Carter promised to remain close to the people. The White House would be, in his words, "the people's White House." Through the art of music, especially, he kept his promise.

Born in Plains, Georgia, Carter was the first chief executive to come to office directly from the Deep South since well before the Civil War. He was a peanut farmer, who served first as state senator and later as governor of Georgia. President Carter's White House was hardly aristocratic or courtly. He dressed informally, often appearing in sport shirt for business, and he entertained middle America with great warmth and sincerity. All were welcome at the White House, it seemed, whether they were 2,000 senior citizens, 1,000 Iowans, Armenian-Americans, the Peanut Brigade, the Country Music Clan, or just 750 friends from New Hampshire or Georgia.

Carter's first attempt to lighten the image of pomp and protocol at the White House resulted in the simplification of ceremonial procedures. Some news reporters mistakenly claimed Carter did away with the playing of "Ruffles and Flourishes" and "Hail to the Chief" when he only eliminated these honors for outdoor arrivals, retaining them for most indoor ceremonies. President Carter did cut the fourteen Herald Trumpeters, however, and the fifty-six servicemen parading state and territorial flags, and he featured only one military band in his no-frills style. But there was no reduction of other aspects of music at the White House. The same president who campaigned wearing an Allman Brothers Band t-shirt brought to the Executive Mansion some of the finest classical artists the residence had ever known. And—more significantly—these artists were now shared with the nation for the first time through the medium of television in a carefully planned series of concerts. It was indeed "The People's White House"—the great stage whose curtains were now drawn open for the entire world to enjoy. Through such music, Carter underscored the point he made in Atlanta in September 1976: "I am vividly aware of the importance of the arts to our communities. I still remember the impact a visiting symphony orchestra made in the county I come from in south Georgia. It was the first time a symphony orchestra had ever played in that area. Everybody, from country merchants to farmers went, listened and enjoyed. The orchestra's visit was the main topic of conversation for weeks afterwards. People felt that something beautiful and full of meaning had touched their lives."[1]

Few presidential families have personally enjoyed classical music as much as the Carters. Even Harry Truman admitted preferring instrumental music to vocal, and the Kennedys' personal tastes ran toward popular classics and programmatic styles. But the Carters were both instrumental and opera devotees. Robert Shaw, conductor of the Atlanta Symphony who organized the musical side of the inaugural receptions, claimed Jimmy Carter's love of music was genuine. "In Atlanta, during his days as Governor," Shaw said, "I'd bring the orchestra up every so often at his request to play for state dinners and such. But he'd also come to our regular concerts all the time—and he'd stand in line and buy tickets."

At the request of Mrs. Carter, Robert Shaw arranged for seven small instrumental ensembles, including the Juilliard and the Cleveland quartets, to perform at various White House receptions after Carter took office. At the diplomatic reception on January 22, when the guests had left, the president asked if the Juilliard Quartet would play for a brief while longer. So they did, for an audience consisting solely of Jimmy and Rosalynn Carter and Robert Shaw. "The Carters sat down," first violinist Robert Mann recalled, "and we played the hymn-like slow movement from Haydn's op. 20, no. 1. We fully expected them to get up in the middle and excuse themselves gracefully. But they sat and listened, really listened—after thirty years of performing, one can sense the kind of quietness that implies deep concentration. There was a silent pause after we finished, a quite wonderful moment, and the President said, 'You know, this is the kind of music that brings tears to the eyes.' "[2] This reaction was obviously a far cry from the image many critics had of Carter. The president's musical preferences were thought to have run along the lines of a tune called "Drop Kick

Me, Jesus, through the Goal Posts of Life," heard on the radio at his brother Billy's filling station in Georgia.

Carter felt his love of music was insured by a superlative, partially crippled school teacher, Julia Coleman, who exposed the young boy in his isolated farm community to classical music and literature. Carter also admitted spending most of his meager earnings as midshipman at Annapolis on classical records. "Other midshipmen would visit our room and we would argue for hours about the relative quality of performance of orchestras and concert soloists. For some reason, each time we reached the final part of 'Tristan and Isolde,' a large group would quietly gather in the corridor to listen to the Liebestod."[3]

But a reference to Wagner impressed Marine Band Leader Colonel John Bourgeois shortly after Carter came to the White House. The conductor of the Marine Band traditionally tries to learn the musical preferences of each new president. "I hope you'll play the Prelude to the third act of *Tristan and Isolde* sometime. I enjoy that very much," Carter told the surprised leader. This was not the usual background music for White House receptions. But then neither were the Bach Brandenburg Concertos. For the Tito state dinner a harpsichord was brought in, and an entire program of J. S. Bach was played in the foyer of the mansion. The press, usually reporters of social, not musical, affairs, did not always understand. What wound up in the society columns might be 99 percent musically incorrect, such as the time the reviewer claimed Mozart's *Eine kleine Nachtmusik* was played "over and over again," when it was actually played once. The reviewer failed to recognize the thematic repetitions characteristic of Viennese classicism.[4]

When the Carters moved into the White House, they were delighted to discover that they had some 2,000 long-playing records to enjoy from Richard Nixon's administration. They selected all the classical discs (numbering about fifty) and extension speakers were installed in the president's study. The main stereo units were kept in the office of Susan Clough, the president's secretary, who ensured that Debussy, Schumann, Bach, and Wagner were on the turntable eight to ten hours a day. Once the music was too loud to enable several senators on the other end of the telephone line to hear what the president wanted of them. "He turned it down until our business was done," Frank Moore, White House congressional liaison chief, recalled.[5]

Almost three-quarters of the musical programs held at the White House under Carter consisted of classical artists and repertory. Pianist Rudolf Serkin played Mendelssohn's Prelude and Fugue in E Minor and Beethoven's "Appassionata" Sonata, op. 57, for the Carter's first state dinner on February 14, 1977, for President and Mrs. López Portillo of Mexico. As an encore, he played the Brahms Intermezzo in C Major, op. 119, no. 3. Mrs. Portillo, a former concert pianist, also played two Chopin selections, an impromptu delight that melded elegance and informality in the typical Carter style. Later that spring Cynthia Gregory and Ted Kivitt danced on the South Lawn stage accompanied by the Marine Band. Some of the other classical artists who entertained during

Carter's administration were Metropolitan Opera's Shirley Verrett; the Dallas Symphony Orchestra Brass Quartet; Tchaikovsky Competition winners Elmar Oliveira and Nathaniel Rose; Isaac Stern, Andre Previn, and Martina Arroyo—all three for the signing of the Panama Treaty on September 7, 1977; and the New York City Ballet for the North Atlantic Alliance summit on May 30, 1978.

But the most exciting innovation during the Carter administration was the Sunday afternoon PBS series of five hour-long programs presented by distinguished solo artists, Vladimir Horowitz, Mstislav Rostropovich, Leontyne Price, Mikhail Baryshnikov, and Andrés Segovia. Broadcast nationally and throughout Europe from the East Room, the programs held the same excitement for the public that diva Emma Albani's concert in the historic room did for the much smaller audience 100 years earlier. As Mrs. Carter explained, "These programs came about because Jimmy and I knew there were so many people who had never been to the White House and would be so thrilled to be able to come. We wanted all of America to enjoy the White House like we did."[6] Via the medium of television, they had their wish.

The first concert, presented by pianist Vladimir Horowitz on February 26, 1978, set the tone and pattern for the succeeding programs. The small platform, lined with flowers, was placed at the east wall with the chairs grouped around it from north to south, thus improving the accoustics of the room immeasurably. The audience of about 300 at Horowitz's request consisted mainly of musicians and arts celebrities ("not politicians who look at their watches to see when I will finish") and included Samuel Barber, William Warfield, Isaac Stern, Constance Keene, Alice Tully, John Steinway, and the new heads of the National Endowment for the Arts and the National Endowment for the Humanities, Livingston L. Biddle and Joseph Duffy.[7] The program was taped live and rebroadcast later that same day.

Horowitz, who had played for Herbert Hoover in 1931, had been asked to play at the White House several times by various administrations but always refused. Carter's concept of the televised concert, rather than a social event, appealed to the great artist, and he timed his historic program to coincide with the fiftieth anniversary of his American debut. He arrived at the White House on February 25 for the rehearsal, graciously declining the president's offer to tour the family living quarters first. A problem arose when the East Room proved too live acoustically for Horowitz. "He didn't realize that when the room is full of people, the echo is eliminated," Chief Usher Rex Scouten recalled. President Carter, dressed in blue jeans, sweater, and suede shoes, ran upstairs, and with Scouten's help they found an oriental rug on the third floor that they brought down and placed before the platform. "Horowitz thought it helped. I didn't notice any difference," Scouten said.[8]

Horowitz, who had brought in his own Steinway for the White House program, selected works characteristic of his repertory: a Chopin group, Schumann's "Träumerei," a Rachmaninoff polka, and his own Variations on a Theme from Bizet's *Carmen*, which he had played at his concert for President Hoover. The critics were ecstatic. They praised his typically supercharged approach to the music and his velvety tone. Some complained about editorial infelicities on the printed program ("Träumerei was misspelled"), or about Horowitz's clangorous piano ("an historical relic"), but did the world really care? It had witnessed an artistic miracle direct from the White House and the chief critic was the president himself. At the close of the concert Jimmy Carter came onstage clearly moved. "It's hard to speak," he said. "The White House has been host to a lot of great people, but never a greater man or greater performance."[9]

The sumptuous musical feast had a bitter aftertaste, however. Horowitz came in for a great deal of criticism from the White House because he received over $150,000 for the foreign distribution rights of the videotape, 10 percent of which would go to WETA, the sponsoring Washington station.[10] For decades artists had donated their performances at the White House, and the administration was clearly not prepared for any departures from this tradition or for the new problems imposed by the mass media. The next four PBS artists were told in no uncertain terms that the White House wanted no further publicity about performers making money from playing at the White House.

It was not until fall when Leontyne Price presented her contribution to the PBS series. On October 8 the famous soprano, accompanied by pianist David Garvey, sang works by Handel, Richard Strauss, and Puccini, closing with a group of American art songs and spirituals. Especially memorable was her brilliant interpretation of songs by three Pulitzer prize winners, Ned Rorem, Dominick Argento, and Samuel Barber. President Carter interrupted his Camp David weekend for the concert and his forthcoming anti-inflation message became the subject of quips by Charles Schultze, chairman of the Council of Economic Advisers. "We'll put it to music," he joked, "perhaps Berlioz's *Symphonie fantastique.*" A music critic nearby added that the French master's huge score would have to be "frugally pared down to bare essentials."[11]

For the third telecast the special stage donated by the Harkness Ballet under Lyndon Johnson was erected. On February 25, 1979, Mikhail Baryshnikov and Patricia McBride dazzled the 130 guests with spins and soared a mere hair's breadth beneath the East Room crystal chandelier. "One had the close-up, surreal sense of watching someone skate on a bathtub rink," observed a *Post* reporter about the small stage, always a problem for dancers.[12] Baryshnikov adjusted to the space after two or three rehearsals, and a special lens made the stage look larger to the television audience. The renowned *premier danceur's* famous defection from the Soviet Union on June 30, 1974, was played down in the White House press releases, perhaps because such mention would violate the spirit of detente. But his dancing, the president said in his introduction, transcended national boundaries and "binds together the human spirits." The program was aired publicly on Easter Sunday, April 15, 1979.

The final two concerts of the series had to be missed by President Carter, who was involved in the Egyptian-Israeli peace negotiations.

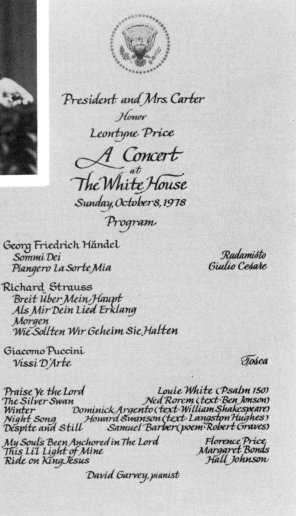

The Presidential Seal

President and Mrs. Carter
Honor
Leontyne Price

A Concert
at
The White House
Sunday, October 8, 1978
Program

Georg Friedrich Händel
  Sommi Dei   *Radamisto*
  Piangero La Sorte Mia   *Giulio Cesare*

Richard Strauss
  Breit Über Mein Haupt
  Als Mir Dein Lied Erklang
  Morgen
  Wie Sollten Wir Geheim Sie Halten

Giacomo Puccini
  Vissi D'Arte   *Tosca*

Praise Ye the Lord   *Louie White (Psalm 150)*
The Silver Swan   *Ned Rorem (text·Ben Jonson)*
Winter   *Dominick Argento (text·William Shakespeare)*
Night Song   *Howard Swanson (text·Langston Hughes)*
Despite and Still   *Samuel Barber (poem·Robert Graves)*

My Soul's Been Anchored in The Lord   *Florence Price*
This Li'l Light of Mine   *Margaret Bonds*
Ride on King Jesus   *Hall Johnson*

David Garvey, pianist

Leontyne Price presented a nationally televised concert in the East Room for the Carters and their guests on October 8, 1978. The American soprano has sung several times in the White House, including for the Carters' Israeli-Egyptian Peace Treaty Signing, for the welcoming ceremonies of Pope John Paul II, and during the Johnson and Reagan administrations.

World-famous cellist and music director of the National Symphony Orchestra, Mstislav Rostropovich, accompanied by his daughter, Elena, played the Adagio from Toccata, Adagio and Fugue in C Major by J. S. Bach; Weber's Adagio and Rondo for Harmonichord arranged for cello by Gregor Piatigorsky; three pieces from Schumann's Fünf Stucke, op. 102, and the Sonata for Cello and Piano, op. 40, by Shostakovich. The latter, Rostropovich claimed, was an acerbic work that Soviet officials of the 1930s held in disfavor and that the cellist had deliberately chosen for the White House. Ostracized by the Soviet Union, "Rostropovich has undergone very much hardship and if anyone understands the meaning of liberty, it is he," Mrs. Carter remarked before the concert.

For Andrés Segovia's program on March 11, Vice-President Walter Mondale substituted for the president, who was in the Middle East. "I know the hopes of all humanity are with the President as he searches for peace," Mondale told the 220 guests. Impeccably, with all the warmth that the White House seemed to evoke from its performers, the eighty-five-year-old classical guitarist played the Spanish music that endeared him to the world—works of de Narvaez, Castelnuovo-Tedesco, Torroba, and Albeniz. Indeed, peace was soon to come, and it would be announced to the world through music in a manner like no other.

"It was a time of filtered joy," stated one report. "The scars of four wars and strain of sixteen tortuous months of negotiations . . . the difficulties that everyone knows lie ahead" were on the faces of the three participants—Egypt's Anwar Sadat, Israel's Menachem Begin, and Jimmy Carter.[13] On March 25, 1979, two weeks after Segovia's telecast, 1,600 White House guests, 5,000 spectators, and a global television audience of millions watched the signing of the Egyptian-Israeli peace treaty. That evening the largest dinner in White House history was held under a forty-five-foot-high tent with candelabra on the tent poles casting a romantic glow across the 134 tables. The musical entertainment for such a historic affair was sheer genius. "Normally we have six to eight weeks to plan the entertainment for a state dinner," Gretchen Poston, the Carters' social secretary, said. "For the peace celebration, we had five days. We didn't know how one artist could represent all three countries, so we asked each nation to bring its own performer. Sadat provided a popular Egyptian trio of guitar, tabla drum and electronic organ; for Israel we had violinists Itzhak Perlman and Pinchas Zukerman (both native Israelis); and to represent our own country, we invited Leontyne Price."[14] The great diva sang the powerful aria "Pace, pace, mio Dio," from Verdi's *La forza del destino*.

Musical units from all four branches of the service performed, and an especially beautiful touch was provided by the U.S. Army Chorus conducted by Major Allen Crowell. Within the course of a few days, Army arranger James Kessler researched a Hebrew song Sadat would have known and came up with "Salma ya Salma," a very old chant from the Egyptian leader's native village. Kessler, who holds a bachelor of music degree in composition from Eastman School of Music, then found a popular Israeli song of the 1960s, "Machar" by Naomi Shemer, with the help of the embassy of Israel and cleverly combined the two tunes in a moving commemoration of the historic event. Both songs had as their subject peace, their modal lines interweaving in simple counterpoint, overlapping on the word "peace" to emphasize the song's poignant message: "Peace will arrive with the morning sun. This is more than the proverb of a dreamer." "As the chorus sang, both Sadat and Begin recognized their tunes," Kessler recalled. "They were obviously delighted."[15]

But there was another side to Carter. He felt that it was important to recognize the ethnic and folk traditions in America, and he did this effectively by dedicating entire programs to one style of American popular or indigenous music. These programs were held on the South Lawn as 800 guests picnicked on paper plates and enjoyed the music in a relaxed setting. Honoring the twenty-fifth anniversary of the Newport Jazz Festival, the White House Jazz Concert, held on June 18, 1978, featured nine decades of this art form with performances by ninety-five-year-old Eubie Blake, Katherine Handy Lewis, Mary Lou Williams, Jo Jones, Clark Terry, Sonny Rollins, Max Roach, Herbie Hancock, Dizzy Gillespie, Ornette Coleman, Lionel Hampton, Stan Getz, and other luminaries. In the audience were Billy Taylor, Gerry Mulligan, John Lewis, Charles Mingus, and others. All totaled, there were about fifty jazz musicians at the White House that day. "Never before has jazz as an art form been honored at such a high level," said Newport Jazz Festival producer George Wein. The concert was broadcast live by National Public Radio and recorded by the Voice of America.

President Carter sat on the lawn in his shirtsleeves, reminiscing about the jazz concerts he had enjoyed while in the Navy, with Mrs. Carter at his side. At one point he asked Dizzy Gillespie to play "Salt Peanuts" and joined the famous bop artist with repeated exclamations of "salt peanuts!" during breaks. Someone made the comment that this must have been the "first Presidential hot chorus in history."[16] After Cecil Taylor's abstract and expressive solo, the president leaped up and pursued the pianist into a clump of trees, talking with him and congratulating him enthusiastically. In his welcome address, Carter noted that "if there ever was an indigenous art form, one that is peculiar to the United States and represents what we are as a country, I would say it is jazz." To the president jazz combined two characteristics that have made America what it is: "individuality and a free expression of one's inner spirit."[17]

This same type of focus was given to black musicians when the Carters held an informal dinner and concert on the lawns the following summer. Once again a huge audience assembled. On June 7, 1979, they heard Chuck Berry, Patti LaBelle, Evelyn "Champagne" King, Andrae Crouch, Billy Eckstine, and others. The event honored the one-year-old Black Music Association, and the press was quick to pick up the political overtones of the occasion. The timing was propitious.

Ninety-five-year-old jazz pianist Eubie Blake plays during a program honoring the Newport Jazz Festival on the White House Lawn to the delight of the Carters and their guests.

Carter, whose credibility had been slipping among blacks, had opposed the lifting of sanctions against Rhodesia in a strong statement issued only hours before the concert.

The "Old Fashioned Gospel Singin'" festival took place the following fall on September 9. The president usually gave an address before these programs, and his comments always brought out his and Rosalynn's personal involvement in the musical styles. Most of the gospel programs the Carters knew were "24-hour sings." They had shortened the White House event to three hours, the president said, and the audience laughed. It was a remarkable program—a White House first and it proved the president's words: "Gospel music is really rural music. It has both black and white derivations; it's not a racial kind of music. . . . it's a music of pain, a music of longing and a music of faith."[18]

Rosalynn Smith Carter, one of our most concerned and politically active first ladies, shared her husband's interests in music. But, unlike the president who did not play the piano (although he said he wished he could), Mrs. Carter often accompanied her daughter Amy on the piano as the little girl practiced her violin under the famous Suzuki method of instruction. Mother and daughter worked together on one of the three White House Steinways, usually the third floor upright. Rosalynn Carter, moreover, managed to save the East Room Steinway, recommending that it be renovated instead of discarded. The action was completely reworked in time for André Watts's program of Scarlatti, Rachmaninoff, Debussy, and Gershwin for the king and queen of Jordan on June 17, 1980. Like the president, Mrs. Carter enjoyed attending the rehearsals for White House concerts. "They loved the programs so much, in fact," said Gretchen Poston, "we couldn't keep them away. I think the presence of the president and first lady beforehand made the artists more relaxed during the evening's performance. They are often very nervous."[19]

The reaction of artists playing the White House seems to take many turns. For some just being a *guest* of the president is disarming. Metropolitan opera singer James McCracken tells of the time he and his wife Sandra Warfield pulled up to the entrance of the White House for a state dinner as the Marine Band lining the stairs started to play. "We got out of the taxi, very excited, and went inside," recalled the tenor. In the foyer they met House Speaker Thomas P. O'Neill who exclaimed, "Hey, aren't you James McCracken?" "Oh boy, isn't this nice," thought the singer, flattered. "My day has been made. Yes, sir," he answered. "Well, you forgot to pay your taxi," said O'Neill. The Speaker, it seems, had paid it for him.[20]

Meeting and performing for the president can be almost overwhelming to the artists. "It is always awesome to be so close to the center of such power, such involvement with so many things that affect our lives daily," says violinist Isaac Stern who has performed for seven presidents. Gretchen Poston recalls the reaction of the late Andre Kostelanetz when he presented his "Promenade at the White House" on May 20, 1978. The great conductor led a program of Mozart and Mendelssohn on the White House lawn, concluding with Tchaikovsky's bombastic *1812 Overture* complete with fireworks. It was his first appearance at the White House. According to Mrs. Poston, "President Carter came to the rehearsal and sat all afternoon in the ninety-degree heat listening. Kostelanetz had been given just about every award by this time, but when he met the president, tears just streamed down his face. He said that at no time in his life did he have anything more exciting happen to him than this. It was always impressive to see how people felt when performing at the White House. And Baryshnikov felt this same way when he danced. I noticed that the artists were almost overwhelmed. The bigger the artist, the humbler they seemed."[21] Kostelanetz conducted a large orchestra of military personnel for members of Congress and their families. "This is a good time for us," remarked the president before the concert. He noted jokingly that Kostelanetz was able to get perfect harmony from three different military services, "something that I have not always been able to achieve." The audience laughed again when he added, "I think that when you hear the last selection, which is the *1812 Overture*, it will remind you of the kind of breakfast that I have with the congressional leaders every two weeks."[22]

Poston was an especially creative social secretary. When Eugene List brought his "Monster Concert" to the White House, she had to position six pianos and twenty-eight pianists in an unprecedented East Room extravaganza à la Gottschalk. "We were not sure if the floors would hold up," she said. The chief usher and his engineers had to test them beforehand. On another occasion the resourceful social secretary stationed thirty-five American poets in ten different rooms of the White House so that they could read their poetry simultaneously during the Carters' "Salute to American Poets." But occasionally there were mix-ups, sometimes funny ones. Soprano Clamma Dale, Poston recalls, was rehearsing in a room below the state dining room during a dinner given for Premier Nicolae Ceausescu of Romania.

> Just as President Carter lifted his glass and opened his mouth to begin the after-dinner toasts we heard 'ah-ah-ah-ah-ah'—scales going up and down. Everybody looked around. The President tried again, and as he lifted his glass once more and opened his mouth to speak, out came the scales again. I was just dumfounded. So I ran upstairs and finally discovered Miss Dale back in the corner of the linen closet, where she thought she was not disturbing anyone. She was, in fact, at the base of the shaft going up to the fireplace directly behind the President as he stood in the state dining room. For a while we thought we had lost our soprano in a fireplace.[23]

As the 1970s came to a close and the 1980s began, mass communication seemed to hold every American in its portentous grasp. The airways were congested with citizen-band radios, video games, stereos, and cordless phones. Television, with its abilities to reach millions, told most of the stories to most of the people most of the time. Soap operas, full-scale ballets, and political debates moved with equal ease into the American living room. And the mass media with its powers to predict, persuade, and promulgate created its own special breed of Pied Piper—the television and recording stars who, among other activities, staged huge, profitable benefits for their favorite political candidates. One reporter called it "celebrity politics." Indeed, country singers like Tom T. Hall and Loretta Lynn were recognized for their campaigning for President Carter in 1976 by fêtes at the White House after he took office. But this was nothing new. Presidents have always been sung into office. Movie stars had lent their support to Truman, just as campaign glee clubs had done for Buchanan nearly 100 years earlier. But in the 1980s there is a difference, for artists and producers have greater visibility and their efforts carry more weight. As the former president of Casablanca Records, Neil Bogart, says, "Winning an election is just as important to me as making a Number One hit record."[24]

For Ronald Reagan television was the natural vehicle to bring to the nation what he considered the joyous symbol of American free enterprise, his inauguration. The country had a 7.4 percent rate of unemployment, but there was enormous resilience within a capitalistic society, he felt. Taste, style, and prosperity could be had by anyone willing to work long and hard enough. In direct contrast with the homespun Carter years (the Carter inauguration held six $25-a-ticket balls and 200 free concerts), Ronald Reagan's first inauguration in 1981 was the most expensive in history, costing $16 million.[25] Structured for television, it was a gigantic four-day celebration that was viewed throughout the entire world. The inaugural galas, produced and directed by Frank Sinatra, featured Bob Hope, Ethel Merman, Donny Osmond, Sinatra himself, and a host of others. In one evening performing arts extravaganzas were held in the three theaters of Kennedy Center. Those who could not afford the seats costing $50 and up could share the nation's jubilation via television for little or nothing. "It's great having an actor in the White House," quipped Bob Hope. "We went from peanuts to popcorn. It's the greatest thing to happen to Hollywood since George Burns played God."

As a former actor and actress, Ronald and Nancy Reagan came to the White House with extensive knowledge of the entertainment world. They were married in 1952 while both were appearing in Hollywood films; it was a second marriage for Ronald whose former wife was film star Jane Wyman. Both of Ronald and Nancy's children have pursued careers in the arts: Ron, a former dancer with the Joffrey II Ballet, is a writer specializing in drama and the performing arts, and Patricia (Patti) is a rock and country singer, author, and song writer.

While Ron recalls his father singing to him as a child, the Reagans' musical talents lie more in the area of creative programming than in performing. "Once when I was a drum major leading my high school band in a parade," the president told several hundred young band members during his second inauguration, "I was aware that the music was growing fainter and fainter behind me. Soon I knew they had gone one way and I another—and I had just marched right out of my musical career." Las Vegas producer Herman Hover once commented that as a nightclub performer Ronald Reagan had practically no talent. "He couldn't dance, he couldn't sing and he couldn't tell jokes." In Warner Brothers' *Million Dollar Baby* (1941), Reagan had to play the piano and his chief recollection of the film was the time he spent trying to master keyboard technique. Having no musical experience, he had to work for two weeks on a dummy keyboard with a pianist from the Warner Brothers music department. "A lot of acting is imitation anyway," said Reagan, "and I became pretty good as long as the piano remained silent. For awhile there I almost convinced myself I could play."[26]

By the time Reagan took office as governor of California in 1966, he had appeared in Hollywood films for over thirty years. But he also had shown a remarkable grasp of human conditions as one of the most successful presidents the Screen Actors' Guild had ever had. "He's always been a politician, even if he didn't know it," said an actress who had known him over the years. "He just happened to spend a number of years making a living as an actor."[27] Reagan has always been especially moved by patriotic music and tells the following vignette about his good friend and colleague, Jeanette McDonald:

> It was early in World War II. Our men were still fighting on Baatan. I was a lieutenant at Fort Mason in San Francisco. There was no USO, nor any program for entertainment in those early days. The commanding general had asked if I could get someone to sing the national Anthem at ceremonies for I Am An American Day. Jeanette said yes without hesitation. . . .
>
> She sang until there weren't any more songs left and still they wanted more. Finally she told them she only knew one more song that was a great favorite of hers, and she started singing the *Battle Hymn of the Republic*. I will never forget her, nor forget how as she sang, these 20,000 boys came to their feet and finished singing the hymn with her.[28]

Under the Reagans the White House reverberates regularly with patriotic musical messages close to the president and first lady—"America the Beautiful," "God Bless America," and other songs that reach out to the American spirit.

Not surprisingly, great film scores have had a characteristic meaning for President Reagan. In the fall of 1982 he sent a letter to each of the sons of the noted composer Erich Korngold (1879–1957), expressing the nation's thanks for the donation of their father's manuscripts to the Library of Congress. Many American lives had been touched by Korngold's music, said the president, including his own "in a special way." Movie aficionados will recall that a fine Korngold score accompanied the film *King's Row*, in which Reagan had given one of the best performances of his acting career.

Nancy Davis Reagan brought to the White House an image of elegance, class, and good taste. But during those early months she was criticized unmercifully for her extravagant refurbishing of the White House, expensive purchases of new china for the mansion, and flamboyant penchant for designer clothes in an era when millions were out of jobs. Poised, petite, with an aura of graceful informality about her,the first lady appears almost delicate—but has proven herself far from fragile. She has used the media and the entertainment world to campaign sincerely for a better America. She narrated a two-hour PBS anti-drug documentary, "The Chemical People"; appeared with Gary Coleman on NBC's sitcom "Diff'rent Strokes" in a story about drug abuse that reached nearly 28 million; and with Frank Sinatra she sang a song called "To Love a Child" for nearly 600 foster grandparents on the White House lawn. Its lyrics, rendered in an unsophisticated voice, summed up her feelings: "To love a child. / You start with a smile, / And after a while, / A hug and a kiss. / It takes no more than this / To love a child."

But it was the spunky song-and-dance routine she rendered that transformed the image of Nancy Reagan. At the annual Gridiron Dinner in April 1982, Washington journalists lampooned the first lady's expensive tastes by singing a satirical parody on James Hanley's "Second Hand Rose." To everyone's surprise Mrs. Reagan showed up onstage wearing a frumpy mismatch of feather boa, white pantaloons, gaudy skirt, and yellow rubber boots. Poking fun at herself, as well as the press, she retorted with *her* version of the song, belting out to the same tune the following lyrics:

> I'm wearing second-hand clothes,
> Second-hand clothes.
> They're quite the style
> In spring fashion shows.
> Even my new trench coat with fur collar
> Ronnie bought for ten cents on the dollar.
> Second hand gowns
> And old hand-me-downs,
> The china is the only thing that's new.
>
> Even though they tell me that I'm no longer
> Queen,
> Did Ronnie have to buy me that new
> Sewing machine?
> I sure hope Ed Meese sews.[29]

As the song ended, the first lady attempted to smash a plate decorated to look like a piece of her $200,000 White House collection.

Nancy Reagan's most impressive performance, however, took place after the death of her friend, the former actress Princess Grace of Monaco, in 1982. Mrs. Reagan substituted for her as the narrator in the National Symphony's performance of *Carnival of the Animals* by Saint-Saëns. As a result, Sulton Qaboos Said of Oman presented the symphony with a $300,000 endowment to establish The Nancy Reagan Chair of Narrative Music. Not only did this gift benefit the arts in Washington substantially, but also it was undoubtedly the most gracious musical tribute to a first lady in history.

Shortly after the Reagans came to the White House, they began plans for a series of televised concerts that would originate for the most part from the East Room. Called "In Performance at the White House," the annual series of four PBS concerts has been among the most visible, imaginative, and wholly successful arts venture to come from the White House. While the Carters' televised programs were formal and classical, the Reagans' added their own special mark by broadening the musical styles to include Broadway, country, jazz, and gospel. "We try to create programs that salute distinguished American performers as well as brilliant young talent which has not yet received recognition in this country," Mabel ("Muffie") Brandon, the former social secretary, emphasized.[30] Thus older, established artists performed with younger talent on these telecasts, which included biographical documentary film. The opening theme music, the joyous finale from Aaron Copland's *The Red Pony*, set the tone for each of the programs, which reverberated with a spirit of youth, grace, and the vibrant musical images of America.

At first the press was skeptical. "The Reagan administration seems to be launching a new campaign to become known for performing arts as well as performing budget cuts," said one reporter.[31] But after the first program it changed its tune. One has to go no further than Mrs. Reagan's opening remarks at the first concert to sense that the long skein of White House musical history had indeed come to a brilliant and vital focal point. And all the musical styles so important to the great mansion's traditions came alive again. "Good evening and a warm welcome to the White House," began Mrs. Reagan.

> Ever since this wonderful house was built, it's been filled with music. Thomas Jefferson played his violin and Harry Truman played his piano in this room. The Marine Band has serenaded countless foreign dignitaries at state dinners and some of the world's most dazzling performers have appeared beneath these chandeliers. That tradition of music continues this evening and in the months ahead. We've invited to the White House four of the greatest artists of our time and we've asked them in turn to bring their nominees for future greatness. I'm delighted that we can use the White House as a showcase for this young talent. The East Room, where we're holding these concerts, has echoed over the years with the sounds of Beethoven, Bach, Eubie Blake. Tonight with the participation of public television, the East Room becomes a concert hall for the entire nation.[32]

The first series was introduced by Beverly Sills, who has served as mistress of ceremonies for each of the programs. The opening concert on November 22, 1981, featured Ida Levin, a 1980 Leventritt Artist, and the veteran pianist Rudolf Serkin. The brilliant eighteen-year-old violinist had studied with Serkin at Vermont's Marlboro School of Music, and the two artists communicated vividly together, despite almost sixty years difference in their ages. Serkin played Beethoven's "Moonlight Sonata," Levin continued with one of the most challenging works in the violin repertory, Ysaÿe's "Ballad," and both artists collaborated in Schubert's spirited Rondo Brilliant. The East Room platform was set up like a living room with flowers, armchairs, and oriental rugs. TV cameras and other vestiges of the media were skillfully hidden among the potted plants. With her secure technical command, singing tone, and compelling personality, Levin was a special treat for the sixty-five invited White House guests and the nation.

Beverly Sills, Ida Levin, and Rudolf Serkin open the young artists' "In Performance at the White House" televised series on November 22, 1981.

On December 20, eight rising young singers, among them soprano Ashley Putnam, baritone Allen Titus, and mezzo-soprano Gail Gilmore, sang arias accompanied by pianist Donald Hassard. The young artists were all members of the New York City Opera, of which Beverly Sills was director. The following spring the East Room stage was erected, and on March 28, 1982, brilliant young dancers from the San Francisco Ballet, Martha Graham Dance Company, and the cast of *Sophisticated Ladies* tapped, shuffled, leaped, and swirled on the surface. "We rehearsed in an even smaller space so when we got to the real thing, it felt luxurious by comparison," said dancers Evelyn Cisneros and Kirk Peterson, who gave the world premier of Stravinsky's *Ragtime* that evening.[33] Gene Kelly, a long-time friend of the Reagans, was the older artist who introduced the young dancers, and eighty-seven-year-old Martha Graham was the honored guest. As she watched Joyce Herring in her starkly moving *Lamentations*, Graham's thoughts must have gone back to the time she herself performed in the White House for Franklin Roosevelt.

The final concert of the 1981–82 series was broadcast from a large ranch adjacent to President Reagan's Western White House in California. It featured country music star Merle Haggard and twenty-year-old champion fiddler Mark O'Connor. Ironically, ten years earlier Reagan had signed a pardon for Haggard, who had spent three years in San Quentin for attempted burglary. At one point in the program, after singing "Tulsa," a song with some fairly low-down lyrics, Haggard remarked with a grin, "Maybe you'll have to pardon me again, Mr. President."[34] For the President and Mrs. Reagan and their guests seated on bales of hay and in Western attire, Haggard played and sang "Pennies from Heaven," his once-controversial "Okie from Muskogee," "Working' Man Blues," and "Rainbow Stew." The latter drew a big laugh from the president when Haggard sang: "When a President goes through a White House door and does what he says he'll do / We'll all be drinkin' free bubble up and eatin' that rainbow stew."

The success of the first four programs prompted the Reagans to continue the series in 1982–83. Once again produced by Peter Weinberg for New York's WNET/13 and Washington's WETA/26, the four telecasts illustrated the Reagans' support and encouragement of outstanding young talent. That year the artists were introduced by Itzhak Perlman, who served as master of ceremonies, but his brief performances during the jazz and Broadway programs seemed somewhat out of place. More in keeping with the great violinist's repertory was the opening concert on November 7, 1982. Twenty-year-old pianist Ken Noda played Mozart and Chopin with extraordinary sensitivity and facility, joining Perlman in Stravinsky's *Suite Italienne* and in works by Fritz Kreisler and Pablo Sarasate. "I'm sure you know how deeply I feel about the power of art," Mrs. Reagan said during her address to the 100 guests and the nation. "I believe that art binds us one to another. . . . What but art can cause tears among strangers?" The next month four generations of jazz artists, among them Dizzy Gillespie, Stan Getz, Chick Corea,

President and Mrs. Reagan enjoy the country music of Merle Haggard with mistress of ceremonies Beverly Sills at a ranch near the Western White House.

and Roy Haynes, performed in the East Room on December 4. Trumpeter Jon Faddis and West Coast singer Diane Schuur, blind from infancy, were the young artists. "I couldn't believe it. I was absolutely stunned," said Schuur as she told of a phone call from Stan Getz inviting her to appear at the White House.[35] With warmth and a wide range of rich color, she sang two of her own compositions and was kissed and embraced by a deeply moved Mrs. Reagan.

In the spring chamber music and Broadway theater were featured on the continuation of the "In Performance" series, on April 6 and June 6, respectively. The first program, which included a documentary showing rehearsals and taped interviews, televised superb performances by the Juilliard String Quartet and the youthful Muir Quartet. The final concert was held outdoors with Mary Martin and John Raitt saluting seven young singers on their way to major careers in the field of American musical theater. Songs by Richard Rodgers, Jerome Kern, Irving Berlin, George Gershwin, Leonard Bernstein, and Richard Adler exhibited the vivid dramatic and musical talents of the young performers as well as those of Martin and Raitt. Little did it matter that the afternoon was interrupted by a sudden downpour. The program was continued the next day with the White House staff as stand-in audience. Few television viewers were aware that the program comprised two separate tapings.

The third series began on September 21, 1983, with soprano Leontyne Price as emcee and James Levine, music director of the Metropolitan Opera, introducing six current and former members of the Met's Young Artist Development Program—a fitting celebration of the Met's 100th anniversary season direct from the White House. The program consisted of arias by Price herself and operatic selections by Brian Schexnayder, Terry Cook, Gail Dubinbaum, Timothy Jenkins, Marvis Martin, and Karen Bureau. Martin, with her velvet-voiced, ravishing interpretation of "Depuis le jour" from Charpentier's *Louise*, brought back memories of the young Leontyne Price, and Wagnerian soprano Karen Bureau dazzled all with her powerful performance of "Dich teu're halle" from Wagner's *Tannhäuser*. The president concluded the program with a wry reference to the old film *Night at the Opera*: "For years I didn't think you could give *Il trovatore* without the Marx Brothers." Then he added:

> It's wonderful today to see the widespread popularity of opera in America from New York to San Francisco and a great many towns and cities in between. You know, for the attentive ear, opera might even be considered a spectator sport. There's a strong element of competition in this art form, the excitement of watching world-recognized professionals at work and the thrilling payoff of years of education and training. All of this plus music, drama and dance add up to a unique and thrilling event. From talent like we've just heard here, drawn from the Met's wonderful training program, opera lovers can be confident of this inspirational art form in the future in America. Again, we can't thank you enough. God bless you all.

Because of equal-time restrictions placed on the presidential candidates' televised appearances during election year, 1984 brought no further PBS concerts. The last program of the three-year series featured talented gospel and spiritual singers, and Leontyne Price again served as mistress of ceremonies at Washington's historic Shiloh Baptist Church on December 14, 1983, with the Reagans attending. The program conjured up images of the gospel hymnody rendered by the Fisk Jubilee Singers for President Chester Arthur a century earlier. Indeed, for all of their appearance of innovation, the Reagans' televised concerts are the continuation of a tradition of almost 100 years—the White House musicale—even to the elegant refreshments offered to the guests in the state dining room after the programs. But while child prodigies and talented young performers have always appeared at the White House, the Reagans' choices are more than mere aspirants to greatness— they *have* arrived and can hold their own with the most seasoned artists of their era. The concept has focus, political strategy—in the noblest sense of the term—and most of all, true artistic merit. The Reagans plan to continue their PBS series, focusing primarily on American music.

But the musicale, a term no longer used at the White House, is not the only cultural tradition kept alive at the mansion. The Reagans hold approximately ten state dinners a year, and all are followed by entertainment. The programs do not consist of mostly Las Vegas–type performers, as the newspapers claimed; indeed, the classical artists outnumber the popular. For example, Isaac Stern, Marvin Hamlisch, Bobby Short, the Twyla Tharp dancers, André-Michel Schub, George Shearing, Anna Moffo, Robert Merrill, Pinchas Zukermann, Byron Janis, Sergio Franchi, Sherrill Milnes, and the Chamber Music Society of Lincoln Center have all performed on separate occasions. And black Metropolitan Opera singer Grace Bumbry entertained the premier of China only weeks after cellist Mstislav Rostropovich performed for Rajiv Gandhi, the prime minister of India, on June 12, 1985. Sometimes small parties are held in the yellow Oval Room upstairs, where Peter Nero played for Chancellor Helmut Kohl of Germany. But rare now are the large extravaganzas of the Kennedy, Johnson, and Nixon years. With the John F. Kennedy Center nearby, the first family can attend elaborate productions with ease, and through the televised Kennedy Center Honors galas they are able to salute America's greatest performers with elegance and visibility.[36] Still, the White House will always be home, and the Reagans' finely orchestrated parties have established them as the nation's first host and hostess. As jazz vibraphone virtuoso Lionel Hampton said when he played with a roster of jazz greats during President Reagan's first summer in office: "During the Carter party we had a barbecue. At this one we have caviar."[37]

The social secretary is still basically White House impresario and today more than ever before has to have some knowledge of the current arts fields and expertise in advising the performers about East Room acoustics and limitations. The final selections of the artists rests with the first lady, however. "Everything we do here is approved by Mrs.

Reagan," says Mabel Brandon, who was succeeded by Gahl Hodges in April 1983 and by Linda Faulkner in July 1985. "Mrs. Reagan is extremely concerned and involved with all the performing artists at the White House."[38] But Nancy Reagan's chief entertainment advisor and liaison is Frank Sinatra. "She's had a crush on him since she was a young girl," said a friend. "Sinatra has become a sort of entertainment clearing house for the White House. If they have trouble getting in touch with a performer for a state dinner, he comes to the rescue."[39] Appropriately, Frank Sinatra and Perry Como sang for President Alessandro Pertini of Italy after a state dinner on March 25, 1982. In May 1985 Sinatra was awarded the Presidential Medal of Freedom.

Occasionally the Reagans invite large groups to perform, but with these artistic pleasures come logistics headaches. Before the New York Philharmonic played outdoors on the evening of July 29, 1982, for Indira Gandhi's visit, conductor Zubin Mehta asked if they could rehearse all afternoon beginning at 1:00. In order to prevent disturbance of the President's cabinet meeting, the orchestra had to rehearse on the South Lawn in the 95° heat. "Luckily we found a lot of volunteers to hold umbrellas over the musicians while they played to protect the instruments from the blazing sun," Chief Usher Rex Scouten said. Then he added thoughtfully, "The White House is not a concert hall, and everything we do here involves some compromise. . . . On the mezzanine levels there are dressing rooms for twenty to twenty-five ladies, but only for about a dozen men. When the New York Philharmonic came, we had to put the men in the family theater to change and the soloist in the East Wing visitors office so that he could have quiet. Every place else in the house was being used for something."[40]

And, while the White House over the years has been ingenious in arranging rehearsals that do not conflict with presidential activities, there have been occasional problems. Mabel Brandon recalls how a group of deaf dancers were rehearsing to a loud, pungent drum beat while the president was in the library below working. What happened? "Oh, word came from downstairs to please stop because the drums were being picked up by the President's tape recorder," she said.[41]

The White House is managed by the chief usher, who coordinates efforts all the way from security to the comforts of the president and first lady. Preparing for the concerts, whether indoors or outdoors, often involves juggling a multiplicity of elements—stages, platforms, chairs, lighting, sound systems, and the diverse accouterments of the electronic media. "Now we spend as much time getting the facilities ready for the press coverage as for the artists," admits Rex Scouten: "The PBS series is a major, major production, but even for the state dinners and other events we have to determine ahead of time, are they going to televise the whole thing, part, or just what? The White House takes care of all its own lighting—spots, colored lights, and so forth—but it's absolutely pointless for us to put in theatrical lighting and have the whole thing washed out with television lights. Often when there is to be a staged production, the guest company sends in their own people to work with our resident staff as far as the lighting is concerned. The White House Communication Agency then works with the sound."[42]

Scouten also feels that with top entertainment "you have to have professionalism all the way through. To the artists performing at the White House is the most important thing they have ever done in their lives." The lighting people, too, know that they are at the White House and are trying to do their best: "They have never been in a situation quite like this," Scouten adds. "So how do you balance all these people and keep them happy? How do you reserve space for the press and their equipment and yet in the end try to have the room as presentable as possible for the President of the United States and his guests to walk into? These are some of the biggest challenges we have.[43]

After the assassination attempt on President Reagan on March 30, 1981, security at the White House was tightened. Entertainers in the modern White House have to go through the same security clearance that everyone else does. Each instrument has to be checked, and when large groups of artists perform, this can take almost an hour. Until Carter took office, everything had to be checked by hand; now there are metal detectors and dogs sniff routinely for suspicious materials. During Ida Levin's rehearsal for her PBS concert with Rudolf Serkin, one could sense all eyes were not on the performers: U.S. Secret Service men scrutinized every corner of the East Room. "We were briefed prior to the rehearsal and told by the security men that the worst thing you can do in the White House is to run," said the young violinist. "It gets the security people terribly excited."[44]

The Reagans have restored the outdoor ceremonial procedures at the White House that President Carter had eliminated or simplified. The Herald Trumpets and Fife and Drum Corps play, and the military bands from the four branches of service alternate for the various welcoming ceremonies for foreign dignitaries. Music is important in establishing good foreign relations, emphasizes Paul Miller, director of ceremonies for the Military District of Washington. "It really does have an effect on diplomacy," he says. "I can recall a foreign head of state coming to Washington to discuss some very, very serious problems. But the fellow was in such a good mood after the ceremony that the negotiations went very well. He said, 'I just want you to know that it had a great deal to do with the music you provided that morning at the arrival ceremony.' "[45]

And just what *is* the right music? Often it is the visiting dignitary's favorite tunes and marches, but sometimes choosing this music is not simple. Mistakes can be made, even with something as vital as a national anthem. The U.S. Army Band maintains an extensive file of virtually every national anthem of the world through information derived from the embassies. One of the band's jobs is to keep the various service bands provided with correct information as well as musical scores. "We had a problem with Romania on this last visit," Miller recalled. "As the band was playing their national anthem at the White House arrival ceremony, one of their officials went up to

Colonel John R. Bourgeois, U.S. Marine Corps, was appointed the twenty-fifth director of the U.S. Marine Band in May 1979. The Marine Band performs more than 150 programs a year at the White House.

the assistant chief of protocol and said, 'You're playing the wrong music. You know, that's a terrible insult.' We learned that Romania had just changed its national anthem. They had forwarded a copy to the embassy but it had not arrived in time to get properly distributed. Very few people at the embassy were aware that the anthem had been changed.'[46]

The nation's oldest continuous musical organization, the U.S. Marine Band numbers 140 musicians who play nearly 600 programs a year, 150 of them at the White House. Conducted by Colonel John Bourgeois, the band plays for White House concerts, dinners, and receptions, accompanies many of the guest artists, and plays for dancing—a special pleasure of the Reagans—just as it had more than 100 years ago. The players of the band are educated at the nation's finest music schools and must be able to sight read a wide variety of music. Many attain high civilian positions when they leave the band, as in the case of violinist Elliot Chapo, who became concertmaster with the New York Philharmonic and later with the Dallas Symphony

Orchestra. Women first joined the band under President Nixon and today number about twenty-four players.

When she first came to the White House as social secretary, Muffie Brandon was presented with a detailed catalogue of the various musical units within the Marine Band with identifying photographs and lists of each unit's representative repertory. Brandon then auditioned several of the units to gain a feeling for their suitability for White House occasions. Today's social secretary has at least sixteen possibilities: Concert Band, Marine Band Combo, Chamber Orchestra (the White House Orchestra of twenty-three players), Cordovox Trio, Piano Trio, Brass Choir, Brass Quintet, Guitarist, Dance Band, Woodwind Quintet, Harpist, Harp and Flute Duo, String Ensemble, Pianist, Dixieland Combo, and Baritone Vocalist. There is no Marine choir, and when such a group is desired, the excellent Army or Navy choirs assist. Strolling strings are provided by the Army and Air Force and have played in the state dining room during dinner from the time of Eisenhower.

Playing background music for a typical state dinner at the White House is often as complex as accompanying a Hollywood film or operatic production. The director must continuously adapt his repertory to shifting moods and casting—with the central characters the president and his honored visitor. "As the guests are arriving," Colonel Bourgeois explains, "the orchestra, stationed in the foyer, might play Gershwin, Leroy Anderson, Mozart, or the second movement of Schubert's C Major Symphony, which has a nice 'walking feeling.' "

> When the guest of honor arrives, we select something rather elegant and joyful—a bourée from one of the Bach suites, perhaps. As the President and his party come down the stairs, "Hail America" by George Drumon is played. This is traditional. The President then poses for the press and before entering the East Room, the band sounds four "Ruffles and Flourishes," the President and First Lady are announced and "Hail to the Chief" follows. There is always considerable tension in getting this timing just right. For the receiving line, marches connected with a sort of cadence tend to move people into dinner. When the President finally leaves for dinner, we bring the volume up to let everyone know he will enter the dining room.[47]

All these comments resemble those of John Philip Sousa when he led the Marine Band under President Hayes over 100 years ago.

Preserving White House traditions is important to the Reagans, and every musical gesture at the mansion today is an echo from the past. Music still celebrates the intriguing mélange of occasions that it always had. But the Reagans have added their own distinctive touch and often there is an aura of history about it. The U.S. premiere of Mozart's recently discovered Symphony in F, K19a, was performed by New York's Mostly Mozart Festival Orchestra on the White House lawn on July 8, 1981, for a distinguished audience of political and artistic leaders.[48] On July 13, 1982, a John Philip Sousa program was

On the occasion of its 100th anniversary, the Boston Pops Orchestra performed at the White House on July 15, 1985. Nancy Reagan is seated with Vice-President and Mrs. George Bush, front row, right.

conducted by Keith Brion, who dressed as the famed bandmaster himself to the delight of the children present. Brion is also a Sousa scholar and has spent many years researching Sousa's composing and conducting techniques. Both nostalgia and more recent history were conjured up when the Beach Boys performed on the South Lawn on June 12, 1983, to help raise money for young mentally retarded athletes in the Special Olympics. Missing from the audience was Secretary of the Interior James Watt, who had said two months earlier that "rock groups attracted the wrong element" and could not play on the Washington mall. But the president intervened.[49]

Ultimately, however, the wonders of the White House programs lie in the music itself, in its kaleidoscopic powers on the human spirit. Isaac Stern once said, "The world weeps, cries, loves and laughs better through music than any other way." At the Reagans' first Christmas party for their senior staff, Michael Deaver, special assistant to the president, played two-pianos with a local pianist, Bob Vagoda. Jim Brady, injured during the assassination attempt on the president, was in his wheelchair. "Christmas carols were played," recalls Mabel Brandon, "and we all stood around the pianos in the grand foyer. It was one of the most beautiful musical moments I have ever known. It was spontaneous, moving and really captured the essence of Christmas."[50] But it also caught the spirit of the White House, where music provides a vital bond among world leaders, princes, diplomats, blacks, whites—or just the family. And while administrations change, tastes shift, and new currents bring fresh musical styles to the White House—in this music the image of America remains, reinforcing our heritage and glorifying our dreams.

CONCLUSION

This book has been a story of "the gradual emergence of the American national character with the growing acceptance of its diverse ethnic treasures and a lessening dependence upon European culture." But it has also been the tale of the American process of music-making—how music in a democracy was absorbed, shaped, transformed, and perceived from post-Revolutionary days to the present. Whether dramatic or abstract, vernacular or cultivated, music is a powerful voice that can charm as forcefully as it can repel. Ultimately, the manner in which music is perceived within the complexities of society determines its absorption, expression, and direction. The ancient Greeks recognized this in their doctrine of *ethos*, which claimed music had a vital effect on human character and conduct. Indeed, Plato in his *Republic* found in music certain mystical properties that could strengthen character, heal illness, spur men to action, and play a dominant role in the education and political system of Greek civilization.

In modern times, echoes from the doctrine of *ethos* appear in many guises—from the patriotic repertory of the U.S. Marine Band to the "subversive" American symphonic music of the 1950s, from the controversial messages of rock to the mind-expanding colors of music video. This book, then, is not only about history, the White House, or even music. It is about the human spirit. And it proves that the art of music can mold the political process, shape a historical event, and capture the human spirit in a manner like no other.

What might we conclude about White House musical history and its relationship to the American experience in its broadest spectrum? A brief glimpse backward into the long skein of American musical life indicates that the process of perceiving and enjoying music in all its diverse styles has been essential to America from its founding days.

The earliest New England colonists enjoyed simple, functional music that was primarily of a religious nature. And although the settlers had no worldly wealth and little leisure time, music was a tool that praised and served God through the noblest forms of human expression—hymns and psalm tunes. It is not surprising, then, that the first American composers were "tunesmiths" such as William Billings, whose fuguing tunes became a staple of New England congregations, singing schools, and social groups. Of strong Puritan heritage, Abigail Adams must have known this music with its sturdy, rugged

American character. It is little wonder that our second first lady "shuddered" when she saw the "shameful" ballets in Paris and the opulent production of Handel's *Messiah* at Westminster Abbey in the 1780s. Emigrant musicians and political figures were also important in the early cultural life of the nation. The best known among the latter were Thomas Jefferson and Francis Hopkinson, one of the earliest American composers and the first secretary of the Navy.

By the postcolonial period, Americans were becoming more economically stable and politically independent. The cities along the eastern seaboard were acquiring wealth and adopted European standards of culture as models of elegance and urbanity. The finest American families regarded French furnishings as a sign of gentility, and the elegant piano, made by Erard frères and brought to the White House from France in 1817, illustrates the sophisticated tastes of the James Monroes. French cultural influences on the White House are also noted in Dolley Madison's unique purchase of music composed, arranged, and published in 1810 by Mme. Le Pelletier, possibly the first woman to compose serious instrumental music in America. As the nineteenth century progressed, America turned more and more to its own rapidly growing industries and enterprises; during the administration of John Quincy Adams, Congress directed that the White House purchase American-made products "as far as practicable."

Public concerts, popular as early as 1730, increased in number after the Revolution, and Alexander Reinagle's City Concerts in Philadelphia were enjoyed by George Washington during the 1780s. But while public secular music was influenced primarily by middle-class patronage, American "aristocratic" music found a home at the Presidential Palace where the first families entertained with elegance, grace, and a touch of homespun pride. With little entertainment of substance in the desolate city of Washington other than the "mishmash" and a few learned pigs, an invitation to a White House drawing room was a treasure indeed. Two volumes of music belonging to Louisa Catherine Adams, wife of John Quincy Adams, as well as the first lady's harp and Babcock piano, attest to the availability of musical instruments and scores in America during the 1820s. But the two volumes also indicate that aristocratic or "courtly" music was no different from the music that most Americans enjoyed during the early nineteenth century.

There is still a great deal to learn about the widespread musical practices of the American family during the nineteenth century. The investigation of family music-making at the White House reveals a dual image: entertainment for guests, a kind of "salon" music performed by "gentlemen (and lady) amateurs"; and private music-making for personal enjoyment. The study of music was considered an important element of education and respectability, and without exception, presidential family members either sang or played instruments, such as harp, guitar, piano, violin, or flute. The piano, however, was the centerpiece of family musical life during the nineteenth and early twentieth centuries; over half of the first ladies during the period played with a degree of proficiency. With the possible exception of Adams's and Jefferson's administrations, the White House was never without at least two pianos, often three or four. And while George Washington was one of the first Americans to purchase an American-made piano (from Thomas Dodds in 1789), after 1830 all the pianos acquired by the White House were American-made. For as the century progressed, ingenious Yankee mass-marketing techniques brought top-quality, domestically made instruments into thousands of American homes.

The collections of music owned by presidential families—notably those of George Washington, Thomas Jefferson, James Madison, Zachary Taylor, Millard Fillmore, James Buchanan, Abraham Lincoln, Rutherford Hayes, and Benjamin Harrison—are fine examples of the urban secular styles enjoyed by the amateur American pianist of the time. Every variety of music is among these pages: opera airs, patriotic music, marches, dances, variations, ballads, and rousing battle pieces. To Oliver Wendell Holmes the piano was a "wondrous box," and another quotation from his poem "The Opening of the Piano" expresses the feelings of many Americans: "For the dear soul knew that music was a very sovereign balm / She had sprinkled it over Sorrow, and seen its brow grow calm."

Few presidents in history have been as sensitive and receptive to music as Abraham Lincoln. But Lincoln lived in an era during which music was a powerful art that sang presidents into office, marched men to war, serenaded the lonely, and protested society's ills with greater intensity than ever before. From the 1840s through the period of the Civil War, America's propensity for self-expression through song seemed to forecast the nation's moods of more than a century later. Sensitive, ingenuous, and urgent, these musical messages took many forms. Lincoln, often moved to tears by the ballads of Stephen Foster and the Hutchinson Family, was equally affected by patriotic songs, such as Julia Ward Howe's "The Battle Hymn of the Republic." Grand opera was also a special pleasure for this president, who attended nineteen productions while he was in office, claiming that "I must have a change or I will die."

Opera in nineteenth-century America was more significant and widespread than some historians have asserted. English light operas with spoken dialogue, known as ballad operas, had been popular especially during the colonial period, just as the operettas of Gilbert and Sullivan captured the American stage in the 1880s and 1890s. But as early as 1810, New Orleans had a permanent grand opera company, and New Yorkers heard their first foreign-language opera in 1825. While grand opera was expensive to produce, many of the latest French, Italian, and German operas were staged in American theaters only months after they received their premieres in Europe. And although opera was enjoyed as a fine social affair, it entertained Americans outside the theater in countless piano arrangements and transcriptions for concert bands that, from about 1840 into the early twentieth century, drew thousands to the community bandstands. The U.S. Marine Band, the White House "court ensemble" since 1801, brought to America music from the latest Italian operas and newest works of Wagner, Brahms, and other European composers. But as early as 1781, a military ensemble had serenaded George Washington and Charles Lee at Valley Forge with excerpts from a new opera by the French composer, André Grétry.

America's enjoyment of theatrical events in mid-century found expression in the dichotomous combination of European romanticism and rugged American humbug. The attractions touted by P. T. Barnum, who introduced soprano Jenny Lind to America, and the "monster" concerts conducted by Louis Antoine Jullien drew throngs and promoted the celebrity image. Despite his showmanship, Jullian frequently encouraged national consciousness by playing music by native American composers. Solo recitals were uncommon at this time, and performers, still mainly from Europe, often had to share their programs with bands, orchestras, and even magicians. Especially popular were the pianist-composers, most notably Anton Philip Heinrich and Louis Moreau Gottschalk, who played for John Tyler and Abraham Lincoln respectively. Through their extravagant ideas, colorful effects, and appeal to mass culture, Heinrich and Gottschalk were among the first musical explorers in the New World concert scene.

But the dazzling theater known as European romantic ballet remained a sterile import, whose daring costumes and sensual gestures discouraged the development of native American dance. In spite of modern claims that she danced at the White House, the voluptuous Fanny Elssler merely *visited* President Van Buren in the 1830s. Indeed, it remained for Martha Graham, encouraged by President and Mrs. Franklin Roosevelt, to establish an internationally recognized style of modern dance in America. As for social dancing, American society has raised an eyebrow on more than one occasion; even George Washington's minuet, Warren Harding's waltz, and John F. Kennedy's twist have come under attack. But it was the nation's joy in dancing that combined with early ragtime and patriotic marches at the close of the century to form a new, indigenous art form—jazz.

The spirit of jazz derives from the American black experience, but its stylistic roots lie in a wide variety of idioms: minstrel-show music, the "hot" rhythms of camp-meeting spirituals, gospel songs, brass bands, ragtime, and the moody inflections of the blues. By 1900 the revolution of American music had begun; the entertainment world would never be the same. Jazz swept the nation during the first decades of the twentieth century, disseminated by radio, films, recordings, and television. It touched the popular songs of Tin Pan Alley, the music of the dance bands, and Broadway theater: jazz had become big business.

The explosion of the music industry seemed to separate American audiences more distinctly than ever before into enthusiasts of either classical or popular music. In the nineteenth century symphonic organizations and concert artists had developed a wide-ranging repertory that appealed to mass audiences. But the White House from Theodore Roosevelt to Franklin Roosevelt preferred classical music performed by the era's most renowned artists—Paderewski, Rachmaninoff, Kreisler,

Schumann-Heink, Horowitz, Ponselle, and others—and rarely programmed commercial music for its distinguished guests. Early jazz forms appeared at the White House occasionally, however. Scott Joplin's popular "Maple Leaf Rag" of 1899 was performed by the Marine Band at the request of President Roosevelt's outgoing daughter, Alice, and a Navy jazz band played for social dancing during Warren Harding's administration. But little conscious visibility was given to jazz until the administration of John F. Kennedy. By the 1960s, jazz had become America's quintessential musical expression and its foremost cultural export.

The history of America's acceptance and appreciation of the black concert and operatic artist is a story worthy of more attention than it has received. The White House respected and encouraged black artists at a time when America barely recognized them outside the confines of the minstrel shows, as illustrated by Marie Selika's historic program for President Hayes in 1878. In the years after the Civil War and throughout Reconstruction, blacks were publicly segregated, hidden, or excluded entirely from the theaters, yet they managed to open theaters of their own and even form their own opera companies. Even as recently as the 1940s, Washington's National Theater allowed no blacks in the audience until George Gershwin's *Porgy and Bess*, with its all-black cast, was produced there.

Blacks were not accepted on the American operatic stage until at least the 1930s, and Eleanor Roosevelt's invitations to several black opera singers to perform in the White House were unprecedented in the twentieth century. The sensational Sissieretta Jones ("Black Patti"), who sang for Presidents William McKinley and Benjamin Harrison, created her own substitute for the legitimate American operatic stage: a dignified troupe of entertainers who prepared the way for the distinction that would come to black artists, such as Marian Anderson, after World War II.

A new national consciousness of the values of culture and of America's own unique musical heritage seemed to escalate after World War II. Both private and government support provided funds for artistic growth in diverse parts of the nation, especially during the 1950s and 1960s. The National Foundation for the Arts and Humanities was inaugurated under President Lyndon Johnson and across the nation arts centers were constructed. President Dwight D. Eisenhower's cultural exchange programs proved that America's idioms and performers were exportable and that the art of music could be a powerful binding force among nations.

All presidents from the time of Harding have publicly recognized the nation's cultural life in their addresses and communications. John Kennedy saw the rise of new hopes and visions for an America that would be remembered "not for our victories or defeats in battle or in politics, but for our contribution to the human spirit." Kennedy established the Presidential Medal of Freedom, and Lyndon Johnson awarded it to Aaron Copland only a decade after a member of Congress had called the renowned American composer a "communist sympathizer." Kennedy's administration also gave the arts a clearly defined focus by establishing the White House as a prominent center for America's cultural achievements. President and Mrs. Ronald Reagan have recognized the performing arts in America in various ways. One of the most effective has been the nationally televised series, "In Performance at the White House," that has featured the finest American performers and music, ranging from chamber music and opera to country music, jazz, and the songs from Broadway. Indeed, in these programs and other state entertainment, the long, colorful legend of America's discovery of itself continues with imagination and fresh momentum.

While the modern White House welcomes the arts of America more vigorously and visibly than ever before, it still maintains a certain moral obligation to the people to offer music that is appropriate or "right." But what is "right" or "wrong" often depends on the viewpoints and vicissitudes of the times. To a congressman of the 1870s, the "Athenian concept of music that ennobled the heart and purified the soul" shaped the music of the White House; to a critic a century later, "distinguished rock" was the cultural high point of the mansion. Might there be an echo from ancient Greece in the White House, then?—an image of a civilization that valued the *polis* or city-state as a source of moral, social, and political strength?—a symbol of a society's conviction that the sensuous powers of music could generate ethical values vital to the well being of the people? The answers are not hard to find. For as society moves into the future, this symbol gains power and vitality as the performing arts of all varieties become allied with American life more intimately than ever before. Thus the ancient image becomes a modern directive, transformed and rejuvenated by new dreams, fresh visions, and always a characteristic American spirit.

NOTES

List of abbreviations used in notes

DDEL	Dwight D. Eisenhower Library, Abilene, Kansas
Eisenhower Papers	Dwight D. Eisenhower Papers, DDEL
ER Papers	Eleanor Roosevelt Papers, FDRL
FDR Papers	Franklin D. Roosevelt Papers, FDRL
FDRL	Franklin D. Roosevelt Library, Hyde Park, New York
GRDN	General Records of the Department of the Navy, NARS
HHPL	Herbert Hoover Presidential Library, West Branch, Iowa
HSTL	Harry S. Truman Library, Independence, Missouri
JFKL	John F. Kennedy Library, Boston, Massachusetts
Johnson Papers	Lyndon B. Johnson Papers, LBJL
Kennedy Papers	John F. Kennedy Papers, JFKL
Lady Bird Johnson Papers	LBJL
LBJL	Lyndon Baines Johnson Library, Austin, Texas
LC	Library of Congress, Washington, D.C.
MBL	Marine Band Library, U.S. Marine Barracks, Washington, D.C.
MCHC	Marine Corps Historical Center, Navy Yard, Washington, D.C.
MLKL	Martin Luther King Memorial Library, Washington, D.C.
MTA	Miscellaneous Treasury Accounts of the President's House, NARS
NARS	National Archives and Records Services, Washington, D.C.
NMAH, SI	National Museum of American History, Smithsonian Institution, Washington, D.C.
OPB&G	Office of Public Building and Grounds, NARS
OWHC	Office of the White House Curator, The White House, Washington, D.C.
OWHSF	Official White House Social Functions, NARS
RHPC	Rutherford B. Hayes Presidential Center, Fremont, Ohio
Truman Papers	Harry S. Truman Papers, HSTL
WHCF	White House Central Files, LBJL

Chapter 1. Musical Life at Home

1. Rufus Wilmot Griswold, *The Republican Court* (New York: Appleton, 1855), 313-14. George Washington Parke Custis, recalling his sister practicing "under the immediate eye of her grandmother," noted, "The poor girl would play and cry, and cry and play" (George Washington Parke Custis, *Recollections and Private Memoirs of Washington* [New York, 1860], 408*n*). For more on the musical life of the Washingtons, see Nicholas E. Tawa, "Music in the Washington Household," *Journal of American Culture* 1 (Spring 1978):21-43.

2. Martha Parke Custis had two children by a previous marriage: John Parke Custis (Jacky) and Martha Parke Custis (Patsy), who died in her teens before Washington became president. John was killed during the Revolution, leaving four children, two of whom President and Mrs. Washington raised (Nelly and Tub). George Washington never had children of his own.

3. Eleanor Parke Custis to Elizabeth Bordley, May 30 [1797], Mt. Vernon Archives, Mt. Vernon, Va.

4. Stephen Decatur, Jr., *Private Affairs of George Washington from the Records and Accounts of Tobias Lear, Esquire, His Secretary* (Boston: Houghton Mifflin, 1933), 45, 74.

5. Raoul F. Camus, *Military Music of the American Revolution* (Chapel Hill: University of North Carolina Press, 1976), 79, 159.

6. The Marine Band undoubtedly can trace its origins even further back; a fife and drum corps was probably formed when the Continental Marines were organized in Philadelphia on Nov. 10, 1775.

7. Decatur, *Private Affairs*, 16, 228-29. See also Oscar Sonneck, "The Musical Side of Our First Presidents," in *Suum Cuique Essays in Music* (Freeport, N.Y.: Books for Libraries Press, 1969), 41, reprinted from *New Music Review*, 1907; and Paul Wilstach, *Mount Vernon: Washington's Home and the Nation's Shrine* (New York: Blue Ribbon Books, 1930), 101-2.

8. Decatur, *Private Affairs*, 15.

9. Anne Hollingsworth Wharton, *Martha Washington* (New York: Scribner's, 1897), 231-32.

10. Donald Jackson and Dorothy Twohig, eds., *The Diaries of George Washington*, 5 (Charlottesville: University Press of Virginia, 1979), 163, 169.

11. Charles Hamm, *Music in the New World* (New York: W. W. Norton, 1983), 104; Decatur, *Private Affairs*, 240, 250, 254-55, 280, 309; "Washington's Household Account Book, 1793-1797," *Pennsylvania Magazine of History and Biography* 31 (1907):62, 70.

12. For more on "The President's March," see Oscar Sonneck, *A Bibliography of Early Secular American Music (18th Century)*, rev. ed. William Upton (Washington, D.C.: Library of Congress, 1945), 341-44.

13. The piece was published in Philadelphia (1789) and sold by H. Rice.

14. Vera Lawrence, *Music for Patriots, Presidents and Politicians* (New York: Macmillan, 1975), 115. John Tasker Howard, "The Music of George Washington's Time," George Washington Bicentennial Lecture-Recital, New York University, Mar. 22, 1932, HHPL. "The President of the United States' March" by a "Mr. Sicard" (Philadelphia: McCulloch) is generally thought to have been composed about the time of Washington's inauguration in 1789 and may predate the Reinagle chorus. Editions of Phile's "President's March" appear to date from the time of Washington's second inauguration in 1793, but it is uncertain when the piece was written. See Sonneck, *Bibliography*, 341-44.

15. Sonneck, "Musical Side," 46-47.

16. Daniel Boorstin quoted in Kenneth W. Leish, ed., *The American*

Heritage Pictorial History of the Presidents of the United States (New York: American Heritage, 1968), 1:12.

17. Washington to Francis Hopkinson, Feb. 5, 1789, in John C. Fitzpatrick, ed., *The Writings of George Washington* . . . (Washington, D.C.: Government Printing Office, 1944), 30:196-97. For more on the Hopkinson songs, see Charles Hamm, *Yesterdays: Popular Song in America* (New York: W. W. Norton, 1979), 89-93.

18. "Invoice of Goods . . .," July 20, 1767, in Fitzpatrick, ed., *Writings of Washington*, 2:463.

19. "Invoice of Sundrys . . .," Oct. 12, 1861, ibid., 370.

20. Minnie Kendall Lowther, *Mount Vernon: Its Children, Its Romances, Its Allied Families and Mansions* (Chicago: John C. Winston, 1930), 126.

21. Decatur, *Private Affairs*, 33-34; a copy of the letter is in the Mt. Vernon Archives.

22. Washington to Clement Biddle, Dec. 21, 1789, in Fitzpatrick, ed., *Writings of Washington*, 30:481.

23. James R. Heintze, "Music of the Washington Family: A Little-Known Collection," *Musical Quarterly* 56 (1970):289.

24. Entries for Nov. 21 and Dec. 28, 1796, "Philadelphia Household Accounts," Mr. Vernon Archives.

25. Decatur, *Private Affairs*, 35.

26. The piano's history after Washington's presidency is obscure. Decatur states it was taken to Mt. Vernon, then to Arlington in the hands of George Washington Parke Custis, then passed to Robert E. Lee. During the Civil War it was broken up by souvenir hunters (*ibid.*). The Metropolitan Museum of Art possesses a Dodds and Claus square pianoforte dating ca. 1791 with sixty keys, a compass of FF-f^3 (five octaves), and an English action without escapement or backcheck. Its original three pedals are missing. An American eagle design is stenciled on the nameboard.

27. Oscar Sonneck, *Early Concert Life in America* (New York: Musurgia, 1949), 130; Judith Britt, typescript inventory, Mar. 1978, NMAH, SI. The guitar is the property of the Lewis Collection, Smithsonian. A wooden flute, now at Mt. Vernon, appears to be later than 1800 and therefore not the flute ordered for John Parke Custis in 1775.

28. Arthur Loesser, *Men, Women and Pianos: A Social History* (New York: Simon and Schuster, 1954), 244.

Chapter 2. The European Touch

1. Abigail Smith Adams, *Letters of Mrs. Adams, the Wife of John Adams*, introduction by Charles Francis Adams (Boston: Little, Brown, 1840), 1:133. On Aug. 27, 1785, Abigail wrote to her sister from London that her favorite Scotch song was "There'e nae Luck about the House." Various arrangements of the song were published between 1812-24 in Baltimore, Philadelphia, and New York. See Richard J. Wolfe, *Secular Music in America, 1801-1825*, 2 (New York: New York Public Library, 1964).

2. Adams, *Letters*, 432-35.

3. Page Smith, *John Adams* (New York: Doubleday, 1962), 1(1735-1784): 685. John Quincy Adams was minister to Berlin at this time. Besides Charles and John Quincy, John and Abigail's children were Susanna, Abigail, and Thomas Boylston. For more on the history of the remarkable Adams family, see Jack Shepherd, *The Adams Chronicles: Four Generations of Greatness* (Boston: Little, Brown, 1975). Some authors, such as Gilson Willets and Marie Smith, claim that Abigail Adams brought to the President's Mansion her

piano, harp, and guitar. They probably confused this first lady with Abigail Filmore, whose daughter Mary Abigail played these instruments in the White House (see ch. 4, herein).

4. "Marine Band Chronology," compilation of clippings and reports from various government documents, July 11, 1798, to Mar. 8, 1954, 121 pp., typescript, MBL.

5. Handwritten list dated 1804 in files of Marine Band, MCHC; *National Intelligencer*, Sept. 25, 1805.

6. Shepherd, *Adams Chronicles*, xxiii.

7. Sonneck, "Musical Side," 37.

8. L. H. Butterfield, ed., *Diary and Autobiography of John Adams* (Cambridge, Mass.: Harvard University Press, 1961), 4:66. For a description of the Concert Spirituel during this period, see *n*23 below.

9. Ibid., 104. John Adams especially enjoyed religious music and attended services of various denominations. His description of an elaborate Catholic ritual in Christ Church, Philadelphia, opens with the music "consisting of an organ, and a choir of singers" that "went all the afternoon except sermon time. And the assembly chanted most sweetly. Here is everything which can lay hold of the eye, ear, and imagination. Everything which can charm and bewitch the simple and ignorant. I wonder how Luther ever broke the spell." (H. Earle Johnson, "The Adams Family and Good Listening," *Journal of the American Musicological Society* 11 [Summer-Fall 1958]:166.)

10. Adams, *Letters*, 83. For more on the operas that Mrs. Adams might have seen, see issues of *Journal de Paris* (Library of Congress, Washington, D.C.) for the period Dec. 1784 through Feb. 1785. While operas by Grétry, Piccinni, Monsigny, and Philador were being produced in Paris during this period, Abigail's reference to the "God or Goddess" seems to indicate the heroic or tragic form. Rameau's *Castor et Pollux* was also being performed at the Académie Royale de Musique at this time.

11. Ibid., 82.

12. Johnson, "Adams Family," 168. Johnson quotes from a letter to Miss E. Cranch, Sept. 2, 1785.

13. Ibid. Two days after the performance, *Porcupines Gazette* announced the publication, at Carr's Musical Repository, of "the very favourite New Federal Song." The first issue of the song bore the image of President John Adams neatly trimmed and pasted on the music above the words "Behold the Chief who now commands!" When Washington was appointed commander in chief of the American forces, on July 3, 1798, Carr substituted a portrait of Washington for Adams. See Oscar Sonneck, "The First Edition of Hail Columbia," *Miscellaneous Studies in the History of Music* (New York: AMS Press, 1970), 180-89; and Wendy C. Wick, *George Washington, an American Icon: The Eighteenth-Century Graphic Portraits* (Washington, D.C.: Barra Foundation, 1982), 125-27.

14. While Paine's verses are forgotten today, those of Francis Scott Key live on. Key's text, also set to the Anacreon tune, was written in 1814 after the bombardment of Fort McHenry by the British and published the same year as "The Star-Spangled Banner." It was not until 1931, however, that it was established as our national anthem (see ch. 9, herein). The earliest setting of the Anacreon tune is listed in Harry Dichter and Elliott Shapiro, *Handbook of Early American Sheet Music, 1768-1889* (New York: Dover, 1977), 35, as " 'Freedom Triumphant,' B. Carr, NY & Phila. [1796]." For more on the origins of "The Star-Spangled Banner," see William Lichtenwanger, "The Music of the Star-Spangled Banner: From Ludgate Hill to Capitol Hill," *Quarterly Journal of the Library of Congress*, July 1977.

15. Charles William Janson, *The Stranger in America, 1793-1806* (New York: Press of the Pioneers, 1935), 213. Reprinted from the London edition of 1807.

16. Nathan Schachner, *Thomas Jefferson: A Biography* (New York: Appleton-Century-Crofts, 1951), 2:690. Meriwether Lewis was one of the leaders of the Lewis and Clark Expedition of 1804-6.

17. John C. Haskins, "Music in the District of Columbia, 1800 to 1814" (M.A. thesis, Catholic University of America, 1952), 19.

18. Jefferson to Nathaniel Burwell, Mar. 14, 1818, in Andrew A. Lipscomb and Albert Ellery Bergh, eds., *The Writings of Thomas Jefferson* (Washington, D.C.: Government Printing Office, 1903-4), 15:135.

19. Claude G. Bowers, *The Young Jefferson, 1743-1789* (Boston: Houghton Mifflin, 1969), 21; Lyon G. Tyler, *Letters and Times of the Tylers* (Richmond, Va.: Whittet and Shepperson, 1884), 2:55.

20. Jefferson's catalogue, the property of the Massachusetts Historical Society, Boston, is reprinted in Helen Cripe, *Thomas Jefferson and Music* (Charlottesville: University Press of Virginia, 1974), appendix I, 97-104.

21. Ibid., 114.

22. Thomas Jefferson to Martha Jefferson, Mar. 28, 1787, quoted in ibid., 30.

23. Ibid., 19-24. The Concert Spirituel was generally regarded as the central institution of Paris's nonoperatic life. Many famous performers appeared there, and their programs played a role in the dissemination of Italian music in Paris. The Concert Spirituel ended in 1790. See Mary Cyr, "Paris," *New Grove Dictionary of Music and Musicians*, 6th ed. (London: Macmillan, 1980), 14:IV, 99-200.

24. Washington was a great stickler for form and ceremony. He rode about in a huge cream-colored coach decorated with cupids in the style of Louis XVI. Though he had never been abroad, he was acquainted with aristocratic English officers and the "pomp and panoply of glorious war." Esther Singleton, *The Story of the White House* (New York: McClure, 1907), 1:22-25.

25. Ibid., 25.

26. Mrs. Samuel Harrison Smith (Margaret Bayard), *The First Forty Years of Washington Society*, ed. Gaillard Hunt (New York: Scribner's, 1906), 399.

27. Ibid., 30.

28. *National Intelligencer*, July 5, 1801. Tingey's fine singing is mentioned in various other sources. Margaret Bayard Smith held a private gathering earlier in the year and recalled: "Captain T. [Tingey] sings a good song, his wife and two daughters accompany him . . . these songs very agreeably supplied the place of conversation" (Smith, *First Forty Years*, 18). As the British were entering Washington on Aug. 24, 1814, Tingey ordered the Navy Yard to be burned before evacuating it.

29. Quoted in Singleton, *White House*, 1:xxiii. The "Porter's Lodge" today is the chief usher's reception room or office.

30. Washington, Jan. 11, 1809, Catherine Mitchell Papers, LC.

31. Jefferson to Fabbroni, June 8, 1778, in Julian P. Boyd et al., eds., *The Papers of Thomas Jefferson* (Princeton, N.J.: Princeton University Press, 1950–   ), 2:196.

32. Remarks of Hon. Fiorello H. LaGuardia, House of Representatives, *Congressional Record*, 71st Cong., 2d sess., Jan. 29, 1930. Mazzei and a group of Tuscan farmers had assisted Jefferson with agricultural experiments in Virginia in 1773. Mazzei also helped Jefferson meet the musicians Piccinni and Caravoglia when he arrived in Europe as minister to France.

33. Hall to Wharton, Feb. 28, 1805 in "Marine Band Chronology," MBL;

Karl Schuon, *Home of the Commandants* (Quantico, Va.: Leatherneck Association, 1966), 67-68; Allen J. Ferguson, "The Band from Catania," *Marine Corps Gazette*, Nov. 1981, 43-45.

34. Wharton to Hall, June 29, 1805, in "Marine Band Chronology."

35. "Narrative of Gaetano Carusi in Support of his Claim Before the Congress of the United States," typescript copy, n.d., 3. Courtesy Charles Lombard, Washington, D.C.

36. "Size Roll of Marines Enlisted by Captain John Hall," May 10, 1805, typescript, MBL; William Burrows to Johnathan Williams, Nov. 6, 1805, MCHC.

37. "Narrative of Gaetano Carusi," 3.

38. For more on Catania, see Herbert Weinstock, *Vincenzo Bellini: His Life and His Operas* (New York: Knopf, 1971), 4-6, and F. de Roberto, *Catania* (Bergamo: Istituto Italiano d'Arti Grafiche, 1907).

39. Wolfe, *Secular Music in America*, 1:171.

40. Ibid.; *National Intelligencer*, Jan. 24, 1831.

41. Gale to Wharton, Dec. 26, 1806, in "Marine Band Chronology," MBL.

42. "Narrative of Gaetano Carusi," 11-12; "Report of the Committee on Naval Affairs," House of Representatives, *Congressional Report*, 24th Cong., 1st sess., Jan. 6, 1836; "Gaetano Carusi," House of Representatives, *Congressional Report*, 29th Cong., 1st sess., June 17, 1846.

43. Order by Wharton, July 31, 1806, quoted in Haskins, "Music in D.C.," 8.

44. John Clagett Proctor, "Dancing When the Capital Was Young," *Washington Sunday Star*, Dec. 3, 1933. The entreprenurial Carusis rented the lower floor of the U.S. post office. When the post office moved out leaving the place in a shambles, the Carusis again sued the government. In the mid-1850s Samuel Carusi became a founder of the short-lived Washington Philharmonic Society. Gaetano's descendent, Eugene C. Carusi, is a noted Washington lawyer, and his wife is active as a patron of the John F. Kennedy Center for the Performing Arts.

45. "It is usual for him to have a dozen or 15 persons to dine every day." Catherine Mitchell to Margaret Miller, Apr. 8, 1806, Mitchell Papers, LC.

46. Schachner, *Jefferson*, 2:68.

47. Cripe, *Jefferson and Music*, 89-90.

48. Claxton to Jefferson, June 13, 1800, Jefferson to Claxton, June 18, 1800, quoted in ibid., 42 (original letters in Massachusetts Historical Society). There is no musical instrument listed in Jefferson's inventory of government purchases for the White House compiled in 1809. The inventory is printed in Marie Kimball, "The Original Furnishings of the White House," Pt. I, *Magazine Antiques*, June 1929.

49. Cripe, *Jefferson and Music*, 57.

50. Astor to Jefferson, Feb. 27, 1808, Jefferson to Astor, Apr. 13, 1808, reels 40 and 41, Thomas Jefferson Papers, LC. According to some sources, John Jacob Astor gave the Madisons a fine dinner set and two fur pieces while they lived in the White House.

51. Frank Kidson/H. G. Farmer, "Astor & Co.," *New Grove*, 6th ed., 1:662-63. Daniel Spillane, *History of the American Pianoforte* (New York: Da Capo, 1969), 68-69. President Monroe and Sarah Childress Polk owned Astor pianofortes (see ch. 3 herein).

52. Cripe, *Jefferson and Music*, 129. The question of Jefferson's violins is discussed in appendix III and on 43-47.

53. The music stand now at Monticello is revolving and has five adjustable music rests. It accommodates four seated players and one standing. In a bound

volume of manuscript music at Charlottesville is a copy of "Variations on the Sicilian Hymn, 'Life Let Us Cherish.' "

54. Jefferson to Martha Jefferson Randolph, Apr. 4, 1790, in Edwin Betts and James Bear, eds., *The Family Letters of Thomas Jefferson* (Columbia: University of Missouri Press, 1966), 51.

55. Dolley Madison remained a beloved social figure in the capital for many years after she left the White House. She died at eighty-one almost a pauper. She and James Monroe were childless. See Conover Hunt Jones, *Dolley and the "Great Little Madison"* (Washington, D.C.: American Institute of Architects Foundation, 1977), and Katherine Anthony, *Dolly Madison: Her Life and Times* (Garden City, N.Y.: Doubleday, 1949).

56. Catherine Mitchell to Margaret Miller, Jan. 2, 1811, Mitchell Papers, LC.

57. Smith to Kirkpatrick, Dec. 5, 1816, in Smith, *First Forty Years*, 131-32.

58. "Social Life in Washington during Mr. Madison's Presidency," *National Intelligencer*, Mar. 11, 1871. Mrs. William Seaton was the wife of the owner and manager of the *National Intelligencer*. Her memory of Mrs. Madison's first reception in the winter of 1812-13 is reprinted in this issue.

59. Latrobe to Dolley Madison, Mar. 17, 1809, in Edward C. Carter II, ed., *The Papers of Benjamin Henry Latrobe*, microfiche edition, 2 vols. (Clifton, N.J.: James T. White, 1976), fiche no. 198, row B, col. 10. Andrew Hazelhurst was the brother of Latrobe's wife, Mary. His father, Isaac Hazelhurst, ran a highly prosperous import/export business in Philadelphia. Correspondence from Latrobe to Dolley Madison, Mar. 22, 1809, indicates that Mary selected a guitar for Mrs. Madison in Philadelphia.

60. The piano was tuned shortly before the great fire, as the following voucher indicates.

Mrs. Madison for the President's House to F.A. Wagler	
1814 Jan 8 to tuning grand piano	$2.00
regulating hammers	.50
1 broken string in the bass	.37 1/2
Aug 5, 1814 Rec. the above	$2.87 1/2

Account #29.494, Record Group 217, MTA, NARS.

61. Jones, *Dolley*, 56.

62. Voucher 13, account #28.634, Record Group 217. Wagler composed "President Monroe's Grand March" and a piece celebrating Andrew Jackson's victories at New Orleans, among other works.

63. United States for the President's House bot of Joseph Milligen [*sic*]

    12 numbers of Madame Le Pelletier's Musical Journal $12

    Delivered Oct. 19, 1810

    Rec. payment Oct. 4, 1813

Account #29.494, Record Group 217.

64. Milligan to James Madison, Oct. 30, 1818, James Madison Papers, LC. There are over fifty letters between Milligan and Jefferson in the Jefferson Papers (reels 43 and 44) dealing with book matters. A bound copy of the entire series is in the Library of Congress. Mrs. Madison's original music would have been burned in the fire. The contents of the *Journal* are listed in Wolfe, *Secular Music*, 458-59.

65. Quoted in Gregory A. Wood, *The French Presence in Maryland, 1524-1800* (Baltimore: Gateway Press, 1978), 124-25.

66. Jones, *Dolley*, 43.

67. Harry Ammon, *James Monroe: The Quest for National Identity* (New York: McGraw Hill, 1971), 400.

68. *National Intelligencer*, May 12, 1817.

69. May 15, 1818, "Marine Band Chronology," MBL. The report states that Pulizzi played the piece at Crawford's Ballroom in Georgetown on the above date.

70. Singleton, *White House*, 134; Ammon, *James Monroe*, 405.

71. Account #37.131, May 8, 1818, Record Group 217. Writing to James Monroe from Le Havre on Sept. 15, 1817, Russell and Le Farge advises: "Being obliged to take piano of Erard, we could not get any other ready made but the one sent. He allowed us a very large discount on account of the many purchases we have made of him."

72. Kenneth Carpenter, "A History of the United States Marine Band" (Ph.D. diss., University of Iowa, 1971), 27, 32; Wharton to Bullus, Aug. 23, 1812, in "Marine Band Chronology," MBL. For more on Janissary music see Camus, *Military Music*, 33-39, and Rosemond Harding, *The Piano-Forte* (Cambridge: Cambridge University Press, 1933), chs. 5, 6. Pianos with Janissary attachments were made in America in the 1830s by Pommer, Reuss and Newman.

73. *National Intelligencer*, Mar. 26, 1819.

74. Johnson, "Adams Family," 165-76. While Adams was minister to England, he gave a frank appraisal of a performance he heard at Drury Lane: "*Israel in Egypt* was in two parts, to which was added a third part, consisting of several foolish ballads, and a grand battle symphony, composed by Beethoven, to show the triumph of the 'Rule Brittania' and 'God Save the King' over 'Malbrook.' Bad music, but patriotic. The house was full; the entertainment, like that of all English oratories [*sic*], dull" (Mar. 13, 1816, in Allan Nevins, ed., *The Diary of John Quincy Adams, 1794-1855* [New York: Ungar, 1951], 170).

75. Nevins, ed., *Diary*, Nov. 7, 1830.

76. *Memoirs of John Quincy Adams* (New York, 1874), 1:98-99, quoted in Johnson, "Adams Family," 172. John Quincy served for seventeen years in the House of Representatives after he left the White House.

77. The diaries of John Quincy Adams are part of the Adams Family Papers, the property of the Massachusetts Historical Society. Hundreds of Louisa Catherine Adams's letters and other writings are part of this collection and are available on microfilm. Reels 264-69 contain her poems and a play, "Records of a Life, or My Story," 1825; "Adventures of a Nobody," begun 1840; and other autobiographical writings.

78. Joan Challinor, "Louisa Catherine Johnson Adams: The Price of Ambition" (Ph.D. diss., American University, 1982), 211.

79. Ibid., 589.

80. Margaret Bayard Smith, quoted in Anne Hollingsworth Wharton, "Social Life at the White House," *The Era*, July 1902, 85.

81. Sept. 6, 1825, in "Marine Band Chronology," MBL. A week later the Marine Band once again looked to Italy for new membership. The commandant ordered Capt. Charles Broom, who was commanding Marines of the Mediterranean squadron to "enlist for the Corps six good musicians, three clarinet players, 2 French horn players, and 1 flute player. They can easily be procured in Sicily or Naples. Ask Commodore Rodgers to send them back on the first national vessel." Sept. 14, 1825, in ibid.

82. "March and Chorus in the Dramatic Romance of the Lady of the Lake, composed by Mr. Sanderson" (Philadelphia: G. E. Black, ca. 1812), LC. See also "Origins of Hail to the Chief," 1 page, typescript, Division of Political History, NMAH, SI.

83. "Oh! Say Not a Woman's Heart Is Bought. A Favorite Ballad as sung

with the greatest applause by Mrs. French, composed by John Whitaker" (Philadelphia: G. E. Blake) in Mrs. Adams's albums of music, property of Division of Political History, NMAH, SI. The larger album contains mainly published works (many by Americans, including Carr, Willig, and Blake); the smaller consists of handscribed pieces.

84. Jefferson disliked Moore because he called the President's House "a very noble structure by no means suited to the philosophical humility of its present possessor, who inhabits but a corner of the mansion himself and abandons the rest to a stage of uncleanly desolation." Moore had many vitrolic viewpoints about America that made their way into his verse (Hamm, *Yesterdays*, 58-59).

85. From Louisa Adams, "Adventures of a Nobody," quoted in Lyman H. Butterfield, "Tending a Dragon-Killer: Notes for the Biographer of Mrs. John Quincy Adams," *Proceedings of the American Philosophical Society* 118 (Apr. 1974):172. Hamm notes that the *Irish Melodies* of Thomas Moore "share the distinction with the songs of Stephen Foster of being the most popular, widely-sung, best-loved, and most durable songs in the English language of the entire nineteenth century" (Hamm, *Yesterdays*, 44). See Hamm's ch. 3 for a discussion of Moore's *Irish Melodies*.

86. Quoted by James Hewitt in Hamm, *Yesterdays*, 50.

87. Margaret Brown Klapthor, *Official White House China 1789 to the Present* (Washington, D.C.: Smithsonian Institution Press, 1975), 49.

88. Spillane, *History of the American Pianoforte*, 84-86. The Babcock piano is a gift to the Smithsonian from the Juilliard School of Music. Association between the Mackay and Adams families goes back as far as Mungo Mackay's contacts with John Adams in 1798. See Dan Berwin Brockman, "Mackay-Hunt Family History," Cohasset, Mass., 1983, typescript, NMAH, SI. In the Smithsonian's Adams-Clement Collection is also a hymnal, *The Christian Psalter*, that contains several metrical versions of the psalms written by John Quincy Adams.

Chapter 3. Politics, Protest, and the Changing American Culture

1. *National Intelligencer*, Mar. 4, 1829. James Monroe was the first president to be honored with an inaugural concert (*National Intelligencer*, Mar. 4, 1817). See also Elise K. Kirk, "Celebrating the Presidency: The Inaugural Concert in the Nineteenth Century," in *Performing Arts Annual* (Washington, D.C.: Library of Congress, 1986).

2. Singleton, *Story of the White House*, 1:198-99.

3. July 4, 1829, in "Marine Band Chronology," MBL.

4. Account #61.369, Record Group 217, MTA, NARS. See also "Furniture of the President's House," House of Representatives, *Congressional Report*, 27th Cong. 2d sess., Apr. 1, 1842. In this report is also listed: "1 music stool for circular room, first story."

5. *National Intelligencer*, Jan. 24, 1831; T & H to Jackson, June 23, 1831, reel 39, Andrew Jackson Papers, LC.

6. Account #61.369, Record Group 217, MTA, NARS. Sorting out the pianos from government vouchers and records of this period is a complicated and often frustrating process. A "small pianof." was tuned for $1 on this same date, and on Dec. 12, 1829, "6 new mahogany feet, one pedal and other repairs and tuning" were provided by Jacob Hilbus for $18 (perhaps for Louisa Adams's Babcock if it had been a government purchase?). President Jackson also had a "grand piano" ("grand" in this case meaning "elegant") delivered on Sept. 9, 1833, and on Oct. 5, he sent it back to Professor Wagler. There is no

indication as to whether this was rented, or bought and returned (voucher 17, #70.467, Record Group 217).

7. Marquis James, *The Life of Andrew Jackson* (New York: Bobbs-Merrill, 1938), 2:595.

8. Lillian Moore, *Images of the Dance: Historical Treasures of the Dance Collection, 1581-1861* (New York: New York Public Library, 1965), 51.

9. Ivor Forbes Guest, *Fanny Elssler* (London: Adam & Black, 1970), 136-38.

10. "Hail to Old Tippecanoe," from *The Tippecanoe Song Book* (1840), in Lawrence, *Music for Patriots*, 276.

11. "Speech of Mr. Ogle of Pennsylvania on The Regal Splendor of the President's Palace," delivered in the House of Representatives, Apr. 14, 1840, 12, 13, Rare Book Collection, LC. On May 31, 1839, the White House paid $1 "for varnishing one piano" ("Furniture," House Report 27/2, Apr. 1, 1842).

12. Benjamin Perley Poore, *Perley's Reminiscences of Sixty Years in the National Metropolis* (Philadelphia: Hubbard Bros., 1886), 1:229.

13. Arrangements of "Hail to the Chief" and "Wha'll be King but Charlie" appear with "The Blue Bells of Montrose" in a small book of piano pieces in the Scala Collection, LC. Francis Scala joined the Marine Band in 1842, but some of the pieces from the earlier years of the band may have made their way into his collection. See David M. Ingals, "Francis Scala: Leader of the Marine Band from 1855 to 1871" (Ph.D. diss., Catholic University of America, 1957).

14. Poore quoted in Lawrence, *Music for Patriots*, 297. Pneumonia was the cause of the president's death, but reports indicate that "they bled, cupped and blistered him, gave him calomel and castor oil and rhubarb" until he was totally worn out from the primitive medical treatment. James Greer, *William Henry Harrison, His Life and Times* (Richmond, Va.: Garrett and Massie, 1941), 400.

15. *New York Herald*, Apr. 9, 1841.

16. Camus, *Military Music*, 116-17. Other presidents who died of illness while in office were Taylor, Harding, and Franklin Roosevelt. Lincoln, Garfield, McKinley, and Kennedy were assassinated.

17. Robert Seager II, *And Tyler Too* (New York: McGraw-Hill, 1963), 13, 558n26. Some sources have erroneously attributed both verse and music to Tyler.

18. "When Tyler Ruled: Recollections of White House Life in the Forties— Told by His Daughter," *Washington Evening Star*, June 10, 1893. Letitia Tyler Semple served briefly as first lady before the president remarried.

19. Seager, *And Tyler, Too*, 350-351.

20. Jessie Benton Frémont, *Souvenirs of My Time* (Boston: D. Lothrop, 1887), 70.

21. Mary Ormsbee Whitton, *First First Ladies* (New York: Hastings House, 1948), 193; Laura C. Holloway, *The Ladies of the White House* (Philadelphia: Brailey & Co., 1881), 395; "Recollections of Scala," *Morning Times*, Jan. 19, 1896, Scala Collection, LC.

22. Scala claims he was appointed leader in 1842, but he probably was recalling his appointment as fife major in 1843 (Ingalls, "Scala," 11). The Ingalls thesis contains an alphabetical catalogue of Scala's works, as well as parts lists.

23. "Recollections."

24. Hopkins to CMC, May 27, 1840, in "Marine Band Chronology," MBL. The total cost of the eighteen instruments listed is $352.

25. Order from Raphael R. Triay, leader of the band, June 13, 1849, in

"Marine Band Chronology," MBL. This order also lists "Music paper—$15.00."

26. Ingalls, "Scala," 132.

27. Voucher 1, account #87.086, Record Group 217, MTA, NARS. The term "concert piano" probably implied a large square at this time. The term "double grand action" undoubtedly means double escapement. "Metallic plate" denotes a metal hitchpin plate. "Tablet front" probably refers to the case style, one in which the keyboard was flanked by rectangular recessed vertical panels (tablets) that were placed slightly forward of the fronts of the keys.

28. John Tasker Howard, *Our American Music* (New York: Crowell, 1946), 230.

29. Ibid., 231-32.

30. Hamm, *Yesterdays*, 156.

31. Carol Ryrie Brink, *Harps in the Wind: The Story of the Singing Hutchinsons* (New York: Macmillan, 1947), 82.

32. "The Old Granite State," words by John Hutchinson in "Music by Hutchinson Family," published by Firth, Hall and Co., 1843.

33. Milo Milton Quaife, ed., *The Diary of James K. Polk during His Presidency, 1845 to 1849* (Chicago: McClurg, 1910), 1:276-78.

34. Charles E. Claghorn, *Biographical Dictionary of American Music* (New York: Parker, 1973), 122.

35. George Clinton Odell, *Annals of the New York Stage* (New York: Columbia University Press, 1927), vols. 4-7.

36. Mrs. Polk's Astor and Harewood square pianoforte (9 Cornhill Rd., London) and her music book are the property of the James K. Polk Home, Columbia, Tenn.

37. Scala, "Recollections."

38. Quaife, ed., *Diary of Polk*, 366-67.

39. Scala, "Recollections."

40. Holman Hamilton, *Zachary Taylor: Soldier in the White House* (Hamden, Conn: Archon Books, 1966), 223.

41. John C. Baker's "The Parting Requiem" and "Where Can the Soul Find Rest" were published separately as "Songs and Glees of the Bakers" (Boston: Keith's Music Publishing House, 1847) and are now in the Library of Congress.

42. Quoted in Samuel Eliot Morison, *The Oxford History of the American People* (New York: Oxford University Press, 1965), 516.

Chapter 4. A House Divided

1. Morison, *Oxford History of the American People*, 574.

2. Sept. 9, 1850, in Allan Nevins and Milton Halsey Thomas, eds., *The Diary of George Templeton Strong* (New York: Octagon Books, 1974), 2:18.

3. Jenny Lind, concert program, Dec. 18, 1850, given at National Hall, Washington, D.C.; a copy of the program is in the Library of Congress.

4. Charles G. Rosenberg, *Jenny Lind in America* (New York: Stringer and Townsend, 1851), 88.

5. Unidentified contemporaneous source quoted in Singleton, *Story of the White House*, 2:14-15.

6. Margaret Brown Klapthor, *The First Ladies* (Washington, D.C.: White House Historical Association, 1975), 35.

7. Holloway, *Ladies of the White House*, 469.

8. Christine Saddler, *Children of the White House* (New York: Putnam, 1969), 135.

9. Volumes 112-15, 118, M1.A15, LC.

10. Voucher 8, account #107.778, Record Group 217, MTA, NARS.

11. Spillane, *History of the American Pianoforte*, 107, 141, 155.

12. Voucher 27, account #109.073, Record Group 217, MTA, NARS.

13. Unidentified newspaper clipping, Scala Collection, LC.

14. *Washington Weekly Star*, May 3, 1856.

15. Virginia Clay Clopton, *A Belle of the Fifties: Memoirs of Mrs. Clay of Alabama Covering Social and Political Life in Washington and the South, 1853-1866* (New York: Doubleday, Page and Co., 1904), 29.

16. "Music for Presidents," anonymous, undated news clipping from the period, Scala Collection, LC.

17. Singleton, *Story of the White House*, 2:52. The Scala Collection contains a copy of "Pick Pocket Quickstep," composer unknown, arranged for band, probably by Scala.

18. Singleton, *Story of the White House*, 2:53-54.

19. "The Blind Boy Pianist," *Dwight's Journal of Music*, Sept. 17, 22, 1860; *The Albany Argus*, Jan. 1866, in "Thomas Greene Bethune (1849-1908)," *Black Perspective in Music* 3(1975).

20. Eileen Southern, *Music of Black Americans* (New York: W. W. Norton, 1971), 252; Richard Badolph, *The New Vanguard* (New York: Vintage Books, 1959), 121.

21. Geneva Southall, "Blind Tom: A Misrepresented and Neglected Composer-Pianist," *Black Perspective in Music* 3(1975). Southall discusses Blind Tom's compositions and musical style (partly deriving from Chopin and Field) and includes musical examples.

22. Ibid. Today Tom would probably be analyzed as an idiot savant, a mentally defective person with rare gifts in a special field.

23. Blake to Chickering, June 22, 1857, Chickering to Blake, June 27, 1857, Blake to Chickering, July 3, 1857, Letters Sent/Received, Record Group 42, OPB&G, NARS. A Chickering grand piano stands today at Buchanan's Wheatland home in Lancaster, Pa.; however, it is believed to have been purchased by Buchanan in 1865 after he left office.

24. *Washington Weekly Star*, Apr. 30, 1859.

25. Harry Eskew, "William B. Bradbury," *New Grove*, 6th ed., 3:150; H. Wiley Hitchcock, *Music in the United States* (Englewood Cliffs, N.J.: Prentice-Hall, 1974), 104.

26. Alistair Cooke, *Alistair Cooke's America* (New York: Knopf, 1977), 200.

27. From Lincoln's campaign speech, June 16, 1858, quoted in Morison, *Oxford History of the American People*, 595.

28. James P. Shenton, preface to William Barney, *Flawed Victory: A New Perspective on the Civil War* (New York: Praeger, 1975), vii. Shenton observed that Americans had inflicted upon one another more casualties than had ever been sustained in a previous, or subsequent, foreign war.

29. Kenneth A. Bernard, *Lincoln and the Music of the Civil War* (Caldwell, Idaho: Caxton Printers, 1966), 312-13.

30. John Lair, *Songs Lincoln Loved* (New York: Duell, Sloan and Pearce, 1954), ix. See also Philip D. Jordan, "Some Lincoln and Civil War Songs," *Abraham Lincoln Quarterly*, Sept. 1942.

31. Noah Brooks, "Personal Recollections of Abraham Lincoln," *The Independent* 31 (July 1865): 222-30.

32. Kenneth A. Bernard, *Abraham Lincoln: The Song in His Heart* (Worcester, Mass.: Achille J. St. Onge, 1970), 49-51. In the Scala Collection are copies for band of "Annie Laurie, as sung in the opera *La dame blanche*. Arr. by P. K. Moran"; "Kathleen Mavourneen" by Frederick Crouch; and

"Mary of Argyle," composer unknown. The last two are arranged by Scala as quicksteps. Other songs especially enjoyed by Lincoln were "The Doxology," Newman's "Lead, Kindly Light," Foster's "Gentle Annie," Dempster's "The Lament of the Irish Immigrant," Hewitt's "Rock Me to Sleep, Mother," Willing's "Twenty Years Ago," Bishop's "Home, Sweet Home," and Hopkins's "Silver Bell Waltz." See Lair, *Songs Lincoln Loved*, and Bernard, *Abraham Lincoln*.

33. Carl Sandburg, *Abrahan Lincoln: The War Years* (New York: Harcourt Brace & Co., 1939), 596-97.

34. Ibid., 597.

35. Lincoln was known to have heard *Faust* three times while he was president. He appeared at the opera twice during the one-week opera season in Washington in April 1863, and in the hectic month of March 1865 he heard three operas the last two days before his departure for City Point (Bernard, *Abraham Lincoln*, 36-39).

36. The cast for that performance comprised largely foreign singers who did not know the words of "The Star-Spangled Banner," which was sung as Lincoln entered the theater. Two young American divas in the cast, however, came to the rescue: Isabelle Hinckley and Adelaide Philips (*New York Herald*, Feb. 21, 1861).

37. Ibid., Apr. 23, 1863.

38. Clara Louise Kellogg, *Memoirs of an American Prima Donna* (orig. publ. 1913; New York: Da Capo, 1978), 56-57.

39. Washington *Daily Morning Chronicle*, Mar. 24, 25, 1864; *National Intelligencer*, Mar. 24, 1864.

40. Irving Lowens, "Louis Moreau Gottschalk," *New Grove*, 6th ed., 7:570-74.

41. Louis Moreau Gottschalk, *Notes of a Pianist*, ed. Clara Gottschalk Peterson (Philadelphia: J. B. Lippincott, 1881), 148-49.

42. W. S. Wood, commissioner of Public Buildings and Grounds, to Henry W. Gray, Esq., June 21, 1861, Letters Sent, Record Group 42, OPB&G, NARS. Another letter (in the Chicago Historical Society) from Stanley McClure to Paul Angle, director, Oct. 1, 1948, indicates that the piano (#1900) was delivered to the White House sometime after June 21, 1861, by the firm of William H. Carryl and Bros., 719 Chestnut Street, Philadelphia. This piano stands in the Chicago Historical Society today.

43. *Philadelphia Press*, Sept. 27, 1865; *National Intelligencer*, Oct. 6, 1862.

44. Ruth Painter Randall, *Mary Lincoln: Biography of a Marriage* (Boston: Little, Brown, 1953), 213.

45. *Washington Sunday Morning Chronicle*, June 30, 1861.

46. Bernard, *Lincoln and the Music of the Civil War*, 36.

47. Mrs. Blanchard's handwritten reply is property Nicolay Papers, Library of Congress. The Lincolns also sent flowers to Viola Hutchinson after she sang in the White House (Brink, *Harps in the Wind*, 206). Lincoln was known to have received other opera singers at the White House: Lillie Hegermann-Lindencrone and Joseph Hermanns, whom Lincoln had recently enjoyed as Mephistopheles in *Faust*. In the Abraham Lincoln Papers, LC, is the earliest letter that we know of from a performing artist to a president: soprano Anna Bishop wrote on Feb. 15, 1861, inviting the president to her performance in the "English Opera" at Niblo's Garden in New York. But the president attended Verdi's *Masked Ball* at the Academy of Music instead.

48. Bernard, *Lincoln and the Music of the Civil War*, 16-17.

49. *National Republican*, Oct. 17, 1862; Bernard, *Lincoln and the Music of the Civil War*, 114-15; *History of Commodore Nutt, Now Exhibiting at*

Barnum's Museum, New York (pamphlet, 1862), Hoblitzelle Theater Arts Library, Austin, Tex.; C. Percy Powell, ed., *Lincoln Day by Day* (Washington: Lincoln Sesquicentennial Commission, 1960), 3:145. The Lincolns also entertained General and Mrs. Tom Thumb at the White House reception in Feb. 1863.

50. "Living Stage Folk Who Knew and Cheered Lincolns," *Montgomery Advertiser*, Feb. 12, 1911. See also M. Milinowski, *Teresa Carreño* (New Haven, Conn.: Yale University Press, 1940), 61-62. Carreño, described at the height of her illustrious career as "the Valkyrie of the piano," also became a fine singer, conductor, and composer. The article in the *Montgomery Advertiser* includes an interview with (supposedly) Adelina Patti, who tells of her performance in the White House for Lincoln. The date of Patti's appearance is not corroborated by her biography, however, which indicates she was in London and Paris during the fall of 1862. There is also nothing mentioned in the papers to substantiate that she was even singing in Washington at this time. There may have been some confusion with Carlotta Patti, also a fine singer, whose career paralleled her sister's. Carlotta was presenting a program in the capital during the period in question.

51. John Wallace Hutchinson, *The Story of the Hutchinsons* (Boston: Lee & Shepherd, 1896), 2:380. The Hutchinsons were in Washington singing for the Union soldiers. During one of their programs they caused a near riot by singing "Hymn of Liberty" with its powerful antislavery lyrics by John Greenleaf Whittier. General George B. McClellan promptly forbad their further appearances before the soldiers, but Lincoln declared he saw nothing wrong with the song and gave permission for the Hutchinsons to continue their programs (Lair, *Songs Lincoln Loved*, 60).

52. Bernard, *Lincoln and the Music of the Civil War*, 298-99. "The first favorite of all is 'Dixie's Land,' and its music has sounded almost day and night until it has taken on a weird, spell-like influence, and it seems a part and a voice of this horrible glamour that sweeps in upon the souls and hearts of men." William O. Stoddard, *Inside the White House in War Times* (New York: Webster, 1890), 17-18.

53. Lair, *Songs Lincoln Loved*, 15. "Your Mission" was composed by S. M. Grannis with words by Mrs. Ellen H. Gates.

54. Ona Griffin Jeffries, *In and Out of the White House* (New York: Wilfred Funk, 1960), 178.

55. Diary account of Secretary Welles, July 11, 1863, "Marine Band Chronology," MBL. The famous War of the Bouffons of 1752 divided the Parisian audiences into two camps: the one (consisting of Louis XV and the aristocracy) favored the serious national French opera, and the other (the queen and various connoisseurs) supported the newer, melodious Italian comic opera.

56. F. B. Carpenter, *The Inner Life of Abraham Lincoln: Six Months at the White House* (New York: Hurd and Houghton, 1867), 143.

57. *Washington Evening Star*, Apr. 20, 25, 1865; *Illinois State Journal*, May 3, 5, 1865.

Chapter 5. Music on the Lighter Side

1. Hamm, *Yesterdays*, 254. The Hutchinsons comprised a seven-member team at this time: "Mr. and Mrs. John W. Hutchinson, Henry Hutchinson, Mrs. Lillie Phillips, Ludlow Patton, Mrs. Abby Hutchinson Patton and C. M. Parks" (*National Republican*, Apr. 19, 1878). Hayes was the last of seven presidents that the famous family entertained during its long career.

2. Klapthor, *First Ladies*, 42.

3. Saddler, *Children of the White House*, 168.

4. The album is the property of the Andrew Johnson National Historic Site, Greeneville, Tennessee. It was common for family or friends to present a young lady pianist with her favorite pieces collected and bound into a book with her name on the cover. Belle's album was probably such a gift. Handwritten inside the cover is the inscription "From her old friend Wm. G. M."—possibly William G. Metzerott, Washington's noted music dealer, who sold Andrew Johnson the Steinway square pianos that the president gave each of his daughters.

5. "Inventory of the President's House," Feb. 28, 1867, Letters Sent/Received, Record Group 42, OPB&G, NARS.

6. B. B. French to Schomacker and Co., Piano Manufacturers, July 14, 1865, Letters Sent, Record Group 42, OPB&G, NARS.

7. The photographs are the property of the Division of Political History, NMAH, SI, and the Prints and Photo Division, LC.

8. Steinway #16,214, property of the Tennessee State Museum, Nashville; a bill of sale for #16,651 (patented in 1859) is at the Andrew Johnson National Historic Site. Each piano has a rosewood veneer case, a seven-octave compass, two pedals, and a one-piece cast iron frame.

9. Francis Scala, "Reminiscences of the Man Who Played at White House When Tyler Was President and for Many Years After," typescript, Scala Collection, LC. Reprinted in the *Washington Times*, Apr. 26, 1903. Eliza McCardle married Andrew Johnson when she was seventeen and taught him writing and arithmetic.

10. Thomas Hillgrove, "A Complete Guide to the Art of Dancing," 1863. Portions of the guide are reprinted in the program booklet for the 100th anniversary of the opening of the Renwick Gallery, Washington, D.C., Feb. 20, 1981, Division of Musical Instruments, NMAH, SI.

11. *Intelligencer* Job Printing House, 375 and 377 D Street, Washington, D.C., $2.00, by James English, voucher 18, account #157.952, Record Group 217, MTA, NARS. A copy is in the Division of Political History, NAMH, SI.

12. *Washington Evening Star*, Dec. 19, 1864.

13. See Odell, *Annals of the New York Stage*, vol. 8, for the Pauls' various engagements in New York City.

14. *Songs Introduced in the Comical and Musical Entertainments Written by Mr. Howard Paul and Which Has Reached in Great Britain Over Three Thousand Representations*, 39th ed. (New York: Published by the Proprietor at Irving Hall, n.d.), copy in the Ford Collection, New York Public Library.

15. *National Intelligencer*, Jan. 21, 1867.

16. Thomas P. Pendel, *Thirty-Six Years in the White House* (Washington: Neale Pub. Co., 1902), 136.

17. Quoted in William Best Hesseltine, *Ulysses S. Grant, Politician* (New York: Ungar, 1935), 295.

18. Ibid., 294.

19. Hutchinson, *Story of the Hutchinsons*, 2:34.

20. Singleton, *Story of the White House*, 2:130.

21. Hamm, *Yesterdays*, 195. See also 196-98 for an excellent discussion of Abt's musical style. President Grant had attended an earlier Peace Jubilee, Gilmore's first attempt at the colossal enterprise, in Boston on June 15-17, 1869. This was hailed as "The Grandest Musical Festival in the History of the World," and utilized a chorus of 10,000 voices and an orchestra of 1,000 instruments with Ole Bull as concertmaster. The sensation of the jubilee was a rendition of Verdi's "Anvil Chorus," which included 100 local firemen in red flannel uniforms pounding real anvils. Another monster concert that the Grants attended was held on May 10, 1876, in Philadelphia. Dom Pedro of Brazil was the honored guest.

22. *Philadelphia Press*, Apr. 29, 1869; Scrapbook, Ulysses S. Grant Col-

lection, Special Collections, George Washington University Library, Washington, D.C.

23. Frank B. Carpenter, *Carp's Washington*, ed. Frances Carpenter (New York: McGraw-Hill, 1960), 50.

24. Quoted in Bess Furman, *White House Profile: A Social History of the White House and Its Occupants* (New York: Bobbs Merrill, 1951), 328-29. Mary Arthur McElroy, youngest sister of Chester Arthur, served as White House hostess for the bachelor president.

25. *Washington Evening Star*, Jan. 20, 1871.

26. For more on the origins of "The Marines' Hymn," see "History of 'The Marines' Hymn,' " typescript, n.d., 3pp., MBL.

27. Ibid., iv. According to Jon Newsom, the word "Hippocorno" is Scala's unique corruption of the term Ebor Corno. This designation was probably established by Allen Dodworth, a New York bandmaster, who dubbed a brass-wind of the E-flat tenor horn family the "New York Horn" (in Latin, the "Novo Eboracii Corno"). "The American Brass Band Movement," *The Quarterly Journal of the Library of Congress* 36 (Spring 1979):119.

28. A list of the parts for Scala's arrangement, dated 1870, of "Coro e Cavatine" from Verdi's *Attila* reads as follows: "Eb flute and piccolo 2div; Eb clarinetto 2 copies; 1 clarinetto; 1 clarinetto ripieno 2div; 2 clarinetto 2div; 3 clarinetto 2div; 1&2 Eb cornetta 2div; 1&2 Bb cornetta 2div; 3&4 Bb cornetta 2div; Eb altos 2div; Eb French horns 2div; Bb tromboni 3div; Bb baritone; Eb tuba; Bass and small drums." Parts list, Scala Collection, LC. See also Ingalls, "Scala," 118.

29. "Entertainment at the White House," *Report of the Board of Indian Commissioners*, Washington, June 9, 1870, a two-page clipping in the file "Washington, D.C.—Social," MLKL.

30. Major Augustus A. Nicholson to Vice-Admiral David P. Porter, Jan. 13, 1870, entry 14, vol. of 1870, Record Group 80, GRDN, NARS. Microfilm copies of documents cited from Record Group 80 are in MCHC. The leader of the Marine Band earned $79 per month, the salary of the leader of the West Point Band.

31. Col. Comdt. McCawley to Secretary of the Navy Thompson, June 25, 1877, entry 14, vol. of Jan.-June 1877, Record Group 80, GRDN, NARS.

32. Ibid. Several letters of this nature requesting discharge were attached to Comdt. McCawley's memo. Members of the band often played outside the military to make extra money, such as for picnics, serenades, swim meets, bicycle races, opera, variety shows, and new store openings.

33. "The Famous Marine Band: A talk with Walter Smith, the well-known cornetist," *Daily Telegraph*, Kalamazoo, Mich., Nov. 10, 1886.

34. McCawley to Thompson, Sept. 11, 1879; bill of lading Goumas & Cie to Louis Schneider, Oct. 9, 1876, both in Record Group 80, GRDN, NARS.

35. John Lapini to Maj. Nicholson, Adjt. and Inspt., USMC, June 24, 1874, B. Constantiney to Adjt. and Inspt. Nicholson, Aug. 17, 1875, both in Record Group 80, GRDN, NARS.

36. Section 12 of Whitthorne's bill printed in the *Army and Navy Journal*, June 1876, in "Marine Band Chronology," MBL.

Chapter 6. Prima Donnas for the President

1. Lillian Hegermann-Lindencrone, *The Sunny Side of Diplomatic Life* (New York: Harper & Bros., 1914), 112.

2. Rutherford B. Hayes to Fanny Hayes, Jan. 24, 1886, RHPC. The earliest of our first ladies to have been a college graduate, Lucy Hayes attended Wesleyan Female College in Cincinnati.

3. Charles Richard Williams, *Diary and Letters of Rutherford Birchard Hayes* (Boston: Houghton Mifflin, 1914), 2:311. Sung one evening in 1878 were "Jesus, Lover of My Soul," "Nearer My God to Thee," and "Tell Me That Old, Old Story." The Hayes Center holds the hymnal *Songs for the Sanctuary* (New York: Barnes, 1872); on the cover stamped in gold letters is "Mrs. Hayes—Executive Mansion."

4. Hayes Scrapbook, 3:2, RHPC.

5. Operti was musical director of the Tammany Society Theater in New York in 1869, directing shows that featured "Mlle. Gertrude and her elfin troupe of learned quadrupeds," and a "spectacular burlesqular extravaganzacular odd-ditty" (Odell, *Annals of the New York Stage*, 8:508). In 1884 (Arthur's administration) he composed the music for *On the Yellowstone—Realistic Scenes of the President's Trip to the National Park*, which the *New York Herald* called a "novel Western patois" (ibid. 12:305).

6. *National Republican*, May 2, 1877.

7. Sadie E. Martin, *The Life and Professional Career of Emma Abbott* (Minneapolis: L. Kimball, 1891), 142-43, 98-99.

8. *National Republican*, Nov. 11, 1884.

9. *Cincinnati Gazette*, Feb. 22, 1879.

10. *National Republican*, Nov. 14, 1878.

11. Harold Rosenthal, ed., *The Mapleson Memoirs: The Career of an Operatic Impresario, 1858-1888* (New York: Appleton-Century, 1966), 218. The original edition was published in two volumes by Remington and Co. in 1888. For more on Marie Selika, see *The Colored American Magazine*, Nov. 1901, 51-52. Two days before her White House appearance the black diva sang in Washington at the First Congregational Church, "supported by Mr. Williams and members of the Washington Harmonica Society" (*Washington Post*, Nov. 11 1878).

12. *Washington Post*, Feb. 27, 1880.

13. Widdows to Rogers, Aug. 4, 1877, RHPC. This should not be confused with the well-known "Rock of Ages" by Thomas Hastings.

14. Hutchinson, *Story of the Hutchinsons*, 1:458-59.

15. *National Republican*, Feb. 19, 1879.

16. *Aptommas' History of the Harp*, "in which is given a comprehensive view of its origin and progress from the Creation to the present time and embracing accounts of its employment respectively by the Antedeluvians, Egyptians, Hebrews, Grecians, Romans, Cimbirans, Celts, French, etc. . . . published by the author" (New York, 1859).

17. The *Album* is property of Library of Congress and was presented to the Music Division by E. H. Droop on Nov. 28, 1931. A notation inside the cover indicates that it was given to Droop "by his friend Leo Wheat on April 12, 1899." E. F. Droop was the Steinway dealer in Washington after the firm of W. G. Metzerott was dissolved in 1884. His son headed a special music committee at the time of McKinley's first inauguration, which featured his composition "Pride of the Nations," conducted by Victor Herbert. Aptommas was the first in a long line of distinguished harpists, including Carlos Salzedo, Melville Clark, Ada Sassoli, and Mildred Dilling, to play in the White House.

18. Widdows to Mrs. Hayes, Feb. 12, 1879, RHPC.

19. Dated July 18, 1879, and quoted in *Hayes Historical Journal* 2, nos. 3-4 (1979).

20. E. Heron-Allen, "Ede Remenyi," *New Grove*, 6th ed., 15:734-35. See also Henry C. Lahee, *Famous Violinists of Today and Yesterday* (Boston: L. C. Page, 1899), 205-15.

21. Lahee, *Famous Violinists*, 1901 ed., 209. Other comments about Remenyi's playing appeared in the *Washington Post* (Mar. 8, 1893), when he

performed at Metzerott Hall during Cleveland's second inauguration—a sample: "He draws upon the instrument sounds the human ear never hears ... he has no rival, one of the meteors that flash at intervals across the sky."

22. *National Republican*, Feb. 10, 1880; "Grand Musical Entertainment: The McGibney Family," [1881-82], Emil Seifert, musical director, formerly concert master of Berlin. The leaflet is the property of the Hoblitzelle Theater Arts Library.

23. Telegram from George A. Gustin to Honorable Carl Schurz, Mar. 1880, RHPC.

24. "Miss Grundy's Letters," Mar. 28, 1878, clipping in Hayes Scrapbooks, Vol. 112, RHPC. Miss Grundy (Austine Snead) was a New York correspondent.

25. Casey to Wm. Knabe & Co., June 25, 1878, Knabe to Casey, June ?, 1878, Letters Sent/Received, Record Group 42, OPB&G, NARS.

26. Casey to Knabe, Mar. 15, 1879, ibid.

27. Knabe to Rockwell, Dec. 11, 1882, ibid. "List of furniture from data furnished by T. J. Pendle, Usher, April 15, 1898." Letters Received, Nov. 21, 1929, ibid. Listed as "Green Room Knabe bought during Arthur." The discarded White House furnishings were usually sold at auction, and the funds received were used to purchase new furniture. Arthur's famous auction of 1882 included twenty-four wagon loads of goods.

28. William Bradbury, who had directed his choir in works by Handel and Rossini for President Buchanan, founded his New York piano company in 1854. Freeborn G. Smith served as Bradbury's superintendent before he purchased the company, continuing the name of Bradbury. In 1917 the Bradbury Piano Company was absorbed by the William Knabe firm.

29. Smith to Babcock, Sept. 30, 1871, Letters Sent, Record Group 42, OPB&G, NARS.

30. Smith to Casey, Mar. 22, 1877, ibid.

31. "Miss Grundy's Letters," Mar. 28, 1878, RHPC. The Bradbury eagle inlay does not show in the sketch made of Carl Schurz playing for the Hayes in the oval library, but artists in those days took many liberties. (Notice Frances Cleveland's wedding gown, which appears different in three newspapers.)

32. The eagle Bradbury stands in the Hayes Presidential Center as a donation from the Girls' Club of Ohio.

33. Casey to Rockwell, commissioner of Public Buildings and Grounds, June 16, 1881, Letters Sent, Record Group 42, OPB&G, NARS. Smith also tried to put a piano in the Soldiers Home where the Hayes spent their summers. The offer was turned down because the home already had a piano.

34. Sumner to Casey, Mar. 2, 1881, Casey to Sumner, Mar. 7, 1881, Sumner to Casey, Mar. 8, 1881, Letters Sent/Received, ibid.

35. "Articles in Serviceable Condition in the Executive Mansion, May 13, 1882." Ledger in files: "Grand piano (ebony) Bradbury, with stool, Red Room." Ibid.

36. *New York Times*, Aug. 23, 1976. Sousa also compiled, at the direction of Secretary of the Navy Tracy, a book of "representative melodies" of the world's cultures, which included "airs" of Abyssinia, Boa Vista, Celebes, Dalecarlia, East Indies, Fiji Isles, Lapland, Moldavia, Nukahivah, Pfalz, and Samoa. See Sousa, *National and Patriotic Airs of All Lands, with copious notes* (Philadelphia: Coleman, 1890). The book is the property of the Benjamin Harrison Home, Indianapolis. Several of Sousa's marches were arranged for dancing; "The Washington Post" was commonly known as the "Two-step" in Europe.

37. John Philip Sousa, *Marching Along: Recollections of Men, Women, and Music* (Boston: Hale, Cushman and Flint, 1928), 70-71.

38. Ibid.

39. *Catalogue of Music, Band, U.S. Marine Corps* (Washington: Government Printing Office, 1885), 18. The number of selections in the other categories, presumably for band, were: overtures, 151; waltzes, 76; songs, duets, trios, and quartets, 68; polkas and galops, 50; gavottes, 9; patrols and dances, 28; miscellaneous (solos, quadrilles, etc.), 21. The *Catalogue* is the property of the Marine Band Library.

40. Emma Foote to Florence Carlisle, Apr. 21, 1877, RHPC. A Navy Department memo of Feb. 25, 1878, indicates that the president was to have "a state dinner at which the Band will be present as an orchestra." It was signed "P. W. Thompson, Sect. of the Navy" (Record Group 80, NARS).

41. "The Famous Marine Band, a Talk with Walter Smith," *Daily Telegraph.*

42. *Star,* Jan. 1, 1884. *Ruy Blas,* MBL. The parts vary in date. Some are arranged for band in manuscript and others printed bearing "arranged by Chas. Godfrey/B.M. Royal Horse Guards" (London: Lafleur and Son, n.d.).

43. Sousa to Col. Comdt. McCawley, Nov. 11, 1882. Sousa's three-page letter was enclosed in a memo McCawley sent to Secretary of the Navy William E. Chandler on Nov. 14, 1882. Entry #14, vol. of 1882, Record Group 80, GRDN, NARS. First-class musicians received $45 per month, second-class, $28.

44. Saddler, *Children of the White House,* 191-92.

45. William H. Crook, *Memories of the White House,* comp. and ed. Henry Rood (Boston: Little, Brown, 1911), 163.

46. Receipts for $25 dues paid to the Mendelssohn Glee Club by Mrs. Chester Arthur on Oct. 6, 1874, Oct. 8, 1875, and Nov. 14, 1876. The society, founded in 1865, gave three concerts a season at Chickering Hall in New York City. Reel 1, Chester A. Arthur Papers, Manuscript Division, LC.

47. "Account Book," William (H. H.) Steward for President Arthur, the Executive Mansion (White House) Washington [n.d but probably 1883], reel 1, Arthur Papers, LC.

48. *Washington Evening Star,* Feb. 24, 1883. Patti called on the president at the White House on Feb. 21, however, and was escorted through the mansion (*National Republican,* Feb. 22, 1883).

49. Rosenthal, ed., *Mapleson Memoirs,* 168.

50. Albani's fine recording of this piece is a collector's item. The soprano died in 1930 at the age of eighty-three. See Emma Albani, *Forty Years of Song, with a discography by W. R. Moran,* ed. Andrew Farkas (New York: Arno Press, 1977).

51. *Washington Post,* Mar. 30, 1883. For more on Nilsson at the White House, see Edna Coleman, *White House Gossip from Andrew Johnson to Calvin Coolidge* (Garden City, N.Y.: Doubleday, Page, 1927), 159, and undated newspaper clipping in White House Social File, MLKL. Another famous singer, Minnie Hauk, saw Arthur at the White House on Oct. 11, 1883, and expressed her hopes that a National Opera Company could be formed similar to those in Europe. "Your idea has my full approbation," said the president, "but you see we are still too young a nation for such an enterprise." Minnie Hauk, *Memories of a Singer* (London: N.p., 1925), 193.

52. James Trotter, *Music and Some Highly Musical People . . . Remarkable Musicians of the Colored Race* (Boston: Lee and Shepherd, 1878), 257-59.

53. *Washington Post,* Feb. 17, 1882.

54. Ibid., Feb. 18, 1882.

55. Sousa, *Marching Along,* 80.

56. Ibid., 85.

57. *Washington Weekly Star,* Apr. 14, 1882.

58. Ibid.

59. *Yale Daily News* 12, no. 134 (Apr. 25, 1889). A complete program is in the Yale University Library, New Haven, Conn., dated Tuesday evening, June 25, 1889.

60. *Washington Weekly Star*, June 4, 1886.

Chapter 7. Familiar Tunes with a New Message

1. William H. Crook, *Memories of the White House* (Boston: Little, Brown, 1911), 177.

2. Carpenter, *Carp's Washington*, 256; *Washington Post*, Mar. 8, 1885.

3. Sousa's catalogue lists eight Gilbert and Sullivan operettas. Other presidents also enjoyed "G and S." Among the family items of James Garfield is a fine leather-bound piano/vocal copy of *Patience* dated 1881, the year of the premiere performance in London. The name "Garfield" is imprinted in gold on the cover. (Published by J. M. Stoddard and Co. [Philadelphia].) It is now the property of the President James A. Garfield Home, Lake County Historical Society, Mentor, Ohio. President Arthur attended a gala performance of *Patience* at the Academy of Music in Baltimore, a benefit for the Home of the Friendless.

4. *Washington Weekly Star*, June 11, 1886. See also Wilbur Cross and Ann Novotny, *White House Weddings* (New York: David McKay, 1967), 120-27.

5. *Washington Weekly Star*, Mar. 26, 1886.

6. May 14, 1886, Letters Received (#368), Record Group 42, OPB&G, NARS. By 1884 the quartet had sung over thirty concerts in Washington and toured several cities receiving excellent reviews.

7. *New York Times*, Sept. 18, 1890.

8. Theodore E. Steinway, *People and Pianos: A Century of Service to Music* (New York: Steinway and Sons, 1961), 39; John Steinway in an interview with Elise Kirk, Steinway Place, New York City, Mar. 14, 1979. The letter from Grover Cleveland to William Steinway expressing appreciation for the wedding gift is at Steinway Hall, New York City. According to Steinway records, the piano came back to the plant as a trade-in as recently as 1951 and was sold to Brodwin Piano Company, now no longer in business. Chester and Ellen Arthur also owned a Steinway piano. Accounts show that it had been tuned on Mar. 15 and Oct. 25, 1880, before Arthur became president and shortly after Ellen died. Receipt, Schlegel, Steinway and Sons, Dec. 31, 1880, reel 1, Arthur Papers, LC.

9. Five years after Grover Cleveland died in 1908, Mrs. Cleveland married Thomas J. Preston, Jr., a professor of archeology. She lived to be eighty-four years old.

10. Frances Cleveland to Leo Wheat, Apr. 1894, in Wheat, *Album*, LC.

11. *Washington Star*, Oct. 5, 1897.

12. *Chicago Daily News*, Sept. 27, 1892, Sousa Papers, MCHC.

13. *Cleveland Daily Telegraph*, Nov. 10, 1886.

14. Damrosch to F. Cleveland, Feb. 25, Mar. ?, 1909; Classen (conductor of the Liederkranz) to F. Cleveland, Mar. 3, 1909, reel 144, Grover Cleveland Papers, LC. Printed concert program, in the Riggs Family Papers, LC.

15. The piano is the property of Benjamin Harrison Memorial Home. See also *Frank Leslie's Illustrated Newspaper*, May 3, 1890, for Russell's letter to the Fisher Company praising the piano.

16. Loesser, *Men, Women and Pianos*, 500. In addition to Gottschalk's "Last Hope," the Harrison Home possesses a two-volume collection of piano

pieces with "Carrie L. Scott" on the covers. These pieces date from the 1840s and 1850s, when Caroline Scott was studying and teaching music. Representative works include: "The Lament of the Irish Immigrant" (Dempster), "Susanna, from Songs of the Sable Harmonists" (Foster), "Empress Henrietta's Waltz" (Herz), "Chasse d'Amour" (Grobe), and various works of Hewitt, Strakosch, Willis, Henry Russell, and others.

17. *Washington Post*, Apr. 24, 1890. Printed dance program for the White House Ball, Apr. 23, 1890, property of the Benjamin Harrison Home.

18. Randolph de Bonneville Keim, *Society in Washington* (Washington, D.C.: Harrisburg Publishing Co., 1887), 227-28. Special Collections of the George Washington University Library.

19. Undated clipping from *The Inland*, Benjamin Harrison Home.

20. Programs in "White House Receptions"—scrapbook, 1889-91, Benjamin Harrison Papers, LC. The musicale did not follow a dinner party, but was the featured evening event with "light refreshments" served afterwards.

21. *Washington Evening Star*, Apr. 19, 1890.

22. *Washington Post*, Oct. 22, 1891; *New York Times*, Sept. 29, 1891.

23. The scrapbook is in the possession of the Moorland-Spingarn Research Center, Howard University, Washington, D.C. See also Willia E. Daughtry, "Sissieretta Jones: A Study of the Negro's Contributions to Nineteenth Century American Concert and Theatrical Life" (Ph.D. diss., Syracuse University, 1957).

24. *Washington Evening Star*, Feb. 5, 1890. The funeral of Caroline Harrison, who died at age sixty, was also held in the East Room (on Oct. 25, 1892). The service was shorter, but the choir of St. John's again sang "Lead, Kindly Light"—"Cardinal Newman's beautiful hymn, which Mrs. Harrison so much admired" (*Washington Post*, Oct. 28, 1892). St. John's Church on Lafayette Square was named "the Church of the Presidents," although neither Benjamin Harrison nor Grover Cleveland worshiped there regularly.

25. *Washington Evening Star*, June 27, 1891.

26. "Memorandum on Winter Receptions at the White House," Nov. 1897. T. A. Bingham Papers, LC.

27. *Washington Post*, Jan. 22, 1898, clipping in Bingham Papers, LC.

28. Typed memo, Jan. 26, 1898, ibid.

29. *Washington Post*, Feb. 3, 1898. The bands for President Dole's receptions played also at the McKinleys' first formal reception on Jan. 20, 1898.

30. "When the Band Plays: In the White House Grounds on Saturday Afternoons," *Washington Evening Star*, June 27, 1891, clipping in White House Social Files, Washingtoniana Collection, MLKL.

31. Ibid.

32. *Richmond Times*, Mar. ?, 1893; scrapbook of programs of U.S. Marine Band, July 30, 1898 to Aug. 27, 1910: programs (typescript) comprise mainly concerts at the White House, U.S. Capitol, and Marine Barracks. Scrapbook, scores, and manuscripts of many of the "descriptives" are the property of the Marine Band Library. A large Fanciulli collection is at the New York Public Library at Lincoln Center.

33. *Washington Post*, June 1, 1897; the article was reprinted in *Post*, May 24, 1981.

34. It is interesting that nowhere within the Commonwealth are drum ruffles and the two-note bugle call used in this manner today, though the tradition is still carried on in our country. Four ruffles and flourishes are rendered to many foreign and American dignitaries and officials. However, these honors are followed by "Hail to the Chief" only for the president of the United States. See "Ruffles and Flourishes," typescript, n.d., MBL; Camus,

Military Music, 114-15; and "Personnel General Salutes, Honors and Visits of Courtesy," Publication Department of the Army, Washington, D.C., Aug. 15, 1980.

35. Reports for dinners at the Executive Mansion, Tues., Nov. 29, 1898: to President Iglesias of Costa Rica; dinner to President Dole of Hawaii, Feb. 1, 1898; dinner to Admiral Dewey, Oct. 3, 1899, all in Bingham Papers, LC.

36. Autograph manuscript possession of Marine Band Library. The library also holds manuscripts, printed scores, and parts for Sousa, Santelmann, and other Marine Band leaders. Additional Sousa materials are at the Library of Congress and the University of Illinois at Urbana–Champaign.

37. Southern, *The Music of Black Americans,* 306. The details of Douglass's performances in the White House are not known.

38. *Washington Post,* Feb. 9, 1898. Ernest Lent was born in Germany in 1856. He toured Europe as a concert cellist before settling in Washington as a teacher in 1884, where he lived until his death in 1922. Arriving in America from Prague, Czechoslovakia, in 1892 as a young man, Joseph Cadek took residence in Chattanooga, Tenn. He died in 1927 after having founded the Chattanooga Conservatory of Music and playing a long and important role in the city's cultural development. See Donald Clyde Runyan, "The Influence of Joseph O. Cadek and His Family on the Musical Life of Chattanooga, Tennessee (1893-1973)" (Ph.D. diss., Vanderbilt University, 1980).

39. Program in Bingham Papers, LC.

40. Droop to Mrs. McKinley, Nov. 5, 1897, William McKinley Papers, LC. Droop delivered a piano stool specifically made by Henry Holtzman and Sons of Columbus, Ohio, to go with the piano. An A. B. Chase electric player piano was presented to President and Mrs. Warren Harding in 1921 and used in the West Sitting Room.

41. The Kimball Company originated in Chicago and concentrated on the production of medium-priced, quick-selling instruments. A Kimball salesman writing in 1880 said that the name of Kimball was as familiar in the western states as that of Grant. McKinley's Kimball developed a crack in the plate and was repaired on Jan. 3, 1901. Conway to McKinley, Feb. 27, 1897, Nov. 1, 1899, Jan. 3, 1901. McKinley Papers, LC. The piano is property of Elizabeth D. Martin of Bolivar, Ohio, a grandniece of Ida McKinley.

42. Davis to McKinley, Sept. 17, 1895, Letters Received, Record Group 42, OPB&G, NARS. A leaflet showing this instrument is enclosed with Davis's correspondence.

43. Droop to Cortelyou, Apr. 24, 1901, McKinley Papers, LC. This letter also contains a reference to the fact that McKinley may have turned down an offer to have a Steinway placed in the White House. McKinley's novel idea of riding in extravagant isolation throughout the country in a luxurious private railroad car was made the topic of political cartoons during the period. See *Washington Evening Star,* June 17, 1899.

44. Program, Feb. 14, 1901, McKinley Papers, LC. Kerry Mills, composer of the hit "Whistlin' Rufus" (1899), was a prolific black composer whose works show a combination of march, cakewalk, and ragtime styles. Another such composer was Abe Holzmann ("Bunch 'o' Blackberries," 1900). See William J. Schafer and Johannes Riedel, *The Art of Ragtime* (Baton Rouge: Louisiana State University Press, 1973), 30-31.

Chapter 8. The Musicale Tradition

1. "White House Social Aides," undated clipping in OWHSF, in Record Group 42, OPB&G, NARS. These records follow the Bingham Papers as a

comprehensive set of sources for White House entertaining from 1902 through 1915. In the twenty-one large, leather-bound scrapbooks are programs, guest lists, invitations, newspaper clippings, correspondence, photographs, and memoranda by the officers in charge. See also Lillian Lohmeyer Soules, "Music at the White House during the Administration of Theodore Roosevelt" (M.M.Ed. thesis, Catholic University of America, 1968).

2. David Phillips, "The Lord Great of the Republic," *Collier's Weekly* 31, no. 6 (1902).

3. Mabel P. Daggett, "Mrs. Roosevelt, the Woman in the Background," *The Delineator*, Mar. 1909, as quoted in Sylvia Jukes Morris, *Edith Kermit Roosevelt: Portrait of a First Lady* (New York: Coward, McCann and Geoghegan, 1980), 541. The president is reputed to have liked Caruso's singing and once commented, "There have been many presidents, but only one Caruso." It is uncertain whether the great tenor ever visited the White House, but he cherished the autographed photo given to him by Roosevelt after the president heard him sing *Tosca* at the National Theater.

4. The letter is dated Aug. 28, 1910. See the copy of John A. Lomax, *Cowboy Songs and Other Frontier Ballads* (New York: Sturgis and Walton, 1916), vii-viii, in the Library of Congress.

5. *The Letters of Archie Butt, Personal Aide to President Roosevelt*, ed. Lawrence F. Abbott (Garden City, N.Y.: Doubleday, 1925), 830. Butt mentions in a letter of July 27, 1908 (#XXIII), that the president "has a poor idea of music for while he sang all the choral parts of the service, he was usually an octave lower than the choir in the hymns, but he did fairly well in the difficult Gregorian chants" (ibid., 80).

6. Ibid., 33-34.

7. The precise details of protocol for the musicales are specified in the typed memoranda in Scrapbook, 1903, OWHSF, Record Group 42, OPB&G, NARS. Edith Roosevelt customarily stood at the entrance to the East Room greeting the guests, then took a large chair provided for her near the door. The president and a selected guest occupied reserved chairs in the front row and were the last to enter the room.

8. "Steinway in the White House," *National Magazine* 50 (May 1921):93.

9. Theodore Roosevelt Papers, LC. The piano is currently in the First Ladies Hall, NMAH, SI.

10. There were at least two other presidential Steinways before Woodrow Wilson left office. William Loeb received a letter on Jan. 6, 1909, from Henry Junge of Steinway stating that "we shall be delighted to rent Mrs. Roosevelt one of our new upright pianos for the price of $15 to $20 per month" (TR Papers). President Wilson had his nine-foot Steinway concert grand (Style D#68,035) shipped from Princeton to the White House in 1912 before his inauguration. We know from correspondence on July 12, 1921, that this piano had been removed from the White House for rebuilding, then returned to Mrs. Wilson after July 16 (Junge to Mrs. Wilson, July 12, 1921, Loeb to Junge, July 16, 1921, Woodrow Wilson Papers, LC). The piano stands in the Woodrow Wilson Home, Washington, D.C.

11. Steinway, *People and Pianos*, 63.

12. The Washington Steinway dealer Edward H. Droop also occasionally assisted with the musical arrangements during this period, which raises the possibility that he may have earlier, too. Accounts are conflicting as to just when Junge began his association with the White House. His obituary (*New York Times*, July 19, 1939) mentions his being in charge of the White House musicales "soon after their beginning under President Theodore Roosevelt." Correspondence in the TR Papers clearly shows only Tiffany's involvement

in the White House programs, but Junge might have served as an advisor or assistant.

13. Cecilia Beaux, *Background with Figures* (New York: Houghton Mifflin, 1930), 230-31, as quoted in Morris, *Edith Kermit Roosevelt*, 236.

14. I. J. Paderewski and Mary Lawton, *The Paderewski Memoirs* (London: Collins, 1939), 365. Paderewski's printed White House Program in Scrapbook, 1902, OWHSF, Record Group 42, OPB&G, NARS.

15. Harold Schonberg, *The Great Pianists* (New York: Simon and Schuster, 1963), 347.

16. Correspondence between Tiffany and Loeb, Dec. 9, 14, 1903, TR Papers, LC.

17. Loeb to Tiffany, Jan. 23, 1904, ibid.

18. The Liederkranz male chorus also sang for Prince Henry of Prussia at the Waldorf Astoria in New York during his U.S. visit, Feb. 22–Mar. 11, 1902. The Arion Society sang again for President Roosevelt on June 3, 1908, and later for Coolidge on May 18, 1928.

19. *Washington Post*, May 7, 1906.

20. Ibid.

21. Margaret Campbell, *Dolmetsch, the Man and His Work* (Seattle: University of Washington Press, 1975), 175.

22. Mabel Dolmetsch, *Personal Recollections of Arnold Dolmetsch* (London: Routledge and Paul, 1958), 170.

23. Pablo Casals, *Joys and Sorrows: Reflections*, as told to Albert E. Kahn (New York: Simon and Schuster, 1970), 109.

24. "White House Social Aides," Scrapbook, 1902, OWHSF, Record Group 42, OPB&G, NARS.

25. David Bispham, *A Quaker Singer's Recollections* (New York: Macmillan, 1920), 317. Printed program in Scrapbook, 1904, OWHSF, Record Group 42, OPB&G, NARS. Set to a text of Rudyard Kipling's, "Danny Deever" (1897) was composed by Walter Damrosch, conductor of the New York Philharmonic.

26. Nov. 19, 1903, TR Papers, LC.

27. Ole May, "How Alice Roosevelt Converted the Marine Band Leader to Ragtime," Nov. 27, 1915, newspaper source unknown, MCHC. The Marine Band archives hold handwritten parts for the "Maple Leaf Rag" that date from 1904. From their 5 × 7 size, they were probably intended for marching band lyres.

28. "White House Gayety," *Washington Post*, Dec. 20, 1903.

29. Only four performances were given, however, and the composer attributed this failure to the hostile anti-American Berlin group. E. E. Hipsher, *American Opera and Its Composers* (Philadelphia: Presser, 1927), 334-43.

30. Doron K. Antrim, "The Part Music Has Played in the Lives of Our Presidents," *Musical Observer* 33 (Oct. 1924).

31. Scrapbook, 1907, OWHSF, Record Group 42, OPB&G, NARS.

32. Memorandum: "The White House," Apr. 23, 1907, 9:30 P.M., WHSF.

33. *Washington Star*, Oct. 17, 1908; *Washington Post*, Oct. 17, 1908.

34. Memorandum: "Performance of the Ben Greet Woodland Players in the White House Grounds, October 16-17, 1908," Scrapbook, 1908, OWHSF, Record Group 42, OPB&G, NARS. Decorative printed program on p. 186.

35. *Washington Herald*, Oct. 17, 1908.

36. *Washington Times*, Oct. 17, 1908.

37. "Musicales at the White House," *Christian Herald*, Apr. 6, 1910. For more on the Baldwin piano, see letters from Lucien Wulsin, chairman of the Baldwin Company, to Mrs. Taft from Feb. 2 to Mar. 29, 1909, located at the Cincinnati Historical Society.

38. Olga Samaroff Stokowski, *An American Musician's Story* (New York: W. W. Norton, 1939), 74.

39. Schonberg, *Great Pianists*, 364. Hofmann became an American citizen in 1926. He performed twice for President Roosevelt in the White House: with Frieda Hempel on Dec. 14, 1933, and at the presentation of the new Steinway piano on Dec. 10, 1938. He died in Los Angeles in 1957 after an illustrious, legendary career.

40. Hofmann's program is in OWHSF, Record Group 42, OPB&G, NARS. Since the program does not specify an opus number for Scriabin's *Poème*, it is impossible to know whether it was Op. 41 (1903), or from Op. 32 (1903) or Op. 44 (1905)—the last two entitled "Two Poems." Perhaps the most interesting musically would have been Op. 44, composed when Scriabin was preoccupied with new ventures that led to the philosophical and mystical aspects of his mature style. His works after about 1908 are characterized by extreme chromaticism and harmonic complexities.

41. "Visit of His Highness, Prince Tsai Tao," Apr. 28, 1910, OWHSF, Record Group 42, OPB&G, NARS.

42. Charles Norton to Tiffany & Company, Apr. 4, 1911, William Howard Taft Papers, LC.

43. Memorandum, Mar. 25, 1911, OWHSF, Record Group 42, OPB&G, NARS.

44. Gwen Bagni and Paul Dubor, *Backstairs at the White House* (New York: Bantam, 1979), 105-6, based upon Lillian Rogers Parks's *My Thirty Years Backstairs at the White House*. Mrs. Parks and her mother, Maggie, served as maids from the Taft through Eisenhower administrations.

45. During this period White House dance programs showed an alternation between the waltz and the two-step, as the plan below typifies when an East Room dance of 1911 was accompanied by the U.S. Engineer Band:

Two-step	Red Wing	Mills
Waltz	Bright Eyes	Hoschana
Two-step	When Jackie Smiles	Caroll
Waltz	Under Love's Window	Linke
Two-step	The Gay Musician	Edwards
Waltz	The Blue Danube	Strauss

OWHSF, Record Group 42, OPB&G, NARS. See also "Mr. Taft Picks a Waltz Partner," Jan. 24, 1910, in *Letters of Archie Butt*, 263-64.

46. "Musicales at the White House," *Washington Star*, n.d., District of Columbia Historical Society.

47. Bagni and Dubor, *Backstairs*, 90.

48. Bispham, *Quaker Singer*, 318; Paderewski and Lawton, *Paderewski Memoirs*, 365. Paderewski played for Wilson in the White House on Feb. 22, 1916, and on May 16, 1919. A patriot and statesman, Paderewski pleaded the cause for Poland; Chief Usher Irwin Hoover thought "he came to the conference just as he does to his concerts . . . he rumples his hair, bows and scrapes, even sits as if he were at the piano, out on the edge of his chair" (Irwin H. Hoover, *Forty-Two Years in the White House* [New York: Houghton Mifflin, 1934], 84.)

49. Doron K. Antrim, "Our Musical Presidents," *Etude*, May 1940. Wilson's violin, as well as his mother's guitar, are in the Woodrow Wilson Birthplace, Staunton, Va. The guitar is a six-stringed instrument, beautifully inlaid and possessing a soft, mellow tone. It was made in France about 1850.

50. Edith Bolling Wilson, "As I Saw It," *Saturday Evening Post* 211 (Jan. 14, 1939): 52; Vincent P. Carosso, "Music and Musicians in the White House," *New York Historical Society Quarterly* 48 (Apr. 1964): 120-21.

51. The first in a series of four musicales to be held during the Wilson terms featured Morgan Kingston, tenor, Beatrice Harrison, cellist, and Ida Sassoli, harpist on Dec. 5, 1913. Memorandum, OWHSF, Record Group 42, OPB&G, NARS.

52. Memorandum and printed program, ibid.

53. Grainger also played for Franklin Roosevelt at the White House on Jan. 6, 1938.

54. Melville Clark, "I Played the Harp for Wilson," *Christian Science Monitor*, May 19, 1945.

55. Edith Wilson, *My Memoir* (Indianapolis: Bobbs-Merrill, 1939), 121.

56. Ibid., 145. The president's Victrola from the White House is believed to be the one in the Wilson Home in Washington, D.C. (Victor Talking Machine Company, Camden, N.J.). A set of eleven volumes of recordings accompanying the machine includes Mme. Schumann-Heink's famous disc, "Stille Nacht," and recordings of Caruso, Zimbalist, Sembrich, Melba, and McCormack. There are several selections by the Victor Dance Orchestra— "Pink Lady Waltzes" and others.

Chapter 9. White House Jesters

1. Clipping file, James M. Goode, "Lost Washington" Collection, Smithsonian Institution. See also Goode, *Capital Losses* (Washington, D.C.: Smithsonian Institution Press, 1979), 376-78.

2. By 1919 the popularity of movies was leaving every other form of entertainment far behind. To console himself in his illness, President Wilson had movies screened for him in the White House two and three times a week. He dubbed his projectionist "my movie doctor."

3. For the first time in history a president publicly eulogized the music industry. President Harding's message to the Convention of Music Trades, Mar. 23, 1921, asserted: "Probably no single force has done more to popularize music, not only in this country but throughout the world, than the enterprise and real artistic genius of the men who have built the great American industry in musical instruments." Warren Harding Papers, LC.

4. The first program featured the returns of the Harding-Cox election. President Coolidge reputedly brought the first radio to the White House (and Harry Truman the first television set). Secretary Hoover's study in the *New York Times*, May 18, 1924, indicates that there were more than 3 million receiving sets in existence in the nation at that time. FDR was the first president to use the media—especially radio—to communicate intimately with the people.

5. Willis F. Johnson, *The Life of Warren G. Harding* (Chicago: Winston, 1923), 24-26; Carosso, "Music and Musicians in the White House," 121.

6. Minstrel and ragtime songs were spirited, often syncopated, reflections of black folk culture. Their earthiness and vitality had great impact on the popular music industry in America at the turn of the century. Reputedly, Roosevelt adopted such a piece—"A Hot Time in the Old Town Tonight" (1896) by Theodore Metz—as the official song of his Rough Riders during the Spanish-American War. Dialect songs generally dealt with minorities, such as the Irish, Germans, or Italians, and were especially popular in beer halls and saloons.

7. Earl Godwin, "They Make our Presidents Laugh," *Philadelphia Public Ledger*, June 14, 1925. Matt Horne had been a policeman for about twenty-five years, then a member of the Department of Justice. The George O'Connor archive consists of three large scrapbooks, photographs, clippings, and song

texts and is the property of the Lauinger Memorial Library, Georgetown University, Washington, D.C.

8. "George O'Connor Entertains with Popular Songs and Keeps Chief Executive in Merry Mood," *Washington Post*, Oct. 29, 1910.

9. Jim Walsh, "Favorite Pioneer Recording Artists: George H. O'Connor," *Hobbies*, Jan. 1955. The article continues in the Feb. and Mar. issues.

10. "Radio Entertainers Attract Crowd as They Go to the White House," *The World*, Mar. 9, 1930.

11. Walsh, "Favorite Recording Artists," Mar. 1955.

12. "Al Jolson Leads Actor Band in Pledge of Support at Breakfast Party," *Washington Star*, Oct. 17, 1924. See also Ishbel Ross, *Grace Coolidge and Her Era* (New York: Dodd, Mead and Co., 1962), 164-65.

13. Michael Freedland, *Jolson* (New York: Stein and Day, 1972), 69-70.

14. "George Cohan Gives President Copy of His Bicentennial Song," *Washington Star*, July 29, 1931.

15. *New York Times*, June 2, 1921.

16. *The World*, Oct. 1, 1928.

17. *New York Times*, June 4, 1921; see also "President Harding to Give His Aid to Music Week" (n.d.), Abbey Gunn Baker Papers, OWHC.

18. Joint Resolution No. 3, signed by Secretary of State David Winebrenner, May 8, 1929. Presidential Subject: National Anthem, The Herbert Hoover Papers, HHL.

19. Baldwin piano #37024, style K. Baldwin Company to McClure, Jan. 24, 1950, OWHC.

20. "Boy Pianist Plays at White House," *New York Herald*, May 18, 1923. Harding Scrapbook, OWHC. Cherkassy later studied with Josef Hofmann at the Curtis Institute in Philadelphia and has given concerts all over the world.

21. "Gifted Musicians Eagerly Await Bid to White House," source unknown, Mar. 15, 1937. White House scrapbook, Washingtoniana Collection, MLKL.

22. *Washington Post*, Apr. 9, 1925.

23. Helen White to Elise Kirk, Apr. 4, 1981.

24. The pianoforte was borrowed on Apr. 4, 1932, and returned to the Smithsonian at the beginning of Franklin D. Roosevelt's administration, probably in 1937 with the other White House furniture on loan from the Smithsonian (receipt, Apr. 4, 1932; memorandum of packing, Apr. 1, 1932; memorandum, Chief Usher Hoover to Goldsmith, Apr. 1, 1932, Accession file #118796, NMAH, SI). James Monroe's Astor is in the James Monroe Museum and Memorial Library, Fredericksburg, Va.

25. Elizabeth Sprague Coolidge (distant relative by marriage to Calvin Coolidge) was responsible for the establishment of the Berkshire Festivals of Chamber Music and for the Elizabeth Sprague Coolidge Foundation at the Library of Congress. Numerous modern composers, including Loeffler, Schoenberg, Bartok, Piston, and Stravinsky, have written works commissioned by the foundation. Through her patronage, Mrs. Coolidge was an important influence on classical and modern chamber music in America and Europe.

26. Susan Dyer, "The Friends of Music at Stanford," *Stanford Alumni Magazine*, 1958, courtesy of Mildred Hall Campbell and Ruth Fesler Lipman, secretaries to Mrs. Hoover at the White House.

27. Marguerite D'Alvarez, the great Peruvian contralto, was the sister of J. Alvarez de Buenavista of the Peruvian Embassy. *Herald*, Mar. 25, 1924. All Harding and Coolidge printed musicale programs, OWHC.

28. Schonberg, *Great Pianists*, 367.

29. Sergei Bertensson and Jay Lerner, *Rachmaninoff: A Lifetime in Music* (New York: New York University Press, 1956), 238.

30. Ibid., 194-95.

31. Schonberg, *Great Pianists*, 371.

32. Ross, *Grace Coolidge*, 162.

33. Two pages of explanatory notes were printed in the small, seven-page program. In listing the selections, Fellowes's name was misspelled, and the word "circa" was appended to Tomkins, as if it were part of his name. However, the program was finely executed and each stringed instrument with its date and maker was included.

34. The viola d'amore was a treble viol instrument played on the shoulder like the violin. It was used mainly during the periods of Bach and Vivaldi and possessed a separate set of strings, which vibrated sympathetically with those above it when bowed.

35. Clark to Coolidge, Mar. 24, 1924, Calvin Coolidge Papers, LC.

36. Mildred Campbell to Elise Kirk, Mar. 9, 1981. Tibbett's program included selections from *The Beggar's Opera*, the prologue from *Pagliacci*, and "On the Road to Mandalay." Actually Tibbett was fulfilling his promise: "When you become President," he had told Hoover, "I want to sing for your first musicale." The president obviously did not forget this. *New York Times*, Apr. 20, 1929.

37. Herbert Hoover, *Memoirs, 1874-1920: Years of Adventure* (New York: Macmillan, 1951), 357. "Mr. Paderewski was not particularly strong as an administrator," Hoover felt. "At his request, we sent a whole staff of expert advisers for his governmental department of finance, railways, and food; in fact, the American advisers practically conducted the whole food administration and reconstruction of the railways." Paderewski had previously played for President Coolidge on Jan. 20, 1928. The Steinway piano he used during his American tours is in the National Museum of American History.

38. Glen Plaskin, *Horowitz, a Biography* (New York: William Morrow, 1983), 142; *New York Times*, Jan. 7, 1931; *Chicago Tribune*, Feb. 25, 1931.

39. Campbell to Kirk, Mar. 9, 1981.

40. Marks to Akerson, June 10, 1929, Akerson to Marks, June 20, 1929. See also "Harmonica Jubilee to be Held at the Bellevue-Stratford on May 8, 1928," leaflet, and "Harmonica Band Movement," *Philadelphia Evening Bulletin*, Apr. 12, 1929. All these are in Presidential Subject—White House—Artists Who Wish to Appear. Herbert Hoover Papers, HHPL. A harmonica craze, plugged by radio, brought orders for 20 million instruments in 1925.

41. Phenix to Hoover, Mar. 18, 1930, Akerson to Phenix, Mar. 20, 1930, ibid.

42. Shieffelin to Wilbur, Dec. 7, 1932, Goss to Joslin, Jan. 19, 1933, ibid.

43. Jerome Kern, *The Jerome Kern Song Book* (New York: Simon and Schuster, 1955), 3.

44. E. Clark to R. Weeks, Dec., 1923, Coolidge Papers, LC.

45. The letters are property of the Herbert Hoover Presidential Library.

Chapter 10. New Music for a New Deal

1. Arthur P. Molella, curator, "Introduction," in *FDR: The Intimate Presidency* (Washington, D.C.: National Museum of American History, Smithsonian Institution, 1982), a catalogue of exhibition commemorating the 100th anniversary of FDR's birth.

2. The Roosevelt Home at Hyde Park, N.Y., contains a large collection of sheet music, early gramophone recordings, and piano rolls typical of the period ca. 1880-1920. It is not always possible to tell who owned or played the music, however. "I'll Sing Thee Songs of Araby" from *Lalla Rookh* (New

York: G. Schirmer, n.d.) bears the penciled inscription "F. D. Roosevelt" at the top right hand corner of the cover. "Valse Romantique" by Friml (Boston: Arthur P. Schmidt, 1908) shows "Anna Eleanor Roosevelt" (President Roosevelt's daughter) written in pencil on the cover and the following remarks in pen: "It is a very hard piece for me, but it will come in time, I hope. Kick me please. No sir!!! Mrs. Robert Raffle is a very good teacher. I don't want to take music unless she teaches me."

3. Diary of Sarah Delano Roosevelt, July 27, 1896, Sarah Delano Roosevelt Papers, Box 67, FDRL. The diaries begin in May 1881 and end January 1905. Describing the performance of *Walküre*, which she attended on Dec. 17, 1904, Sarah writes, "I loved the beautiful music." Sarah Roosevelt's mother-of-pearl opera glasses are the property of the home at Hyde Park.

4. Oct. 18, 1899, in Elliott Roosevelt, ed., *FDR: His Personal Letters, Early Years* (New York: Duell, Sloan and Pearce, 1947), 347.

5. Ibid., 284, 286.

6. Printed program (May 17, 1901), courtesy of Harvard University Library, Cambridge, Mass.

7. Some of the works in the collection include Benjamin Carr's "The Siege of Tripoli," a programmatic piano piece ca. 1805; "The Lighthouse" with verses by Thomas Moore; "Battle of Port Royal"; "Decatur's Victory"; "Atlantic's Return"—a schottische showing the great side-wheeler on the open seas in the colored lithographed cover; and "Oh, What a Row! or the Adventures of a Steam Packet, a new comic song as sung by Mr. Barnes," all in FDRL.

8. Memos, D. J. to McIntyre and McIntyre to McSweeney, Jan. 24, 1934, PPF 1219, FDR Papers; see also Early to Donally, Jan. 28, 1936, Official Files [OF] 50-C, FDR Papers.

9. Roosevelt, ed., *Early Years*, 79.

10. FDR to Sarnoff, Jan. 31, 1940, PPF 764, FDR Papers.

11. "Three Favorite Hymns Are Listed by Roosevelt," *New York Times*, Mar. 16, 1935.

12. FDR to Davenport, May 4, 1942, President's Personal Files [PPF] 100, FDR Papers. Printed program, "A Thanksgiving Day Service at the White House," Wilkinson Collection, Division of Political History, NMAH, SI. The Marine Band played during this service as William Santelmann relates: "The minister told me to be sure to interpret the hymns as spirited songs of joy ... but after the service the President in his wheelchair came up to me and reprimanded, 'Young man, why do you jazz up the hymns like that!? ... Learn to play hymns the way they were supposed to be played!' Then he left, stopped a moment, turned back to us, smiled and wished us all 'a very happy Thanksgiving.' " William Santelmann in an interview with Elise Kirk, Jan. 21, 1982. All other programs mentioned in this chapter are the property of the FDRL and NMAH, SI.

13. James Roosevelt and Sidney Shalett, *Affectionately FDR* (New York: Harcourt, Brace, 1959), 69.

14. Interview with Marian Anderson by Mary McAlpine for the Canadian Broadcasting Co., Sept. 26, 1973, FDR Papers; Mrs. Roosevelt's "My Day" column often contained comments about her White House musicales.

15. Article written for Frank B. Cookson of the *Educational Music Magazine*, July 22, 1938, Eleanor Roosevelt [ER] Papers 3031-51, FDRL. Especially interesting are Mrs. Roosevelt's handwritten revisions on this typescript, characteristic of her personal interest in the content and expression of her texts.

16. John Steinway in an interview with Elise Kirk, Steinway & Sons, New York City, Mar. 14, 1979.

17. J. Edgar Hoover to Marvin McIntyre, Nov. 15, 1938, PPF 3380, FDR Papers. The "anonymous letter" also alleged that Germans had adopted a policy of introducing pro-German musicians into the Metropolitan Opera. The Hoover report observed that from a prospectus for the 1938-39 season, the company repertory listed fourteen German, eleven French, two Russian, and seventeen Italian operas. The general manager of the Met was Edward Johnson, an American, who had featured young American singers, such as John Carter, Leonard Warren, and Risë Stevens. While the first opera of the season *Tristan und Isolde* was "written by a German," the report continued, "it starred Kirsten Flagstad, a Scandinavian and Lauritz Melchior, a Dane."

18. Junge to Mrs. Roosevelt, Dec. 13, 1937, ER Papers, 80.3, #986.

19. For the 1938-39 season a list of seventy names of performers with Junge's comments ("Nice for Lent," "Too many pianists already," "Solo sax-ophonist—a novel idea") was submitted to Mrs. Roosevelt for her perusal.

20. Junge to Helm, Oct. 19, 1934, ER Papers, 80.3, #986.

21. Junge to Mrs. Roosevelt, Apr. 12, 1939, Junge to Helm, Apr. 3, 1934, White House Office of Chief of Social Entertainments, Box 204, Junge, ER Papers.

22. All letters Helm to Junge, ER Papers, 80.3, #986. Edith Helm had been social secretary under Woodrow Wilson and would also serve under the Trumans.

23. Junge to Schneider, Feb. 22, 1936, ER Papers, 80.3, #986.

24. Tibbett to President and Mrs. Roosevelt, July 7, 1939, ER Papers, #1529. Tibbett at this time was the highest paid among concert singers, earning $2,500 per performance. Abel Green and Joe Laurie, Jr., *Show Biz: From Vaude to Video* (New York: Doubleday, 1953), 407.

25. Iturbi to Mrs. Roosevelt, Nov. 10, 1934, ER Papers, 80.3, #986.

26. May 24, 1939, ER Papers, 60.9.

27. *New York Times*, Jan. 21, 1935. The Gullah Negros reputedly originated the popular new dance of the 1930s, the "Big Apple," which they danced barefoot. Green and Laurie, *Show Biz*, 418.

28. Leontyne Price, *Highlights of a Prima Donna* (New York: Vantage Press, 1973), 194.

29. D. Junge to Helm, Mar. 8, 1935, Helm to D. Junge, Mar. 9, 1935, ER Papers, 80.3, #986.

30. Todd Duncan in an interview with Elise Kirk, Washington, D.C., Feb. 24, 1982.

31. Anderson/McAlpine interview.

32. Graham to Mrs. Roosevelt, Feb. 22, 1937, Helm to Hawkins, Feb. 25, 1937, ER Papers, 80.9, #993.

33. Junge to Helm, Oct. 19, 1934, ER Papers, 80.3, #986.

34. Crim to Greiner, Nov. 8, 1939, Steinway and Sons, New York City.

35. Junge to FDR, Dec. 12, 1936, Steinway and Sons. Mrs. Roosevelt purchased a slightly used Steinway baby grand for her Val Kill cottage at Hyde Park for $500. It was delivered courtesy Steinway in June 1937. Junge to Mrs. Roosevelt, June 25, 1937, ER Papers, 80.3.

36. Steinway/Kirk interview.

37. *New York Times*, Dec. 18, 1938.

38. Recorded comments by Wendy Marshall and her sister, Helen Marshall Borchard, 1981, in NMAH, SI.

39. FDR to Paul Green, Mar. 2, 1934, reprinted in "Folk Music in the Roosevelt White House: An Evening of Song, Recollections and Dance," a booklet accompanying the concert held at the National Museum of American

History, Smithsonian Institution, Jan. 31, 1982. The twenty-eight-page booklet contains excellent oral histories of Alan Lomax, Wade Mainer, Lily May Ledford, and Charles Seegar.

40. Junge to Muir, Feb. 24, 1935. See also Mallon to Roberts, Jan. 15, 1934, ER Papers, 80.3, #986. Iva Roberts played on Feb. 26, 1935. See also Schneider to Niles, Apr. 12, 1934, and Niles to Mrs. Roosevelt (n.d.), ER Papers, 80.3, #991. A dulcimer, a gift from Niles to FDR, is at the museum at Hyde Park.

41. Charles Seeger, "Folk Music and the New Deal," in "Folk Music in the Roosevelt White House," 22.

42. Lomax to Mrs. Roosevelt, July 6, 1939, ER Papers, 50.2, #386. Lomax is a widely recognized scholar in the field of folk music research. Junge to Mrs. Roosevelt, Dec. 17, 1938, in Of. Ch. Soc. Entertainments, Box 204, ER Papers.

43. Helm to Dornbush, Mar. 5, 1939, Of. Ch. Soc. Entertainments 91-197, Helm to Junge, Nov. 2, 1935, Of. Soc. Entertainments, Box 204, ER Papers.

44. Helm to Dornbush, Apr. 13, 1939, Of. Ch. Soc. Entertainments 91-197. See also Dornbush to Mrs. Roosevelt, Apr. 18, 1939. Transportation and per diem was $5 apiece. Cost for the Negro chorus was given as $2040.30; the Coon Creek Girls, $390; the Cowboy Singers, $1298.40. The expenses were to be paid by the State Department.

45. Junge to Helm, May 23, June 1, and June 3, 1939, ER Papers, 80.3, #986. See also June 6, 1939, Of. Ch. Soc. Entertainments, 91-197. Junge also brought two American Indian singers to Hyde Park for the picnic for the king and queen on June 11, 1939; Princess Te Ata and Ish-Ti-Opi.

46. The complete program has been reprinted in "Folk Music in the Roosevelt White House," 23-28.

47. The Lincoln Memorial program was arranged after Anderson was refused a singing engagement at DAR's Constitution Hall because she was black. Mrs. Roosevelt resigned from membership in the Daughters of the American Revolution as a result of this infamous incident.

48. "Folk Music in the Roosevelt White House," 12, 22, 13. Lily May adds: "After we got off stage and went back to our dressing room, we noticed that Sis had a $20 bill that had slipped down her leg and was flattened out right in front under the silk hose. She had put it in her garter for safe keeping, before performing, and it had worked loose. Now we realized that it had been there while we were out on stage and it had been seen by all!"

49. U.S. Marine Band Leaders' Logs, Dec. 7, 1941, MBL.

50. Hamm, *Yesterdays*, 377-79.

51. "Roosevelt Praises Inspirational Songs," *New York Times*, July 29, 1942; FDR to Romberg, July 27, 1942, PPF 100, FDR Papers.

52. "Folk Music in the Roosevelt White House," 16-17. Several pieces from this historic program were recreated by Josh White, Jr., Wade Mainer, and others at the concert, Jan. 31, 1982, NMAH.

53. All letters are the property of the FDRL. The collection also includes correspondence between the president and Lauritz Melchior, Basil O'Connor, Jose Iturbi, Ignacy Jan Paderewski, Ernestine Schumann-Heink, Lawrence Tibbett, Hans Kindler, Douglas Fairbanks, Rosa Ponselle, Edwin Hughes, and Schuyler Chapin.

54. William Santelmann in an interview with Elise Kirk, Arlington, Va., Jan. 21, 1982.

55. Lt. Col. William F. Santelmann, USMC (Retd.), "My Eight Terms in the White House," typescript, Apr. 21, 1955, 18, MCHC.

56. U.S. Marine Band Leaders' Logs, Aug. 31, 1942, MBL. Entertaining at the president's last inaugural festivity, Jan. 20, 1945, were Eddie Cantor, Jimmy Durante, Lena Horne, Rex Ingram, Danny Kaye, Zero Mostel, Earl Robinson, and Frank Sinatra.

57. Barnett Lester, "What the Roosevelts Like in Swing Music," *The Senator* (June 17, 1939): 23-24, Washingtoniana Division, MLKL. After someone once sent him a copy of Alex Templeton's new recording, "Bach Goes to Town," the president commented that he hoped he'd never be converted "from Bach to Boogie-Woogie." Struther PPF 100.

58. "1600 Peppermint Lounge," *Washington Evening Star*, Nov. 13, 1961. Seideman also recalls playing for the Hoovers while they danced the Charleston.

59. "Grave Is in Garden," *New York Times*, Apr. 16, 1945.

Chapter 11. A Study in Contrasts

1. HST to Mrs. John Truman and Mary Jane, June 13, 1945, Truman Papers. The portion of this chapter dealing with Harry Truman is reprinted with modification in Brian Lingham, ed., *Harry Truman: The Man . . . His Music* (Kansas City: Lowell, 1985).

2. HST to Mrs. John Truman and Mary Jane, Apr. 16, 1945, Truman Papers. Truman mentions in his diary entry for Apr. 12 that he thought the president was in town for Bishop Atwood's funeral and wanted to see him before returning to Warm Springs, Ga.

3. HST to Mary Jane, Apr. 12, 1948, ibid.

4. HST to Margaret Truman, Feb. 14, 1948, ibid.

5. HST to Bessie Wallace, Jan. 10, 1910, ibid.

6. Rex Scouten, in an interview with Elise Kirk, The White House, Aug. 5, 1982.

7. "Music and Art," p. 8 of a nine-page typed questionnaire, n.d., President's Personal Files (PPF), Truman Papers. Truman jotted down, in his usual terse, breezy style, his own views on subjects ranging from his health and dress to music and painting; also Margaret Truman, in a telephone conversation with Elise Kirk, Apr. 6, 1982.

8. Henry S. Bundschu, "Harry S. Truman, the Missourian," reprinted from the *Kansas City Star*, Dec. 26, 1948, HSTL.

9. "Music and Art," 8.

10. Truman's remarks to Guy Lombardo are quoted in Robert H. Farrell, *Off the Record: The Private Papers of Harry S. Truman* (New York: Harper and Row, 1980), 356. Frederic Logan's "The Missouri Waltz" (1914) became the official state song on June 30, 1949.

11. Ibid., 23.

12. Truman calls this sonata "No. 9," undoubtedly according to the edition he used.

13. Ibid. For more on Truman's training and tastes in music, see Anthony Leviero, "Harry Truman, Musician and Music Lover," *New York Times*, June 18, 1950, and Leroy V. Brant, "Music's Significant Place in Modern Life, from a Discussion with President Harry S Truman," *Etude*, Oct. 1946.

14. Margaret Truman, *Harry S. Truman* (New York: William Morrow, 1973), 336.

15. Howard Mitchell, in an interview with Elise Kirk, Apr. 18, 1982. A White House memo pertaining to the Trumans attending *The Beggar's Opera* specifies that "this is not to be announced in advance and it is, of course, to be handled 'off the record,' as is usually done." MJC to Perlmeter et al., Sept. 23, 1952, PPF, Truman Papers.

16. "President Attends New Porgy and Bess," *New York Times*, Aug. 6, 1952; files of Eben A. Ayers, asst. press secretary to HST, Jan. 22, 1947, HSTL. Another controversy, reminiscent of Marian Anderson's, took place when singer Hazel Scott was not allowed to sing at DAR's Constitutional Hall. Mrs. Truman kept her previous commitment to attend the DAR tea in spite of the vehement protests of Scott's husband, Representative Adam Powell of New York. She claimed her acceptance was not related to the "merits of the issue. I deplore," she said, "any action which denies artistic talent an opportunity to express itself because of prejudice against race or origin." Ayers Files, Oct. 12, Mar. 26. Truman later barred Powell from the White House because of his harsh words to Mrs. Truman during the controversy.

17. Leviero column in *New York Times*, Mar. 19, 1950.

18. EH to BT, Oct. 8, 1946, Truman Papers. Greiner, suspected of being pro-Nazi, was cleared by an FBI study that found that the funds he had been sending to Germany were in support of an aged aunt. Leonard P. Hutchinson, Protective Research Section, U.S. Secret Service, to Adrian Tolley, The White House Social Office, Oct. 3, 1946, ibid. See also *New York Times*, Apr. 22, 1958.

19. HST to MT, Oct. 23, 1946, ibid. Greiner's list included sixteen pianists, eight violinists, and twenty-four vocalists. Those who were available were marked "A." The president's original choices for pianists were: 1. Eugene List, 2. Sylvia Zaremba, 3. Rudolph Ganz, 4. Percy Grainger, 5. William Kapell. Violinists marked were: 1. Jascha Heifetz, 2. Yehudi Menuhin, 3. Albert Spalding, 4. Patricia Travers. Margaret had not yet checked her choices for the singers.

20. John Steinway, in an interview with Elise Kirk, Steinway Place, Long Island, N.Y., Mar. 14, 1979.

21. HST to BT and Mary, Jan. 30, 1947, Truman Papers.

22. Eugene List, in an interview with Elise Kirk, Dallas, Mar. 21, 1981. After List's performance, Truman played Paderewski's "Minuet," often confused in accounts of this event with Beethoven's "Minuet in G." In a typed copy of a letter to his mother and sister, Truman has crossed off the reference to Beethoven and written in "Paderewski." See also "Log of the President's Trip to the Berlin Conference (July 6 to Aug. 7, 1945)" compiled by Lt. William M. Rigdon, USN, typescripts, HSTL. A copy of the Chopin score, played by List and later autographed by him, was presented to the president on Jan. 4, 1946.

23. Truman, *Harry S. Truman*, 280; HST to BT, July 22, 1945, Truman Papers.

24. Ayers Files; Aug. 26, 1945, Truman Papers. The dates of the programs were as follows: Air Force Band, July 6, 1945; Naval Academy Choir, Feb. 9, 1947; Olsen and Johnson, June 4, 1945; and Hildegarde, Aug. 26, 1945.

25. Marie NcNair, "Gaiety Reigned at the White House: First Dancing Party in Eight Years Thrills Capital's Younger Set," *Washington Evening Star*, Feb. 7, 1946.

26. Bess Truman died on Oct. 18, 1982, at age ninety-seven—our longest-living first lady.

27. Truman, *Harry S. Truman*, 342.

28. Hume's review appeared in the *Washington Post* on Dec. 6, 1950. With Truman's reply it was reprinted in the *New York Times*, Dec. 9, 1950, and in other papers across the country. Truman's original letter eventually made its way to the collection of a New Haven businessman and was auctioned for $15,000 in 1967.

29. R. Anderson to Truman, n.d., PPF, Truman Papers.

30. HST to Philip Graham, Feb. 4, 1952, ibid. The documents concerning this incident are clipped together with the top page marked "Music—Personal. See me. *Important—Personal*," in Truman's hand.

31. The distinguishing feature of the Baldwin was its large sterling silver spread eagle and thirteen stars on the fallboard, designed by Sidney Waugh with the approval of the president. On the back of the fallboard was the presidential seal. After the piano was moved to the White House Library in March 1953, the press of Cincinnati, the home of the Baldwin firm, expressed indignation over the instrument's new location in the "basement." In 1965 the piano was loaned to the State Department and an identical copy placed in the Harry S. Truman Library (also a gift of the Baldwin Company). Records of the Cincinnati Historical Society. See also "White House Tour: Music by Truman," *New York Times*, May 4, 1952, and "A Tale of Truman and that Piano," *Cincinnati Enquirer*, Dec. 28, 1972, HSTL. Truman also received an upright piano from the National Press Club, and, during Inter-American Music Week in May 1951, a spinet made of raw materials from many member countries of the United Nations. Neither was used in the White House. Two Steinway baby grands and a Gulbranson spinet were already on the second floor when Truman became president.

32. The first collection contains "Der Schäfer und der Reiter," "Lob der Tränen," and "Der Alpenjäger" (Vienna, Cappi & Diabelli, 1822) and the second "Der Wanderer," "Morgenlied," and "Wanderers Nachtlied" (also Cappi & Diabelli, 1821). All gifts are the property of the HSTL.

33. On the title page of the book is the following: "*Songs in the New Opera Called Camilla* as they are performed at the Theatre Royall. Sold by I Walsh Musicall Instrument maker in Ordinary to her Majesty, at the Golden Harpe and Ho-boy in Catherine Street near Sommerset House in the Strand." Fifty-one arias from the opera are included. The gift was presented to the president and his family by the Italian ambassador and the secretary of state.

34. The collection of contracts also contains a photostat of the letter of agreement for Charles Gounod's "Ave Maria." See also David L. Bazelon to Matthew J. Connelly, July 27, 1949, Truman Papers.

35. Entry for June 4, 1956, in Ferrell, *Off the Record*, 331.

36. Julia Pels, "Art for Whose Sake?" *American Legion Magazine*, Oct. 1955, Box 209, 236J, Eisenhower Papers.

37. A recording of Eisenhower singing "God Bless America" with Waring (EL-D12-38) was made following Irving Berlin's tribute at the rally on Oct. 30, 1952 (Audio visual archive, Eisenhower Library). In July 1954 Berlin received the Congressional Medal for his patriotic songs.

38. Mary Jane McCaffree (Mrs. Henry Monroe, Jr.), in an interview with Elise Kirk, Washington, D.C., Mar. 10, 1982. Mrs. McCaffree was not only social secretary but also press and personal secretary for Mrs. Eisenhower.

39. Howard Mitchell, in a telephone interview with Elise Kirk, Washington, D.C., Apr. 18, 1982.

40. Santelmann, "My Eight Terms in the White House," 29-30.

41. William Santelmann, in an interview with Elise Kirk, Arlington, Va., Jan. 21, 1982.

42. Four-page memo, "White House Musicales," n.d., typescript, Steinway & Sons, New York. Howell Crim retired as chief usher in May 1957 and was succeeded by Bernard West.

43. "White House Vaudeville," *Newsweek*, Mar. 10, 1959. The president enjoyed playing golf regularly with Lawrence Welk and Fred Waring.

44. Mary Jane McCaffree interview. Wiley Buchanan, *Red Carpet at the White House* (New York: Dutton, 1964), 232. The program was larger than the usual 3 1/2 × 5 inches, had a drawing of the White House on the cover,

and was decorated with a red, white, and blue ribbon. All Eisenhower White House programs in Mamie Dowd Eisenhower Papers, Social Records, DDEL.

45. "White House Guests See Broadway Acts," *New York Times*, May 9, 1958; Harry MacArthur, "White House Musicale Was Well-Kept Secret," *Washington Sunday Star*, May 11, 1958.

46. For the Broadway program on May 8, 1958, a separate list for the musicale was compiled. In attendance were 134 guests, eighteen press, and twenty-four performers with spouses and friends, totaling 176. The Eisenhowers invited society reporters to cover the state dinners, but they were allowed to come only before the dinner and return for the musicale.

47. Betty Beale. "Music Advisory Committee Suggested for White House," *Washington Evening Star*, Feb. 8, 1959.

48. Steinway/Kirk interview. Thirty-year-old Fleisher became the first American to win a major foreign competition when he was awarded the Queen of Belgium Prize in 1952. Another Steinway artist and 1960 Belgium prize winner, Malcolm Frager, performed for the king of Denmark at a state dinner on Oct. 11, 1960.

49. Greiner to Henry Steinway, May 3, 1957, Steinway & Sons.

50. Piatigorsky had been first cellist with the Imperial Opera, Moscow, at the age of fifteen. It is said that after his arrival in the United States in 1929, he brought about a cello renaissance. He was considered the greatest cellist after Casals.

51. MJM to JE, Mar. 10, 1960, OF 101-B-6, DDE to Bernstein, Apr. 6, 1960, OF 101-B-6, Eisenhower Papers.

52. Memo for the Record, Office of the Assistant to the President, Jan. 11, 1955, OF 236-J, ibid.

53. William K. Wyant, Jr., "Federal Aid for the Arts," *Music and the Arts*, Dec. 9, 1956, reprinted from the St. Louis *Post-Dispatch*, Eisenhower Papers. An attempt was made to bring the entire *Porgy and Bess* company to the White House to be received by the president, but this did not materialize. See Robert Breen to Maxwell M. Rabb, May 31, 1956, and ff., OF 111, ibid.

Chapter 12. *The Value of Culture for All*

1. Mahalia Jackson, *Movin' On Up* (New York: Hawthorn Books, 1966), 139.

2. From words of John F. Kennedy written on the facade of the John F. Kennedy Center for the Performing Arts, Washington, D.C.

3. "John F. Kennedy: Government and the Arts," *John F. Kennedy Center for the Performing Arts Inaugural Program*, Sept. 8, 1971.

4. Oral history interview with Leonard Bernstein, composer and music director of the New York Philharmonic, by Nelson Aldrich, July 21, 1965, New York, 2-4, Kennedy Papers.

5. August Heckscher, "Kennedy: The Man Who Lives On," typescript address, Larchmont Temple, Nov. 20, 1964, 6-7, August Heckscher Papers, JFKL.

6. Letitia Baldridge, *Of Diamonds and Diplomats* (New York: Ballantine Books, 1968), 185. However, to many Americans "culture" could be a "smelly word" with a "faint scent of communism to it," Tish Baldridge, Mrs. Kennedy's social secretary added. Another criticism of the New Frontier's promotion of the arts came from American artist, Thomas Hart Benton, who felt that the White House was "making a dilettante show of it . . . the art that I am expressing has nothing to do with high society . . . I get more out of a backwoods saloon than at the White House." *New York Times*, May 14, 1962.

7. This concept was formulated by Salinger, Schlesinger, and Mrs. Kennedy

shortly after the inauguration. Arthur and Barbara Gelb, "Culture Makes a Hit at the White House," *New York Times*, Jan. 28, 1962. Stephen Birmingham in his *Jacqueline Bouvier Kennedy Onassis* (New York: Grosset & Dunlap, 1978), 106, notes that Jacqueline Kennedy was a decided political asset to the president, and he let her do pretty much what she wanted.

8. Jacqueline Kennedy Onassis to Elise Kirk, Feb. 3, 1984.

9. The program on Apr. 30, 1963, was presented for Grand Duchess Charlotte of Luxembourg by Basil Rathbone and the Consort Players. The early music group was organized in 1953 by Sydney Beck, head of the Rare Book and Manuscript Section of the Music Division of the New York Public Library. Another tribute to musical scholarship took place when the president sent a letter to the Eighth Congress of the International Musicological Society congratulating the IMS on its achievements.

10. Oral history interview with August Heckscher, by Wolf von Eckhardt, Dec. 10, 1965, New York, Kennedy Papers.

11. *New York Times*, Aug. 10, 1962.

12. Evelyn Lincoln to Helga Sandburg, May 3, 1962, President's Official File [POF], Kennedy Papers.

13. Heckscher/Eckhardt interview, 14-15. *Washington Post* music critic, Paul Hume, learned from Mrs. Kennedy that both she and the president liked symphonic music with extramusical associations, such as Tchaikowsky's *Romeo and Juliet* Overture and Debussy's Prelude to "Afternoon of a Faun." William Lichtenwanger to Edward Kennedy, Mar. 17, 1971, Music Division, Library of Congress.

14. Bernard West in an interview with Elise Kirk, Washington, D.C., July 22, 1981; Klapthor, *First Ladies*, 79. See also "Jackie Brings Culture to the White House," *New York–Journal American*, Nov. 23, 1960. "A Tour of the White House with Mrs. John F. Kennedy" was broadcast on the CBS Television Network, Feb. 14, 1962.

15. Onassis to Kirk. Mrs. Kennedy also founded the Office of the Curator of the White House, the Committee for the Preservation of the White House, and the White House Historical Association in 1961. While the Office of the Curator was approved by law on Sept. 22, 1961, it received precise standing through an Executive Order issued by President Lyndon Johnson in 1964.

16. Heckscher/Eckhardt interview, 3.

17. John Steinway to Henry Steinway, May 12, 1961, Steinway & Sons. The memo comments also on Mrs. Kennedy's dislike of the design of the state piano in the East Room and her request that a smaller grand be placed on the main floor. This she felt could be easily moved into the other rooms for small affairs. The Steinways complied with a Hepplewhite console, which was kept on the second floor and moved downstairs when needed. It was eventually replaced by a larger upright still in use under the Reagans.

18. Heckscher/Eckhardt interview, 51.

19. Bernstein/Aldrich interview, 8-9.

20. *New York Times*, Nov. 14, 1961. Reprinted in program notes, "A Concert at the White House," Columbia AKL5726. See also *Washington Post*, Nov. 14, 1961.

21. Col. John Bourgeois, in an interview with Elise Kirk, Washington, D.C., Feb. 12, 1982.

22. Casals to John F. Kennedy, Nov. 17, 1961, Kennedy Papers. For more on Casals event, see Marta Istomin interview with Elise Kirk, Washington, D.C., July 20, 1982; Casals, *Joys and Sorrows*, 289-94; and jacket notes "Concert at the White House."

23. Herbert S. Parmet, *JFK: The Presidency of John F. Kennedy* (New York: The Dial Press, 1983), 129.

24. Ibid.

25. Bernstein/Aldrich interview, 13; *New York Times*, Jan. 19, 1962.

26. Baldridge, *Diamonds and Diplomats*, 178.

27. Marjorie Hunter, "Mozart and Milk Offered to White House Visitors," *New York Times*, Feb. 8, 1962. The performance used piano accompaniment.

28. *New York Times*, Nov. 20, 1962; press release, Office of the Assistant Social Secretary for the Press, The White House, Oct. 31, 1962, Music Division, LC.

29. Irving Lowens, "White House Guests Thrilled by Bumbry," *Washington Evening Star*, Feb. 21, 1962. The Kennedys had done away with separate state dinners for the vice-president, Speaker, and chief justice and combined the events into a single evening. Tish Baldridge recalls this concert as one of the highlights of the Kennedy years. Letitia Baldridge to Elise Kirk, Jan. 30, 1985.

30. Betty Beale and Daisy Cleland, "Kennedys Are Hosts," *Washington Evening Star*, Feb. 21, 1962.

31. Baldridge, *Diamonds and Diplomats*, 207.

32. Ibid., 186, 187.

33. Lowens, "Move to East Room Solves 'Magic Flute,'" *Washington Evening Star*, June 4, 1963.

34. Baldridge, *Diamonds and Diplomats*, 196-97.

35. Ibid., 194.

36. Tish Baldridge to Evelyn Lincoln, memo, Sept. 25, 1961, POF—staff memos, Kennedy Papers.

37. Tish Baldridge to President and Mrs. Kennedy, memo (nd), POF—staff memos, ibid. The list was compiled for the dinner on Feb. 20, 1962, for the vice-president, Speaker, and chief justice at which black mezzo-soprano Grace Bumbry made her U.S. debut.

38. Tish Baldridge to Evelyn Lincoln, memo, Feb. 20, 1961, POF—staff memos, ibid. During FDR's administration the White House donated $2.50 to the National Symphony.

39. Tish Baldridge to the President, memo, Apr. 26, 1963, POF—staff memos, ibid.

40. Heckscher/Eckhardt interview, 56.

41. Bourgeois/Kirk interview.

42. West/Kirk interview.

43. Baldridge, *Diamonds and Diplomats*, 159-60.

44. Ibid.

45. Betty Beale, "Dancing at the White House: Adlai Stevenson Honored," *Washington Evening Star*, Nov. 13, 1961.

46. "Reminder Service," typescript, Apr. 20, 1962, *Washington Star* Archives, MLKL; *Washington Evening Star*, Apr. 3, 1962. Robbins was choreographer for the film version of *West Side Story*, produced by United Artists.

47. Frank Sinatra to Pierre Salinger, Mar. 30, 1961, White House Central Files—"Entertainers," Kennedy Papers. "Political Blows Give '64 Preview," *New York Times*, Oct. 17, 1963; Tony Scaduto, *Frank Sinatra* (London: Michael Joseph, 1976), 43-59; Baldridge/Kirk, Jan. 30, 1985.

48. Memo from Evelyn Lincoln, Sept. 18, 1961, The White House, POF—staff memos, Kennedy Papers.

49. Ann H. Lincoln, *The Kennedy White House Parties* (New York: Viking, 1967), 176.

50. The complete listing of the musical selections and organizations performing on the day of the funeral appears in the *Washington Star*, Dec. 1, 1963, compiled by Irving Lowens. Capt. Gilbert H. Mitchell, assistant conductor of the Army Band, served as music coordinator for the Military District of Washington during the ceremonies.

51. J. Edwards, *Military Customs*, 5th ed (New York: Aldershot, Gale & Polden, 1961), 202. For more on the Kennedy assassination and funeral see *Four Days: The Historical Record of the Death of President Kennedy*, comp. United Press International and American Heritage Magazine (New York: American Heritage, 1964).

52. *New York Times*, July 12, 1964.

53. *New York Times*, Nov. 27, 1963.

54. Copyright © 1965 by W. H. Auden. Reprinted from Edward Mendelson, ed., *W. H. Auden: Collected Poems*, by permission of Random House, Inc.

55. Jack Valenti, *A Very Human President* (New York: W. W. Norton, 1975).

56. Mrs. Lyndon Johnson to Elise Kirk, Aug. 20, 1980.

57. Roger Stevens, "Report on the Formation of the Arts Foundation," typescript, 20, File—National Endowment for the Arts (NEA), Administrative History, White House Central Files [WHCF], Johnson Papers, LBJL, Austin, Tex. See also Elise Kirk, "Presidents and the Performing Arts—a Tribute to LBJ," *Dallas Civic Opera Magazine* 3 (1980): 72; Roger Stevens, "The First Annual Report of the National Council on the Arts, 1964-1965," typescript, File—NEA, Ad. Hist., WHCF, Johnson Papers. Sixty-three million dollars was appropriated to finance the first three years of the foundation program.

58. Isaac Stern in an interview with Elise Kirk, Dallas, Jan. 15, 1983. Abe Fortas, an old and valued friend of Stern, played duets with the noted artist on informal occasions at the White House.

59. Transcript, oral history interview with Abe Fortas by Joe Frantz, on Aug. 14, 1969, 19, Johnson Papers.

60. Transcript, oral history interview with S. Dillon Ripley by Thomas H. Baker, n.d., 7, ibid.

61. Juanita Roberts to George Thow, researcher, productions staff, the Lawrence Welk Show, May 5, 1964, GEN PPF 15-8, WHCF, ibid.

62. Lady Bird Johnson, *A White House Diary* (New York: Holt, Rinehart & Winston, 1970), 25-26. The barbecue was held on Dec. 29, 1963.

63. Irving Lowens, "Merrill and Minstrels Sing at White House," *Washington Star*, Jan. 15, 1964.

64. Paul Hume, "Light Years from Real Folk Song," *Washington Post*, Jan. 15, 1964.

65. Irving Lowens to Elise Kirk, Mar. 5, 1983; Harold Schonberg to Elise Kirk, Jan. 29, 1985.

66. *Washington Post*, Dec. 12, 1968.

67. Luci Johnson Turpin to Elise Kirk during "Modern First Ladies" conference, Gerald R. Ford Museum, Grand Rapids, Mich., Apr. 18-20, 1984.

68. Valenti, *Human President*, 78.

69. Keehn to Stegall, Nov. 16, 1964, Folder—Carol Channing, Social Files—Alpha, Box 327, Lady Bird Johnson Papers, LBJL.

70. Transcript, oral history interview with Erich Leinsdorf by Joe B. Frantz, Mar. 18, 1969, 7, 10, 11, Johnson Papers. See also miscellaneous correspondence in Leinsdorf Name File, Jan. 13, 1966–Feb. 23, 1968, WHCF, ibid.

71. Memo, Office of the White House Press Secretary, July 2, 1964, Social Files, Liz Carpenter's Files, Lady Bird Johnson Papers. Among the other recipients were Helen Keller, Carl Sandburg, T. S. Eliot, Walter Disney, Paul Dudley White, Reinhold Niebuhr, and Helen Taussig.

72. Remarks at a Reception Honoring American Artists, Winners in the Tchaikovsky International Music Competition in Moscow, September 7, 1966, *Public Papers of the Presidents of the United States*, vol. of 1966, Pt. II (Washington: Government Printing Office, 1966), 440-41.

73. Johnson to Kirk, Aug. 20, 1980.

74. Steinway/Kirk interview. Van Cliburn played Beethoven's Sonata in E-flat Major, op. 31, no. 3, and several Chopin selections on Apr. 10, 1968. Washington at the time was beset with uprisings. Crowds of 75,000 marched on Apr. 9, the day of King's funeral.

75. Elizabeth Carpenter, *Ruffles and Flourishes* (New York: Doubleday, 1970), 200-201. Merrill's program with Veronica Tyler was on Feb. 8, 1968. The president joked about the fuss made on the morning radio during his toast to the prime minister that evening: "Well, there they go again, always wanting me to dance to their tune." Press release, Feb. 8, 1968, Office of the White House Press Secretary, Social Files—Bess Abell, Box 23, Lady Bird Johnson Papers.

76. LBJ to Merrill, Oct. 8, 1965, Name File, WHCF, Johnson Papers.

77. Typed script, Salute to Congress File, Social Files—Bess Abell, Box 6. NBC-TV planned to cover portions of the event for inclusion in a special preconvention show on Aug. 19.

78. Nat Greenblatt to Barbara Keehn, Sept. 8, 1964, Nash Castro to Bess Abell, memo, Aug. 31, 1964, Salute to Congress File, Social Files—Bess Abell, Box 6, Lady Bird Johnson Papers. A program of quite a different nature was proposed by Secretary of the Interior Stewart Udall to Secretary of State Dean Rusk. Udall thought that the cabinet itself might sponsor an event that would include recitals by Pablo Casals and Leontyne Price with readings by Alfred Lunt and Sidney Poitier. See "Proposed Letter to Secretary Rusk and Other Cabinet Members," from Dean Rusk, Salute to Congress File, Social Files—Carpenter, Box 10, Lady Bird Johnson Papers.

79. Memorandum, n.d., Social Files—Bess Abell, Box 29, #4014, ibid.; press release, Office of the Press Secretary to Mrs. Johnson, Dec. 7, 1968, James Webb Folder, Social Files—Carpenter, Box 58, ibid.

80. Johnson, *White House Diary*, 738; Johnson to Kirk.

81. *Washington Post*, Sept. 30, 1965; "Fact Sheet on New Stage for East Room," Sept. 27, 1965, Social Files—Carpenter Press Releases, Lady Bird Johnson Papers; West/Kirk interview.

82. Office memorandum, U.S. government, memo for the record from Miss Paine, Jan. 2, 1964, MBHC.

83. Edie Adams, oral history interview with Joe B. Frantz, May 13, 1970, Johnson Papers; *New York Times*, Feb. 12, 14, Mar. 23, 1964.

84. Excerpt from Carpenter, *Ruffles and Flourishes*, reprinted in *Washington Evening Star*, Feb. 3, 1970.

85. *New York Times*, Jan. 19-23, 27, 1968; *Washington Evening Star*, Jan. 19, 1968; Carpenter, *Ruffles and Flourishes*, 206-7.

86. Letter to Mrs. Johnson, Jan. 23, 1968, Social Files, Alpha—Eartha Kitt, Box 1305, Lady Bird Johnson Papers.

87. Barbaralee D. Diamonstein to Eric F. Goldman, "Some Recollections of the White House Festival of the Arts" (typescript), May 11, 1966, GEN AR 7/26/65, Box 2, WHCF, Johnson Papers.

88. Ellington had played for President Eisenhower at a White House Correspondents dinner in Washington about ten years earlier. For more on Ellington at the White House, see Edward Kennedy Ellington, *Music Is My Mistress* (New York: Doubleday, 1973), 424-33.

89. To Mrs. Abell [*sic*] from American Embassy, Tokyo, June 3, 1965, White House Festival of the Arts Folder, Social Files—Bess Abell, Box 11, Lady Bird Johnson Papers.

90. Abell to Carpenter, hand-draft of memo, n.d., ibid. Carpenter, *Ruffles and Flourishes*, 208; Abell to Goldman, May 28, 1965, GEN AR 7/26/65, Box 2, WHCF, Johnson Papers.

91. Goldman to LBJ, Feb. 25, 1965, GEN AR 7/26/65, Box 2, WHCF, Johnson Papers.

92. *New York Herald Tribune*, June 15, 1965.

Chapter 13. Evenings at the White House

1. Paul Miller, in an interview with Elise Kirk, Ft. McNair, Washington, D.C., July 21, 1982.

2. Isabelle Shelton, "The President's Trumpeters," *Washington Sunday Star*, Mar. 22, 1970. See also George Farmer, *Rise and Development of Military Music* (London: W. Reeves, 1912), 18-19.

3. *The Memoirs of Richard Nixon* (New York: Grosset and Dunlap, 1978), 9, 14, 17.

4. Rex Scouten, in an interview with Elise Kirk, The White House, Aug. 5, 1982.

5. *Memoirs of Nixon*, 9.

6. The RIAA supplemented the recordings in 1980 during the Carter administration, and the entire collection remains in the White House today. A duplicate set is in Performing Arts Library of the John F. Kennedy Center.

7. Frank Getlein, "Nixon and the Arts," *New York Times Magazine*, Feb. 14, 1971.

8. Billy Taylor, in an interview with Elise Kirk, Washington, D.C., June 24, 1982.

9. Thomas Meehan, "Washington Society Isn't Exactly Swinging," *New York Times Magazine*, Mar. 8, 1970.

10. *Memoirs of Nixon*, 539.

11. Mel Gussow, "Mrs. Stuart: White House Impresario," *New York Times*, Feb. 24, 1970. Connie Stuart also served as Mrs. Nixon's press secretary until she was succeeded by Helen Smith in early 1973.

12. Donnie Radcliffe, "No House for Show Biz," *Washington Post*, July 27, 1973.

13. Vera Glaser and Malvina Stephenson, "Watchdogs at the White House," *Washington Evening Star*, Dec. 21, 1969.

14. *New York Times*, Jan. 23, 1970; *Washington Evening Star*, Jan. 20, 1970.

15. Alan Frank, *Sinatra* (New York: Hamlyn, 1978), 140-41. Anthony Ripley, "Sinatra at White House Gets Standing Ovation," *New York Times*, Apr. 18, 1973.

16. Nixon had twenty-six non-denominational Sunday worship services at the White House during his period in office. The Vienna Choir Boys, Danish Boys' Choir, several Hebrew choruses, and many other choirs performed. Programs are the property of the Office of the White House Curator.

17. *Memoirs of Nixon*, 540.

18. Taylor/Kirk interview; *New York Times*, Apr. 30, 1969; *Washington Evening Star*, Apr. 29, 1969. Duke Ellington died in New York City on May 24, 1974, at age seventy-five.

19. Glaser and Stephenson, "Watchdogs." Another important jazz program took place on Oct. 21, 1969, when the Modern Jazz Quartet played for the shah of Iran. President Nixon announced that after the concert there would be dancing to the "best Marine combo in the country." Apparently he had not been told that, for the first time in the memory of anyone, the Navy Band would be playing after a state dinner in the foyer.

20. Ted Thackery, Jr., "Star-Spangled Fete for Moon Pioneers," *Los Angeles Times*, Aug. 14, 1969.

21. Property of the U.S. Army Chorus, Brucker Hall, Ft. Myer, Arlington, Va.

22. Rex Scouten and Nelson Pierce, in an interview with Elise Kirk, The White House, Aug. 5, 1982. The Fords had Scouten construct a tent with a floor and carpet for the queen of England's visit, in order to avoid the muddy ground and guests' ruined shoes when Ford was vice-president.

23. James McCracken in an interview with Elise Kirk, Dallas, Nov. 11, 1982. See also Elise Kirk, "Playing the White House," *American Way* (Apr. 1983):149.

24. Rudolf Serkin performed Beethoven's Sonata in C Minor, op. 13 ("Pathetique"); and three Preludes from op. 28 and Polonaise in A-flat Major, op. 53, by Chopin on Feb. 19, 1970. The occasion was to open an exhibition of the paintings of Andrew Wyeth at the White House—the first time the presidential mansion had recognized a single living artist with a showing.

25. Eugene List, in an interview with Elise Kirk, Dallas, Mar. 21, 1981.

26. Isabella Shelton, "Music Salutes Israel's Leader," *Washington Evening Star*, Sept. 26, 1969.

27. Steinway to List, June 16, 1969, Steinway & Sons.

28. Steinway to Scouten, Apr. 23, 1969, Steinway & Sons.

29. Steinway/Kirk interview.

30. Scouten to Steinway, Apr. 23, 1970, property of Steinway & Sons

31. Steinway/Kirk interview.

32. *Washington Evening Star*, Feb. 6, Jan. 29, 1972.

33. Betty Beale, "Topless at the White House?" *Washington Sunday Star*, Feb. 6, 1972; Isabelle Shelton, "Moffo's Moorings Slip," *Washington Evening Star*, Oct. 27, 1970; Carpenter, *Ruffles and Flourishes*, 201; Christopher Lydon, "Beverly Sills Sings at the White House," *New York Times*, Feb. 3, 1971; Beverly Sills to Elise Kirk, Nov. 20, 1981.

34. Sally Quinn, "Bill Schustick Yo-Ho-Hos at the White House," *Washington Post*, Nov. 5, 1971.

35. Ibid.

36. Bruce Howard, "Whiffenpoofs Turn Deaf Ear to Nixon," *Washington Star-News*, Dec. 14, 1973.

37. List/Kirk interview.

38. Isabelle Shelton, "Host on the Ivories," *Washington Evening Star*, Mar. 8, 1974; "Notes on People," *New York Times*, Mar. 22, 1973.

39. Andrew Glass, "The Fords as Impresarios: Who Plays the White House— And Why?" *New York Times*, Sept. 14, 1975.

40. Ibid.

41. *New York Times*, June 13, 1975.

42. Betty Ford, *The Times of My Life* (New York: Harper and Row, 1978), 230.

43. Ibid., 231; Isabelle Shelton, "The Best Show Was the Late Show," *Washington Evening Star*, June 17, 1975.

44. Ford, *Times of My Life*, 229.

45. Ibid., 221.

46. *Washington Post*, Mar. 16, 1975. Mrs. Ford refused to accept the State Department's "leftover guest lists." "The State Department used to send over proposed guest lists," she said, "and they were so dreary we hardly ever used them, because State tried to hold back all the glittering people for themselves, for Henry Kissinger's famous luncheons." Ford, *Times of My Life*, 223.

47. Taylor/Kirk interview.

48. Video cassette of the program, property of the Gerald R. Ford Library, Ann Arbor, Mich. Bob Hope, a native of England, was master of ceremonies.

There was no biographical information about Captain and Tennille on the printed program, but Hope had four long paragraphs, "the only performer who has triumphed in all five show business media: vaudeville, stage, radio, motion pictures and television."

49. "Remarks upon Presenting the Presidential Medal of Freedom to Artur Rubinstein," Apr. 1, 1976, in *Public Papers of the Presidents of the United States: Gerald R. Ford*, 1 (Washington: Government Printing Office, 1979), 881-82.

50. Artur Rubinstein's response to the president's remarks appear on an audio recording cassette, the property of the Ford Library.

51. Anna Kisselgolff, "Martha Graham Hailed by Nation; Given Freedom Medal by Ford," *New York Times*, Oct. 15, 1976. "It is interesting that Martha Graham had pursued her career almost exclusively without government subsidy until only recently," the *Times* reported. The day that Ford presented the Medal of Freedom to Graham he announced at a news conference that he was asking Congress for $50 million more for a new "challenge" grant program for the NEA.

52. Betty Beale, " 'Lowbrow' Entertainment at the White House," *Washington Sunday Star*, July 29, 1973; Charlie McCollum, "What's the Matter with Rock at the White House Anyway?" *Washington Sunday Star*, July 18, 1976.

53. Ibid.

Chapter 14. Music, Mass Media, and the Modern White House

1. Message to the National Assembly of State Arts Agencies in *Carter on the Arts* (New York: ACA Publications, 1977), 44.

2. "President is serious about music," Springfield (Mass.) *Morning Union*, Mar. 4, 1977.

3. *Carter on the Arts*, 17.

4. Col. John Bourgeois in an interview with Elise Kirk, Marine Barracks, Washington, D.C., Feb. 12, 1982. Bourgeois was especially impressed with the genuine attention and recognition President Carter gave the Marine Band.

5. Andrew Glass, "Sound of Music—Culture in the Carter White House," *New York Times*, Mar. 13, 1977.

6. Rosalynn Carter in a telephone interview with Elise Kirk, Dallas/Atlanta, Feb. 22, 1984. See also Rosalynn Carter, *First Lady from Plains* (Boston: Houghton Mifflin, 1984).

7. Guest list for Horowitz concert, courtesy of Irving and Margery Lowens. See also Glenn Plaskin, *Horowitz* (New York: William Morrow, 1983), 435.

8. Scouten/Kirk interview; Carter/Kirk interview.

9. Harold Schonberg, "Horowitz Plays for Carter," *New York Times*, Feb. 27, 1978. "For this event, they roll out the carpet," *Washington Star*, Feb. 27, 1978; Irving Lowens review in ibid.

10. Linda Charlton, "Horowitz Deal Disclosed," *New York Times*, May 12, 1978.

11. Donnie Radcliffe, "Diva and the President," *Washington Post*, Oct. 9, 1978.

12. Paul Henderson, "Light and Magic in the East Room," ibid., Feb. 26, 1979. See also video cassette of rehearsal, Feb. 23, 1979, Carter Projects, NARS.

13. Hugh Sidney, "In Celebration of Peace," *Time*, Apr. 9, 1979.

14. Gretchen Poston in an interview with Elise Kirk, Washington, D.C., July 7, 1981.

15. MSgt. James Kessler in an interview with Elise Kirk, Brucker Hall, Ft. Myer, Va., Aug. 6, 1982.

16. John Wilson, "Carter Opens Home to Jazz as an Art," *New York Times*, June 19, 1978. See also Jacqueline Trescott and Joseph McLellan, "A Who's Who of Jazz on the South Lawn," *Washington Post*, June 19, 1978, and Taylor/Kirk interview.

17. Wilson, "Carter Opens Home."

18. Gospel Music Association. Remarks at a White House Performance, Sept. 9, 1979, in *Public Papers of the Presidents of the United States: Jimmy Carter* (Washington: Government Printing Office, 1979-80), 2:1614-15.

19. Poston/Kirk interview.

20. McCracken/Kirk interview.

21. Poston/Kirk interview.

22. White House Promenade. Remarks at the Reception for Members of Congress and Their Families, May 20, 1978, in *Public Papers: Carter*, 1:944-45.

23. Poston/Kirk interview.

24. Up Front. "The New Star Wars: Celebrity Politics Becomes Part of the Game," *People*, Mar. 1982.

25. Laurence Leamer, *Make Believe: The Story of Nancy and Ronald Reagan* (New York: Harper & Row, 1983), 2.

26. Tony Thomas, *The Films of Ronald Reagan* (Secaucus, N.J.: Citadel Press, 1980), 119.

27. Ibid., 9.

28. Sharon Rich, *Jeanette McDonald: A Pictorial Treasury* (Los Angeles: Time Mirror Press, 1973), 211.

29. *Newsweek*, Apr. 12, 1982; Elisabeth Burmiller and Donnie Radcliffe, "Nancy Reagan, the First Two Years," *Washington Post*, Jan. 23, 1983; Donnie Radcliffe, "First Lady Steals Show," ibid., Mar. 29, 1982.

30. Mabel Brandon in an interview with Elise Kirk, the White House, Jan. 8, 1982.

31. *Christian Science Monitor*, Sept. 18, 1981.

32. Remarks made by Mrs. Reagan introducing the program, "In Performance at the White House," Nov. 22, 1981. Unless otherwise indicated, all quotations and information from the "In Performance at the White House" series have been drawn from the author's attendance at the concerts and rehearsals as well as viewing the telecasts.

33. For more on this program, see Alan M. Kriegsman, "Dazzlers on Their Toes," *Washington Post*, Mar. 30, 1982; Irving Molotsky, "Gene Kelly Brings Young Dancers to White House," *New York Times*, Mar. 29, 1982.

34. John Ardoin, "The Haggard Style Captivates Reagans," *Dallas Morning News*, Apr. 23, 1982; *Newsweek*, Mar. 22, 1982.

35. "Chance to Appear on 'In Performance at the White House' is Break of a Lifetime for Two Young Jazz Musicians," News release, WETA, Washington, D.C., Dec. 1982.

36. Occupying the special presidential box, the Reagans traditionally attend the two and one-half-hour gala at the Kennedy Center, which presents the five honorees who had been recognized at a White House reception beforehand. The first recipients (in 1978) were Marian Anderson, Fred Astaire, George Balanchine, Richard Rodgers, and Artur Rubinstein.

37. Richard Harrington, "Lionel Hampton's South Lawn Serenade," *Washington Post*, Sept. 11, 1981.

38. Brandon/Kirk interview.

39. Burmiller/Radcliffe, "Nancy Reagan."

40. Scouten/Kirk interview.

41. Brandon/Kirk interview.

42. Scouten/Kirk interview.

43. Ibid. Rex Scouten was succeeded by the new chief usher, Gary Walters, in January 1986.

44. *New York Times*, Dec. 25, 1981.

45. Paul Miller in an interview with Elise Kirk, Ft. McNair, Washington, D.C., July 21, 1982.

46. Ibid.

47. Bourgeois/Kirk interview.

48. The following details were part of the notes printed on the White House program for this concert: "Presumed lost for more than two centuries, the Symphony was written in 1765, when Mozart was nine years old. It was known only as a fifteen-measure fragment scribbled in his father's hand on the back of another composition's title page until it was discovered among some private papers in West Germany last fall. The original manuscript was subsequently sold to the Bavarian State Library, and arrangements for the Mostly Mozart Festival performances have been made through the German music publishing house of Barenreiter Verlag, owners of the worldwide copyright."

49. *Washington Post*, June 13, 14, 1983.

50. Brandon/Kirk interview.

BIBLIOGRAPHICAL ESSAY

Accompanying each chapter of this text, notes present details of the sources most directly related to the project. This survey is offered primarily to guide the reader through the general categories of materials consulted, at the same time noting their relevance and accessibility. The most important single tool for researching White House history is Ann Duncan Brown's *The White House: A Bibliographical List* (Washington, D.C.: Library of Congress, 1953; suppl., 1960), which contains almost every article, book, and monograph on the White House furnishings, the presidents, first families, and life at the mansion. This valuable index needs to be updated, however, and also to include works relating to music. The important materials that should be added are Helen Cripe's *Thomas Jefferson and Music* (Charlottesville: University Press of Virginia, 1974); Kenneth Bernard's *Lincoln and the Music of the Civil War* (Caldwell, Idaho: Caxton, 1966); and H. Earle Johnson's "The Adams Family and Good Listening" (*JAMS*, summer-fall, 1958). For George Washington, Nicholas Tawa's "Music in the Washington Household" (*Journal of American Culture* [Spring 1978]) and Judith Britt's *Nothing More Agreeable* (Mt. Vernon: Mt. Vernon Ladies Association, 1984) are relevant.

The handful of other books and articles on early White House social life, including a few articles on presidents and music, must be read with caution, since the authors rarely have considered primary sources and tend to pass down the same anecdotal errors (the production of *La traviata* for James Buchanan, for instance). The best single book on the White House is Esther Singleton's pioneer study, *The Story of the White House*, 2 volumes (New York: McClure, 1907). While this was a fine source for its day and utilizes primary materials, it lacks documentation and leaves the reader wondering where all those marvelous quotations originated. The series of guide books published by the White House Historical Association are excellent for the general reader. The association has also issued a new journal, *White House History*, and plans to publish a comprehensive history of the mansion. But the most outstanding book on the White House is Margaret Klapthor's scholarly and fascinating *Official White House China 1789 to the Present* (Washington, D.C.: Smithsonian Institution Press, 1975). For government records relating to the mansion's furnishings, this study is a remarkable source. These records led me to the identification

of numerous pianos that were placed in the White House during the
nineteenth century and thus reinforced my conviction that the mansion
was indeed a musically active home from its earliest days.

To locate information about the pianos (often derived from tuning
receipts), and anything else musical that I could find, I spent several
months plowing through inventories at the National Archives. These
records included the vouchers and expense accounts of Record Group
217, Miscellaneous Treasury Accounts for the President's House (1800–
1867) and Record Group 42, correspondence relating to purchases filed
with the Office of Public Buildings and Grounds (1867–1901). In order
to locate the account, one must be familiar with the names of those
who served as commissioners of public buildings during the early
history of Washington, and here Klapthor's book and her personal
suggestions were invaluable. Somehow through all of this I kept hearing
the late Irving Lowens's words that I would encounter a great deal of
"negative" research in writing on White House musical history. No
truer words were spoken. And so I opened with great care the hundreds
of musty, crumbling inventories with their chipped wax seals, untying
their faded red ribbons hopefully. If I found few piano vouchers, I was
sure I had located the *original* government "red tape." Among all
these White House expenses were every gold spittoon, picture hook,
and chimney sweeping and water closet repair bill possible. Imagine
my delight when there appeared evidence of the earliest collection of
music purchased for the mansion—Madame Le Pelletier's exquisite
Journal of Musick, published in Philadelphia in 1810!

Other important materials consulted were the biographies, diaries,
memoirs, and state papers, both published and in manuscript, of the
presidents and first ladies. The most useful of *The Public Papers of
the Presidents of the United States*, comprising speeches, statements,
and reports arranged chronologically for each president, were the later
series for Lyndon Johnson, Richard Nixon, Gerald Ford, Jimmy Carter,
and Ronald Reagan, in which the various presidents' remarks about
music were often included. But the real gems were found in the un-
published papers. In myriads of fascinating nooks, crannies, and byways
lay the memos, correspondence, clippings, programs, and guest lists
relating to musical events at the White House. The papers of the
presidents before Herbert Hoover are housed at the Library of Congress
(the Adams family at the Massachusetts Historical Society) and available
on microfilm. Indices to the papers are helpful, but frequently a musical
matter will be hidden in letters to now obscure personages.

The true legwork for my research began with extended visits to
each of the presidential libraries where the archives of the modern
chief executives are housed. Beginning with Herbert Hoover, these
libraries with their accompanying museums are located in towns and
cities associated with the presidents and are spread across the country.
Aside from my having to walk a good distance along the highway
each day in snowy minus-four-degree weather to reach the Hoover
Library in West Branch, Iowa, the locations of the libraries (Hoover,
Roosevelt, Truman, Eisenhower, Kennedy, Johnson, and Ford) enabled

me to sense the immediacy of the presidential office and become familiar with the flow of changing administrations, unequaled by any other means. The papers for Nixon and Carter are contained in the National Archives, and only the audio-visual materials are open to the public at the present time; the Carter library is being built in Atlanta, Georgia, however, and is scheduled for completion in 1986. Systems of filing and retrieving information vary from library to library and grow more complex with the later administrations. At the Johnson library, for example, the White House Central Files, which contain most of the presidential papers, are subdivided according to Name, Subject (Executive and General), and Confidential files with a detailed system of cross-reference. One must learn the names of important members of the White House staffs under each administration, moreover, since needed materials are often filed under their names.

There were moments when I had the feeling I was spying on the intricate memoing network of the White House. Where else could one find, on an official memo that had passed through several channels, the president's own handwriting vetoing a musical group that asked to play at the White House? The Papers of Harry S. Truman, moreover, are especially revealing. Reflecting his keen interest in music, President Truman's letters, diaries, and memoranda in his own hand occasionally contain some titillating notes: on one file, "Music—Personal. See me. *Important—Personal.*" Another fascinating body of materials in the presidential libraries comprises the autograph letters from prominent concert artists, composers, and entertainers filed alphabetically—and inconspicuously—along with John Doe and everyone else in America who wrote to the president.

For White House programs and details surrounding a musical event, the superb staffs of each of the libraries managed to review and pull materials for me from files not yet opened, mainly those of the first ladies. Only Eleanor Roosevelt's papers are available at present, although those of Mrs. Lyndon Johnson and Mrs. Herbert Hoover are currently being opened for general research. Perusing the day-by-day schedules of each of the presidents, moreover, reveals that the musical life of the mansion seemed to go on regardless of the onerous duties of the chief of state.

A study of the audio-visual materials in the presidential libraries illustrates the increased importance and visibility of the concerts from the period of John F. Kennedy onward. Photographs of performers appearing at the White House do not exist before this administration. Beginning with Lyndon Johnson, recordings and films were made of selected programs by the White House Communications Agency; however, the sound was often discontinued after the president's speech, leaving singers with their mouths open and famous pianists with their arms wildly thrashing. Tape recordings of many of the concerts during the 1960s are in the Music Division of the Library of Congress, and the Pablo Casals concert under the Kennedys is available commercially (Co. AKL5926). Historic early engravings, lithographs, photographs, and drawings were found in the collections of the Library of Congress,

New York Public Library, Associated Press, United Press International, White House Curator's Office, Bettmann Archive, the Marine Band Library, Smithsonian Institution, Hoblitzelle Theater Arts Library, and other sources listed in the Picture Credits.

Like the photographs and recordings, newspaper coverage of White House entertainment reflects changing attitudes on the part of both the public and the first families as to their significance. Rutherford Hayes, conscious of his dignified image after the corruptions of the Ulysses Grant administration, probably encouraged the press to cover his many musicales, because the *National Republican* of this period scarcely missed an event. Reporters began regularly reviewing the state dinners as social affairs under William McKinley, but music was rarely mentioned. Calvin Coolidge flatly refused to allow a choir concert to be broadcast from the White House via radio, and FDR, first of the "media monarchs," allowed not one of the 300 musicales to be covered by the papers, although Eleanor Roosevelt mentioned many of them in her "My Day" column. The first music critics came under Dwight Eisenhower's last years during America's great cultural boom, continued prominently through Kennedy's administration, but reviewed only occasionally under Johnson's tenure. The Nixon, Ford, and Carter programs received front-page coverage with photographs, but the Reagan state dinner concerts have had less press attention. As former film personalities, the president and first lady have chosen an artistic and effective alternative to show their support of the performing arts through their fine series of PBS telecasts, which are reviewed regularly.

The printed programs for White House musical entertainment are obviously rich sources for the study of the repertory itself. The earliest in this genre is the program of dances for Andrew Johnson's Juvenile Soirée on December 28, 1868, property of the White House Curator's Office. Programs for the musicales began with those printed on satin during the Benjamin Harrison period and are located among the Harrison Presidential Papers housed at the Library of Congress. For programs during the administrations of McKinley through Coolidge the presidential papers are also useful, as are the manuscript collections of White House social aides, T. A. Bingham and Irwin Hood Hoover, also in the Library of Congress. From the turn of the century to the present, White House entertainment records and programs were pasted into large leather-bound scrapbooks. The first of these series is entitled "Official White House Social Functions" (1902–15) and comprises twenty-one volumes contained in the National Archives relating to the active social life of Theodore Roosevelt, William Howard Taft, and Woodrow Wilson's earlier years. The remaining series are in the White House Curator's Office and the various presidential libraries. A collection of programs from various administrations beginning with Franklin Roosevelt is in the Ralph E. Becker Collection, Division of Political History at the Smithsonian. For the Reagan administration I received printed programs from the White House Social Office and from three events that I attended: the Itzak Perlman/Ken Noda "Young Performers" telecast on November 7, 1982; the Congressional Children's concert on July 13, 1982; and the arrival ceremony for Prime Minister Indira Gandhi of India on the South Lawn, July 28, 1982. The thrill of watching research into 180 years of music history come alive before my eyes matched my gratitude in being allowed to witness these fine events.

To locate musical instruments, scores, and memorabilia associated with presidential families, I wrote to over 200 historic sites commemorating the presidency—birthplaces, residences, monuments, and other structures—most operated by the National Park Service. The result was gratifying, but the most important collections of music were found at Mt. Vernon, Woodlawn Plantation, Harvard University, and the Library of Congress (Nelly Custis's music); the White House Curator's Office (Zachary Taylor's family music); the Smithsonian (Louisa Catherine Adams's scores), and the Library of Congress (Abigail Fillmore's music). The Rutherford B. Hayes Presidential Center holds hymnals of the Hayeses during their White House years as well as the unique, beautifully illuminated 110-page Social Register kept by O. L. Pruden under the direction of Webb Hayes, the president's son and personal secretary. The music at the presidential libraries from Hoover on, especially the large collection of scores at the Truman and FDR libraries, ranges from pieces sent in by the public to early family sheet music. All were not necessarily used at the White House. Sorting out the function and significance of this music was problematic, often frustrating.

An important collection for this study was the records of the U.S. Marine Band housed in the Marine Band Library and at the Marine Corps Historical Center. These archives contain scores, early band programs, government records on microfilm, leader's logs from 1917 to the present, a compendium of useful clippings entitled "Marine Band Chronology, 1798–1954," and other items valuable for rounding out the ceremonial and musical history of the White House. Additional sources for this project are too numerous to cite in detail. They comprise American political and musical histories; early histories of military bands in both Europe and America; studies of social and theatrical life in Washington, D.C.; theses; congressional records; recollections and diaries of former first ladies, Washington socialites, diplomats, and reporters; and various oral histories located in the presidential libraries. Published biographies of famous performers often mention a program they presented at the White House, and I had a busy one year and four summers in Washington, linking and verifying leads, clues, and hunches in the manuscripts housed in the magnificent Jefferson, Adams, and Madison buildings of the Library of Congress. The joy of having at my disposal the wonders of those resources cannot be overemphasized, and the recollections, moods, and ambience of our nation's capital will remain key elements in the message of this book.

ACKNOWLEDGMENTS

This book could not have been realized without the help and support of many curators, archivists, librarians, friends, and others who generously shared with me their recollections about White House musical life. Regretfully, I cannot mention them all without embarking on another book in itself, but their dedication and assistance have been deeply appreciated. The main organization that sponsored my project was the Smithsonian Institution. A postdoctoral fellowship enabled me to spend a year and four summers in the Division of Political History, National Museum of American History, consulting with the excellent staff and utilizing the vast resources of this prestigious museum. I am also grateful to the Lyndon Baines Johnson Foundation for its assistance and to Southern Methodist University for granting me a leave from teaching for two semesters to work on my project in Washington.

A word of thanks is hardly adequate to express to Margaret Klapthor—my advisor, mentor, and friend at the Smithsonian—all that her help has meant to my spirit as well as scholarship. As curator emeritus of the Division of Political History, Mrs. Klapthor has been responsible for the First Ladies Hall for many years, and her knowledge and writings on the White House are well known. In spite of rigorous professional demands on her time, she was never too busy to talk with me, answer questions, and care about my work when I needed such assurance desperately. Other Smithsonian curators to whom I am indebted are Herbert Collins (Political History), Helen Hollis and Bob Sheldon (Musical Instruments), Carl Scheele (Community Life), Harold Langley (Naval History), and Rodris Roth (Domestic Life). Eleanor Boynge, former secretary of the Division of Political History, kindly answered phone calls and took messages that kept me in touch with the outside world while I was buried in secluded archives.

In addition to the Smithsonian, the White House staff itself was a patient, supportive, and authoritative pillar for my work. The associate curator, Betty Monkman, not only allowed me to consult and photocopy programs, records of social events, photographs, and documents in the Office of the White House Curator, but also answered my questions about the mansion with her characteristic expertise. The first social secretary under the Reagans, Mabel ("Muffie") Brandon, and her assistant, Linda Faulkner, who became social secretary in 1985, provided programs and arranged for me to attend certain White House rehearsals and concerts and—most exciting of all—to meet the president and first lady. Diane Powers and Carol Greenawalt in the White House Photo Office were most gracious, and my long interview with the chief usher, Rex Scouten, and his assistant, Nelson Pierce, was invaluable.

Interviewing important personalities added a touch of humanity to my manuscript that cannot be measured. I recall with sincerest gratitude my long conversation with Rosalynn Carter and interviews with Todd Duncan, Eugene List, James McCracken, Mstislav Rostropovich, Isaac Stern, Billy Taylor, and many other artists. The following persons also associated with White House entertainment kindly allowed me to interview them:

Letitia Baldridge, social secretary under John F. Kennedy
Colonel John Bourgeois, leader, U.S. Marine Band
Mabel Brandon, social secretary under Ronald Reagan
Mildred Hall Campbell, secretary for Mrs. Herbert Hoover
Marta Istomin, artistic director, John F. Kennedy Center
Mary Jane McCaffree (Mrs. Henry Monroe, Jr.), secretary for Mrs. Dwight Eisenhower
Paul Miller, director of ceremonies, Military District of Washington
Gilbert Mitchell, coordinator of music, funeral of John F. Kennedy
Howard Mitchell, former conductor, National Symphony Orchestra
Gretchen Poston, social secretary under Jimmy Carter
William Santelmann, former leader, U.S. Marine Band
John Steinway, former chairman, Steinway & Sons, New York
Bernard M. West, former chief usher, the White House.

Impressive to me was the personal attention I received from archivists associated with specific resources. Special thanks is offered to Frank Byrne, chief librarian of the Marine Band Library, for his fine cooperation and to the following helpful individuals associated with the presidential libraries.

Cora F. Pederson and Dale Mayer, Herbert Hoover Library, West Branch, Iowa
John Ferris and Mark Renovitch, Franklin D. Roosevelt Library; Susan Brown, Roosevelt Home, Hyde Park, New York
Elizabeth Safly, Warren Ohrvall, and Erwin Mueller, Harry S. Truman Library, Independence, Missouri
James Leyerzapf and Kathy Novak, Dwight D. Eisenhower Library, Abilene, Kansas
William Johnson, Megan Desnoyers, and Allan Goodrich, John F. Kennedy Library, Boston, Massachusetts
Nancy Smith, Tina Lawson, Linda Hanson, and E. Philip Scott, Lyndon B. Johnson Library, Austin, Texas
Holley Wilson, Richard NcNiel, Fynette Eaton, and Robert Bohanan, Nixon and Carter Projects, National Archives and Records Services, Washington, D.C.

Leesa Tobin, Dennis Daellenbach, and Richard Holzhausen, Gerald R. Ford Library, Ann Arbor, Michigan.

Other individuals were also of great assistance:

Esme E. Bahn, Mooreland-Spingarn Research Center, Howard University, Washington, D.C.

Paul M. Bailey, Hoblitzelle Theater Arts Library, University of Texas, Austin

Joseph Barnes, chief musician, Public Affairs, U.S. Navy Band, Washington, D.C.

James A. Bear, Jr., curator, Monticello, Virginia

Judson E. Bennett, Richard Long, Charles Wood, and Carol Nowicke, Marine Corps Historical Center, Washington, D.C.

Robert L. Brubaker, curator of Special Collections, Chicago Historical Society

Thomas Burney, Rare Books; Oliver Orr, Lincoln specialist; and John McConough, director, Manuscript Division, Library of Congress

Sally Smith Cahalan, James Buchanan, Foundation for the Preservation of Wheatland, Lancaster, Pennsylvania

Theora David, White House Photographers Association, Washington, D.C.

Roxanna Dean, supervisor, Washingtoniana Collection, Martin Luther King Memorial Library, Washington, D.C.

Perry Gerard Fisher, executive director, Columbia Historical Society, Washington, D.C.

Joyce Goulait, Photographic Services, Smithsonian Institution

Wilhelmina S. Harris, Adams National Historic Site, Quincy, Massachusetts

James J. Hestin, former director, New–York Historical Society

Jane Holahan, Fine Arts Division, Dallas Public Library

Richard Jackson, head, Americana Division, Music Reading Room, Performing Arts Research Center, New York Public Library

James Kessler, arranger, U.S. Army Band, Ft. Myer, Virginia

James Ketchum, curator of the Senate, U.S. Capitol

Hugh A. Lawing, park historian, Andrew Johnson National Historic Site, Greeneville, Tennessee

Donald Leavitt, chief, Jon Newsom and staff, Music Division, Library of Congress

Watt P. Marchman, former director, and Leslie H. Fishel, director, Rutherford B. Hayes Presidential Center, Fremont, Ohio

Frances D. McClure, Walter Havighurst Special Collections, Miami University, Oxford, Ohio.

Bernard Meyer, executive vice-president, White House Historical Association, Washington, D.C.

George H. O'Connor, George O'Connor Collection, Lauinger Memorial Library, Georgetown University, Washington, D.C.

Genevieve Oswald, Dance Collection, Performing Arts Research Center, New York Public Library

Dorothy Provine, Record Group 42, National Archives and Records Service

Francis Rainey, Home of James K. Polk, Columbia, Tennessee

Pat Ronsheim, President Benjamin Harrison Memorial Home, Indianapolis, Indiana

Herman Sass, senior librarian, Buffalo and Erie County Historical Association, Buffalo, New York

Anne B. Shepherd, curator of manuscripts, Cincinnati Historical Society

Florian Thayne, architect of the Capitol, U.S. Capitol

Wendy Weber, Mrs. Reagan's Press Office, The White House

David Zeidberg, director, Special Collections, George Washington University Library, Washington, D.C.

To the following individuals, who kindly answered my queries and provided important, specific pieces of information, many, many thanks: Elizabeth C. Abell (Bess), Mary Aladj, Ralph Becker, Judith Britt, John S. Burroughs, Joan Challinor, Eliott Chapo, Francis Grover Cleveland, John Coolidge, Clement Conger, Margaret Truman Daniel, Mrs. Gerald Ford, Malcolm Frager, Martha Graham, Dale Harpham, Queen Noor al Hussein of the Hashimite Kingdom of Jordan, Mrs. Lyndon Johnson, Gene Kelly, Estelle Ball Kuhl, William Lichtenwanger, Ruth Lipman, Irving and Margery Lowens, Charles Francis Lombard, Betty Martin, Mrs. Jacqueline Onassis, Vivian Perlis, Roberta Peters, Ronald Prescott Reagan, James Roosevelt, Francis B. Sayer, Harold Schonberg, Eleanor Seagraves, Beverly Sills, Bobby Short, Henry Z. Steinway, John R. Truman, Nancy Tuckerman, Luci Johnson Turpin, D. Gardiner Tyler, Fred Waring, Helen White, and the fine staffs of numerous presidential historic sites.

I am grateful to the following publications for material that I drew from my own articles: *Opera News* ("Nightingales at the White House," Nov. 1, 1980); *American Way* ("Playing the White House," Apr. 1983); *The Magazine Antiques* ("Pianos in the White House," May 1984); *Kennedy Center Stagebill* ("American Celebration," Jan. 21, 1985); and the Library of Congress's *Performing Arts Annual*, premiere issue ("The Inaugural Concert in the Nineteenth Century," 1986). I also appreciate the helpful comments of Gilbert Chase, Dena Epstein, and Margaret Klapthor, who all read my manuscript with care and perception, and the capable work of the staff of the University of Illinois Press. Finally, I offer thanks to my family and many friends, whose interest and enthusiasm provided a loving, human continuum during the many years of my research for *Music at the White House.*

PICTURE CREDITS

The black-and-white illustrations used in *Music at the White House* are courtesy of: page 8, New-York Historical Society; page 10, Library of Congress; page 12, Music Division, New York Public Library at Lincoln Center, Astor, Lenox and Tilden Foundations; page 15, Library of Congress; page 16, Mt. Vernon Ladies Association; pages 17 and 21, Library of Congress; page 25, White House Collection; page 27, Thomas Jefferson Memorial Foundation; page 29, Naval Historical Center; page 33, National Museum of American History, Smithsonian Institution; page 36, New-York Historical Society; page 38, Library of Congress; page 40, Colt Clavier Collection, Bethersden (Ashford), England; page 44, Library of Congress; pages 46 and 47, Adams-Clement Collection, National Museum of American History, Smithsonian Institution; pages 50 and 52, Library of Congress; page 54, Franklin D. Roosevelt Library; page 59, Music Division, New York Public Library at Lincoln Center, Astor, Lenox and Tilden Foundations; page 60, Hoblitzelle Theater Arts Collection; page 63, Library of Congress; page 65, Lester Levy Sheet Music Collection, Milton S. Eisenhower Library, Johns Hopkins University; page 66, Library of Congress; page 71, Buffalo and Erie County Historical Society; page 73, Library of Congress; pages 76 and 77, Music Division, New York Public Library at Lincoln Center, Astor, Lenox and Tilden Foundations; page 79, White House Collection; page 82, Chicago Historical Society; page 84, Library of Congress; page 87, Record Group 42, OPB&G, National Archives and Records Services; page 88, Library of Congress; page 101, Print Division, New York Public Library; page 104, Library of Congress; page 105, Record Group 42, OPB&G, National Archives and Records Services; page 108, Library of Congress; page 109, Marine Band Library; page 110, Library of Congress; pages 115 and 118, Library of Congress; page 119, Hoblitzelle Theater Arts Collection; page 122, Library of Congress; pages 123 and 125, Hoblitzelle Theater Arts Collection; page 130, Department of Defense photograph (Marine Corps), Marine Band Library; page 134, top and bottom, Hoblitzelle Theater Arts Collection; pages 139, 141, 142, 143, 145, top and bottom, Library of Congress; page 149, Benjamin Harrison Papers, Library of Congress; page 152, Music Division, New York Public Library at Lincoln Center, Astor, Lenox and Tilden Foundations; page 155, Library of Congress; page 159, Moorland-Spingarn Research Center; page 160, Library of Congress; page 173, top and bottom, National Museum of American History, Smithsonian Institution; page 175, photograph by London Stereoscopic Co., Music Division, New York Public Library at Lincoln Center, Astor, Lenox and Tilden Foundations; page 177, Hoblitzelle Theater Arts Collection; page 178, top, middle, and bottom, T. A. Bingham Papers, Library of Congress; page 181, photograph by Apeda of New York, Hoblitzelle Theater Arts Collection; page 184, Carnegie Library of Pittsburgh; page 187, left and right, Record Group 42, OPB&G, National Archives and

Records Services; pages 190 and 191, Hoblitzelle Theater Arts Collection; page 193, photograph by Pach Brothers of New York, Library of Congress; page 195, Music Division, New York Public Library at Lincoln Center, Astor, Lenox and Tilden Foundations; page 201, UPI/Bettmann Archive; page 203, National Photo Company; page 204, World Wide Photo, Franklin D. Roosevelt Library; page 205, Naval Historical Center; page 209, National Museum of American History, Smithsonian Institution; page 211, top, Hoblitzelle Theater Arts Collection; page 211, bottom, White House Collection; page 213, top and bottom, Hoblitzelle Theater Arts Collection; page 215, top and bottom, White House Collection; page 216, Library of Congress; page 218, top, middle, and bottom, Hoblitzelle Theater Arts Collection; page 231, Bettmann Archive; page 232, Music Division, New York Public Library at Lincoln Center, Astor, Lenox and Tilden Foundations; page 233, Franklin D. Roosevelt Library; page 235, Bettmann Archive; page 237, top and bottom, Franklin D. Roosevelt Library; page 238, White House Collection; page 241, Library of Congress; page 242, Music Division, New York Public Library at Lincoln Center, Astor, Lenox and Tilden Foundations; page 243, World Wide Photo, Franklin D. Roosevelt Library; page 244, National Archives and Records Services; page 246, Bettmann Archive; page 247, Hoblitzelle Theater Arts Collection; page 249, Franklin D. Roosevelt Library; page 251, *Time* photograph, Franklin D. Roosevelt Library; page 255, Montreal *Gazette*, Harry Truman Library; page 257, World Wide Photo, Harry Truman Library; page 261, St. Louis *Post Dispatch*, Oct. 30, 1949, Harry Truman Library; page 262, United Press International, Jan. 4, 1946, Harry Truman Library; page 263, Acme Newspictures, United Press International, Harry Truman Library; page 265, World Wide Photo, Harry Truman Library; page 269, United Press International, Dwight D. Eisenhower Library; pages 270 and 273, Dwight D. Eisenhower Library; page 275, Hoblitzelle Theater Arts Collection; page 276, Music Division, New York Public Library at Lincoln Center, Astor, Lenox and Tilden Foundations; pages 291 and 292, John F. Kennedy Library; page 294, Abbie Rowe photograph, John F. Kennedy Library; pages 296 and 297, John F. Kennedy Library; page 303, Boosey and Hawkes Inc.; page 304, © News Group Chicago, Inc., Jacob Burck, Chicago *Sun-Times*; page 307, Lyndon Baines Johnson Library; page 311, Knudsen photograph, Lyndon Baines Johnson Library; pages 321, 323, and 326, Nixon Projects, National Archives and Records Services; page 331, Gerald R. Ford Library; page 341, top and bottom, Carter Projects, National Archives and Records Services; page 344, Donald J. Crump, *National Geographic* staff, White House Historical Association; page 351, Bill Fitz-Patrick, The White House; page 352, Michael Evans, The White House; page 357, Marine Band Library; page 359, Steven Purcell, The White House.

The color illustrations in signature one are courtesy of: first page, top, Mount Vernon Ladies Association; first page, bottom, National Museum of American History, Smithsonian Institution; second page, top, I. N. Phelps Stokes Collection, New York Public Library at Lincoln Center, Astor, Lenox and Tilden Foundations; second page, bottom, Adams-Clement Collection, National Museum of American Art; third page, Dance Collections, New York Public Library at Lincoln Center, Astor, Lenox and Tilden Foundations; fourth page, Music Division, New York Public Library at Lincoln Center, Astor, Lenox and Tilden Foundations; fifth page, Hoblitzelle Theater Arts Collection; sixth page, Rutherford B. Hayes Presidential Center; seventh page, top, Hoblitzelle Theater Arts Collection; seventh page, bottom, White House Historical Society; eighth page, Marine Band Library.

The color illustrations in signature two are courtesy of: first page, top and bottom, John F. Kennedy Library; second page, top, Lyndon Baines Johnson Library; second page, bottom, Joseph J. Scherschel, White House Historical Association; third page, top and bottom, Nixon Projects, National Archives and Records Services; fourth page, top and bottom, Gerald R. Ford Library; fifth page, Gerald R. Ford Library; sixth page, top and bottom, Carter Projects, National Archives and Records Services; seventh page, Jack Kightlinger, The White House; eighth page, top and bottom, Jack Kightlinger, The White House.

INDEX

Note on the Author

Elise K. Kirk, Ph.D., is an author, lecturer, and musicologist who has taught at Southern Methodist University and the City University of New York. She studied music at the University of Michigan, Catholic University of America, and the University of Zurich, Switzerland. Her research in music and its cultural milieu has led to awards from the Smithsonian Institution, the Lyndon Baines Johnson Foundation, and the American Council of Learned Societies. Elise Kirk is founder and former editor of *Dallas Opera Magazine*. She served on the National Advisory Board for the John F. Kennedy Center for the Performing Arts and writes for many national publications, including *Musical Quarterly, Opera News, Bulletin for Research in the Humanities*, and the Library of Congress *Performing Arts Annual*. She is the author of *Steinway at the White House: One Hundred Years of Music* and co-editor of *Opera and Vivaldi*, essays derived from the international symposium held concurrently with the Dallas Opera's American premiere of Vivaldi's *Orlando furioso*, featuring Marilyn Horne.